CURIOUS CUSTOMS OF
SEX &
MARRIAGE

GRETNA GREEN, or the RED-HOT MARRIAGE.

CURIOUS CUSTOMS OF
SEX &
MARRIAGE

GEORGE RYLEY SCOTT

SENATE

Curious Customs of Sex and Marriage

First published in 1953 by Torchstream Books, London

This edition published in 1995 by Senate, an imprint of
Studio Editions Ltd, Princess House, 50 Eastcastle Street,
London W1N 7AP, England

Reprinted 1995

ISBN 1 85958 027 0

Printed and bound in Guernsey by
The Guernsey Press Co. Ltd.

I

THE facile critical evaluation of past events, customs, and methods as being without any value or appeal other than an antiquarian one, is illustrative of that supposedly realistic approach which, in these modern days, so often and so increasingly covers blatant ignorance with a thin veneer of neo-sophisticated pseudo-pantologism. In complete opposition to any such viewpoint, it is my firm contention, as I have been at some considerable pains to state, and even to reiterate, in connexion with previous works, that the degree of any person's understanding of an existing state of affairs, and of its future potentialities, is in direct ratio to the extent of one's knowledge regarding its genesis and development.

It has long been axiomatic in medical circles that the successful treatment of disease is largely dependent upon a thorough grasp of the patient's medical history; so much so, indeed, that in recent decades, and particularly in the fields of psychiatry and psycho-analysis, exhaustive knowledge of the patient's past life is of paramount importance in treating an existent neurosis. The gulf between the psychological state of an individual and a sociological manifestation in a nation or a race may at first sight seem to be one of gargantuan proportions, but a little intelligent reflection will show that, in essence, this difference is mainly inexistent. What, after all, is a nation but a collection of individuals? How often have the ideological concepts (sane or insane, beneficial or harmful) of an individual been accepted, tolerated, or approved by a large proportion, or even by the whole, of the inhabitants of a country or a continent? Witness the wholesale permeation of Europe and America by the mysticism of St. Paul, of Emanuel Swedenborg, of Mrs. Eddy, *et al.* The unearthing of the reasons why, in the past, a cult emerged, gained credence, and grew world-wide in its scope and influence, may be of profound importance in the correct understanding of its present significance and its future possibilities.

II

The idea of marriage as a purely private and domestic affair, the basic function of which was to " multiply and replenish the earth," permeated early thought to such an extent that to the ancient Jews a marriage that proved barren ceased to be regarded as a marriage at all. The basic simplicity of the affair, in those early days when marriage was merely a means of regulating procreation, will be apparent from a study of the pages of this work.

In the earliest stages of society, any form of union for the purpose of sexual expression, whether or not procreation was recognised as a definite objective, where it transcended that of mere gregarious promiscuity, was often beset with difficulties, and certainly in some tribes strong retardatory influences were at work. In order to make the marital union something even remotely resembling a permanent alliance the superstition which led to the avoidance of marriage had to be overcome by a more powerful superstition designed to outweigh and destroy each and every anti-marital concept, such for instance as some means of overcoming or annulling the evil, which, almost universally, in primitive society, was and is held to result from the mere physical contact of the sexes.

Even so, in many races, man showed a marked disinclination to marry. So widespread was this disinclination that at one time and another it was deemed necessary to take steps calculated to induce the acceptance of the matrimonial state, even to the extent of using what was little removed from an act of *force majeure*. The Lacedemonians, for instance, instituted various penalties designed to make a single man's life intolerable. Among these measures, says Little, was one which ordained that all unattached adult males must, on one occasion during each winter, in a state of nudity, run around the forum and sing songs specially composed for the occasion and designed to expose the singers to ridicule. In other cases the bachelors were dragged around an altar and beaten with sticks by a number of young women. In addition, these unmarried men, whatever their rank or position, were given no measure of respect by those younger than themselves. It was for this reason, says Plutarch, that no one had a word of censure or rebuke for a young man who, at an assembly, on the entrance of the celebrated Dercyllidas, did not rise, but said : " Sir, you must not expect that honour from me, though young, which cannot be returned to me by a child of yours when I am old." At one time, even more stringent measures were taken : according to Hermippus, the young and unmarried of both sexes were locked up together in a dark chamber, and each male was obliged to take as wife the first female he placed his hand upon.

The Spartans, perhaps, took the most comprehensive steps to regulate marriage in a manner calculated to encourage the only object allowed or conceded. Thus action might be taken by the State not only against those who remained unmarried, but also against those who made unsuitable alliances, i.e. marriages unlikely to produce vigorous offspring. For the Spartans, says Müller, " considered marriage, not as a *private relation*, about which the State had little or no interest, but as a *public institution*, in order to rear up a strong and healthy progeny to the nation."[1] Among many other races, marriages between infants were arranged by their parents as a means of overcoming the adult male's disinclination to enter into any matrimonial alliance.

In civilised nations the problem was of a different kind, but problem it was nevertheless. After experiments with polygyny and polyandry, monogamy was accepted almost universally, in practice if not in theory, as the perfect form of marital union, and as such, it was portrayed, romanticized and propagandized in every conceivable way, by Church and State alike. Yet, strangely enough, monogamy was and still remains, in many respects, in conflict with the basic sexual urge of mankind, and for this reason it has always been necessary for the State to take steps designed specifically towards the idealization of this form of marriage, and to induce, in a variety of ways, its general acceptance and approval. These efforts, which have been made through the ages, to popularize the monogamic concept, present a panorama of absorbing interest and outstanding importance.

---

[1] C. O. Müller, *The History and Antiquities of the Doric Race*, 1839. Vol. II, p. 295.

III

Fifteen centuries of Christian civilization had to go into the limbo of the past before the Church made any serious and determined attempt to gain control over marriage, by making an ecclesiastical ceremony a necessary prologue.

Church and State concentrated on making the union, as far as possible, and in the vast majority of cases, an indissoluble one. Hence the evolution of marriage ceremonies calculated to stress the " till death doth us part " aspect ; hence the appeal to superstition ; hence the formulation of laws designed to put every conceivable bar in the way of dissolution.

Inevitably difficulties were encountered. Always has there been a risk that in the attempt to make the marital alliance permanent, in combination with the responsibilities inherent in the contract, society might conceivably drive man into promiscuity as an alternative means of satisfying a biological urge. This risk, from time to time, has been underlined by the steps which it was sometimes considered necessary to take, even in civilized communities, to make men marry. Thus in seventeenth century New England the life of a bachelor was made most ignominious by his subjection to many forms of persecution.[1] In Hartford, for instance, the penalty for remaining unmarried was the payment of twenty shillings a week to the town.[2] In other towns, single men were compelled to live in houses assigned to them ; they were continually spied upon ; and their lives generally made miserable. " In those days," said Alice Morse Earle, " a man gained instead of losing his freedom by marrying."[3]

---

[1] Even to-day in some parts of the world indirect coercion is not unknown. In the *Daily Mail* (March 24, 1951) appears the following paragraph : " Tirana, Albania.—A tax on bachelors between 20 and 50, and unmarried and childless women between 20 and 40, has been imposed by the Albanian Government. Reuter."

[2] Alice Morse Earle, *Customs and Fashions in Old New England*, 1893, p. 36.

[3] Ibid., p. 37.

IV

The major disadvantages of modern marriage are concerned with the loss of freedom which is an inevitable concomitant of any such union, and the indissolubility, in all but exceptional circumstances, of the contract. In primitive races marriages were little more than temporary alliances dissolvable at will. Even in the days of Moses the position was not much different. Thus the defects to which I have referred really came into being as part and parcel of marriage when Church and State, in view of the advance of civilization, and the increasing importance of property rights, decided that the need to prove paternity had become essential. With the help of the Church, and the vast improvement in the economic conditions of society as a whole, monogamy as a permanent form of union, cemented by improved standards of morality and increased respectability, came into its own.

For generations these conditions continued to improve. But with the birth of the twentieth century, disturbing and hitherto unknown and probably unthought of influences arose. In recent years these influences have been intensified to such a degree that the concept of monogamy is again in some danger. The decline in orthodox religion, which has been so manifest in the past half-century, the development of birth control, and the emancipation of women, have, in a cumulative sense, played havoc with Victorian and even Edwardian standards. As a result, the Church and the State have been led to make certain concessions. They have revised the regulations governing the marriage contract, mainly in regard to the factor of indissolubility. In other words they have increased, not only the reasons, but also the facilities within the limits imposed by these specific reasons, for terminating the contract.

What of the future ? Will monogamy in its present amended, and it must be conceded, saner form be able to continue ; or will it shrink until it becomes little more than a shadow of its once glorified, tyrannical and arbitrary self ? Will it, in turn, be compelled to give way to some revised form featuring additional modifications, or may it be displaced by some completely different kind of marital union ? The divorce rate is dismayingly heavy ; the trend is toward an extension of its incidence. Is monogamy to become, then, little more than a beatific state for the aged? Truly, these are questions which are difficult to answer, problems which are difficult to solve; and while I am making no attempt to answer or to solve them, in any conclusive, dogmatic or explicit sense; a study of the pages that follow will, I think and hope, do much to place the intelligent reader in a position to arrive at certain tentative answers and solutions, to all these, and possibly to other subsidiary and implicatory, questions and problems. For to end these prefatory remarks with a sentence from the opening paragraphs, the degree of any person's understanding of an existing state of affairs, and of its future potentialities, is in direct ratio to the extent of one's knowledge regarding its genesis and development.

GEORGE RYLEY SCOTT.

CONTENTS

PAGE

INTRODUCTION - - - - - - - v

PART I

CURIOUS CUSTOMS AND RITES RELATING TO COURTSHIP AND THE PRE-MARITAL PERIOD

CHAPTER

I. CURIOUS COURTSHIP AND BETROTHAL CUSTOMS   3

The Significance of Courtship—Betrothal in Infancy or Childhood—The Manner of Betrothal —The Role of the Matchmaker—Symbols of Betrothal.

II. LOVE CHARMS AND PHILTRES - - - 16

Charms for enabling one to look into the Future —Philtres for Enticing or Developing Love.

III. VIRGINITY: ITS VALUE AND OTHERWISE - 33

Virginity as a Highly-prized Possession—Virginity as a Despised Possession.

IV. BUNDLING, ITS ANALOGUES AND OTHER CURIOUS METHODS OF COURTSHIP - - - 39

The Genesis, Development, and Significance of Bundling—Other Strange Methods of Courtship.

PART II

VARIOUS FORMS OF MARRIAGE

V. MARRIAGE BY CAPTURE - - - - 53

Rarity of the Practice in its True Sense— " Marriage by Capture " as a Ceremonial Procedure.

xi

CHAPTER   PAGE

VI.   MARRIAGE BY PURCHASE   -   -   -   -   64

    Origin and Antiquity of Purchasing a Wife—The
    Dowry as a Form of Purchasing a Husband.

VII. JUVENILE MARRIAGES   -   -   -   -   -   72

    The Origin and Incidence of Juvenile Marriage—
    The Evils of Infantile Marriage.

VIII. PLURAL MARRIAGE IN ITS VARIOUS FORMS   -   80

    Polygamy: Its Origin and Incidence—Mormonism.

IX.   MONOGAMY IN ITS VARIOUS PHASES   -   -   90

    The Genesis of Monogamy—Trial and Com-
    panionate Marriage.

X.   VARIOUS OTHER FORMS OF MARRIAGE -   -   96

    Group and Communal Marriage—Marriage to
    Gods and Devils—The Levirate—Spiritual Wives
    —Concubinage—Pseudo-Marriages.

PART III

CURIOUS FERTILITY RITES AND OTHER CUSTOMS CONNECTED WITH MARRIAGE

XI.   MAGICAL RITES RELATING TO MARRIAGE   -   115

    The Cult of Fertility—Warding off the Attacks of
    Evil Spirits—Other Curious Superstitions.

XII. CHASTITY IN THE MARRIED STATE AND ITS
       ENFORCEMENT   -   -   -   -   -   128

    The Emergence of Chastity as a Treasured Posses-
    sion—Methods of Securing Chastity.

XIII. SELLING, LOANING, AND EXCHANGING WIVES   134

    The Sale of Wives—The Loan and Exchange of
    Wives.

XIV. THE COUVADE AND OTHER CURIOUS PRACTICES -   141

    The Couvade—*Jus Primæ Noctis*—Infanticide—
    Wife-beating—Other Curious Practices.

PART IV

CURIOUS RITES IN CONNEXION WITH THE CELEBRATION OF MARRIAGE

CHAPTER · · · · · · · PAGE

XV. MARRIAGE RITES OF THE HEBREWS AND THEIR CONTEMPORARIES - - - - 159

Ceremonies of the Jews—Rites of Contemporary Races—Rites of the Ancient Greeks and Romans.

XVI. MARRIAGE RITES OF OTHER RACES AND IN VARIOUS COUNTRIES - - - - 167

Ceremonial Marriage in India, Persia, etc.—Marriage Rites of Egypt, Morocco, etc.—Marriage Rites of China and Japan—Marriage Rites in Other Countries.

XVII. MARRIAGE RITES OF PRIMITIVE AND SAVAGE TRIBES - - - - - - 199

Curious Ceremonies practised in the Old World—Curious Ceremonies practised in the New World.

XVIII. MARRIAGE CUSTOMS OF GREAT BRITAIN AND AMERICA IN OLDEN TIMES - - 211

Curious old Wedding Customs—Customs connected with the Wedding Cake, Ring, &c.

XIX. CLANDESTINE MARRIAGES - - - - 243

The Notorious Fleet Marriages—The Marriages of Gretna Green.

PART V

PROHIBITIONS AND TABOOS RELATING TO MARRIAGE

XX. TABOOS IN CONNEXION WITH MARRIAGE - - 269

The Emergence and Development of the Incest Taboo—The Condemnation and Punishment of Adultery—Taboos concerning Menstruation and Pregnancy—The Taboo on the Re-marriage of Widows.

XXI. THE END OF THE MARITAL CONTRACT - - 288

Curious Divorce Customs—The Suttee.

BIBLIOGRAPHY - - - - - - 298

INDEX - - - - - - - 305

PART ONE

CURIOUS CUSTOMS AND RITES RELATING TO COURTSHIP AND THE PRE-MARITAL PERIOD

CHAPTER I

CURIOUS COURTSHIP AND BETROTHAL CUSTOMS

I

The Significance of Courtship

COURTSHIP may represent a short or a long period, its duration being dependent on many factors. It is supposed to represent a period during which the two parties have an opportunity of getting to know each other intimately, and in the process discovering whether the initial attraction will develop or wane.

In actual truth, however, it is a time when the courter and the courted, owing to the very fact of being in love, are in no state to arrive at any logical or realistic valuation of each other. In many cases both parties are infatuated, and it is quite impossible for the cold light of reason to enter into the matter at all.

The courting period is inevitably a time of make-belief, and usually disingenuous or unconsciously-motivated make-belief at that. Naturally the lovesick youth or maiden wishes to create a favourable impression, and to this end the whole period that elapses before marriage is punctuated with subterfuge, pretence, evasion, repression and simulation.

Despite such a state of affairs, or perhaps because of it, the courting time is often the happiest of all periods in a person's life. Especially is this the case where the two parties are really unsuitably mated, and such instances are unfortunately extremely numerous. For no period of courtship, however protracted it may be, and however close the relationship between the engaged parties, can prove as revealing as one single week of actual marriage.

One of the features of courtship is the showering of gifts on the girl by her fiancé. Even among the poorer classes the male usually gives such presents to the extent of his means. In most cases, too, the girl makes occasional gifts to her fiancé.

Among many races, primitive and otherwise, it was, and in

many cases still is, customary for the male, during his courting period, to give presents, not to the girl, but to her parents.

Courting, even in civilized countries, was not always so free from danger to the enterprising youngster as it is to-day. In seventeenth-century New England, for instance, unless a young man made sure that he had full permission to pay court to a girl, he might very easily land himself into grievous trouble. The Puritans, who were responsible for the regulations then in force, frowned upon anything that smacked of irresponsible or un-authorized love-making. The "petting", "necking", and other flirtatious practices of twentieth-century America would have ranked as serious crimes to the law-makers of Boston and other New England towns. Had anyone dared to adopt such courting methods they would have been punished by whipping or im-prisonment, with probably a fine thrown in for good measure. In Alice Morse Earle's extremely interesting study of New Eng-land customs, we find many references to these laws. Thus in the year 1672 at Plymouth, Jonathan Coventry was indicted for "making a motion of marriage" to Katharine Dudley, having neglected to obtain "formal consent." In 1660, Arthur Hubbard, for "disorderly and unrighteously endeavouring to gain the affections of Mistress Elizabeth Prence," was prosecuted by the girl's father, and fined £5 by the court.[1]

The austerity of these Puritans was, too, responsible for a strange method of courtship reputed to have been employed in the Connecticut Valley during the eighteenth century. Re-ferring to this practice, the before-mentioned authority on New England customs, says : " other sweethearts are said to have been forced to a most ceremonious courtship, to whisper their tender nothings through a ' courting-stick ', a hollow stick about an inch in diameter and six or eight feet long, fitted with mouth-and ear-pieces. In the presence of the entire family, lovers, seated formally on either side of the great fireplace, carried on this chilly telephonic love-making. One of these bâtons of propriety is still preserved in Long-Meadow, Mass."[1]

[1] Alice Morse Earle, *Customs and Fashions in Old New England*, London, 1893, pp. 40-41.
[1] Ibid, p. 64.

II

Betrothal in Infancy or Childhood

In many races it is customary for betrothal to take place during infancy, and indeed there are instances where this occurs at the moment of birth and sometimes, strange as it may seem, while a child is in its mother's womb.

In all such instances, of course, the betrothal arrangements are made either directly by the parents or through the offices of a professional matchmaker. In particular the services of a matchmaker are usually enlisted where the female infant is literally sold, as a prospective bride, to an aged male ; in cases where a substantial dowry is involved ; and also where the match is to the financial or social interests of both parties.

Although it often happens that the female infant is betrothed to a male of approximately equivalent age, there are numerous departures from this practice. Thus it is by no means unusual for parents to arrange for their baby girl to be affianced to a male who has already reached puberty ; or, in some instances to a middle-aged or even an elderly man, the marriage to take place when the girl arrives at maturity.

Inevitably, in all cases of infant betrothal, there are risks that the arrangements will come to nothing. Infant mortality, especially among races which adopt such betrothal methods, is abnormally high. Further, where the child is affianced to an adult there is a big risk that by the time it reaches marriageable age the chosen husband will be dead. Special precautions are taken to meet these circumstances, should they arise. In order to ensure that when the male infant reaches the age at which he can marry, a girl will be available without the need for a fresh search, it is usual to delegate to him at birth two, or even more than two, female infants. Similarly one girl may be affianced to two, or more than two, males. In all such cases, it is understood that if all the parties are living when maturity is attained, the first individual on the list to which the male or the female is betrothed has the right to fulfil the contract.

Among the Kaffirs, says Thompson, " The young females are often betrothed before they arrive at marriageable state. The marriages are generally made by the parents, and it is not unusual for them to send one of their daughters to a family when there is a young man of fit age to be married. With the young girl some attendants are sent ; and if the father of the youth is pleased with the maiden, and consents to give the number of cattle required by her family, there is a beast slaughtered, and after several days spent in feasting and dancing, the young couple are acknowledged as man and wife. The price generally paid by the family of the bridegroom to that of the bride is ten oxen ; but the chiefs, when they marry wives of high lineage, must sometimes give five or six times that number."[1]

Writing of the Indians of Northern Canada, Samuel Hearne stated that the girls were always betrothed well before reaching puberty, but never to males of equal ages.

Of the few who go so far as to anticipate birth in the betrothal of female offspring are certain tribes indigenous to Australia and the islands constituting Polynesia. Almost without exception, in these cases, are these pre-natal betrothals of presumptive girls made to males of maturity. If an error has been made and the child turns out to be of the wrong sex, the experiment is repeated should an already-born female of suitable ancestry not be available.

According to Malinowsky, so far as the natives inhabiting the Trobriand Islands are concerned, there is little difference between the betrothal of the infants and marriage itself. From birth, or the time immediately after birth, when the betrothal occurs, the boy and girl concerned are regarded and even addressed as husband and wife.

When we come to look for the reasons for these infant betrothals we are confronted with several, prominent among which is the financial aspect. As will be apparent when we come to consider marriage by purchase and its analogues, the question of finance is very often an all-important one in connexion with marital unions arranged by parents or others. Naturally, an infant girl, in view of the possibilities of death occurring before the attainment of marriageable age and the inevitable risks relating to appearance, etc., is purchaseable for a considerably lower sum than is the maiden who has attained puberty and whose beauty is ascertainable and assured. Thus the man who is prepared to take chances as regards these matters, and who is prepared to wait, can secure a potential wife for a very small

---

[1] George Thompson, *Travels and Adventures in Southern Africa*, second edition, Vol. II, p. 355.

sum indeed. Similarly the parents of an infant son can provide for his future wedded life at comparatively little cost.

The betrothal of children was not always restricted to savage or primitive tribes. At one time the practice seems to have been general. Apropos of this, Alexander says : " In an early period of the world, the interest, and sometimes the inclination, of parents, when they had lived in friendly manner with, and contracted a regard for, their neighbours, naturally prompted them to wish that a marriage between their children might take place to strengthen the alliance of the families ; and as this wish was frequently formed before the parties were of an age proper for such a junction, they fell upon a method of securing them to each other, by what is called in the sacred writings, betrothing ; which was agreeing on a price to be paid for the bride, the time when it should be paid, and when she should be delivered into the hands of her husband."[1] So, too, Fullom, who says : " Marriages are contracted in the East at a very early age, and the Jewish maidens, like those of the neighbouring nations, are often betrothed in their twelfth year."[2]

III

The Manner of Betrothal

According to the Talmudists, there were in Biblical times, three ways of betrothing : (1) by a written agreement ; (2) by word of mouth, together with the presentation to the female party of a silver coin ; and (3) by an act of cohabitation. Where the espousal took the form of an agreement in writing, the document read : " On such a day of such a month, in such a year, A. the son of B. has said to C. the daughter of D. be thou my spouse according to the law of Moses and the Israelites, and I will give thee, for the portion of thy virginity, the sum of two hundred zuzim, as it is ordained by the law. And the said C. has consented to become his spouse upon these conditions, which the said A. has promised to perform upon the day of marriage. To this the said A. obliges himself : and for this

---

[1] William Alexander, *The History of Woman*, 1779, Vol. II, p. 252.
[2] S. W. Fullom, *The History of Woman*, third edition, 1855, p. 47.

he engages all his goods, even as far as the cloak which he wears upon his shoulder. Moreover he promises to perform all that is intended in contracts of marriage in favour of the Israelitish women. Witness A.B.C."[1]

Where, in the absence of a written contract, the betrothal was agreed upon by word of mouth, and the presentation of a silver coin to the female party, the man, in the presence of witnesses, said : "Accept this silver coin as a pledge that I will one day take thee as my wife." As regards betrothal by cohabitation, although legal, this method was frowned upon, because of the abuses inseparable from it.

The custom of making betrothals verbally, in the presence of witnesses, prevailed long into the Christian era. Usually the mere joining of hands by the two parties to the contract was taken to be a sign of confirmation.

The Medes had a curious betrothal ceremony. The couple, in the presence of relatives and friends, made incisions in each other's arms, allowing the blood to flow and mix in a goblet, and then drinking from it in turn. In this manner was the engagement registered.

In Lapland it was customary, according to Moore, for a young man to punctuate his courtship with presents to the girl's father of bottles of brandy, apart from and in addition to the presents given to the girl herself, which usually took the form of eatables. He was allowed to visit his fiancée as often as he liked, but on each occasion a bottle of brandy was an essential paternal perquisite, and because this spiritous liquor was so highly esteemed the father usually delayed the fixing of the wedding day by every conceivable means and for as long as possible.

In Scotland, a strange method of betrothal was at one time in vogue. On the acceptance by the girl of her lover's proposal, the couple went at night to the nearest stream, where, after washing their hands in the current, they sealed their engagement by clasping hands across the stream, with the moon as witness. It was in this manner that Burns, the Scots poet, was affianced to Mary Campbell. Another curious method, to which members of the rural population were addicted, is described by Rogers, thus : " The fond swain, who had resolved to make proposals, sent for the object of his affection to the village alehouse, previously informing the landlady of his intentions. The damsel,

[1] *Calmet's Dictionary of the Bible*, 1841.

who knew the purpose of the message, busked herself in her best attire, and waited on her admirer. She was entertained with a glass of ale ; then the swain proceeded with his tale of love. A dialogue like the following ensued :—' I'm gaun to speir whether ye will tak' me, Jenny ? ' ' Deed, Jock, I thocht ye micht hae speir't that lang syne.' ' They said ye wad refuse me, lassie.' ' Then they're leers, Jock.' 'An' so ye'll no refuse me, lassie ? ' ' I've tell't ye that twice owre already, Jock.' Then came the formal act of betrothal. The parties licked the thumbs of their right hands, which they pressed together, and vowed fidelity. The ceremony possessed the solemnity of an oath, the violator of such an engagement being considered guilty of perjury. In allusion to this practice, a favourite Scottish song commences :

' There's my thumb, I'll ne'er beguile thee.'

The pressure of moistened thumbs, as the solemn ratification of an engagement, was used in other contracts. The practice, as confirmatory of an agreement, existed both among the Celts and Goths. The records of the Scottish courts contain examples of sales being confirmed by the judges, on the production of evidence that the parties had licked and pressed their thumbs on the occasion of the bargain. The Highlander and the Lowland schoolboy still lick thumbs in bargain making."[1]

In the Orkney Islands, it was once customary for couples to call upon the ancient Scandinavian deity, Odin, to witness their betrothals. In the light of the moon they visited the Temple of Odin at Stennis, and through one of the great perforated stones clasped hands and made their pledge, which was held to be legal.[2]

A strange custom formerly peculiar to Gipsy courtships, was that the betrothal or marriage of a younger daughter was not permissible before the elder. Simson, who made inquiries into this matter, says that he was informed that this practice " had been the cause of many unhappy marriages."[3]

Other curious customs are founded on superstition. In some districts of Scotland it was considered essential, if good luck were to attend the union, that before the ceremony, all knots

[1] Rev. Charles Rogers, *Scotland, Social and Domestic*, 1869, p. 110.

[2] Constance F. Gordon Cumming, *From the Hebrides to the Himalayas*, 1876. Vol. I, p. 274.

[3] Walter Simson, *A History of the Gipsies*, 1865, p. 258.

of whatever kind in the apparel of both bride and bridegroom should be loosened. May was considered an unlucky month in which to marry. In many counties Friday was deemed to be a day of ill-omen ; but in Ross-shire it was favoured as the most auspicious day of the week. Some of these superstitions still survive in remote districts.

IV

The Role of the Matchmaker

In those countries where the parties to be united have little to do with the arrangements for either betrothal or marriage, often the services of a professional matchmaker are engaged by the parents of the young man or of the girl. In other cases the young man's mother or some other female relative acts the part of matchmaker. Thus, Lane, in reference to the Egyptians, says : " Most commonly, the mother, or some other near female relation, of the youth or man who is desirous of obtaining a wife describes to him the personal and other qualifications of the young women with whom she is acquainted, or he employs a *khatbeh* (a woman whose regular business is to assist men in such cases). Sometimes two or more women of this profession are employed. A *khatbeh* gives her report confidentially, describing one girl as being like a gazelle, pretty and elegant and young ; and another, as not pretty, but rich, and so forth. If the man has a mother and other near female relations, two or three of these usually go with the *khatbeh* to pay visits to several *hhareems*, to which she has access in her professional character of a matchmaker ; for she is employed as much by the women as by the men. She sometimes also exercises the trade of a broker for the sale of ornaments, clothing, etc., which procures her admission into almost every *hhareem*. The women who accompany her in search of a wife for their relation are introduced to the different *hhareems* merely as ordinary visitors ; and as such, if disappointed, they soon take their leave, though the object of their visit is of course understood by the other party : but if they find among the females of a family (and they are sure to see all who are marriageable) a girl or young woman having the necessary personal qualifications, they state the motive of their visit, and ask, if the proposed match be not at once disapproved of, what property, ornaments, etc., the object of their wishes may possess. If the father of the intended bride be dead, she may perhaps possess one or more houses, shops, etc. ; and in almost every case, a marriageable girl of the middle or higher ranks has a set of ornaments of gold and jewels. The women-visitors, having asked these and other questions, bring their report to the expectant youth or man. If satisfied with their report, he gives a present to the *khatbeh*, and sends her again to the family of his intended wife, to make known to them his wishes. She generally gives an exaggerated description of his personal attractions, wealth, etc. For instance, she will say, of a very ordinary young man, of scarcely any property, and of whose disposition she knows nothing : ' My daughter, the youth who wishes to marry you is young, graceful, elegant, beardless, has plenty of money, dresses handsomely, is fond of delicacies, but cannot enjoy his luxuries alone ; he wants you as his companion ; he will give you everything that money can procure ; he is a stayer-at-home, and will spend his whole time with you, caressing and fondling you.' The parents may betroth their daughter to whom they please, and marry her to him without her consent, if she be not arrived at the age of puberty ; but after she has attained that age, she may choose a husband for herself, and appoint any man to arrange and effect her marriage. In the former case, however, the *khatbeh* and the relations of a girl sought in marriage usually endeavour to obtain her consent to the proposed union. Very often a father objects to giving a daughter in marriage to a man who is not of the same profession or trade as himself, and to marrying a younger daughter before an elder. The bridegroom can scarcely ever obtain even a surreptitious glance at the features of his bride, until he finds her in his absolute possession, unless she belong to the lower classes of society, in which case, it is easy enough for him to see her face. When a female is about to marry, she should have a deputy to settle the compact, and conclude the contract for her, with her proposed husband. If she be under the age of puberty, this is absolutely necessary ; and in this case, her father, if living, or (if he be dead), her paternal grandfather, or a guardian appointed by will, or by the *ckadee*, performs the office of deputy ; but if she be of age, she appoints her own deputy, or may even make the contract herself, though this is seldom done."[1]

It is in China, however, that the system of arranging marriages without consulting either of the parties has reached the highest degree of ecumenity. In fact, for centuries the services of a professional matchmaker or go-between have been considered an essential part of the negotiations for a betrothal. This negotiation, affirms Davis, is called *ping*. The go-between may be either a man or a woman. Professional matchmakers of both sexes are available, though for the most part they are women of mature age. " Parents who seek to affiance their children," says Gray, " usually make application to one of this class, and the go-between consults the list, which she always carries about with her, of the names of eligible ladies and gentlemen. The age at which young people are affianced is from seven to fourteen years."[2] Usually the initial step in the matter is taken by the parents of the young man, for it is of the greatest importance in China that arrangements for the speedy marriage of a son should be made without any delay. As soon as the go-between has found a suitable girl, the services of a fortune-teller are next enlisted. From the year, month, day and hour of birth in each case a horoscope is prepared. The two horoscopes are compared, and if the report of the fortune-teller is a favourable one, the engagement is well on the way to ratification. Only a stroke of bad luck would cause the negotiations to come to nothing, and the go-between then be called upon to make another search. For, according to Doolittle : " If for the space of three days, while the betrothal is under consideration in each of the families, after the card having the eight characters has been received from the other family, anything reckoned unlucky—such as breaking a bowl or the losing of an article—should occur, the negotiations would be broken off at once, and the card would be returned to the party which sent it. The card during this time is usually placed under the censer, standing in front of the ancestral tablets belonging to the family. When it is deposited there, incense and candles are lighted before these tablets."[3]

---

[1] Edward William Lane, *An Account of the Manners and Customs of the Modern Egyptians*, 1868.

[2] John Henry Gray, *China*, 1878, p. 189.

[3] Rev. Justus Doolittle, *Social Life of the Chinese*, Sampson Low & Marston, 1866, p. 66.

SPANISH CUSTOM OF SERENADING

From *Marriage Rites, Customs and Ceremonies
of All Nations, 1824*

RED INDIAN COURTING SCENES

(*Right*) The Approach; (*Left*) The couple
wrapped in one blanket

From a drawing by Big Back, a Cheyenne Indian,
in Col. Dodge's *Our Wild Indians, 1882*

V

Symbols of Betrothal

Since the days when the custom of betrothal was first instituted it has been usual to seal the bargain or contract by means of something tangible.   We have seen that where the contract was a purely verbal one, the man presented to the lady of his choice, in the presence of witnesses, a silver coin.   A variant, or perhaps an extension of this practice, was the breaking into two halves of a piece of gold or silver, each party to the agreement retaining one of the pieces.

There is a reference to this custom in Doggett's *Country Wake* (1696) in which a character named Hob, in referring to a girl called Mary, to whom he is betrothed, says : " I ask't her the question last Lammas, and at Allhallow's-tide we broke a piece of money, and if I had liv'd till last Sunday, we had been ask'd in the church."   Crooked coins were preferred because of the good luck supposed to be connected with them.   Gay writes :

> "A ninepence bent
> A token kind to Bumkinet is sent."

Also Samuel Butler refers to the crooked coin in the lines :

> " His wit was sent him for a token
> But in the carriage crack'd and broken.
> Like commendation ninepence crook'd,
> With—To and from my love—it look'd."

Although a coin, whole or broken, was used in some countries for many centuries, in other places, even in ancient times, a ring was already the customary token.   According to Tertullian, a ring of gold was given personally or sent by the man to the woman to whom he was engaged, as a pledge.   And gradually the ring achieved almost universal popularity.

A thirteenth-century writer, Vincent de Beauvais, said that betrothing was a contract of future marriage, made by a simple promise, by security given, by a ring, or by an oath.   If, as often was the case, the celebration took place in a church, four observances were usually included in the ceremony, thus : (1) the joining of hands ; (2) the mutually given kiss ; (3) the interchange of rings ; and (4) the testimony of witnesses. In Shakespeare's *Twelfth Night* we find the passage :—

> "A contract of eternal bond of love
> Confirm'd by mutual joinder of your hands,
> Attested by the holy close of lips,
> Strengthened by interchangement of your rings ;
> And all the ceremony of this compact
> Seal'd in my function, by my testimony."

The oath administered on such an occasion, was as follows : " You swear by God and his holy saints herein and by all the saints of Paradise, that you will take this woman whose name is N. to wife within forty days, if holy Church will permit." The priest then joining their hands, said : "And thus you affiance yourselves " ; to which the parties answered, "Yes, sir."[1]

The practice of public betrothing, however, had evil consequences ; the engaged couple frequently considering that it justified cohabitation without waiting for marriage. Whether the custom was discontinued because of this practice is not clear, but in any case it seems to have fallen into disuse by the end of the fifteenth century.

At one time the use of a treble ring, termed the gimmal, was favoured for sealing the betrothal pact. It really consisted of three rings fastened together by a small rivet in such a way as to be easily disjointed. Each ring was engraved with a portion of a design, so that the complete figure was formed only when the three rings were in apposition. At the time of betrothal, the ring was split into its three component parts, one of which was worn by the man, one by the girl to whom he had become engaged, and one by a close friend who was present. At the marriage celebration, the three separate rings were again fastened together to form a wedding-ring for the bride. A variant of the threefold ring was one consisting of two parts, one for each of the contracting parties. In one of his poems Dryden refers to the gimmal ring thus :—

---

[1] Quoted from Douce's *Illustrations*, Vol. I, p. 113 by Nathan Drake in *Shakespeare and His Times*, 1817.

"A curious artist wrought 'em
  With joynts as not to be perceiv'd ;
  Yet are they both each other's counterpart—
  (Her part had Juan inscribed, and his had Zayda,
  You know those names were theirs); and in the midst
  A heart divided in two halves was plac'd.
  Now, if the rivets of these rings inclosed
  Fit not each other, I have forged this tye."

The custom died the death, however, and for several centuries now, in the English-speaking, and in many foreign, countries it has been usual for the man to present his fiancée, on the occasion of their betrothal, with what is termed an engagement ring.   Originally it was usual for the lady to wear this ring on her right hand, but subsequently custom decreed its transference to the left.   In many cases the girl presented a ring to her fiancé, but this was not, nor is it now, obligatory.

CHAPTER II

LOVE CHARMS AND PHILTRES

I

Charms for Enabling one to Look into the Future

YOUNG unmarried women, from the earliest days of civilisation, have eagerly accepted the beliefs respecting the effect of various charms in bringing about a visualization of their husbands-to-be. The powers of divination, in this respect, which various plants were at one time or another supposed to possess, are prominent in the folklore of various countries. And even to this day, in rural parts, many of these beliefs still find credence among the most ignorant and unsophisticated.

Perhaps the most frequent of the various ways of manifesting divinatory power is in the inducement of dreams wherein visions of the sleeper's future partner will occur. Thus, in Halliwell's *Popular Rhymes and Nursery Tales* (page 220) we read: "On Valentine's day take two bay leaves, sprinkle them with rose-water, and lay them across your pillow in the evening. When you go to bed, put on a clean nightgown turned wrong side outwards, and, lying down, say these words softly to yourself :—

> Good Valentine, be kind to me,
> In dreams let me my true love see.

After this go to sleep as soon as you can, and you will see in a dream your future husband."

Again, in the same compendium, appears the following: "A girl must pluck a leaf from the even-ash, and, holding it in her hand, say :—

> This even-ash I hold in my hand
> The first I meet is my true man.

She carries it in her hand a short distance, and if she meets a young man, he will be her future husband. If not, she must put the leaf in her glove, and say :—

16

> This even-ash I hold in my glove,
> The first I meet is my true love.

She carries it in her glove a short time, with the same intention as before, but if she meets no one, she places the leaf in her bosom, saying :—

> This even-ash I hold in my bosom
> The first I meet is my husband.

And the first young man she meets after this will infallibly be her future partner. There are a great variety of rhymes relating to the even-ash. Another is :—

> If you find even-ash or four-leaved clover,
> You will see your love afore the day's over."[1]

Another method calls for the use of butterdock seeds. The young woman must scatter the seeds on the grass half an hour before sunrise on a Friday morning. While doing this she must chant the following words :—

> " I sow, I sow !
> Then, my own dear,
> Come here, come here,
> And mow, and mow ! "

On the completion of the sowing process, her future husband will be seen mowing with a scythe a little distance away.

It will be noted that in regard to the afore-mentioned methods of divination, the herb in itself is not enough to bring about the result desired : much depends upon the use to which the plant is put, and the words and actions of the one who seeks to possess the hidden knowledge. This is particularly observable when an apple is used for the purpose. On October 28 the girl who seeks information respecting the man she is to marry, holds the paring of an apple in her right hand, and taking up a position in the centre of the room, recites the following lines :—

> " St. Simon and Jude, on you I intrude,
> By this paring I hold to discover,
> Without any delay, to tell me this day,
> The first letter of my own true lover."

After turning around three times, she throws the paring over her left shoulder, and on falling to the floor it should form a letter,

---

[1] J. O. Halliwell, *Popular Rhymes and Nursery Tales*, 1849, pp. 222-3.

which will be the initial of her future husband's name. If the paring breaks into pieces or falls in such a way as to form no decipherable letter, the thrower will remain unmarried.[1]

It will be noted, in the afore-mentioned method of divination, the operations must be carried out on a specific date, to wit, October 28. No reason for this is given, but apparently the question of time is considered to be important, as it is by no means unusual for a particular day to figure as part of the *modus operandi* in these divinatory processes. Thus, again consulting the revealing pages of Halliwell, we read : " On St. Agnes' day, take a sprig of rosemary, and another of thyme, and sprinkle them thrice with water. In the evening put one in each shoe, placing a shoe on each side of the bed, and when you retire to rest, say the following lines, and your future husband will appear visible :—

> St. Agnes, that's to lovers kind,
> Come ease the trouble of my mind."

The same authority quotes another instance from Aubrey's *Miscellanies* (ed. 1696, p. 105), thus : " The women have several magical secrets handed down to them by tradition for this purpose, as, on St. Agnes' night, 21 January, take a row of pins, and pull out every one, one after another, saying a Pater Noster, or 'Our Father', sticking a pin in your sleeve, and you will dream of him or her you shall marry. Or, you must lie in another county, and knit the left garter about the right-legged stocking (let the other garter and stocking alone), and as you rehearse these following verses, at every comma knit a knot :—

> This knot I knit
> To know the thing I know not yet :
> That I may see
> The man (woman) that shall my husband (wife) be,
> How he goes and what he wears,
> And what he does, all the days and years.

Accordingly in your dream you will see him, if a musician with a lute or other instrument ; if a scholar, with a book or papers. A gentlewoman that I knew confessed in my hearing that she used this method, and dreamt of her husband whom she had never seen. About two or three years after, as she was on Sunday at church, up pops a young Oxonian in the pulpit. She cries out

[1] Halliwell, op. cit., p. 216.

presently to her sister, 'This is the very face of the man that
I saw in my dream.' Sir William Soames's Lady did the like."
Ben Jonson alludes to the custom in the following lines :—

> "And on sweet Saint Agnes night
> Please you with the promis'd sight ;
> Some of husbands, some of lovers,
> Which an empty dream discovers."

At the time of Shakespeare there was a belief current that
by a process of fasting and the observance of certain ceremonies
on Midsummer Eve (Eve of St. John the Baptist), it was possible
for one's future husband or wife to be discovered. The method
as then practised was simple enough in all conscience, for, we
are told, if a maiden, fasting on Midsummer Eve, laid a clean
cloth at midnight, with bread, cheese, and ale, and sat down
with the street door open, the person whom she was fated to
marry would enter the room, fill the glass, drink to her, bow
and retire. Similarly, the visionary appearance of the destined
bridegroom was supposed to follow the sowing of hempseed
on this night, either in a field or in the churchyard.[1] Strutt
(*Queenhoo-Hall*, Vol. I, p. 136), gives the following fifteenth
century charm :—

> "Around the church see that you go,
>   With kirtle white and girdle blue,
> At midnight thrice, and hempseed sow ;
>   Calling upon your lover true,
>   Thus shalt thou say ;
> These seeds I sow : swift let them grow,
>   Till he, who must my husband me,
>   Shall follow me and mow."

Hobnelia, in John Gay's *Shepherds' Week*, says :—

> "At eve last midsummer no sleep I sought,
> But to the field a bag of hempseed brought ;
> I scatter'd round the seed on every side,
> And three times in a trembling accent cried,
> ' This hempseed with my virgin hand I sow,
> Who shall my true-love be, the crop shall mow.'
> I straight look'd back, and if my eyes speak truth,
> With his keen scythe behind me came the youth."

To the same period belongs the belief in the power of what
was termed "plantain coal" to bring about similar visions.

---

[1] Nathan Drake, *Shakespeare and His Times*, 1817, Vol. I, p. 332.

In reference to this, Aubrey writes : " The last summer, on the day of St. John Baptist, 1694, I accidentally was walking in the pasture behind Mantague-house : it was twelve o'clock. I saw there about two or three and twenty young women, most of them well habited, on their knees, very busy, as if they had been weeding. I could not presently learn what the matter was ; at last, a young man told me that they were looking for coal under the root of a plantain, to put under their heads that night, and they should dream who would be their husbands : it was to be sought for that day and hour."[1]

Then there were the remarkable superstitions of this nature connected with All-Hallows Eve, superstitions which were common both in England and Scotland, as Shakespeare and Burns have recorded. To Nathan Drake's excellent work, *Shakespeare and His Times*, I am indebted for the following information : " The *first* ceremony of Hallow-Eve consisted in the lads and lasses pulling each a *stock*, or plant of kail. They were to go out, hand in hand, with eyes shut, and to pull the first they met with. Its being big or little, straight or crooked, was prophetic of the size and shape of the grand object of all their spells—the husband or wife. If any *yird*, or earth, stuck to the root, that was considered as the *tocher*, or fortune ; and the taste of the *custoc*, that is, the heart of the stem, was deemed indicative of the natural temper and disposition. Lastly, the stems, or, to give them their ordinary appellation, the runts, were placed somewhere above the head of the door, and the Christian names of the people whom chance brought into the house, were, according to the priority of placing the *runts*, the names in question. In the *second*, the lasses were to go to the barnyard, and pull each, at three several times, a stalk of oats. If the third stalk wanted the *top-pickle*, that is, the grain at the top of the stalk, the party in question would come to the marriage-bed anything but a maid. The *third* depended on the burning of nuts, and was a favourite charm both in England and Scotland. A lad and lass were named to each particular nut, as they laid them in the fire, and accordingly as they burnt quietly together, or started from beside each other, the course and issue of the courtship were to be determined. In the *fourth*, success could only be obtained by strictly adhering to the following directions. Steal out, all alone, to the *kiln*, and, darkling, throw into the *pot*,

[1] John Aubrey, *Miscellanies*, 1696.

a clue of blue yarn; wind it in a new clue off the old one: and, towards the latter end, something will hold the thread; demand, who holds it? And an answer will be returned from the kiln-pot, by naming the Christian and surname of your future spouse. To perform the *fifth*, you were to take a candle, and go alone to a looking-glass; you were then to eat an apple before it, combing your hair all the time; when the face of your conjugal companion *to be*, will be seen in the glass, as if peeping over your shoulder. The *sixth* was likewise a solitary charm, in which it was necessary to go *alone* and *unperceived* to the *barn*, and open both doors, taking them off the hinges, if possible, lest the *being*, about to appear, should shut the doors, and do you some mischief. Then you were to take the machine used in winnowing the corn, and go through all the attitudes of letting down the grain against the wind; and on the third repetition of this ceremony, an apparition would be seen passing through the barn, in at the windy door, and out at the other, having both the figure of your future companion for life, and also the appearance or retinue, marking the employment or station in life. To secure an effective result from the *seventh*, you were ordered to take an opportunity of going, unnoticed, to a *Bear-stack*, and fathom it three times round; when during the last fathom of the last time, you would be sure to catch in your arms the appearance of your destined yokefellow. In order to carry the *eighth* into execution, one or more were injoined to seek a south-running spring or rivulet, where ' three lairds' lands meet ', and to dip into it the left shirt-sleeve. You were then to go to bed in sight of a fire, and to hang the wet sleeve before it to dry; it was necessary, however, to be awake, when at midnight, an apparition, having the exact figure of the future husband or wife, would come, and turn the sleeve, as if to dry the other side of it. It is in relation to this particular spell that Burns wrote the following lines :—

> " A wanton widow Leezie was
> As canty as a kittlen;
> But och! that night, among the shaws,
> She got a fearfu' settlin !
> She thro' the whins, an' by the cairn,
> An' owre the hill gaed scrievin,
> Where three lairds land met at a burn,
> To dip her left sark-sleeve in,
> Was bent that night.

Whyles owre a linn the burnie plays
        As thro' the glen it wimpl't;
Whyles round a rocky scar it strays;
        Whyles in a wiel it dimpl't;
Whyles glitter'd to the nightly rays,
        Wi' bickering, dancing dazzle;
Whyles cookit underneath the braes,
        Below the spreading hazle,
                Unseen that night.

Among the brachens, on the brae,
        Between her an' the moon,
The deil, or else an outler quey,
        Gat up an' gae a croon:
Poor Leezie's heart maist lap the hool;
        Near lav'rock-height she jumpit,
But mist a fit, an' in the pool,
        Out-owre the lugs she plumpit
                Wi' a plunge that night."

For the due performance of the *ninth*, you were directed to take
three dishes; to put clean water in one, foul water in another,
and to leave the third empty: you were then to blindfold a
person, and lead him to the hearth where the dishes were ranged,
ordering him to dip the left hand; if this happened to be in the
clean water, it was a sign that the future conjugal mate would
come to the bar of matrimony a maid; if in the foul, a widow;
if in the empty dish, it foretold, with equal certainty, no marriage at all. This ceremony was to be repeated three times,
and every time the arrangement of the dishes was to be
altered."

An old Scots Hallowe'en custom is that known as "Eating
the Herring." A cooked salt herring is eaten immediately before
retiring for the night, and in the dream which follows the future
partner of the sleeper will bring a drink of water to quench
his or her thirst. Guthrie, to whom I am indebted for particulars
concerning the above-mentioned practice, mentions another
which is called "Pricking the Egg." The procedure is to pierce
the shell with a pin and allow the white to drop into a wine-glass
containing water, take some of the mixture in one's mouth,
then go for a walk, and the first person's name one hears called
aloud will be the name of one's future partner in marriage.
Apropos of this particular practice, and as illustrative of the
credulity of the people, this Scots writer says: "An old woman

solemnly assured the editor she had, in her youthful days, engaged in this Hallowe'en frolic, and the name of Archibald (her husband's name) 'came up as it were from the very ground.' "[1]

A queer charm (remarkable also for the strange nature of the concoction's constituents) is given by Halliwell, who writes : " On St. Luke's day, says Mother Bunch, take marigold flowers, a sprig of marjoram, thyme, and a little wormwood ; dry them before a fire, rub them to powder ; then sift it through a fine piece of lawn, and simmer over a slow fire, adding a small quantity of virgin honey, and vinegar. Anoint yourself with this when you go to bed, saying the following lines three times, and you will dream of your partner that is to be :—

> St. Luke, St. Luke, be kind to me,
> In dreams let me my true love see."[2]

Yet another of these charm-divinations which is restricted to a specific day, the 6th of October, is given by the same authority. "A cake of flour, spring water, salt and sugar, is made by three girls, each having an equal hand in the composition. It is then baked in a Dutch oven, silence being strictly preserved, and turned thrice by each person. When it is well baked, it must be divided into three equal parts, and each girl must cut her share into nine pieces, drawing every piece through a wedding-ring which had been borrowed from a woman who has been married seven years. Each girl must eat her pieces of cake while she is undressing, and repeat the following verses :—

> O good St. Faith, be kind tonight,
> And bring to me my heart's delight ;
> Let me my future husband view,
> And be my visions chaste and true.

All three must then get into one bed, with the ring suspended by a string to the head of the couch. They will then dream of their future husbands."[3]

Although, apparently, the day is of no importance, the time factor enters into the following curious method. " Two young unmarried girls must sit together in a room by themselves,

---

[1] E. J. Guthrie, *Old Scottish Customs*, 1885, p. 75.
[2] Halliwell, op. cit., p. 217.
[3] Halliwell, op. cit., p. 216.

from 12 o'clock at night till one o'clock the next morning, without speaking a word. During this time each of them must take as many hairs from her head as she is years old, and, having put them into a linen cloth with some of the herb truelove, as soon as the clock strikes one, she must burn every hair separately, saying :—

> I offer this my sacrifice
> To him most precious in my eyes ;
> I charge thee now come forth to me,
> That I this minute may thee see.

Upon which her first husband will appear, walk round the room, and then vanish. The same event happens to both the girls, but neither see the other's lover."[1]

The importance of extraneous factors is clearly evidenced when kale or broth is employed as a means of divination. The custom was at one time in frequent use in the North of England, and indeed is still occasionally met with. The procedure is for the girl, immediately before retiring for the night, to stand on something she has never stood upon before, and with a pot of cold broth held in one hand, to utter the following lines :—

> " Hot kale or cold kale, I drink thee ;
> If ever I marry a man, or a man marry me,
> I wish this night I may him see,
>   Tomorrow may him ken.
> In church, fair, or market,
>   Above all other men."

At the conclusion of the recital, she drinks from the pot nine successive draughts, and walks backwards to her bed. During the night, she dreams of her future husband.[2]

II

Philtres for Enticing or Developing Love

Numerous as have been the methods employed, and the beliefs current, respecting the envisioning of one's future husband, these are as nothing in comparison with the magical and other

[1] Halliwell, op. cit, p. 215.
[2] Halliwell, op. cit., p. 219.

methods for causing another party to fall in love with one, or to develop or extend existing or waning passion. Moreover, while divination respecting future love affairs was, and is, apparently restricted in its employment to the female sex, no such restriction is called for or employed in regard to love-philtres.

The use of charms to create love is and always has been well-nigh universal. Many of these charms are purely magical in their significance and influence. Particularly is this noticeable in regard to the methods adopted by savages. Mostly the technique is concerned with obtaining possession, temporarily or otherwise, of some object of a personal nature belonging to the party whose love one wishes to arouse or inflame; or, alternatively, of influencing, in some way, something with which contact is likely to be made by the other party. The principle in all cases is connected with the sympathetic magic which plays so curious and so powerful a part in the life of savages. Thus in Baru, says Crawley, when it is desired to excite the love of a member of the opposite sex, one utters a charm over some betel before placing it in a betel box, and " when the man or woman against whom the charm is directed makes use of this betel, he or she falls in love with the owner."[1] One can produce similar results, says the same authority, by uttering charms " over the oil which the woman uses for her hair, or over a piece of hair one has got from a woman."[2]

Human liver was considered by the ancients to be a love-charm of extreme efficacy. It is claimed by some writers that liver was not a charm but an aphrodisiac, but here they err. The reason for this reputed efficacy was based upon the belief, current in those early days of civilization, that the liver was that part of the human organism in which desire of all kinds originated and developed. In accordance with the principle of sympathetic magic, therefore, the liver of a young person full of desire constituted a love-charm of the first magnitude.

It would appear that the ancients believed implicitly in the efficacy of these charms whether their supposed power was derived from sympathetic magic and philtres or aphrodisiacal qualities. The Greeks were addicted to the use of these potions. Both sexes employed them assiduously. Like the savages, they based most of their methods on the principle of sympathetic

[1] Ernest Crawley, *The Mystic Rose*, Methuen, 1927, Vol. I, p. 222.
[2] Crawley, op. cit., Vol. I, p. 222.

magic. When more ordinary methods failed, they roasted images of wax, representing the objects of their love, before the fire, and they firmly believed that as these images became warm, the persons represented by them would be proportionately warmed by love for the individuals conducting the operations. When a lover could obtain anything belonging to his mistress, he looked upon this as constituting a singular advantage, and buried it in the earth beneath the threshold of her door.

Among the various ingredients used in the love-magic of the ancient Greeks were calf's brains, hair from a wolf's tail, the blood of doves, the bones of snakes, the feathers of screech-owls, relics of various kinds, and portions of cadavers. Of the practices of the enchantress we read in Horace :—

> " Canidia crown'd with wreathing snakes
> Dishevell'd, thus the silence breaks :
> ' Now the magic fire prepare,
> And from graves uprooted tear
> Trees, whose horrors gloomy spread
> Round the mansions of the dead ;
> Bring the eggs and plumage foul
> Of a midnight shrieking owl ;
> Be they well besmear'd with blood
> Of the blackest venom'd toad ;
> Bring the choicest drugs of Spain,
> Produce of the poisonous plain ;
> Then into the charm be thrown,
> Snatch'd from famish'd bitch, a bone ;
> Burn them all with magic flame,
> Kindled first by Colchian dame."

The udder of a hyena, tied about the left arm, was thought to entice the affection of any woman one fixed one's eyes upon.[1] Sometimes enchanted medicaments were sprinkled on some part of the house where the loved one resided, as Theocritus's enchantress commands :

> " Now take these poisons, I procure you more,
> And strew them at the threshold of his door,
> That door where violent love hath fix'd my mind,
> Though he regard not, cruel and unkind !
> Strew them, and spitting, say in angry tones,
> I scatter Delphid's, perjur'd Delphid's bones."

---

[1] John Potter, *Archæologia Grecia, or the Antiquities of Greece*, Edinburgh, 1827. Vol. II., p. 250.

The possessor of any article that had belonged to the person whose love was desired, ranked as being of peculiar potency. Even the gods were, on occasion, called upon for aid ; thus Theocritus's Simoetha invoked the help of the moon and Hecate :

> " Moon, shine bright and clear :
> To thee I will direct my secret prayer ;
> To thee and Hecate, whom dogs do dread,
> When stain'd with gore, she stalks amidst the dead.
> Hail, frightful Hecate, assist me still,
> Make mine as green as fam'd Medea's skill."

Another practice was to melt wax over a fire, with the object of softening the heart of the person loved, while, as the wax melted the following lines were recited :

> "As this devoted wax melts o'er the fire,
> Let Myndian Delphis melt with soft desire."

Or laurel was burned to the chanting of these lines :

> " First, Delphid injur'd me, he rais'd my flame,
> And now I burn this bow in Delphid's name ;
> As this doth blaze and break away in fume,
> How soon it takes, let Delphid's flesh consume."

The writings of Virgil and others provide evidence in all abundance that the ancient Romans, like the Greeks, were addicted to the use of love-charms and philtres. Some of these potions were evidently dangerous, for, according to Plutarch and Cornelius Nepos, the Roman general, Lucullus was rendered unconscious by one such ; while Caius Caligula, avers the historian Suetonius, was thrown into a fit by a potion which was intended, by his wife Caesonia, merely to arouse his love. There is evidence, too, that Lucretius lost his life through a potion of an aphrodisiacal nature being given him. Similar fatal results are said to have frequently followed the use of love philtres by the women of Thessaly. As a result of such lethal effects, in Rome, at one time, the use of a love potion was a punishable offence, and in certain cases, as where a man's death was directly attributable to a philtre received from a woman, the penalty was a capital one. The law-makers of later years took very similar views as to the seriousness of the crime of administering such potions, whether or not they effected their purpose.

Beans had some reputation, among the Romans, for their love-stimulative properties. According to Carena, for having endeavoured to conciliate the affections of a young man, through the medium of some beans over which Mass had been celebrated, an old woman was whipped through the streets of Cremona.[1]

The use of charms and philtres was common in Great Britain, as well as in other countries, during the Middle Ages. While the majority were probably harmless, certain dangerous drugs of an aphrodisiacal nature were used, as well as other questionable means. Many references to these charms and philtres are to be found in criminal records. One such case, which occurred in Scotland, is given by Dalyell. I present it in his own words : " Sir John Colquhoun of Luss had married Lady Lilias Graham, eldest daughter of John, fourth Earl of Montrose, and sister of the celebrated marquis bearing that title, previous to the year 1633. Having received Lady Katherine, his sister-in-law, as an inmate of his family at ' Roisdew ', he cast the eyes of unlawful affection upon her : and not forgetting the ordinary arts of seduction, which require little tuition, he ' in craftie and politique manner, first insinuat himselff be subtile and entyseing speiches,' into her favour. But the delusion of these proving ineffectual, the seducer availed himself of the mystical expedients then in vogue, to spread a new snare for her virtue, with necromantic aid. He had a servant, an adept in occult charms, whom, among others, he consulted on his project ; and ' procureit from him, ane necromancer, certain philtra, or poysones, or poysonable and inchantit toakynes of love : speciallie ane jewall of gold, set with divers pretious diamantis, or rubeis, quhilk was poysonet or intoxicat be the said necromancer, and had the secreit and devillische force, of allureing and forceing the persone ressauer thairof, to expose hir bodie, fame, and credeit, to the will and unlauchfull plesour of the gevar and propyner thairof.' Having obtained this marvellous talisman, the seducer did not neglect to profit by its occult qualities :—nor do these seem to have been exaggerated, judging at least by the issue—for after having delivered the ' jewell of gold, set with the said rubeis and diamondis, devillischlie intoxicat and inchantit, as said is, —scho was so bewitchit and transpoirtit, that scho had no power

---

[1] John Graham Dalyell, *The Darker Superstitions of Scotland*, Glasgow, 1835, p. 219.

of hirselff' to refuse the said Sir John Colquhoun. After carrying on their intrigue at home, the parties eloped to London, where they continued to live together : the aggressor was outlawed, for he prudently avoided exposing himself to a criminal trial, his offence being aggravated by the affinity of his paramour. Whatever might have been the consequences in respect to him, the tenor of a charge against the necromancer, his accomplice, renders it probable that sentence would have followed conviction."[1]

References to love inspired by occult practices figure in the witchcraft trials of the Middle Ages. As transpired at the trial of Katherein Craigie, on June 16, 1640, the witch said to a widow : " Tell me if you have a mynd to have Harie Bellendyne to be your huisband, I will give you a gras, which being usit at my directioun, it will cause him to have no other woman but you."

Dalyell mentions a method of inspiring mutual love, in which a circle was drawn on a wafer with blood secured from the ring finger. The wafer was then consecrated, and after other ceremonies had occurred, half this wafer was taken by the person enamoured, and the other half pulverized and administered to the object of affection.[2]

Perhaps the most widely employed of all love charms was the mandrake, the fame of which had been handed down from Biblical times. Its reputation was largely based upon the resemblance of the root of this plant, in shape, to that of the human body; a resemblance which, it is suggested, has often been heightened by artifice.

In ancient times love philtres in both liquid and powder form were in frequent use in Ireland. There are many references to such philtres in folklore and literature. But the most curious of the lot, and, according to Lady Wilde, " the most awful " was the " dead strip ". This writer says : " Girls have been known to go to a graveyard at night, exhume a corpse that had been nine days buried, and tear down a strip of the skin from head to foot; this they manage to tie round the leg or arm of the man they love while he sleeps, taking care to remove it before his awaking. And so long as the girl keeps this strip

---

[1] John Graham Dalyell, *The Darker Superstitions of Scotland*, Glasgow, 1835, pp. 210, 211.
[2] Dalyell, op. cit., p. 288.

of skin in her possession, secretly hidden from all eyes, so long will she retain the man's love."[1]

Shakespeare, in his *Midsummer Night's Dream* refers to the use of the pansy as a love philtre, in the following passage from Act I, Scene 2 :—

> *Oberon.*   That very time I saw (but thou could'st not),
>   Flying between the cold moon and the earth,
>   Cupid all armed.   A certain aim he took
>   At a fair vestal, throned by the west,
>   And loos'd his love-shaft smartly from the bow,
>   As it should pierce a hundred thousand hearts,
>   But I might see young Cupid's fiery shaft
>   Quench'd in the chaste beams of the watery moon,
>   And the imperial vot'ress pass'd on
>   In maiden meditation fancy-free.
>   Yet mark'd I where the bolt of Cupid fell :
>   It fell upon a little western flower—
>   Before milk-white, now purpled with Love's wound—
>   And maidens call it Love-in-Idleness.
>   Fetch me that flower—the herb I show'd thee once ;
>   The juice of it on sleeping eyelids laid
>   Will make a man or woman madly dote
>   Upon the next live creature that it sees.
>   Fetch me this herb, and be thou here again
>   Ere the leviathan can swim a league.
>
> *Puck.*   I'll put a girdle round about the earth
>   In forty minutes.
>
> *Oberon.*   Having once this juice,
>   I'll watch Titania when she is asleep,
>   And drop the liquor of it in her eyes.
>   The next thing that she, waking, looks upon
>   (Be it on lion, bear, or wolf, or bull,
>   On meddling monkey, or on busy ape)
>   She shall pursue it with the soul of love.
>   And ere I take this charm off from her sight
>   (As I can take it with another herb),
>   I'll make her render up her page to me.

Other passages in Shakespeare allude to the use of philtres. Thus, in *Othello*, we find :—

> " Thou hast practis'd on her with foul charms ;
>   Abus'd her delicate youth with drugs, or minerals
>   That waken motion."

---

[1] Lady Wilde, *Ancient Cures, Charms, and Usages of Ireland*, 1890, p. 32.

And in another place in the same play :—

> " She is abus'd, stol'n from me, and corrupted
>   By spells and medicines bought of mountebanks."

Nor is Shakespeare the only writer to mention these practices. In John Gay's *Shepherd's Week* we read :—

> " Strait to the 'pothecary's shop I went,
>   And in love powder all my money spent ;
>   Behap what will, next Sunday after prayers,
>   When to the alehouse Lubberkin repairs,
>   These golden flies into his mug I'll throw,
>   And soon the swain with fervent love shall glow."

Brand refers to a statement in the *Connoisseur* (No. 56) to the effect that " there was publicly advertised among the other extraordinary medicines whose wonderful qualities are daily related in the last page of a newspaper, a most efficacious love powder, by which a despairing lover might create affection in the bosom of the most cruel mistress."[1] The same authority quotes from Newton's *Tryall of a Man's Owne Selfe*, 1602, " Whether by any secret sleight, or cunning, as drinkes, drugges, medicines, charmed potions, amatorious philtres, figures, characters, or any such like paltering instruments, devises, or practises, thou hast gone about to procure others to doate for love of thee."

According to Bloch (*History of English Sexual Morals*) Richard the Third accused Lady Elizabeth Grey of having enticed, with the aid of love potions, King Edward the Fourth into marriage. Any survey of the love philtres and aphrodisiacs used by many races, savage and civilized, in widely separated parts of the world would lack comprehensiveness if mention, however unsavoury it may be, were not made of the employment of urine and fæces of human beings and animals. There are references to these scatalogic or coprophagous philtres and aphrodisiacs by Paracelsus, Pliny, Beckherius, Reginald Scot, Frommann, John Leo, and others ; from the writings of whom Bourke cites numerous examples. In reference to the North American Indians, this authority says : " The witches and wizards of the Apache tribe

---

[1] John Brand, *Observations on the Popular Antiquities of Great Britain*, 1893. Vol. III, p. 306.

make a confection or philtre, one of the ingredients of which is generally human ordure, as the author learned from some of them a few years since. The Navajoes, of same blood and language as the Apaches, employ the dung of cows."[1] The Hottentots and others are addicted to the use of urine in connexion with their marriage rites as a means of promoting fertility (see page 200).

---

[1] Captain John G. Bourke, *Scatalogic Rites of all Nations*, Washington, D.C., 1891, p. 216.

CHAPTER III

VIRGINITY: ITS VALUE AND OTHERWISE

I

Virginity as a Highly-prized Possession

THE high value which is placed upon the virgin state of the bride is no product of modern civilization. It was at least equalled, if not exceeded, in the early days of Christianity, in the Mosaic times described in the Old Testament, and it has always been a feature of certain primitive tribes. The members of at least one ancient religious sect, the Skoptzies, made a practice of cutting away the labia majora, as a means of ensuring virginity for all time.

Evidence of the value placed upon virginity is provided by the fact that in so many cases proof was required that the bride was a virgin at the time of marriage, and severe punishments were devised for the girl or the woman who elected to marry when she was not *virgo intacta*. In the Bible we read that a bride who was found to have lost her virginity was stoned to death.[1]

The proof usually demanded by the husband and his relations was the absence of signs of defloration when the marriage was consummated. The sanguinary discharge following the rupture of the hymen constituted the evidence called for, hence the anxious examination of the bedclothes and under-garments of the bride, to which reference is made in the Bible, thus :—

> If any man take a wife, and go in unto her, and hate her, and give occasions of speech against her, and bring up an evil name upon her, and say, I took this woman, and when I came to her, I found her not a maid ;
> Then shall the father of the damsel, and her mother, take and bring forth the tokens of the damsel's virginity unto

[1] Deuteronomy, xxii, 21.

33

the elders of the city in the gate : and the damsel's father shall say unto the elders, I gave my daughter unto this man to wife, and he hateth her ;

And, lo, he hath given occasions of speech against her, saying, I found not thy daughter a maid ; and yet these are the tokens of my daughter's virginity. And they shall spread the cloth before the elders of the city.

And the elders of that city shall take that man and chastise him. And they shall amerce him in an hundred shekels of silver, and give them unto the father of the damsel, because he hath brought up an evil name upon a virgin of Israel : and she shall be his wife ; he may not put her away all his days.

But if this thing is true, and the tokens of virginity be not found for the damsel ; then they shall bring out the damsel to the door of her father's house, and the men of her city shall stone her with stones that she die.

In ancient Greece it was customary for the godfather and godmother of the bridegroom to satisfy themselves as to the virginity of the bride, and announce their satisfaction to those awaiting the news.   In ancient Egypt and some parts of Turkey it was usual to exhibit proof to the relatives and friends of the bridegroom. So, too, in Morocco. In accordance with the laws of Manu, a Hindu could reject his bride, if proof of her virginity were not forthcoming.

Mungo Park, in reference to the marriage rites of the Mandingoes in the interior of Africa, says : " The new-married couple are always disturbed toward morning by the women, who assemble to inspect the nuptial sheet (according to the manners of the ancient Hebrews as recorded in Scripture), and dance around it. This ceremony is thought indispensably necessary nor is the marriage considered valid without it."[1]

Although neither the presence of an unruptured hymen nor a discharge on the bridal night, is a certain indication of virginity, the absence of hemorrhage is, even to-day, popularly considered to provide evidence of pre-marital intercourse.[2]

Other methods were used by the ancients to ascertain whether

---

[1] Mungo Park, *Travels in the Interior Districts of Africa*, 1816. Vol. I, p. 399.
[2] The hymenal membrane may be of a type that permits intercourse without rupture, or the opening may have been widened by surgical or digital means, or the rupture of the membrane may have occurred accidentally.

or not the young woman was a virgin at the time of marriage. In the days of ancient Rome it was thought that the loss of virginity was followed by an increase in the girl's neck measurement, and this fallacy persists in some quarters to this day. A test, used in the fourteenth century, according to Konrad von Megenberg, was the ability of the girl to drink water in which black amber had been steeped for three days, without anything happening : in the event of her claim to be a virgin proving untrue, this would be at once demonstrated by her inability to hold her own water.[1]

The fact that virginity has, in so many countries, been regarded highly has led to attempts being made at simulation or restoration. These measures usually take the form of tightening up the relaxed vaginal walls by the application of astringent lotions, or surgical restoration of virginal conditions by suturing.

II

Virginity as a Despised Possession

Strange as it may seem to those unversed in anthropological lore, the possession of virginity has not always been something to boast of or to regard as being of great value. On the contrary, in many ancient tribes it was looked upon as a decided disadvantage ; in many primitive races even to this day the woman who is the possessor of an intact hymen is not wanted as a bride.

Ignorance and superstition, which invariably go hand in hand, were and are the causes of this viewpoint. The belief in the pernicious effects of menstrual blood—a belief that persists in many quarters even now—was universal in the early days of civilization as well as among savage tribes, and the common failure to differentiate between the blood accompanying defloration and the menstrual discharge, led to the belief that defloration itself was injurious to the male. Among those races, in particular, where it was considered that such bleeding was due to the presence of, or an attack by, an evil spirit, the risk of intercourse resulting

[1] Ploss and Bartels, *Woman, An Historical Gynecological and Anthropological Compendium*, (edited by E. J. Dingwall) ; Heinemann (Medical Books), London, 1935. Vol. II, p. 37.

in grave danger, or even death, to the male partner, as a consequence of contact with the female's blood, was ever present.

Because of these beliefs it is understandable that a man preferred to take as his wife a female who had already lost her virginity, and it may be imagined that, in many cases, the precise manner in which defloration had occurred was, from his point of view, of little moment. Even in those tribes where promiscuity was frowned upon, the bridegroom was nonetheless averse to running the risk which was thought to be connected with defloration. To avoid this risk, it was customary either to hire someone to perform the act or to have recourse to some form of artificial defloration. It is presumable that there were usually available men willing to take the risk provided the fee offered was sufficiently tempting ; in other cases, slaves, criminals, or even prisoners taken from enemy tribes, were compelled to perform the act. Inhabitants of alien lands, too, were, when opportunity offered, invited to undertake this office ; and as, for some extraordinary reason, a denizen of another land was believed to enjoy a degree of immunity that enabled him to scorn any such danger, it was usual for an invitation of this nature to be accepted with alacrity. Albeit, there were occasions no doubt when the stranger was given little choice in the matter.

There have been instances, too, where apart from or in addition to the above-mentioned risk, it was thought desirable for a girl to go through a form of marriage with a stranger in the first instance. According to Little, in the Island of Mitylene, a singular custom of this nature, by which a girl of marriageable age was enabled to lose her virginity, was observed. This custom, at the time of which Little writes, was known to be a very ancient one. Any stranger visiting the town where it was observed was compelled to enter into a temporary marital union with one of the young women residing there. In some cases, especially if the visitor was a man of some rank or standing, he was permitted to make his choice from a number of young ladies ; but others were given no choice whatever and had to take what was offered, however unhandsome or of whatever age. The marriage ceremony was duly performed by a priest and a nuptial feast held. The following morning the husband was at liberty to depart, nothing further being demanded of him, though a wealthy or influential man would sometimes give the lady a present, often of considerable value, before leaving

A NUDIST WEDDING

her. As for the wife, she considered herself well rewarded by being delivered from the reproach of virginity, which, says Little, it was "ignominious to retain or to surrender to a Mytelenian,"[1] as the preservation of her honour depended upon her being first married to a stranger. It mattered little whether he remained for a time, or whether he returned or not. After one year had elapsed she was free to contract a new marriage with anyone who proposed to her ; and, in the event of her former husband appearing on the scene, he had no legal claim on her : this much was made clear at the time of the first marriage. It is true that Little makes no mention of the point, but apart from any other contributory reasons, it seems to me that the idea of the immunity so generally credited to the stranger accounting in large measure for this practice, has at least a strong degree of probability in its favour.

Don Ulloa records that the ancient inhabitants of Peru would not, except in ignorance, marry virgins, and if it were discovered that any girl had failed to disclose the fact before marriage, the man considered he had been cheated. Similarly, in Tibet a virgin was thought to be unfit to become a wife. Westermarck mentions that the men of the Akamba tribe in British East Africa, consider a pregnant girl to be " a most eligible spouse ; " while the Chibchas and Caribs of America, writes Sir Richard Burton, were accustomed to look upon " virginity as a reproach, proving that the maiden had never inspired love."

In many of the tribes of Australia, the hymen is artificially perforated, and this act is followed, as part of the marriage rites by intercourse with a man other than the husband. " The object of the custom," said Crawley, " is clearly to remove the danger of sexual intercourse for the husband, and perhaps also for the wife, by a ceremonial previous rehearsal of it."[2] The same authority, quoting de Morga, mentions that in the Philippines certain men made a profession of deflowering brides.[3]

Not always, however, is perforation left until the time of marriage. In many tribes it is customary for dilatation to be performed on arrival at puberty, or even before.

Often defloration was really either wholly or in part a sacrificial

[1] Thomas Little, *The Beauty, Marriage-Ceremonies, and Intercourse of the Sexes in all Nations*, 1824. Vol. II, p. 151.
[2] A. E. Crawley, *The Mystic Rose*. Vol. II, p. 67.
[3] Ibid. Vol. II, p. 69.

rite. It was particularly associated with the worship of the
phallic god Mutunus. In other cases the perforation was not
artificially induced, but a priest, acting on behalf of the god,
performed the defloration.

Allied to sacrificial defloration was the act of circumcision
performed, as it usually was in olden days, not as a hygienic
or prophylactic measure, but as a religious rite.

The Abbé Dubois mentioned a post mortem marriage custom
peculiar to the Nambudiri caste. In accordance with this
custom, where a girl died a virgin, dishonour was the lot of
her parents and relatives unless some man could be hired or
otherwise induced not only to go through a form of marriage
with the corpse before it was burned but actually to consummate
the marriage. It has been stated, however, that whatever may
have been customary over a century ago, in more recent years
the extraordinary and repulsive act to which Dubois referred,
did not take place. In a footnote to Beauchamp's translation
of the Abbé's work, we read that no rites, other than those
usually observed at a Hindu marriage, are practised ; and that :
" By marriage here is meant merely the tying of the *tali* (the
emblem of marriage) and not the act of consummation of
marriage."[1]

In many cases where promiscuity is universal the loss of
virginity is thought nothing of. Here it is not so much a case
of desirability as of acquiescence in a state of affairs where
custom has robbed virginity of its value or attraction. In
reference to the Tahitians, Ida Pfeiffer says : " Little girls of
seven or eight years old have their lovers of twelve or fourteen,
and their parents are quite proud of the fact. The more lovers
a girl has the more she is respected. As long as she is not
married she leads a most dissolute life, and it is said that not
all the married women make the most faithful wives possible."[2]

---

[1] *Hindu Manners, Customs and Ceremonies*, by the Abbé J. A. Dubois, translated by Henry K. Beauchamp, c.i.e., third edition, Clarendon Press, Oxford,
1905., pp. 16-17.
[2] Ida Pfeiffer, *A Woman's Journey Round the World*, c. 1852, p. 74

CHAPTER IV

BUNDLING, ITS ANALOGUES, AND OTHER CURIOUS METHODS OF COURTSHIP

I

The Genesis, Development, and Significance of Bundling

THE strange custom of bundling, or courting in bed, is of far more ancient origin than is generally supposed. Many writers contend that the practice originated in Europe and was thence introduced to the Eastern parts of North America. There is evidence that it existed, not exactly in the precise form described by eighteenth-century travellers, but in a more primitive and less methodical manner, as long ago as the time of the ancient Roman Empire, and that in some form or other it was practised by savages in many parts of the world.

It is clear that the custom was not, either in its earliest forms or in its subsequent developments, in any way considered to be connected with or the outcome of licentiousness. In fact, in the early days of Christianity, a practice indistinguishable from bundling, except that there was no thought of subsequent marriage, formed part of that period of temptation to which the more rigid of the ascetics were wont to submit themselves, though how far and in how many cases, in actual practice, morality triumphed, we can only surmise. The fact that so many members of the sects which at that time rejected marriage as something evil and sinful, had associations of, ostensibly, an asexual character with various females, is a point the significance of which cannot be ignored or overlooked.

Evidence of the existence of some form of bundling, though it was not known by this name, in various ancient races, is available in some abundance. In parts of Finland, many centuries ago, it was customary for a couple to sleep together for a week or so before the day fixed for the wedding, the only stipulation being that both parties should retain some of their clothes.

There is evidence that a form of bundling was practised by many tribes of North American Indians. According to Alexander,[1] it was customary for the young man to visit his inamorata at night in her hut, preceding his actual entrance by signs made from the doorway. On the girl giving him permission to enter, he made his way to her side, and without further ado they got into bed together. If she gave the young man anything to eat or drink, this very act constituted a refusal for the courtship to proceed further, and after finishing the repast, " he retired in silence." A variation of this practice, mentioned by other writers, was where the young Indian entered the hut of his loved one, lighted a stick at the fire, and then went to the girl's bed with the burning brand in his hand. Should she blow out the light, it was an intimation that she favoured his court, and forthwith he lay down at her side ; if she pulled the covers over her face, it was a sign that she wished to have nothing to do with him, and he retired at once.

Masson, the traveller and explorer, states that some tribes in Afghanistan have a method of bundling known to them by the name of *mamzat bezé*. " The lover presents himself at the house of his betrothed with a suitable gift, and in return is allowed to pass the night with her, on the understanding that innocent endearments are not to be exceeded."[2]

At later stages of European civilization bundling took a different form, becoming a practice carried out by avowed lovers. The young man visited his fiancée at night and spent the time in her bedroom, either sitting on the bed or getting into it ; in the latter case both parties retaining their clothes. There was nothing secret in connexion with it ; the parents of both boy and girl knew all about the practice and gave it their approval.

The consensus of authoritative opinion regarding the origin of the custom as a method of courting is that poverty was the true cause, a theory which has much to support it in the fact that bundling was virtually restricted to the lower classes of society in each country where it was practised. In the colder months it was not practicable for a couple to pursue their love-making in the open, and the poorer members of the population could not afford fires for long periods : sheer discomfort induced

---

[1] William Alexander, *The History of Women*. Vol. II, p. 213.
[2] Charles Masson, *Journeys in Baloochistan, Afghanistan, The Punjab*, 1842.

the older people to retire to bed at a very early hour, and similarly it caused the lovers to seek the warmth of the girl's bed too. The only point in its favour, and it was a small one at that, was the fact that, as already mentioned, the lovers had no recourse to subterfuge or secrecy.

Apparently bundling reached its greatest popularity in Great Britain, Ireland, Holland, Scandinavia, Switzerland, and, in North America. Sumner[1] says that the houses in Holland, during the seventeenth century, had windows constructed so as to allow convenient entry.

Reference to the custom as practised in Wales, is made by a Mr. Pratt, in a book of travels published in the last decade of the eighteenth century. He says: "The lower order of people do actually carry on their love affairs in bed, and what would extremely astonish more polished lovers, they are carried on honourably, it being, at least, as usual for the Pastoras of the mountains to go from the bed of courtship to the bed of marriage as unpolluted and maidenly as the Chloes of fashion; and yet you are not to conclude that this proceeds from their being less susceptible of the *belle-passion* than their betters; or that the cold air which they breathe has froze ' the genial current of their souls.' " Mr. Pratt, according to his own statement, went to a considerable amount of trouble in an effort to investigate this curious custom; and, he continues, "after being assured, by many, of its veracity, I had an opportunity of attesting its existence with my own eyes." It appears that in a house at which he was staying, in Caernarvonshire, the servant girl had a lover "who walked eleven long miles every Sunday morning to favour his suit, and regularly returned the same night through all weathers, to be ready for Monday's employment in the fields, being simply a day labourer. He usually arrived in time for morning service, which he constantly attended, after which he escorted his Dulcinea home to the house of her master, by whose permission they as constantly passed the succeeding hour in bed, according to the custom of the country. These tender sabbatical preliminaries continued without any interruption near two years, when the treaty of alliance was solemnized; and, so far from any breach of articles happening in the intermediate time, it is most likely that it was considered by both parties

---

[1] W. G. Sumner, *Folkways*, Boston, 1907, p. 527.

as a matter of course, without exciting any other idea. On speaking to my friend on the subject, he observed that, though it certainly appeared a dangerous mode of making love, he had seen so few *living* abuses of it, during six and thirty years' residence in that country, where it nevertheless had always, more or less, prevailed, he must conclude it was as innocent as any other."   After indulging in some banal and trite remarks respecting the connexion between ethics and convention, Mr. Pratt concludes with the following casuistic observations : " The power of habit is perhaps stronger than the power of passion, or even than of the charms which inspire it ; and it is sufficient, almost, to say a thing is the custom of a country, to clear it from any reproach that would attach to an innovation. Were it the practice of a few only, and to be gratified by stealth, there would, from the strange construction of human nature, be more cause of suspicion ; but being ancient, general, and carried on without difficulty, it is probably as little dangerous as a *tête-à-tête* in a drawing-room, or in any other full-dress place where young people meet to say soft things to each other. A moonlight walk in Papa's garden where Miss steals out to meet her lover *without the consent of her parents*, which is, of course, extremely agreeable to the young people, has ten times the peril."[1]

It would appear that the people of Wales were for the most part loath to admit the existence of this custom, for another writer, and a contemporary of Pratt, says in reference to bundling : " Our companion like everyone else that we spoke with in Wales on the subject, at once denied the existence of this custom : that maids in many instances admitted male bedfellows, he did not doubt, but that the procedure was sanctioned by tolerated custom he considered a gross misrepresentation. Yet in Anglesea and some parts of North Wales, where the original simplicity of manners and a high sense of chastity of the natives is retained, he admitted something of the kind might appear. In those thinly-inhabited districts a peasant often has several miles to walk after the hours of labour, to visit his mistress ; those who have reciprocally entertained the *belle passion* will easily imagine that before the lovers grow tired of each other's company the night will be far enough advanced ; nor is it surprising that a tender-hearted damsel should be

[1] *Gleanings Through Wales, Holland, and Westphalia,* London, 1795, pp. 110-113.

disinclined to turn her lover out over bogs and mountains until the dawn of day."[1]

It is noteworthy that Mr. Barbor, following in the footsteps of Mr. Pratt, refers to the harmlessness and innocence of the practice, stating that, to use his own words, " it is averred that the moving tale of love is agitated in that situation without endangering a breach in the preliminaries," and further that, the practice of shifting from a sitting position near the hearth to " a heap of straw or fern covered with two or three blankets in a neighbouring corner " only took place with a " view of accommodation." Now, whether Mr. Pratt and Mr. Barbor really believed that normal human beings actuated by the throes of passionate love, could, in such circumstances observe the proprieties, or whether both these observers were writing with their tongues in their cheeks, I have no means of knowing, but I can say that from a lifetime's study of sexological problems I am unable to subscribe to so naive a viewpoint. In support of my attitude it may perhaps be worth while quoting from another account by a contemporary observer, a clergyman named Bingley, who writes : " The peasantry of part of Caernarvonshire, Anglesea, and Merionethshire adopt a mode of courtship which, till within the last few years, was scarcely even heard of in England. It is the same that is common in many parts of America, and termed by the inhabitants of that continent, bundling. The lover steals, under the shadow of the night, to the bed of his fair one, into which (retaining an essential part of his dress) he is admitted without any shyness or reserve. Saturday or Sunday nights are the principal times when this courtship takes place, and on these nights the men sometimes walk from a distance of ten miles or more to visit their favourite damsels. This strange custom seems to have originated in the scarcity of fuel, and in the consequent unpleasantness of sitting together in the colder parts of the year without a fire. Much has been said of the innocence with which these meetings are conducted. This may be the case in some instances, but it is a very common thing for the consequence of the intercourse to make its appearance in the world within two or three months after the marriage ceremony has taken place. The subject excites

[1] J. T. Barbor, *A Tour Throughout North Wales and Monmouthshire*, 1803, p. 103. (Quoted by Henry Reed Stiles in *Bundling, Its Origin, Progress and Decline in America*, New York, 1934).

no particular attention among the neighbours, provided the marriage be made good before the living witness is brought to light. Since this custom is entirely confined to the labouring classes of the community, it is not so pregnant with danger as, on a first supposition, it might seem. Both parties are so poor that they are necessarily constrained to render their issue legitimate, in order to secure their reputation, and with it a mode of obtaining a livelihood."[1]

It is further noteworthy that American legal opinion did not accept the view that the practice was so innocent as was assumed or claimed by so many of its practitioners and supporters in both the Old and New Worlds. Stiles, in his exceedingly interesting book on the subject, mentions the case of Seger v. Slingerland, in which it was held by the Supreme Court in the State of New York, " That although bundling was admitted to be the custom in some parts of the State, it being proven that the parents of the girl, for whose seduction the suit was brought, countenanced her practising it, they had no right to complain, or ask satisfaction for the consequences, which, the Court say, naturally followed it ! "[2]

An interesting reference to bundling as practised in Ireland occurs in a book entitled *The Stranger in Ireland*, written by John Carr, who says : " One evening, at an inn where we halted, we heard a considerable bustle in the kitchen, and, upon enquiry, I was let into a secret worth knowing. The landlord had been scolding one of his maids, a very pretty plump little girl, for not having done her work ; and the reason which she alleged for her idleness was, that her master having locked the street door at night, had prevented her lover enjoying the rights and delights of bundling, an amatory indulgence which, considering that it is sanctioned by custom, may be regarded as somewhat singular, although it is not exclusively of Welsh growth. The process is very simple : the gay Lothario, when all is silent, steals into the chamber of his mistress, who receives him in bed, but with the modest precaution of wearing her under-petticoat, which is always fastened at the bottom, not infrequently, I am told, by a sliding knot. It may astonish a London gallant to be

---

[1] Rev. W. Bingley, *North Wales*, second edition ; London, 1814. Vol. II, pp. 504-505.

[2] Quoted by Henry Reed Stiles in *Bundling, Its Origin, Progress and Decline in America*, from Caines' Cases, II, p. 219.

told that this extraordinary experiment often ends in a down-right wedlock—the knot which cannot slide. A gentleman of respectability also assured me that he was obliged to indulge his female servants in these nocturnal interviews, and that, too, at all hours of the night, otherwise his whole family would be thrown into disorder by their neglect; the carpet would not be dusted, nor would the kettle boil."

Richard Twiss, in his book *A Tour in Ireland in 1775*, also says that bundling was prevalent among the common people in some parts of Ireland; and as evidence of a similar custom existing in Holland, quotes the following passage from the *Travels of Van Egmont and Heyman*: "In the island of Texel, in North Holland, the women are very fond of courtship, which among the youth of the peasantry is carried on in a manner like *Queesting*. This is an ancient custom of evening visits and courtships among the young people in the islands of Vlie and Wieringen, but especially in the Texel. It is indeed of an antiquity the date of which cannot be traced. The spark comes into the house at night, either by the door, which is left upon the latch, or half open; by one of the windows; or through the stable; and makes his way to the bed-chamber of his sweetheart, who is already in bed. After a compliment or two, he begs leave that he may pull off his upper garment, and come upon the bed to her. This being of course granted, he lifts up the quilt or rug, lays himself under it, and then *queests* or chats with her till he thinks it time to depart, which is invariably done by the same entrance he came in at. This is a custom from which the natives will not soon depart; the parents thinking it equit-able not to deny their children a freedom they themselves were indulged in. Their innate tenacious parsimony also finds its account in this custom, which dispenses with the articles of fire and candle in the long winter evenings and nights."

At about the same time that the Welsh, Scots, and Irish peasantry were busy practising bundling, a similar custom was in vogue three thousand miles away on the North Atlantic coast of America. There is evidence in abundance that in Massachusetts and Connecticut, among the poorer people, courting in bed was popular. It was usually referred to as tarrying, though Washington Irving, in his *History of New York*, used the name favoured in Britain. He mentions a singular custom " which was probably borrowed from the ancient republic of Sparta;

where we are told the young ladies, either from being great romps and hoydens, or else, like many modern heroines, very fond of meddling with matters that did not appertain to their sex, used frequently to engage with the men in wrestling and other athletic exercises of the gymnasium." Irving goes on to say that " The custom to which I allude was vulgarly known by the name of bundling—a superstitious rite observed by the young people of both sexes, with which they usually terminated their festivities ; and which was kept up with religious strictness, by the more bigoted and vulgar part of the community. This ceremony was likewise, in those primitive times, considered as an indispensable preliminary to matrimony; their court-ships commencing where ours usually finish. By which means they acquired that intimate acquaintance with each others' good qualities before marriage, which has been pronounced by philosophers the sure basis of a happy union. Thus early did this cunning and ingenious people display a shrewdness at making a bargain, which has ever since distinguished them—and a strict adherence to the good old vulgar maxim about ' buying a pig in a poke '." Irving, who displays none of the naivete which was so marked a feature of the observations of many earlier writers on the subject of bundling, continues : " To this sagacious custom, therefore, do I chiefly attribute the unparalleled increase of the Yanokie or Yankee tribe ; for it is a certain fact, well authenticated by Court records and parish registers, that wherever the practice of bundling prevailed, there was an amazing number of sturdy brats annually born into the State, without the licence of the law, or the benefit of clergy ; and it is truly astonishing that the learned Malthus, in his treatise on population, has entirely overlooked this singular fact. Neither did the irregularity of their birth operate in the least to their disparagement. On the contrary, they grew up a long-sided, raw-boned, hardy race of whoreson whalers, wood-cutters, fishermen, and pedlars, and strapping corn-fed wenches ; who, by their united efforts, tended marvellously towards populating those notable tracts of country called Nantucket, Piscataway, and Cape Cod."[1]

The Reverend Andrew Burnaby in his *Travels in North America* refers to the practice of a modified form of bundling. He writes :

[1] Diedrich Knickerbocker (Washington Irving), *A History of New York*, Tegg & Son, London, 1836, pp. 140-141.

"A very extraordinary method of courtship is sometimes practised among the lower people in Massachusetts Bay, called *Tarrying*. When a man is enamoured of a young woman and wishes to marry her, he proposes the affair to her parents, without whose consent no marriage in this colony can take place. If they have no objection, they allow him to *tarry* with her one night, in order to make his court to her. At the usual time, the old couple retire to bed, leaving the young ones to settle matters as they can ; who, after having sat up as long as they think proper, get into bed together also, but without pulling off their under-garments, in order to prevent scandal. If the parties agree, it is all very well ; the banns are published, and they are married without delay ; if not, they part, and possibly never see each other again ; unless, which is an accident that seldom happens, the forsaken fair one proves pregnant, and then the man is obliged to marry her, under pain of excommunication." In almost identical words, Anburey described this same practice, and remarks on its prevalence along the sea-coast, where he infers it displaced the former practice of bundling.

At times it would appear that the practice degenerated into something little removed from promiscuity, the " bundlers " being lovers for the time only, in contradistinction to those cases where the practice was continued by the courting couple over a protracted period. There is a reference by Captain Thomas Anburey, to bundling as a social pleasantry offered to a guest.[1] Writing in the closing years of the eighteenth century, Anburey observes : " The night before we came to this town (Williamstown, Mass.), being quartered at a small log-hut, I was convinced in how innocent a view the Americans look upon that indelicate custom they call *bundling* : though they have remarkably good feather beds, and are extremely neat and clean, still I preferred my hard mattress, as being accustomed to it ; this evening, however, owing to the badness of the roads, and the weakness of my mare, my servant had not arrived with my

---

[1] There is evidence that this incident related by Captain Anburey was neither uncommon nor unusual in the period and district to which he referred. The Rev. Andrew Burnaby mentions that a gentleman travelling on the frontiers of Virginia, finding himself stranded, was compelled to put up for the night at a plantation. He was given a bed, into which later, to his astonishment, the owner, his wife and sixteen-year-old daughter, crept also. Richard Twiss, in referring to this statement, says : " I only mention this, in order to remark that I was assured the like custom is frequently practised in these parts, though I never experienced it myself " (*A Tour in Ireland in* 1775, p. 106).

baggage at the time for retiring to rest; there being only two beds in the house, I inquired which I was to sleep in, when the old woman replied, ' Mr. Ensign,' (here I should observe to you, that the New England people are very inquisitive as to the rank you have in the army).   ' Mr. Ensign,' says she, ' our Jonathan and I will sleep in this, and our Jemima and you shall sleep in that.'   I was much astonished at such a proposal, and offered to sit up all night, when Jonathan immediately replied, ' Oh, la !   Mr. Ensign, you won't be the first man our Jemima has bundled with, will he, Jemima ? ' when little Jemima, who, by the bye, was a very pretty, black-eyed girl, of about sixteen or seventeen, archly replied, ' No, father, not by many, but it will be the first Britainer ' (the name they give to Englishmen). In this dilemma, what could I do ?—the smiling invitation of pretty Jemima—the eye, the lip, the—Lord ha' mercy, where am I going to ?—but wherever I may be going to now, I did not go to bundle with her—in the same room with her father and mother, my kind host and hostess too !—I thought of that —I thought of more besides—to struggle with the passions of nature ; to clasp Jemima in my arms—to—do what ? you'll ask —why, to do—nothing ! for if amid all these temptations, the lovely Jemima had melted into kindness, she had been an outcast from the world—treated with contempt, abused by violence, and left perhaps to perish !—No, Jemima ; I could have endured all this to have been blest with you, but it was too vast a sacrifice, when you were to be the victim !—Suppose how great the test of virtue must be, or how cold the American constitution, when this unaccountable custom is in hospitable repute, and perpetual practice."[1]

II

Other Strange Methods of Courtship

Alexander, in his remarkable compendium, *The History of Women*, describes a curious method of courtship at one time practised in Spain, the most extraordinary feature of which was the masochistic element displayed.   But I will let the historian

[1] Anburey, *Travels Through the Interior Parts of America*, in *A Series of Letters*, 1781.   Vol. II, pp. 37-40.

speak for himself : " The Spaniards, finding that the same causes must produce the same effects on the tender and compassionate natures of women, endeavour, instead of attaching them by pleasure, as in other countries, to secure them by exciting their pity and compassion, not only through every part of the courtship, but still more forcibly in a custom which they practised some time ago at Madrid, and in other parts of Spain ; when a company of people, who called themselves disciplinants, or whippers, partly instigated by superstition, and partly by love, paraded the streets every Good Friday, attended by all the religious orders, several of the courts of judicature, all the Companies of trades, and sometimes the King and all his Court. The whippers are arrayed in long caps in the form of a sugar-loaf, with white gloves, and shoes of the same colour ; a waistcoat, the sleeves of which were tied with ribbons of such colours as they thought most agreeable to the fancy of the ladies they adored ; and in their hands were whips made of small cords, to the ends of which were cemented little bits of wax stuck with pieces of broken glass ; with these they whipped themselves as they went along, and he who showed the least mercy to his carcase, was sure of the greatest pity from his dulcinea. When they happened to meet a handsome woman in the street, some one of them took care to whip himself so as to make his blood spurt upon her ; an honour for which she never failed humbly to thank him. When any of them came opposite to the window of his mistress, he began to lay upon himself with redoubled fury, while she, from her balcony, looked complacently on the horrid scene, and knowing it was acted in honour of her charms, thought herself greatly obliged to her lover, and seldom failed to reward accordingly."[1]

Of a somewhat similar nature was the practice, in connexion with ceremonial processions in Constantinople, described by Lady Montagu, of men causing self-injuries by piercing their arms with arrow-heads. " I am told," says this famous narrator, " that some make use of it to advance their love, and when they come near the window where their mistress stands, all the women being veiled to see this spectacle, they stick another arrow for her sake, who gives some sign of approbation and encouragement to this kind of gallantry."

A curious custom prevails in some parts of Persia, according

---

[1] William Alexander, *The History of Women*, Dublin, 1779. Vol. II, p. 226.

to Tegg.   Any young man of initiative and audacity can marry the object of his affections, without the consent of, or in defiance of, her parents.   All he has to do is to seize a suitable opportunity for cutting off a lock of her hair; then, tearing away the veil that covers her face, he throws a sheet over her head and proclaims her to be his affianced wife.   Usually the girl makes no protest at such a method of betrothal; indeed the whole procedure is apparently carried out with her connivance.   The main object is to prevent any other young man proposing to her: as a rule the parents of the girl would forthwith accept him as her fiancé; but, says Tegg, " as they would not exempt him from the necessity of paying some price, and, as they [these proceedings] might be taken up as an affront by the relations, they are not often resorted to; and, when the consent of the parents cannot be obtained, the most common expedient is to elope with the girl."[1]

An even stranger custom is said to be practised by a tribe inhabiting the mountains on the borders of Persia and India. The members of this tribe are called Vizerees. Should a woman be attracted to a man, she instructs the drummer of the camp to attach to the man's cap, by means of a pin, a handkerchief which she has used to bind up her hair. Watching his opportunity the drummer discharges his task in full view of the people, at the same time stating who is the owner of the handkerchief. Custom ordains that the man must marry immediately the lady in question, provided that he is in a position to pay the price demanded by her father.

¹ William Tegg, *The Knot Tied*, 1877, p. 156.

PART TWO

VARIOUS FORMS OF MARRIAGE

CHAPTER V

MARRIAGE BY CAPTURE

I

Rarity of the Practice in its True Sense

It is a common assumption that in savagery, and in the early days of civilization, men were accustomed to capture from neighbouring tribes or countries the women whom they married. Many early historians testified to the widespread existence of the practice.

From a study of Mosaic law as adduced in Deuteronomy, the marrying of women captured in war was allowable. In the Book of Judges, too, there is an account of the Rape of the Sabine virgins. According to the historian Alexander, " When Romulus, the founder of Rome, had formed his infant republic, finding that he had no women, and that none of the neighbouring nations would give their daughters in marriage to men whom they considered a set of lawless bandetti ; he was obliged by stratagem to procure for his citizens, what he could not obtain for them by intreaty. Accordingly, having proclaimed a solemn feast, and an exhibition of games in honour of Equestrian Neptune, and by that means gathered a great number of people together ; on a signal given, the Romans, with drawn swords in their hands, rushed among the strangers, and forcibly carried away a great number of their daughters to Rome. The next day Romulus himself distributed them as wives to those of his citizens who had thus by violence carried them away."[1]

It is a hotly disputed point whether or not exogamy, which was practised by so many ancient more or less civilized nations, and is in vogue among some savage and primitive tribes to-day, led to the introduction of marriage by capture. M'Lennan, one of the leading exponents of the close relationship between

[1] William Alexander, *The History of Women*, p. 150.

marriage by capture and exogamy, contends that in many tribes where female infanticide had been practised, the lack of women to preserve the continuance of the race, led the men to seek wives from tribes other than their own. He observes that "if it could be shown that exogamous tribes existed, and that the usual relations of savage tribes to each other were those of hostility, we should have found a social condition in which it was inevitable that wives should systematically be procured by capture. It also appeared that if the existence of exogamous tribes either actually capturing their wives, or observing the symbol of capture in their marriage ceremonies, should be established in a reasonable number of cases, it would be a legitimate inference that exogamy had prevailed wherever we find a system of capture, or the form of capture, existing. . . . We may conclude that wherever capture, or the form of capture, prevails, or has prevailed, there prevails, or has prevailed, exogamy. Conversely, we may say that, wherever exogamy can be found, we may confidently expect to find, after due investigation, at least traces of a system of capture."[1]

On the other hand, Westermarck, Crawley, and others, with equal certitude, contend that so far from marriage by capture being general among savage tribes, it was and is essentially rare. Many of the instances given by M'Lennan are not marriage by capture in the true sense of the term, but are really elopements. The fact that a young woman was, or is, carried off by her lover without the consent of her parents or other near relatives, does not constitute marriage by capture: to do this the girl, in addition, must be taken *without her consent and by force*. Strictly speaking, in the majority of cases where women are removed by force from their homes during the course of an invasion, or by a marauding force, which are the only cases where women are captured, the question of marriage does not enter into the matter, the women being forced to submit to the demands of their captors in circumstances which amount to rape: the instances in which the women, subsequent to being carried off, *willingly* marry their captors are few and far between.

"There is ample reason to believe," says M'Lennan, "that the practice [of capturing wives] was general among the nations of the north of Europe and Asia. Olaus Magnus, indeed,

[1] John F. M'Lennan, *Primitive Marriage*, Adam and Charles Black, Edinburgh, 1865, pp. 136-7.

represents the tribes of the north as having been continually at war with one another either on account of stolen women, or with the object of stealing women. . . . His brother Johannes dilates on the same topic, and mentions numerous cases in which the plunderers were of the royal houses of Denmark or Sweden. As did the kings, so did their subjects. Among the Scandinavians, before they became Christians, wives were almost invariably fought for and wedded at the sword-point. In Sweden, even long after the introduction of Christianity, women were often carried off when on the way to the church to be married. A wedding cortège was a party of armed men, and for greater security marriages were generally celebrated at night. A pile of lances is said to be still preserved in the ancient church of Husaby in Gothland, into which were fitted torches; these weapons were borne by the groomsmen, and served the double purpose of giving light and protection."[1]

The Maoris as well as the Fijians relied upon securing wives when on forays against other tribes for the purpose of indulging their anthropophagic appetites. But of all the savage races, the Australian Blacks appear to stand out, for sheer brutality and crudeness in taking their wives by force, as the following account, by an anonymous writer, which appeared in *Chambers's Journal* (October 22, 1864), clearly shows : " In nothing is the brutality of their nature more clearly shown than in their treatment of their females. Among them, women are considered as an inferior class, and are used almost as beasts of burden ; so that it is not at all uncommon to meet a huge black fellow travelling merrily along with no load but his spear or war-club, whilst his unfortunate *leubra* is panting under the weight of their goods and chattels, which she is compelled to carry from camp to camp. Courtship, as the precursor to marriage, is unknown among them. When a young warrior is desirous of procuring a wife, he generally obtains one by giving in exchange for her a sister, or some other female relative of his own ; but if there should happen to be no eligible damsel disengaged in the tribe to which he belongs, then he hovers round the encampment of some other blacks until he gets an opportunity of seizing one of their *leubras*, whom perhaps he has seen and admired when attending one of the grand corroborries. His mode of paying his addresses is simple and efficacious. With a blow of his

[1] M'Lennan, op. cit., pp. 70-71.

nulla-nulla (war club), he stuns the object of his ' affections ', and drags her insensible body away to some retired spot, whence, as soon as she recovers her senses, he brings her home to his own gunyah in triumph.   Sometimes two join in an expedition for the same purpose, and then for several days they watch the movements of their intended victims, using the utmost skill in concealing their presence.   When they have obtained the know-ledge they require, they wait for a dark, windy night; then quite naked, and carrying only their long ' jag-spears ', they crawl stealthily through the bush until they reach the immediate vicinity of the camp-fires, in front of which the girls they are in search of are sleeping.   Slowly and silently, they creep close enough to distinguish the figure of one of these *leubras*; then one of the intruders stretches out his spear, and inserts its barbed point among her thick flowing locks; turning the spear slowly round, some of her hair speedily becomes entangled with it; then, with a sudden jerk, she is aroused from her slumber, and as her eyes open, she feels the sharp point of another weapon pressed against her throat.   She neither faints nor screams; she knows well that the slightest attempt at escape or alarm will cause her instant death, so, like a sensible woman, she makes a virtue of necessity, and rising silently, she follows her captors. They lead her away to a considerable distance, tie her to a tree, and return to ensnare their other victims in like manner.   Then, when they have accomplished their design, they hurry off to their own camp, where they are received with universal applause, and highly honoured for their *gallant* exploit.   Occasionally an alarm is given, but even then the wife-stealers easily escape amidst the confusion, to renew their attempt at some future period.   When a distinguished warrior carries off a bride from a strange tribe, he will frequently volunteer to undergo ' the trial of spears ', in order to prevent the necessity of his people going to war in his defence; then both the tribes meet, and ten of their smartest and youngest young men are picked out by the aggrieved party.   These are each provided with three reed-spears, and a *wommera*, or throwing-stick; and the offender, armed only with his *heiliman* (a bark-shield eighteen inches long by six wide), is led out in front, and placed at a distance of forty yards.   Then, at a given signal, the thirty spears are launched at him in rapid succession; these he receives and parries with his shield, and so skilful are the blacks in the use of their own

MARRIAGE BY CAPTURE. A CIRCASSIAN BRIDE'S RIDE

From G. T. Bettany's *The World's Inhabitants*, 1888

weapons, that very seldom is any wound inflicted. Having successfully passed through this ordeal, the warrior is considered to have fairly earned his *leubra*, and to have atoned for his offence in carrying her off; so the ceremony generally concludes by the two tribes feasting together in perfect harmony."[1]

Commenting on the above, M'Lennan says : "It is impossible, in reading this account of the Australian mode of capturing women, not to recall what Plutarch says of the ceremonies of Roman marriage, apropos of the Rape of the Sabines : ' It is a custom still observed for the bride not to go over the threshold of her husband's house herself, but to be carried over; because the Sabine virgins did not go voluntarily, but were carried in by violence. *Some add that the bride's hair is parted with the point of a spear, in memory of the first marriages being brought about in a warlike manner*'."[2] (In this connexion cf. p. 166.)

To what extent marriage by capture still exists in isolated places, or as a sporadic practice, it is impossible to say. It does, however, exist in the Arctic regions, according to Louise Jordan Miln, who says the young Eskimo drags by her long hair or her fur garments, the woman whom he intends to make his wife, taking " her to his lair of ice or tent of skin."[3] The Greenlander " will employ or depute a party of friends to seize the woman for him ; "[4] and, says this same authority, marriage by capture still exists in some parts of South America.

II

"Marriage by Capture " as a Ceremonial Procedure

From the earliest days, and in many races in various parts of the world, it has always been customary for maidens to make a show of refusing to marry their lovers, thus causing the young man similarly to make a show of using force to overcome her resistance. In some cases there is actually a sham battle between the friends and relatives of the girl and those of the man. The

---

[1] Quoted by J. F. M'Lennan in *Primitive Marriage*, pp. 306-307.
[2] M'Lennan, op. cit., p. 307.
[3] Louise Jordan Miln, *Wooings and Weddings in Many Climes*, C. A. Pearson, 1900, p. 3.
[4] Ibid., p. 4.

practice at one and the same time is thought to demonstrate the modesty of the female, and the determination, resource, and courage of the male.

It is important to distinguish clearly this practice from marriage by abduction. In all cases where the capture of the woman is a sham affair, the marriage has already been arranged between the two parties or their parents, and the actual pretended resistance or flight on the part of the woman, and the pursuit and seizure on the part of the man, are purely ceremonial or symbolic in character.

In ancient Sparta, according to Plutarch, although the girl was carried off by force, the whole affair, despite its show of actual violence, was planned by the two parties; and Müller, in commenting on this practice, tells us that it "was clearly an ancient national custom, founded on the idea that the young woman could not surrender her freedom and virgin purity unless compelled by the violence of the stronger sex."[1] Similarly, in that section of the race of ancient Greeks, known as the Dorians, marriage was inevitably preceded by the seizure by force of the bride. The plebeian marriages in ancient Rome were carried out along these same lines.

Burckhardt gives an interesting description of this type of marriage as practised among the Arabs of Sinai. "The young maid comes home in the evening with the cattle. At a short distance from the camp she is met by the future spouse, and a couple of his young friends, and carried off by force to her father's tent. If she entertains any suspicion of their designs, she defends herself with stones, and often inflicts wounds on the young men, even though she does not dislike the lover; for, according to custom, the more she struggles, bites, kicks, cries, and strikes, the more she is applauded ever after by her own companions."[2]

In India it is part of the marriage ceremony among the Khonds. Major-General John Campbell, writing in the year 1864, mentions the procedure, regarding which he says: "On one occasion I heard loud cries proceeding from a village close at hand. Fearing some quarrel, I rode to the spot, and there I saw a man

---

[1] C. O. Müller, *History and Antiquity of the Doric Race*, 1839. Second edition. Vol. II, p. 293.

[2] John Lewis Burckhardt, *Notes on the Bedouins and Wahabys*, 1831. Vol. I, p. 264.

bearing away upon his back something enveloped in an ample covering of scarlet cloth; he was surrounded by twenty or thirty young fellows, and by them protected from the desperate attacks made upon him by a party of young women. On seeking an explanation of this novel scene, I was told that the man had just been married, and his precious burden was his blooming bride, whom he was conveying to his own village. Her youthful friends—as, it appears, is the custom—were seeking to regain possession of her, and hurled stones and bamboos at the head of the devoted bridegroom, until he reached the confines of his own village. Then the tables were turned, and the bride was fairly won; and off her young friends scampered, screaming and laughing, but not relaxing their speed till they reached their own village."[1]

The Kalmucks have a similar custom, as the observations of De Hell show. When the arrangements for the marriage have been completed, arrangements chiefly of a pecuniary nature, the young man, accompanied by a party of his friends, set off on horseback to carry off the girl. Her relatives and friends put up a show of resistance, after which she is seized and borne away by her lover in triumph.

Erman, in his *Travels in Siberia*, avers that among the Tunguses and Kamchadales, the girl must resist to the fullest possible extent as part of the preliminaries to marriage, and that only after her clothing has been torn is it concluded that her lover has succeeded in claiming her as his bride.

Apparently in some cases, this show of force is not exercised by the girl's fiancé, but by her friends, female or otherwise. Thus, Burckhardt, writing of the Bedouins, tells us that, " the bashful girl runs from the tent of one friend to another's, till she is caught at last, and conducted in triumph by a few women to the bridegroom's tent; he receives her at the entrance, and forces her into it; the women who had accompanied her then depart. The novelty of her situation naturally induces a young virgin to exclaim; and this is considered by her friends as a sufficient evidence of maiden timidity."[2] Much the same custom is practised in Greenland, according to Cranz, who says that

---

[1] Major-General John Campbell, *Thirteen Years' Service among the Tribes of Khondistan*, 1864.

[2] John Lewis Burckhardt, *Notes on the Bedouins and Wahabys*, 1831. Vol. I, p. 108.

when, as is usual, two old women start negotiations with the girl's parents, and she discovers what is afoot, she runs away, affecting aversion to any proposal of marriage, and has to be dragged to the house of her suitor.[1]

Turning to places nearer home, M'Lennan, on the authority of Gaya, mentions that, in seventeenth century France, it was customary in some provinces for the female to show reluctance to such an extent as to force her fiancé to take her by force. Lord Kames refers to a somewhat similar ceremony being in vogue in Wales until just before the time of writing, which was at the commencement of the nineteenth century. This curious procedure he describes in the following words : " On the morning of the wedding-day, the bridegroom, accompanied with his friends on horseback, demands the bride. Her friends, who are likewise on horseback, give a positive refusal, upon which a mock scuffle ensues. The bride, mounted behind her nearest kinsman, is carried off, and is pursued by the bridegroom and his friends, with loud shouts. It is not uncommon on such an occasion to see two or three hundred sturdy Cambro-Britons riding at full speed, crossing and jostling, to the no small amusement of the spectators. When they have fatigued themselves and their horses, the bridegroom is suffered to overtake his bride. He leads her away in triumph, and the scene is concluded with feasting and festivity. The same marriage ceremony was usual in Muscovy, Lithuania, and Livonia, as reported by Olaus Magnus."[2]

In Ireland at one time it was considered fitting, according to Sampson, that the groom should " run away with the bride." Jeaffreson, in his interesting work *Brides and Bridals*, mentions a curious practice observed some two centuries ago in West Meath, in which a number of the bridegroom's friends approached the bride's party, when it was usual " to make a sportive show of hostility to the cavaliers who advanced on horseback for the purpose of surrendering her to their hands. ' Being come near each other,' says Piers, ' the custom was of old to cast short darts at the company that attended the bride, but at such distance that seldom any hurt ensued. Yet it is not out of the memory of man that the Lord of Hoath on such an occasion lost an eye.' "[3]

---

[1] D. Cranz, *The History of Greenland*, 1870. Vol. I, p. 146.
[2] Lord Kames, *Sketches of the History of Man*, 1798. Vol. II, p. 60.
[3] John Cordy Jeaffreson, *Brides and Bridals*, Hurst and Blackett, 1872, p. 29.

From the accounts of contemporary writers it is apparent that in connexion with these Irish weddings, however good might be the match, it was thought little of if the bridegroom did not first seize and carry off the bride. The couple spent some days, marked by jollification, among friends of the bridegroom, and then returned to the home of the bride's parents. Here they were visited by relations and friends laden with gifts, for the most part consisting of bottles of whisky, as contributions to a second jollification; on the conclusion of which the couple proceeded to their new home, to commence their married life together.

A somewhat similar custom was practised in Connecticut in the eighteenth century. Immediately after the conclusion of the marriage ceremony, a party of young men carried the bride off by force, taking her to a country tavern. The bridegroom, at the head of a number of his friends, rode after the kidnappers, and by providing them with a meal, secured the release of the bride. Alice Morse Earle, to whom I am indebted for this interesting information, says : " The last bride stolen in Hadley was Mrs. Job Marsh, in the year 1783. To this day, however, in certain localities in Rhode Island, the young men of the neighbourhood invade the bridal chamber and pull the bride downstairs, and even out-of-doors, thus forcing the husband to follow to her rescue. If the room or house-door be locked against their invasion, the rough visitors break the lock."[1]

In Great Britain at one time the abduction and marriage of young women, especially heiresses, were frequent occurrences despite the fact that, in accordance with the statute 3 Henry VII 1487, the offence ranked as a felony, and by the 39th Elizabeth 1596 anyone adjudged guilty was denied benefit of clergy. During the Commonwealth and the Protectorate further special steps were taken to deal with the evil. Among the many *causes célèbres* was one which occurred in 1649. The daughter of Sir Thomas Puckeringe, a single girl and an heiress, was walking in Greenwich Park with her maid, when a party of mounted men, led by one Joseph Walsh, seized and carried her off, eventually taking her across the Channel to Dunkirk, and thence to Nieuport, in Flanders, where she was shut up in a religious house. Steps were immediately taken to secure the return of the girl and the arrest of her abductors, but it was not until some eight years

---

[1] Alice Morse Earle, *Customs and Fashions in Old New England*, 1893, p. 77.

later that Jane Puckeringe returned to England in a man-of-war ; while Walsh, who maintained that a marriage ceremony had been performed, and his associates, were surrendered to the English authorities and indicted for felony.

Some of the notorious Fleet marriages were in reality little removed from abductions, as will be evident from a study of the evidence presented in a later chapter of this work. Similarly with certain of the Gretna Green affairs, notably the marriage between the Quaker, Edward Gibbon Wakefield, and the pretty sixteen years' old heiress, Ellen Turner. As a result of an ingenious plot, carried out with considerable skill, the girl, then at a Liverpool school, by means of a note purporting to be from a physician, to the effect that her mother, who was in London, had been suddenly afflicted with a dangerous malady, was induced to accompany the servant who presented the note and travel to London in the carriage thoughtfully sent by the doctor for the purpose. In Manchester, where the carriage stopped for a time, Edward Gibbon Wakefield and his brother, William, put in an appearance. They persuaded Miss Turner to accompany them to Carlisle, ostensibly to meet her father, and then, driving through to Gretna, Edward Gibbon Wakefield and Ellen Turner were made man and wife. Wakefield started the return journey immediately and at considerable speed, ultimately crossing to Calais with his bride. In the meantime the mistress of the school, having become suspicious, journeyed to the Turner home, with the result that the law was set in motion, and within a few days Wakefield was arrested in Calais, and brought back to England, while his wife was returned to her parents. And then, on March 26, 1827, at Lancaster Spring Assizes there commenced the famous trial, which resulted in the brothers Wakefield being sentenced to three years' imprisonment[1] for conspiracy, while the marriage, which had never been consummated, was annulled by a special Act of Parliament. It was during the course of this trial that David Laing, the Gretna ' parson ' who solemnized the marriage, gave, under cross-examination by Lord Brougham, some interesting evidence, thus :—

[1] At the trial, Sergeant (afterwards Sir John Cross), for the prosecution said : " Had this offence been committed on English ground (instead of at Gretna Green, in Scotland), two at least of these defendants (Edward Gibbon Wakefield and his brother) would, in due course of law, have been condemned to an ignominious death."

Are you a Scotch clergyman?—No, I am not.

What are you? Are you any trade at all?—Nothing at all.

Do you mean to say you never were an ostler?—Me, an ostler! No.

How long have you been engaged in this traffic of making this sort of certificate?—Eight-and-forty years.

How old are you?—I am beyond seventy-five.

Well, before the last eight-and-forty years what did you do to get your livelihood? that is my question.—Why, I was a gentleman : sometimes poor and sometimes rich.

Well, when you were poor, what did you do to get your bread? What occupation did you follow?—I followed many occupations.

Let me hear one of them.—I was a merchant.

What do you mean by a merchant : a travelling merchant : a pedlar?—Yes.

What else were you? Were you anything else?—Never.[1]

Another earlier and no less sensational case of abduction was that of Miss Wharton, heiress of the House of Wharton. This young lady was carried off by force and married to a Captain Campbell. The originator and prime mover in this conspiracy, Sir John Johnston, was hanged ; while the marriage was annulled by Act of Parliament in 1690.

[1] Peter Orlando Hutchinson, *Chronicles of Gretna Green*, 1844.

Chapter VI

MARRIAGE BY PURCHASE

I

Origin and Antiquity of Purchasing a Wife

FROM the time when man claimed the exclusive possession of a woman as his companion in life and the mother of his children, the property right in a wife was recognised. It was conceded by the early law-makers of almost all nations and tribes that in such circumstances any marriageable woman represented to her parents something of value. The fact that a wife was a form of property in precisely the same way as an ox, a horse, a house, or any other possession, was not considered to cast a slur upon the woman in any sense. To the decided contrary, in any society where the female of marriageable age was not purchasable, or for any reason did not cause or tempt a male to make a bid for her exclusive possession, this very fact was considered to constitute a slur upon her character or to provide evidence of her worthlessness.

On the other hand it is easy to understand that the purchase of a wife, with all its implications, was likely to appeal to the husband. For not only did this method of marrying increase his power over his wife, but it provided greater security for her good behaviour: he could, in these circumstances, confine her movements if necessary or advisable, and upon proof of her being guilty of any major offence, he could bring the marriage contract to an end.

Another reason for the purchase of wives is given by Olaus Magnus, who says: "Among the Goths, a man gave a dowry for his bride, instead of receiving one with her; to prevent pride and insolence, that commonly accompany riches on the woman's part."

In ancient Assyria the young ladies who were eligible for marriage were each year sold in the public market to the highest bidders. These females were the property of the State, which cared little for the age or character of the buyers, the only stipulation apparently being that, in each case, the buyer must marry the girl he purchased. Heredotus says the most beautiful were offered for sale first, and the rich Babylonians who were in search of wives, bid against one another for these gems of the collection, who invariably brought high prices. Judging from this account and from the records of other historians, the Assyrians would appear to have brought the sale of girls for the purpose of marriage to a degree of perfection never surpassed before or since. For they had evolved a scheme by which it was possible to find purchasers not only for the most beautiful maidens of the year but also for the plain ones and even for the ugly or the repulsive. Their manner of bringing this about was as simple as it was effective. When the requirements of the rich men, the old, the middle-aged, and the young, had been satisfied, a portion of the money received for the pretty damsels was used as bait to secure husbands for those less favoured in the matter of looks. Each of these girls was put up for auction, the condition of sale being that the girl would be knocked down to the man who was prepared to take her as his bride with the smallest sum of money as an inducement.

Nor was the selling of maidens by the State confined to ancient Assyria. The Thracians adopted a similar method, although in this case there seems to be no indication that the rejected were given a marriage portion to tempt purchasers.

In most countries, of course, the money received went to the girls' parents. Naturally and inevitably the price asked varied greatly in different races, and even in the same race according to the age, rank, beauty, etc., of the girl, and the financial or social position of the suitor. In the early days of civilization, as well as in most savage tribes, the purchase price was paid in the form of cattle or goods.

A typical example of the method adopted in Biblical times is provided in the story of the marriage of Rebekah and Isaac, which was preceded by the sending of valuable presents by Abraham to the girl's family, "such things as were there in esteem, on account that they either rarely or never were seen in that country." Then there was Sechem, so infatuated with Jacob's daughter that, whatever the price asked, he was determined to make her his wife. For in asking for Dinah, Sechem said: "Ask me never so much dowry and gift, and I will give according as ye shall say unto me; but give me the damsel to wife."[1] In

---

[1] Genesis xxxiv, 12.

response to the request for his daughter, by David, Saul said : " The king desireth not any dowry, but an hundred foreskins of the Philistines."[1]

Not unnaturally, the greed for money or its equivalent being as universally present in ancient times as in these enlightened years, parents were in the habit of employing every means within their power to enhance the charm and increase the beauty of their daughters. In Circassia, for instance, female children were looked upon as assets of much potential value, and were bred, reared and educated for the express purpose of being sold to rich men in search of wives. It was affirmed that the price requested and obtained for his sister by the prince of the Circassians from the prince of Mingrelia was no less than one hundred tapestry-laden slaves, and the same number of oxen, of horses, and of cows. The Arabs fully realized the advantage of possessing such saleable commodities as daughters, according to the following passage from De la Roque : " Fathers among the Arabs are never more happy than when they have many daughters. This is the principal part of the riches of a house. Accordingly, when a young man would treat with a person whose daughter he is inclined to marry, he says to him, ' Will you give me your daughter for fifty sheep ; for six camels ; or for a dozen cows ? ' If he be not rich enough to make such offers, he will propose the giving her to him for a mare, or a young colt ; considering in the offer the merit of the young woman, the rank of her family, and the circumstances of him that desires to marry her. When they are agreed on both sides, the contract is drawn up by him that acts as cadi or judge among these Arabs."[2]

There are clear indications that the practice existed in Hindustan, some parts of Africa, Turkey, Spain, and other countries. Burckhardt, in describing the marriage customs in Egypt says : " When a girl is to be asked in matrimony, a friend or relation, or the sheikh of the young man (who has instructed him in reading the Koran), goes to the girl's father, and makes a bargain for her. It is a real bargain, for the girl's affections are never consulted, and the amount of the price to be paid for her is the only matter taken into consideration, provided the stations in life of both parties sufficiently correspond ; but even in this

[1] 1 Samuel xviii, 25.
[2] Quoted by Samuel Burder in *Oriental Customs*, p. 269.

respect the Egyptians are not very scrupulous, and a man of low extraction or profession who possesses wealth often marries into a high class. The price paid for the girl to her father, or, if he be dead, to the nearest male relation, varies according to her rank, fortune, or reputation for beauty. Among the first-rate merchants the price is from two hundred to three hundred dollars; among those of the second class, from sixty to eighty; and the lower classes often pay no more than from three to five dollars. It is usual to pay half of the money immediately in advance, this sum becomes the property of the father; the other half remains in the bridegroom's hands, and reverts to his wife if he should die or divorce her; but if she herself sues for a divorce she forfeits her claim to the money."[1]

In China, says Huc, "the young girl is simply an object of traffic, an article of merchandise to be sold to the highest bidder, without her having the right to ask a single question concerning the merit or quality of her purchaser. On the day of the wedding there is great anxiety to adorn and beautify her. She is clad in splendid robes of silk, glittering with gold and jewels; her beautiful plaits of raven hair are ornamented with flowers and precious stones; she is carried away in great pomp, and musicians surround the brilliant palanquin, where she sits in state like a queen on her throne. You think, perhaps, on witnessing all this grandeur and rejoicing, that now, at last, her period of happiness is about to begin. But, alas! a young married woman is but a victim adorned for the sacrifice. She is quitting a home where, however neglected, she was in the society of relations to whom she had been accustomed from her infancy. She is now thrown, young, feeble, and inexperienced, among total strangers, to suffer privation and contempt, and be altogether at the mercy of her purchaser."[2]

At one time it was customary to send pretty girls from small towns and remote districts to places where they were most likely to be seen by well-to-do men in search of wives. Colonel Cunynghame, writing just about a century ago, refers to this practice. His observations are well worth recording here: "The harbour at Hong Kong was generally very crowded with Chinese native craft. The gayest and most highly decorated boats which arrived at our port were those which brought from

---

[1] John Lewis Burckhardt, *Arabic Proverbs*, second edition, London, 1875, p. 134.
[2] M. Huc, *The Chinese Empire*, 1855.

Canton a mercantile commodity very commonly trafficked in by the Chinese. These were young ladies who were bent upon the speculation of marriage, and were brought from the exuberant population of the interior towns to supply this deficiency amongst the numerous Chinese settlers who had come from the continent to our new colony, vast numbers of every trade and occupation having already flocked to the island. These boats arrived with drums and gongs beating, and colours flying, generally coming to an anchor immediately under my own window; tea-tables were soon arranged, and the young ladies, from twenty to forty in number, arrayed in their smartest jackets and trousers, might be seen endeavouring to bewitch those visitors who flocked to the boats. I am informed that the price, generally speaking, averaged from 100 to 200 dollars : this money was transferred to the mother of the young lady, a due proportion being deducted for the expenses attendant upon the voyage, together with commission, etc., upon the bargain."[1]

Some of the North American tribes were accustomed to practise wife-selling. In the Mandan village on the Upper Missouri river, Catlin[2] says often the girl was never so much as consulted, the bargain being made with the father, who invariably held out for the highest price securable.

In that part of Europe anciently known as Gaul, during the fifth century, writes Alexander : " the princess Clotilda, daughter of Gondebaud, King of the Bergundians, being married to Clovis by proxy, the proxy presented her with a sol and a denier, as the price of her virginity, a custom which existed among that people long afterward."[3]

In England, under the Anglo-Saxon laws, a stipulated sum of money must be paid to the father of every young woman by the man who elected to marry her. Should the father be dead, this purchase price, which was termed " compensation ", must be paid to her brother, or, in the event of there being no brother, to her nearest male relative. The price was fixed in accordance with her rank and station in life, any marriage entered into without such payment having been made resulted in the husband losing many of the rights usually connected with

[1] Colonel Arthur Cunynghame, *An Aide-de-Camp's Recollections of Service in China, A Residence in Hong-Kong, and Visits to other Islands in the Chinese Seas* ; Richard Bentley, London, 1853, pp. 233-234.
[2] George Catlin, *North American Indians*, 1876. Vol. I, p. 120.
[3] William Alexander, *The History of Women*, 1776. Vol. II, p. 272.

WELSH WEDDING: RUNNING AWAY WITH THE BRIDE
From a lithograph published in 1850, after a drawing by J. C. Rowland

marriage : that is, the possession of his wife's property, and the right to any compensation allowable by law for an affront to her personally. In the event of the suitor changing his mind and failing to marry the girl, he was called upon to pay a consideration fee to her father or guardian, and, in addition, to forfeit the purchase price already paid. In accordance with the same ancient laws a widow, for whom similarly a price had to be paid, was a much more economical proposition, the sum demanded being only half that required for a woman who had not previously been married. These regulations continued in force until the time of Canute, who made two important alterations ; to wit, that there should be no compulsion in regard to the purchase price, which should be a gift of a purely voluntary nature ; and, more importantly, that the father or guardian should have no power to force a girl to marry anyone against her will.

Alexander mentions that in the reign of Edward the Third, Richard de Neville gave a present of twenty palfreys (saddle-horses) to the King in order to obtain his request to Isola Bisset that she should accept him as her husband ; while Roger Fitz-Walter presented three palfreys to secure the King's letter to a lady (the mother of Roger Bertram), requesting her to marry him. " In those times," says Alexander, " when the Kings of England exercised so unlimited a power over their subjects, the King's request, or his letter, amounted to an absolute command, and the money paid to obtain these, was as literally the purchase of a wife, as if it had been paid for her at a public sale."[1]

Not all men were, however, in a position to pay ready-money or its equivalent for a wife, however much they desired to have the woman as a life companion. In many of these cases the difficulty was overcome by the man giving his services for a period to the girl's father or guardian. From the Bible we learn that for each of his wives, Jacob served Laban a term of seven years. The passage reads : "Laban had two daughters : the name of the elder was Leah, and the name of the younger was Rachel. Leah was tender-eyed, but Rachel was beautiful and well favoured. And Jacob loved Rachel, and said, I will serve thee seven years for Rachel, thy younger daughter. And Laban said, It is better that I give her to thee, than that I should give her to another man : abide with me."[2]

---

[1] William Alexander, *The History of Women.* Vol. II, p. 272.
[2] Genesis xxix, 16–19.

II

The Dowry as a Form of Purchasing a Husband

The giving of money or its equivalent by a father to his daughter, on the occasion of her marriage, has been a common custom from the earliest days, and in such countries where, and at such times when, the selection of a partner in marriage was something with which the female invariably, and the male often, had nothing whatever to do, the arrangement resolved itself virtually into the purchase of a husband, the price paid being the marriage portion, or dowry, given by the father to his daughter. For as all money or goods belonging to the bride became the property of her husband the father's wedding gift to his daughter was indistinguishable from a gift to her husband. Thus the city of Gazar was the portion which Pharaoh bestowed on his daughter when she married King Solomon.

In Greece, so long ago as before the time of Christ, it was customary for wives to bring dowries to their husbands. In the case of an orphan virgin without a portion, her next of kin was obliged to marry her himself, or settle a portion on her according to rank ; if there were several males of an equal degree of consanguinity, each of them contributed to the dowry. In the event of there being more than one virgin, the nearest kinsman was called upon to marry or portion one of them : should he refuse, any person was at liberty to cite him before the archon, on which he was fined 1,000 drachms, this fine being consecrated to Juno, the goddess of marriage. When, as sometimes happened, the daughters of eminent men found themselves with neither money nor relatives to provide for them, the State usually gave them portions. Thus, to each of the two daughters of Aristides, the sum of 300 drachms to provide a marriage portion, was presented out of the city funds.

In comparatively modern times, according to Dodswell (*Tour Through Greece*) single Albanian girls were addicted to wearing red skull-caps, decorated with silver coins of various denominations, overlapping each other like scales, representing their dowries. Daughters of wealthy parents often had gold coins either in place of or interspersed with silver ones. These girls attracted many admirers.

In Ancient Ireland the marriage gift at first, states O'Curry,

" probably consisted exclusively of clothes, household furniture, and live chattels, as in Wales, Scandinavia, etc. ; but at some very early period land might also be given."[1] As regards the amount of the marriage-portion, according to the same authority, this was governed by the rank of the parties, but " usually was one-third of the personal property of the bride's father."[2] Part of the gift which was made by the bridegroom to his wife after the marriage, went, in conformity to Irish law, to her father.

In England it was at one time customary to raise the money to provide portions for the king's daughters by a tribute exacted from every hide of land. This oppressive measure, observes Malcolm, " seems to have been derived from the suggestion of Henry Beauclerc, who demanded three shillings from each hide, to accumulate one [a portion] for Maud on her marriage to the Emperor Henry."[3]

Commenting on the practice in England, Sir William Temple says : " I think I remember, within less than fifty years, the first noble families that married into the city for money ; and thereby introduced, by degrees, this public grievance, which has since ruined so many estates, by the necessity of giving great portions to daughters ; impaired many families, by the weak or mean productions of marriages, made without any of that warmth and spirit that is given 'em by force of inclination and personal choice ; and extinguished many great ones, by the aversion of the persons who should have continued 'em."

In closing this chapter it is worthy of note that in some countries it was customary for young women contemplating marriage to engage in temporary prostitution for the purpose of obtaining their dowries. We have it on the authority of the historian Herodotus that, in ancient Lydia, without exception, before marriage, the daughters, who were required to furnish their own trousseaux, earned the money for this purpose and acquired dowries, by adopting for a time the profession of the prostitute. The same writer refers to a similar custom being prevalent in Cyprus. Valerius Maximus asserts that girls of all classes of the Ulad-Nail tribe did precisely the same thing, despite the fact that prostitution in any form came in for severe denunciation by all the principles of Islamic morality.

[1] Eugene O'Curry, *On the Manner and Customs of the Ancient Irish*, Williams and Norgate, 1873. Vol. I, p. clxxii.
[2] Ibid.
[3] J. P. Malcolm, *Anecdotes, Manners and Customs of London*, Vol. I, p. 68.

CHAPTER VII

JUVENILE MARRIAGES

I

The Origin and Incidence of Juvenile Marriage

IT would appear that at one time and another marriages of children have been common among a large number of races and in many parts of the world. There are for the finding instances of child marriage in the Bible. When King Josiah reached the age of 16, his wife gave birth to a son : Josiah died at 39 ; his son, aged 23, succeeding to the kingship at his father's death (see 2 Kings xxiii. 26). Then there was King Ahaz, whose death occurred at the age of 36, leaving a son aged 25 (see 2 Kings xvi. 2 ; xviii. 2) ; and Solomon who became a father at the age of 11—he died at 52, when Rehoboam had reached the age of 41 (see 1 Kings ii. 42 ; xiv. 21).

The reasons for such marriages may be either religious or economic. In India, for instance, where the children of almost all sects are married at very early ages, it is of the highest importance that every male should commence siring children at the earliest possible moment. His hopes of an after-life in the Hindu heaven are dependent upon the activities of his son or sons. Seeing that it is of first importance that he should have a male descendant who will live at least long enough to produce a son himself, one can well understand his anxiety to raise a crop of children ; the more so in view of the possibilities as regards the female sex preponderating and the risks connected with the rearing of youngsters in a country having so high an infantile death rate. Owing to this religious viewpoint, the demand for female children to provide partners for the males is considerable, and it is as much a duty of parents to see that their daughters are married at the earliest possible age as it is for the parents of boys to ensure this. The adult young woman who remains unmarried is just as likely to come in for censure or ostracism as is the adult male celibate.

According to the laws of Manu : "A man, aged thirty years, is to marry a girl of twelve, or a man of twenty-four years a damsel of eight : a breach of this rule makes a man sinful." But Angira declares : " Damsels of eight, nine, and ten years are respectively named Gauri, Rohini, and Kanya, and all girls above ten are called Rajaswala or women in their catamenia : when therefore a girl has reached her tenth year, she is to be immediately disposed of in marriage, and such marriage, even though celebrated in an interdicted nuptial season, will not be held culpable." Commenting on this, Vidyasagar says : " It thus appears that Angira has fixed the eighth, ninth and tenth years as the proper marriageable age of a girl ; and so great is his apprehension, lest she should continue a virgin after her tenth year, that he enjoins the marriage of a decennarian damsel even in times when weddings are forbidden ; but with respect to males, he assigns neither twenty-four nor thirty years, nor any period for their marriageable age. Nor, it should be observed, whether or not, the above texts of Manu and Angira contradict each other : Manu fixes either the eighth or twelfth year as the marriageable age of a girl, any deviation from which is declared by him to be sinful ; while Angira directs that a damsel may be married in her eighth, ninth or tenth year, the last of which is declared to be the farthest limit, at which her marriage is indispensable and not to be deferred : hence, according to his opinion the twelfth year is by no means the proper marriageable age. The actual practice nowadays is founded on the ordinance of Angira and disrespects the law of Manu."[1]

In many countries, however, the practice has nothing whatever to do with religion, but is of a purely commercial nature, the parents being anxious to sell their daughters for the best price procurable and without the slightest possible delay. According to some writers, in certain tribes where abduction was frequent, the parents sold their daughters at an early age to obviate such a possibility. In Britain child marriages were often arranged between families of rank and position for the express purpose of joining together two properties.

It is therefore not alone in India that one frequently comes across girls of seven to nine years who are already married,

---

[1] Eshwar Chandra Vidyasagar, *Marriage of Hindu Widows*, Sanscrit Press, Calcutta, 1856, p. 31.

and most have said good-bye to the single state by the time they have reached the age of twelve. According to Brett, it is no uncommon thing for an Indian in Guiana, already having a wife and children, to bring up a little girl who is to become his second wife. This odious practice is repeated a few years later.[1] Among many African and American tribes, children are married at extremely early ages and are bearing infants themselves immediately after puberty.

In China juvenile marriages have always been of frequent occurrence. " Nothing is more common," says Huc, " than to arrange a marriage during the infancy of the parties, or even before their birth. Two friends make a solemn promise, or even take an oath, to unite in marriage the children of different sexes that may be born to them ; and the solemnity of the engagement is marked by their tearing reciprocally a piece out of their tunics, and giving it to each other. Marriages contracted in this manner cannot, of course, be founded on congeniality of character ; this can seldom happen, as the parties have not usually seen each other beforehand ; the will of the parent being the sole reason for the formation of the nuptial tie."[2]

Egyptian girls marry at the age of twelve or thirteen ; and " some remarkably precocious " ones at the age of ten.[3] Few are unmarried after sixteen.

It must be borne in mind, however, that in tropical and semi-tropical climates, where development is much more rapid than in countries where more temperate conditions prevail, girls arrive at maturity at an age when, in England and other European countries, they are still children in every sense of the term. Further, in many of the countries where juvenile marriages are customary, as in India and China, there is no actual consummation until the girl has reached the pubertal stage of development. Usually there are strict laws to ensure this, the most satisfactory being where the girl, following marriage at the early age of six or seven years, must remain with her parents until another six years or so have elapsed. Even so, these very early tropical marriages produce much that is evil. Such unions are rarely conducive to happiness in later life ; and, as a result, the husbands are unfaithful and addicted to promiscuity, while

[1] W. H. Brett, *The Indian Tribes of Guiana*, 1868, p. 352.
[2] M. Huc, *The Chinese Empire*, 1855.
[3] E. W. Lane, *An Account of the Manners and Customs of the Modern Egyptians*, 1836.

many of the wives become widows at early ages and end up in becoming prostitutes.

It will no doubt come as a surprise to many readers to learn that in Britain at one time child marriages were by no means uncommon. There is a wealth of evidence in support of this statement. In the *Penny Cyclopædia* appears the following revealing passage : " Temporary disability from defect of age does not invalidate a marriage, but it leaves the party or parties at liberty to avoid or to confirm such premature action on attaining the age of consent, which for males is 14, and for females 12. Before the abolition of feudal tenures, when lords were entitled to sell the marriages of their male and female wards, infantile marriages were very common ; fathers were anxious to prevent wives and husbands being forced upon their children after their death, and lords being eager either to secure the prize for their own family or to realise the profit arising from a sale. Strype, in his time, complained of the scandal arising from the frequency of divorces, especially among the richer sort, who used often to marry their children when they were boys and girls, that they might join land to land, and they, being grown up, many times disliked each other, and then separation and divorce followed, to the breaking of espousals and the displeasure of God."

In the fifteenth, sixteenth and seventeenth centuries juvenile marriages were most common in both England and Scotland. An interesting account of one of these is given in Pepys' *Diary* : "A Bluecoat boy and girl were each left a fortune by two wealthy citizens. The extraordinariness of this occurrence led some of the magistrates to carry it to a match, which ended in a public wedding—he in his habit of blue satin, led by two of the girls, she in blue, with an apron green and petticoat yellow, all of sarsenet, led by two of the girls of the house, through Cheapside to Guildhall Chapel, where they were married by the Dean of St. Paul's, she being given away by the Lord Mayor. The wedding dinner was kept in the Hospital Hall. The date of this juvenile wedding was September 20th, 1695."

It is truly astonishing to find how many of these child marriages *did* actually occur in England. In a manuscript volume entitled " Depositions in Trials in the Bishop's Court from November 1561 to March 1565–6 ", F. J. Furnivall discovered a remarkable array of 27 such unions. There was the strange case of John Somerford, aged three, and Jane Brerton, aged two, both of whom were taken to the parish church and a marriage between them solemnized, the "words of matrimony" being spoken by friends who carried the children in their arms; there was the case of Grace Boyes, aged ten, married to Robert Talbot, aged thirteen, the girl, while visiting at the Talbot home, being taken to the church and married to the boy without her consent; and there was the case where a girl married James Ballard, aged between ten and eleven, the girl in this instance having enticed the boy with two apples, " to go with her to Colne and to marry her."

It is important to remember that these 27 cases figuring in the Chester Depositions probably represent but a small proportion of the child marriages which occurred at that time. These are the marriages which, in the period from 1561 to 1566, proved to be failures, and the parties to them were separated on attaining the age of consent, which was, in the case of the boy, fourteen, and in the case of the girl, twelve years. Proceedings to this end could be taken in the Bishop's Court, provided that the marriage had not been completed by the couple living together as man and wife or by sexual intercourse. If the marriage had been consummated then divorce was only securable on grounds of adultery.

John Smith of Nibley in his *Lives of the Berkeleys*, writing of the third Lord, says: "Then was this lord Maurice born in the year 1281, being the ninth of King Edward the first, and near the month of Aprill wherein his grandfather the lord Maurice dyed; and was, by his father the last lord Thomas, marryed at eight yeares old, in the 17th, of that King, to Eve, daughter of Ewdo lord Zouch and of the Lady Millicent de monte alto his wife; and was by her made father of Thomas, his eldest son, before hee was fourteen years old himself : neither was his wife above that age." In the reign of James the First, George, Lord Berkeley, aged thirteen, married Sir Michael Stanhope's daughter Elizabeth, aged nine; while Maurice, fourth Lord Berkeley, was married to Elizabeth, daughter of Hugh, Lord Spenser, both being nine years of age.

On February 9, 1659, the Countess of Buccleugh, at the age of eleven, married Walter Scott, aged fourteen; on June 8, 1721, the fourteen-year-old daughter of Sir Thomas Powel, Bart., was married to Charles Powel, aged eleven. And there

CHILD WEDDING IN PAKISTAN
The bride is eight years old

were innumerable other cases. The practice persisted through
the centuries in all its frequency, as the Reports of the Registrar-
General for the 31 years, 1851–81 conclusively show. In this
period 154 boys married before *seventeen*, and 862 girls before
sixteen. Of these, eleven boys of *fifteen* married girls of *fifteen*;
(four cases), 16, 18; (two cases), 20 and 21. Three girls of
fourteen married men of 18, 21, and 25. Five girls of *fifteen*
married boys of *sixteen*; in 29 marriages, both girl and boy
were *sixteen*."[1]

As regards the reasons for these English marriages Mr.
Furnivall has this to say: "Property-arrangements were one
cause. Another—and perhaps the chief one—was, I suspect,
the desire to evade the feudal law of the sovereign's guardianship
of all infants. When a father died, the Crown had the right
to hold the person and estate of the propertied orphan until it
came of age, and it could be sold in marriage for the benefit
of the Crown or its grantee. If the orphan refused such a
marriage with a person of its own rank, it had to pay its guardian
a heavy fine for refusing his choice, and selecting a spouse of
its own."[2] There are records of many such cases. To cite
one instance, William Fitz Nigel was compelled to pay King
John for permission to please himself in marriage.

II

The Evils of Infantile Marriage

It was not until a little over a century ago, to be precise
in the year 1846, that those responsible for the Indian Penal
Code recognized the potential evils inherent in infantile marriage
sufficiently to be induced to place some legal restriction upon
the age at which such a union might be consummated, so much
so indeed that it was made a criminal offence, carrying a severe
penalty, for such consummation to be made before the girl wife
reached the age of ten. Nearly fifty years later this age restriction
was altered to twelve years.

[1] *Child Marriages, &c*, 1897, p. xxxiii. Particulars quoted from " Notes and
Queries," IX, 236.
[2] The reader who is interested in further details of these juvenile marriages
is referred to that admirable book *Child Marriages, &c.* (from which this quotation is made), edited by F. J. Furnivall, and published for the Early English
Text Society by Kegan Paul, Trench, Trübner & Co.

These measures were in turn enacted in efforts to remove, at any rate to some extent, some of the more blatant evils inseparable from juvenile marriages, especially in those cases where the girl was an infant, in terms of the law, while her husband was a mature and in some cases an elderly man.

Despite the law, however, the evils to a very big extent, remained. I have already mentioned that in civilized, as opposed to purely savage, races, there has always been a certain amount of regulation in this respect, and it was taken for granted that the age of consummation was postponed until the girl-wife reached sexual maturity. Obviously, however, any such arrangement, with the exception only of those cases where the girl remained in the household of her parents until the time of puberty, left the door wide open for a breach of the custom or the law on the part of the husband. The truth of this was evidenced when, in 1929, the Joshi Report, or to give its full name, the Report of the Age of Consent Committee, was published.

In the course of the investigation which culminated in the issue of the Report, it was discovered that the existence of the law of 1891, prohibiting intercourse of a sexual nature with a female, either married or unmarried, who had not reached the age of twelve, was known to very few members of the lay public. Apart from this lack of knowledge the investigators discovered a reluctance on the part of the girl-wives and their parents to make any complaints against their husbands, and particularly to give evidence in a court of law. Moreover, any wife who testified against her husband, would have to run the risk of being discarded by him, which would prevent her re-marrying and possibly involve social ostracism as well.

The evils which are inseparable from these child marriages are both of a physical and mental character. Development is checked; there is premature ageing; tuberculosis is not uncommon; osteomalacia is a frequent aftermath of repeated pregnancies immediately following the arrival of puberty.

The statements of the witnesses who gave evidence before the committee stressed and underlined these evils. One witness said that cohabitation often occurred among the lower classes before puberty, and that he was " personally aware of four or five girls who had cohabitation at ten and eleven and became mothers."[1]

---

[1] Joshi Report, quoted by Eleanor F. Rathbone in *Child Marriage*, to which book I am greatly indebted for information on this important subject.

Another witness stated that " girls are married at all ages, even at two and three, among the lower classes of Muslims, that immediately after puberty, which happens at eleven or twelve, the girl is sent to the husband's house and that he is aware of girls who became mothers at thirteen or fourteen."[1]   Little wonder that the committee in its final report should have thought fit to utter these grave words : " In the case of early maternity, the evil is widespread and affects such a large number of women both among Hindus and Muslims, as to necessitate redress. It is so extensive as to affect the whole framework of society. After going through the ordeal, if a woman survives to the age of thirty, she is in many cases an old woman, almost a shadow of her former self. Her life is a long lingering misery and she is a sacrifice at the altar of custom. The evil is so insidious in all the manifold aspects of social life that people have ceased to think of its shocking effects on the whole social fabric."

In England the youngest age at which anyone can be married to-day is sixteen, and then only with the consent of her parents. In Northern Ireland, however, the position is a different one. Child marriages can, and do, occur there. A girl aged fourteen was married in 1951 by the Superintendent of the Portadown Methodist Circuit, according to an article entitled " Child Brides " in the *Sunday Pictorial* (March 4, 1951). The writer of the article rightly condemns these marriages.

[1] Rathbone, op. cit.

CHAPTER VIII

PLURAL MARRIAGE IN ITS VARIOUS FORMS

I

Polygamy : Its Origin and Incidence

HOWEVER unpalatable, from the standpoint of modern ethical ideals, the statement may be, it is a fact that man, biologically and inherently, is polygynous. The promiscuity which is so prominent and so characteristic a feature of savagery provides unmistakable evidence of the truth of this. No feature of mankind has provided religion and morality with so many difficulties, not in connexion with its prohibition, which is plainly an impossibility, but in its curbing. In modern civilization, the monogamic concept in combination with the laws relating to marriage, have succeeded only to the extent that economic conditions have been able to fortify them.

It should be noted that in these remarks I am referring to the polygynous nature of the male rather than to the polygamous feature of the human race as a whole. The distinction is important. Polygamy, contrary to popular opinion, involves more than the marrying of a number of women by one male ; it includes the analogous appetite displayed by the female for a number of husbands. Polyandry, as this latter phenomenon is termed, is nothing like so pronounced or so widespread a characteristic in the female as polygyny is in the male. In fact it may be looked upon as abnormal or exceptional, for whatever may be its incidence in those early days when promiscuity was the order of the day, polyandry has proved to be capable of regulation or prohibition in a manner which is impossible with polygyny. Moreover, even in primitive society, it is a much rarer phenomenon than polygyny, being virtually restricted to societies where the number of females is much fewer than that of males, or where poverty of an extreme nature is widespread. In some North American tribes it was customary for a woman to have several husbands; as also in Tibet and Bantan. According to Father Tanchard, in Calicat, he came across women with as many as ten husbands, all of whom were looked upon as so many slaves.

In the Old Testament we have plenty of evidence of the existence of polygyny. Esau undoubtedly was a polygynist; so, too, Adam's son, Lamech; King Solomon, also, had a number of wives. Indeed, there can be little doubt that polygyny was widely practised in the time of Moses, and his supposed prohibition of multiple marriages, as instanced in the passage: "Neither shalt thou take a wife to her sister to vex her, to uncover her nakedness, besides the other in her lifetime," has been the cause of considerable controversy, as in the case of so many other Biblical commands and prohibitions. Apropos of this passage, Dr. Gardner says: "Michaelis, following the *Talmud*, alleges that the Mosaic law does not prohibit more than one wife, although he admits that it does not sanction a man having as many wives as he pleased. Selden, in his learned work *De Uxore Hebraica (On the Hebrew Wife)*, informs us, that the Jewish Rabbis held the prohibition of Moses to extend only beyond four wives. And Mohammed, following as he did in many cases the Rabbanical interpretations, fixed upon four as the number of wives to be allowed to the faithful, and commands that that number should not be exceeded."[1]

For centuries the ancient Romans prohibited polygyny, the Justinian Code proclaiming it to be a punishable offence. Later Mark Antony caused the rule to be altered: he took two wives himself.

In ancient Egypt all men other than those of the poorer classes, who could not afford a plurality of wives, and the priests, who were prohibited from having them, were accustomed to practise polygyny; although, according to Kenrick, one of the wives, under the title of Lady of the House, "enjoyed a superiority in honour and authority over the rest."[2] A similar custom prevailed among the Turkish princes, says Burder, where it was usual "to have one among their many wives superior to all the rest in dignity."[3]

According to Huc, polygyny is a legal institution in China.[4]

---

[1] James Gardner, *Faiths of the World*. Vol. II, p. 679.
[2] John Kenrick, *Ancient Egypt under the Pharoahs*, 1850. Vol. II, p. 58.
[3] Samuel Burder, *Oriental Customs*, 1840, p. 277.
[4] M. Huc, *The Chinese Empire*, 1855.

At one time the practice was restricted to Mandarins and childless forty-year-olds, but more recently the taking of secondary wives has become general.   Here, as in Egypt and some other countries, the first wife is the mistress of the house, all others holding subordinate positions.

In many of the tribes of North American Indians polygyny was practised.   Catlin said it was " no uncommon thing to find a chief with six, eight, or ten, and some with twelve or fourteen wives in his lodge."[1]   Among the Indians of Guiana, the more wives a man possesses the more is he esteemed by his fellow-men.[2]

A form of polygyny practised by many primitive races is the custom of marrying sisters, known as sororate.   However many daughters there are in a family, the man who marries one marries the lot.   It is found among the North American Indians, the Australian Blacks, and the Kaffirs of Africa.

In Tibet, somewhat surprisingly, polygyny and polyandry are both widely practised.   According to Henry Savage Landor, the arrangement is a somewhat complicated one.[3]   A man who marries the eldest of a number of sisters acquires the lot as wives, that is, providing the younger ones are unmarried ; but if he chooses to marry a younger sister in the family he has no claim to the elder sister or sisters, whether or not she or they be single. On the other hand, the girl who marries one of a number of brothers, becomes the wife of them all.   In some parts of the country, owing to the extreme poverty of the inhabitants, the wife-sharing method is apparently the only form of married life possible.   In addition to the question of economics, the dangers to which women who have to be left alone are inevitably exposed, make polyandry a matter of expediency.   It is not likely, in such circumstances, that a wife will be without companionship and protection where there are two or more husbands in the household, a point which may well be brought forward " in defence of even so startling a social arrangement as this, at least among races of so phlegmatic a temperament as the Tibetans."[4]   Moreover, apart from any need for protection, it would appear that

[1] George Catlin, North American Indians, 1876, p. 118.
[2] W. H. Brett, The Indian Tribes of Guiana, 1868, p. 351.
[3] A. Henry Savage Landor, In the Forbidden Land ; An Account of a Journey in Tibet, Capture by the Tibetan Authorities, Imprisonment, Torture, and Ultimate Release, Heinemann, 1898. Vol. II, pp. 61–63.
[4] Constance F. Gordon Cumming, From the Hebrides to the Himalayas : A Sketch of Eighteen Months' Wanderings in Western Isles and Eastern Highlands, Sampson Low, London, 1876. Vol. I, p. 204.

the women of this remote country are not without skill in handling a plurality of husbands. As a rule a wife displays considerable ingenuity in seeing that they are not all at home at the same time. Says Landor : " Only one remains and he is for the time being her husband; then when another returns he has to leave his place and become a bachelor, and so on, till all the brothers have, during the year, had an equal period of marital life with their single wife."[1]

Polygyny is inherently evil, and it can only produce evil results. So true is this, that in China many women will go to any lengths to avoid marriage with a man given to its practice. Some shut themselves up in nunneries; others take their own lives. Gray tells us that " during the reign of Taou-Kwang, fifteen virgins whom their parents had affianced, met together upon learning the fact, and resolved to commit suicide. They flung themselves into a tributary stream of the Canton river, in the vicinity of the village where they lived. The tomb in which the corpses were interred is near Fo-Chune, and is called the Tomb of the Virgins."[2] The same authority mentions another multiple suicide for a similar reason. It occurred in the month of July, 1873. In this instance the affianced girls, numbering eight, had bound themselves together, before jumping into the river.

II

Mormonism

Never has a system of polygyny become so much a part of the social life of the people, and so universally practised, as under the Church of Jesus Christ of Latter Day Saints, founded on the revelations contained in the Book of Mormon. For here polygyny was held to be an essential part of a religious system, as was sufficiently indicated in the speeches made by leading female Mormons at a mass meeting held in Salt Lake City on November 16th, 1878. This meeting, which was attended by 1,500 women, was convened to protest against what were termed

[1] Landor, op. cit. Vol. II, p. 63.
[2] J. H. Gray, *China*, 1878, p. 185.

the Misrepresentations of the Anti-polygamy[1] crusade. The unanimity of the opinions expressed is indicated in the following extracts from the speeches.

"I am proud to state," said Mrs. Eliza R. Snow, "before this large and honourable assembly, that I believe in the principle of plural marriage just as sacredly as I believe in any other institution which God has revealed. I believe it to be necessary for the redemption of the human family from the low state of corruption into which it has sunken. And I truly believe that a Congress composed of polygamic men who are true to their wives, would confer a far higher honour upon a nation, and would perform better service to their country than a Congress composed of monogamic, unreliable husbands. Virtue is the foundation of the prosperity of any nation; and this sacred principle of plural marriage tends to virtue, purity and holiness." Mrs. Zina D. Young, another speaker, in a burst of enthusiastic approval of polygamy, said: "The principle of plural marriage is honourable, it is a principle of the Gods—it is heaven-born. God revealed it to us, among other things, as a saving principle; we have accepted it as such, as we know it is of him, for the fruits of it are holy. Worthy men and women of old practised it, even the Saviour himself traces his lineage back to polygamic parents. We are proud of the principle because we understand its true worth, and we want our children to practice it, that through us a race of men and women may grow up, possessing sound minds in sound bodies, who shall 'live to the age of a tree.'" And then there was the testimony of Mrs. Margaret T. Smoot: "With regard to the principle of plural marriage, I wish to say, that I have had experience in its practice over thirty years. I am the wife of a polygamist, I believe in the principle, and I know it to be pure and chaste; and I know that those who practise it in the spirit of the Gospel, of which it is a part, are pure and virtuous. And I know, too, that purer men and women do not live upon God's footstool than those who live in this order of marriage. I have seen the Prophet

---

[1] Strictly speaking the system of plural marriage adopted by the Latter Day Saints was *polygyny*. The term *polygamy*, which was and is popularly used in referring to the old Mormon practice, and indeed to all forms of marriage in which there is a plurality of wives, is incorrect. *Polygamy* includes *polygyny* (the condition in which a man has two, or more than two, wives at the same time), and *polyandry* (the condition in which a woman has two, or more than two, husbands at the same time). In the following pages devoted to Mormonism, however (in view of the usage by the Mormons themselves and by others quoted) to avoid confusion, the term *polygamy* is also used by myself in this, its popular significance.

Joseph, through whom this principle was revealed; I have listened to his teachings, I have known for myself of his virtue, of his purity, of his goodness, of his desire to elevate and bless the human family, and what I say, many of you, my sisters, can bear witness of. I know, too, that virtue, and goodness, and purity, are the watchwords of our brethren; I say I *know*; I do not say I believe it, but I do know for myself that what I say is true. I know it by the revelations of the Spirit of the living God—the comforter that was promised by the Saviour, and it is confirmed by my long experience. I have lived now nearly seventy years on this earth, and forty-four of them have been spent serving my God in this new and everlasting covenant. My husband, as I have intimated, is a polygamist; his other wives and his children by those are just as much a part of his family as me and mine, I being his first wife; and his other wives are just as lawful and honourable in the sight of God as I am, and his children I consider to be just as lawful and honourable as any children born in wedlock. These are not only my feelings, but I know them to be the feelings of many others who occupy a position like that which I occupy, and I believe them to be the feelings of this whole community, who would, if they had the privilege, speak in their own defence."[1]

Now it is an incontrovertible fact that in every household where there is a plurality of wives, there is nothing but jealousy, conflict and unhappiness among the women concerned. Polygamy is abhorred by women in every country in which it exists. As we have already seen, in China women have been known to commit suicide rather than be married to a polygamous husband (see page 83). This being the case, and few women at any rate will deny its obviousness, how did it come about that plural marriages flourished in the Mormon State for so long a period, and indeed were only brought to an end by the pressure of outside public opinion and the action of the United States Government? The answer is simple. It had the backing of religion: polygamy was so interconnected with Mormonism as then propounded by Joseph Smith, Brigham Young, *et al.*, as to be looked upon as an essential feature of the life of the community of Latter Day Saints. This was driven home by

---

[1] This and the two preceding quotations are taken from an undated pamphlet entitled *"Mormon" Women on Plural Marriage*, which relates to a Mass Meeting in the Theatre, Salt Lake City, Utah, Saturday, November 16th, 1878. (Reported by G. F. Gibbs.)

promises in connexion with a future life on the one hand and threats on the other. All this is clear from Judge Cradlebaugh's denunciatory criticism of Mormonism. In one notable passage he said : " Mormonism repudiates the celibacy imposed by the Catholic religion upon its priesthood, and takes in its stead the voluptuous impositions of the Mohammedan Church. It preaches openly that the more wives and children its men have in this world, the purer, more influential and conspicuous will they be in the next ; that wives, children, and property will not only be restored but doubled in the resurrection. . . . So at variance is the practice of polygamy with all the instincts of humanity, that it has to be pressed upon the people with the greatest assiduity as a part of their religious duty. It is astonishing with what pertinacity through all their ' sermons and discourses ' it is justified and insisted on. Threats, entreaties, persuasions, and commands, are continually brought in play to enforce its cheerful observance."[1]

Even so, there is evidence of the existence of much unhappiness among the Mormon people as a result of the system of plural marriages. Despite the fulminations of the Mormon elders, news of this unhappiness seeped out. Indeed, even the redoubtable Brigham Young, in a sermon delivered on September 21, 1856, admitted : " it is frequently happening that women say that they are unhappy. Men will say, ' my wife, though a most excellent woman, has not seen a happy day since I took my second wife ; no, not a happy day for a year.' It is said that women are tied down and abused ; that they are misused, and have not the liberty they ought to have ; that many of them are wading through a perfect flood of tears, because of the conduct of some men, together with their own folly. . . . I do know that there is no cessation to the everlasting whinings of many of the women of this Territory. And if the women will turn from the commandments of God and continue to despise the order of Heaven, I will pray that the curse of the Almighty may be close to their heels, and that it may be following them all the day long. And those that enter into it and are faithful, I will promise them that they shall be queens in heaven and rulers for all eternity."[2]

In such circumstances, it is not to be wondered at that the

---

[1] *Mormonism Unveiled*, St. Louis, 1891, pp. 22–23.
[2] Quoted from the *Deseret News* (Vol. VI, p. 235) in *Mormonism Unveiled*.

women of Salt Lake City, for the most part simple mortals, full of faith in what they looked upon as the inspired words contained in the Book of Mormon, and believing implicitly in the virtue, honour and veracity of their leader, were loath to express openly any dissatisfaction with the lives they led. But, as always, there were a few cases in which no considerations of religion or anything else sufficed to close their mouths. Their sufferings were such that the threats of terrors to be experienced in a future hellfire could not prevent them doing something to alleviate the few years remaining on this earth. One such case was that of Mrs. Brig Hampton, who applied to President John Taylor for a divorce from her husband Brigham Y. Hampton. In what is truly termed " a remarkable letter to the Inter-Ocean," a correspondent, signing himself " J.W.R.", presents some extraordinary revelations made to him by Helen Hampton, whom he refers to as one of " the thousands of unfortunate victims of polygamy in Utah."

" I found her living in a little house on the outskirts of the city, where she supports her two children, born of Brig Hampton, by sewing, and is to all appearances, and I believe from assurances of this lady who accompanied me, and other Gentile ladies in Salt Lake City, an honest and reliable woman. She is about forty years of age, and bears upon her face marks of the great suffering she has passed through. It was only by the most earnest persuasion, however, that I could get her to talk of her former troubles. She showed me the scars upon her hands from blows received from Brig Hampton, and which were spoken of in this complaint. I asked her if she would tell me how any woman of the intelligence she evidently possessed, could be induced to marry Hampton, knowing he had another wife. Her reply was : ' It will be impossible for me to show you. It is something that you cannot understand, and something that you will not sympathize with.'

" ' What was the argument they used to force you to do this ? ' She replied : ' The argument was that I would be damned if I didn't do it. That was the argument. Brig Hampton's wife, extraordinary as it may seem to you, assisted him in inducing me to marry him. Brigham Young brought his persuasion and his authority to bear upon me. You can form no conception of the kind of persuasion, promises and threats that were used to induce me to become his wife. There were no Gentiles here then as there are now. There were no opportunities of my getting advice, nor what I needed still more, because I had my own scruples, of getting assistance to enable me to withstand this pressure. I was made to believe, a believer as I was then in the Mormon religion, that I would be damned, and that all my salvation would be destroyed if I refused to accede to the wishes of Hampton and of the leaders of the church, and this, you must know was terrible to a young girl of my age. I finally consented. After I left the Endowment House, I felt, in spite of all the confidence I had in the Mormon leaders, that I had done a terrible crime; and on my way to what was to be our home I cried. Brig Hampton's first wife said, ' If anyone should cry it ought to be me.' ' But I would not have married him if you had not urged me,' I said. She replied, ' I didn't want you, and I want you to understand now that I did this to please him, and that I despise polygamy, and all that I have said to you in its favour and the hopes I have held out to you of happiness and peace were false.' "[1]

The writer of this document, after giving some details of life in the Hampton home, goes on to say that in the course of the interview Mrs. Hampton mentioned one feature of polygamy under Mormonism that was new to him. It is of considerable interest, not only because of its novelty but also owing to the light it throws on the methods adopted by the Mormon leaders to secure the obedience of their followers, and for these reasons is well worth reproduction here. She said: " The endowment robe consists of several garments. One of these is a white headgear for the women, which has a flowing cape falling down from the back. During the ceremony this cape is thrown over the woman's face. At some point in the ceremony, the man she has married raises that cape from her face, and no other person is permitted to do it. When the woman dies she is buried in her endowment robes, with this cape on her head, and when she is laid in her coffin the cape is thrown over her face. The teachings of the Mormon leaders are that she cannot be resurrected until the husband raises this cape from her face; that if he pleases and is satisfied that she has been a faithful and obedient wife and true to him, he will raise this cape, and she may be resurrected, but if he is not satisfied of this, then he refuses to do this, and she cannot be resurrected. One of the

---

[1] From the Appendix to *Mormonism Unveiled*, St. Louis, 1891, pp. 410–411.

[Picture Post Library

A CARTOON PUBLISHED AFTER THE DEATH OF BRIGHAM YOUNG

most common threats, Mrs. Hampton said, by which Brig. Hampton used to compel her to obedience, was that if she didn't obey him ' she would never be resurrected,' that he would not raise the cape from her head on the morning of the resurrection. This threat, Mrs. Hampton said, at one time had great terrors for her, but that she had learned now, of course, to regard it as harmless."[1]

---

[1] Op. cit., p. 412.

CHAPTER IX

MONOGAMY IN ITS VARIOUS PHASES

I

The Genesis of Monogamy

A STUDY of sociological development reveals that monogamy was invariably preceded by promiscuity, and usually by polygyny or polyandry. Ashamedness of or dislike for these preceding forms of marriage are only apparent in a community where monogamy is the legal or approved type of marital union. In other words, until the emergence of monogamy the objections to or drawbacks connected with promiscuity on the one hand and polygamy on the other were not realised by either of the sexes.

It is probable that monogamy was practised long before its claims as an alternative to either promiscuity or polygyny were seriously considered. It is invariably practised in all civilized countries where polygyny is customary and legal, for the simple reason that in all societies other than those of a most primitive character, where the principle of might is right in its crudest form reigns supreme, the question of expense causes the poorer men to limit the practice of polygyny to such an extent that they slide into monogamy without being aware of the fact that they are adopting a different form of marriage. As society becomes more civilized the economical aspect looms larger until inevitably polygyny is restricted in its practice to the wealthy and powerful. Side by side with the advance of civilization in any community is the creation or extension of property rights, a factor which increases and underlines the difficulties inherent in a polygynous society. In these circumstances any man whose offspring from a number of wives became numerous found himself involved in legal as well as economical difficulties.

Where polygyny was universal and no alternative was known, it is reasonable to suppose the women showed no discontent with their lot. It is even understandable that a girl showed preference for marrying a man with a number of wives, seeing that in a polygynous society his social position was dependent upon the size of his harem. But once monogamy appeared as an alternative system of marriage, woman's outlook slowly but surely began to change. Not long could it be kept from her that a monogamous alliance had many and definite advantages. It was only a matter of time for monogamy to sweep aside and outmode any and every form of plural marriage.

The emancipation of woman swept along side by side with the development of monogamy. For obviously only under a system of monogamous union was it possible for woman to enjoy any form of liberty and to possess any rights comparable with those enjoyed by man.

In its highest form monogamy resolves itself into a form of marriage in which both parties have equality of rights. Sumner has called such an alliance a " pair marriage." He says : " The term ' pair marriage ' is needed as a technical term for the form of marriage which is as exclusive and permanent for the man as for the woman, which one enters on the same plane of free agreement as the other, and in which all the rights and duties are mutual. In such a union there may be a complete fusion of two lives and interests. In no other form of union is such a fusion possible."[1]

In this ideal conception as a system of marriage carrying absolute equality of rights, monogamy is stupendously rare, and has concomitants that are, ironically enough, more difficult to realise in the highest society than in lower grades. Even in modern so-called democracy there are difficulties in the way. To-day, therefore, despite the much trumpeted equality of the sexes, which, true enough, in so many spheres of life, does exist to a relatively large extent, absolute equality of rights in marriage is seldom realised. In a few countries attempts have been made to give the idealistic concept a practical basis. Thus, in present-day Sweden, husband and wife rank as joint possessors of the home, and no piece of furniture of any kind or of whatever value, can be sold, given away, or otherwise disposed of except by mutual consent. In this way a marital arrangement in which the woman enjoys rights on a par with the man is claimed to have been achieved ; but any such state of economic equality

[1] W. G. Sumner, *Folkways*, Boston, 1907, p. 374.

inevitably in itself must rank as a possible and probable cause of disruptive factors arising which may very well prove to be of a more serious nature than those which have been destroyed.

II

Trial and Companionate Marriage

The form of marital union known as trial marriage is of ancient origin. It was practised extensively by the Egyptians. Alexander says : " The most ancient kind of marriage among the Romans was that in which a man and woman had come together, without any previous bargain ; and having lived together for some time, became at last unwilling to part, as they found themselves insensibly become necessary to each other : and among the Kalmuc Tartars, a young couple agreeing between themselves, retire for one year as husband and wife ; if, in that time, the woman brings forth a child, they remain together ; if not, they either make trial of another year, or agree to part. In the island of Otaheite, the inhabitants pursue incontinent gratifications, wherever inclination leads them ; but when a woman becomes pregnant, the father of her child thereby becomes her husband."[1]

The chiefs of the ancient Singhalese practised a form of trial marriage, though the period of trial was a singularly brief one. The couple lived together for two weeks and at the end of this period, if they were in mutual agreement that a continuance of the union was desirable, a strange ceremony was carried out : the man poured water upon the woman's head, they exchanged rings, had their little fingers tied together, and at the conclusion of this ceremony they were united for life. Certain tribes of North American Indians, notably the Wyandots, were addicted to trial marriage.

Bartels[2] mentions the practice being common among the peasants of East Prussia about the middle of the nineteenth century ; and Pastor Höhn says the custom persisted in South

---

[1] William Alexander, *The History of Women*, 1776.   Vol. II, p. 244.
[2] Ploss and Bartels, *Woman* (edited by E. J. Dingwall), Heinemann (Medical Books), London, 1935.   Vol. II, p. 218.

Germany until as recently as 1912.[1] In England, according to G. v. Bunsen, trial marriage was practised in Yorkshire in the nineteenth century, and should the man abandon the girl when she became pregnant severe punishment was inflicted upon him by the neighbours.[2]

Apparently in some cases the alliance was terminated after a prolonged trial, whether or not the girl became pregnant. For instance, in ancient Ireland, it was quite common for these trial marriages to be entered into for a period of one year. It was customary for the arrangements to be made at the Beltane Festival, celebrated on the 1st of May, and terminated at the Festival held exactly one year later.

Similar to this old Irish custom was the Scottish " handfasting " or " hand in fist ", which consisted of a cohabitation agreement being made between a man and a woman at a public fair, for a period of one year, after which they could, if the experiment had proved satisfactory, get married, or otherwise separate.

In Scott's *Monastery* there is a passage reading : " This custom of handfasting actually prevailed in the upland days. It arose partly from the want of priests. While the convents subsisted, monks were detached on regular circuits through the wilder districts, to marry those who had lived in this species of connexion. A practice of the same kind existed in the Isle of Portland."

James Browne, the Scottish advocate and historian, refers to " a singular custom regarding marriage, retained till a late period amongst the Highlanders, and clearly indicating that their law of marriage originally differed in some essential points from that established under the feudal system." He goes on to say that " this custom was termed handfasting, and consisted of a species of contract between two chiefs, by which it was agreed that the heir of one should live with the daughter of the other as her husband for twelve months and a day. If, in that time, the lady became a mother, or proved to be with child, the marriage became good in law, even although no priest had performed the marriage ceremony in due form ; but should there not have occurred any appearance of issue, the contract was considered at an end, and each party was at liberty to marry

---

[1] Ploss and Bartels, op. cit., p. 219.
[2] Ploss and Bartels, op. cit., p. 218.

or handfast with any other. It is manifest that the practice of so peculiar a species of marriage must have been in terms of original law among the Highlanders, otherwise it would be difficult to conceive how such a custom could have originated, and it is in fact one which seems naturally to have arisen from the form of their society, which rendered it a matter of such vital importance to secure the lineal succession of their chiefs. It is perhaps not improbable that it was this peculiar custom which gave rise to the report handed down by the Roman and other historians, that the ancient inhabitants of Great Britain had their wives in common, or that it was the foundation of that law of Scotland by which natural children became legitimatized by subsequent marriage. And as this custom remained in the Highlands until a very late period, the sanction of ancient custom was sufficient to induce them to persist in regarding the offspring of such marriages as legitimate."[1]

Guthrie says the origin of handfasting was supposed to have been due to the lack of clergy.[2] The most famous of the fairs where the unmarried selected their mates, says the same authority, was, according to tradition, one held at " a spot at the junction of waters known as the Black and White Esk."[3] Forsyth says the place is only a short distance from the Roman encampment of Castle-O'er. He further states : " In later times, when this part of the country belonged to the Abbacy of Melrose, a priest, to whom they gave the name of *book-i-the-bosom* (either because he carried in his bosom a Bible, or perhaps a register of marriages), came from time to time to confirm the marriages."[4] The custom was on occasion adopted by members of the aristocracy. Thus, says Lindsay, " James, sixth Earl of Murray, had a son by Isabel Innes, daughter of the Laird of Innes, Alexander Dunbar, a man of singular wit and courage. This Isabel was but handfasted to him, and deceased before the marriage."

Rogers, commenting on the practice, says : " From the monasteries, friars were despatched into the rural districts to inquire concerning handfasted persons, and to bestow the clerical benediction on those who chose to exchange their exceptional condition for a state of matrimony. Handfasting was one of

[1] Jas Browne, *A History of the Highlands and of the Highland Clans*, 1853. Vol. IV, p. 398.
[2] E. J. Guthrie, *Old Scottish Customs*, 1885, p. 46.
[3] Ibid., p. 47.
[4] R. Forsyth, *The Beauties of Scotland*, 1806. Vol. II, p. 284.

the social irregularities which the Reformers sought to suppress. In 1562 the Kirk-session of Aberdeen decreed, that persons who had been cohabiting under handfast engagements should forthwith be joined in wedlock. Except in Highland districts, where it lingered, handfasting ceased within twenty years after the Reformation."[1]

A curious form of trial marriage was common in ancient Wales, according to Giraldus Cambrensis. He says that it was usual for parents to let out their daughters to prospective husbands on trial, for which privilege a sum of money was paid down, with an arrangement that a further fee be paid if the girl were found to be unsuitable and returned to her parents. The practice was so common, affirms this authority, that a girl hardly ever married without a prior cohabitation.

Although this old concept of trial marriage was denounced by critics as an abrogation of every principle of Christian marriage, and those who practised or supported it, were held to have the morals of the farmyard, there was unquestionably a lot to be said in its favour. In those cases where no pregnancy complicated the problem, the system did permit a couple to find out whether or not they were sufficiently suited to warrant a permanent alliance, and if not, it enabled them to go their ways.

In modern times, there is even more to be said in favour of such an arrangement, whether it be termed trial marriage or companionate marriage. In advocating companionate marriage, Judge Ben Lindsey with much truth, says : " We ought to recognize the childless marriage as a separate thing from the procreative marriage, instead of stupidly treating them as if they were one and the same thing. We ought to recognize that regulations which are perfectly reasonable in the one are absurd and irrational in the other."[2]

---

[1] Charles Rogers, *Scotland, Social and Domestic*, 1869, p. 109.
[2] Judge Ben B. Lindsey and Wainwright Evans, *The Companionate Marriage*.

CHAPTER X

VARIOUS OTHER FORMS OF MARRIAGE

I

Group and Communal Marriage

In many early and primitive races it was customary for promiscuous intercourse to precede any form of marriage. Alexander says that " The Ausi, a people of Lybia, cohabited so promiscuously with their women, that the whole of the children of the State were considered as a community till they were able to walk alone, when, being brought by their mothers into a public assembly of the people, the man to whom a child first spoke was obliged to acknowledge himself its father."[1] In most races, however, this promiscuity crystallized itself into a form of group marriage, restricted to a number of clans, families, or collections of persons having some form of relationship or community of interests. In other instances the inhabitants of one village would form such a group. According to Thompson, the ancient Britons practised group or communal marriage. He says " a number of men would band together and would take in turn an equal number of wives in common, and whatever number of children were born were reputed to belong to all of them."[2] Inevitably there were a good many incestuous unions in such circumstances, and the effects of uncontrolled consanguinity were speedily apparent. There is some ground for the belief that these group or communal alliances were in some instances initiated as alternatives to other forms of marriage. Alexander, for one, is of this opinion. He says : " The Messagetæ, a people of Scythia, being confined to one wife, while the nations around them were indulged with the liberty of polygamy and concubinage ; in order to put themselves in some degree on a footing

---

[1] William Alexander, *The History of Women*, Vol. I, p. 277.
[2] C. J. S. Thompson, *Love, Marriage and Romance in Old London*, Heath Cranton, London, 1936, p. 14.

with their neighbours, introduced a kind of community of wives, and a man who had an inclination to the wife of his friend, only carried her into his waggon or hut, and hung up a quiver while she was there, as a sign, that they might not be interrupted."[1]

Before leaving the subject of communal marriage it is fitting to glance for a moment at the remarkable experiment carried out in the early years of the nineteenth century by the Oneida Community. The Society of Perfectionists was an American communistic organization started by John Humphrey Noyes, in 1838. The first venue of the Society was in the State of Vermont, but a few years later a move was made to Oneida, in Madison County, New York State, and from that time it was popularly known as the Oneida Community. Noyes proclaimed the objects of the Perfectionists to be as follows : " We are not opposed to procreation. But we are opposed to involuntary procreation. We are opposed to excessive and, of course, oppressive procreation, which is almost universal. We are opposed to random procreation, which is unavoidable in the marriage system. But we are in favour of intelligent, well-ordered procreation. We believe the time will come when scientific combination will be applied to human generation as freely and successfully as it is to that of other animals."

The novel features connected with this system of group marriage or polygamy in the true sense of the term (involving polygyny and polyandry), advocated and practised by Noyes and his associates, were in the eugenic measures that were adopted in connexion with it. Despite the allegations of those who denounced the project, there was no suspicion of promiscuity, while permission to have children was only granted, by what was termed the " Stirpicultural Committee ", to men and women who were physically and mentally healthy. It was in some respects a replica of the system advocated by Lycurgus, two thousand years before; while in other respects it anticipated the proposals of many present-day eugenists. In this respect, my comments on stirpiculture, written some years ago, may be suitably repeated here : " It will be noted that Noyes's system was really the application, in the case of human beings, of those principles of selective in-breeding practised by breeders of pedigree livestock in all parts of the world. It called for the

<hr>

[1] Alexander, op. cit., Vol. I, p. 270.

selection of breeding stock and in-breeding, the two essential principles recognized by breeders of exhibition stock. The main obstacle to any such form of breeding applied to mankind was overcome by Noyes through the adoption of birth control as a means of restricting the number of progeny produced by desirable breeders and preventing the offspring of undesirable breeders."[1]

II

Marriage to Gods and Devils

To the ancients the beliefs in the existence and activities of evil and good spirits were as real and as much a part of the ideology of the age as are these same beliefs among savage and primitive races. The sacred books of all nations teem with reference to these spirits, which in the guise of angels or demons as the case might be, interfered with, for good or for evil, the lives of ordinary people. In such circumstances it was perfectly natural that these spirits should be thought to have the ability to engage in sexual commerce with men and women; and the stories of nocturnal visitations by incubi and succubi were accepted as incidents which were to be expected. An early instance is the story of Adam's visitation by the demon Lilith.

The belief in the power of the Devil to assume at will the form of a human being or an animal, which was so pronounced in the days of the witchcraft prosecutions, was largely responsible for the widespread acceptance of accounts of intercourse occurring between the Devil and men or women. At various trials held in the seventeenth century, these powers of metamorphosis were affirmed, admitted, and accepted by judges, prosecutors, and defendants alike. At the trial of Margaret Smaill in Scotland, on September 13, 1678, it was stated that the Devil appeared to Jonet Barker, Margaret Lauder, and Jonet Cranstoun "in lyknes of ane tryme gentillman, and drank with thame all three, and imbracit Margaret Lauder in his airmes." Margaret Sonnes (tried on November 4, 1678) failing to follow him speedily enough, the Devil " did drag her be the coat, and brak the band thereof."

[1] George Ryley Scott, *Scott's Encyclopædia of Sex*, Werner Laurie, 1939, p. 310.

Dalyell says : " The presence of the *incubi* and *succubi* denotes amorous illusions only. Among the incidents of the fifteenth century, Boethius relates that the kindred of a damsel of illustrious birth who had refused several noble alliances, taxing her with incontinence, she admitted that a youth, wonderfully handsome, repaired sometimes to her chamber in the night : but whence he came, or whither he went, she knew not. Provided with torches they entered the apartment, where she was seen in the arms of a monster, so horrid as to exceed human imagination. Many flocked to behold the disgusting spectacle, and with them a priest of sanctified character, who began to recite the gospel of St. John, as the others retreated timorously, or stood speechless. When reaching the passage, *verbum caro factum est*, the demon fled with a terrible outcry, unroofing the chamber and setting its furniture on fire in his exit. In the course of three days a monster was born, and burnt to preserve the credit of the family."[1]

It was the conviction that such intercourse resulted in the birth of monsters, that led to the destruction, immediately following emergence from the womb, of many abnormal infants.

A feature of early civilization was the dedication of virgin girls to their God. Herodotus tells us that one of the temples in the Tower of Babel contained a bed reserved for the use of one woman, chosen by the god himself, according to the asseverations of the Chaldean priests. These priests, says the historian, " maintain this, of which I am not yet convinced, that the God himself comes to the temple and rests upon the couch just in the same way as in the Egyptian Thebes, according to the assertion of the Egyptians; for there, too, a woman sleeps in the temple. Both these women have no intercourse with men, we are told. So, too, in the Lycian Patara does the priestess of the god Apollo act at the time of the oracles, for these do not always take place : but when they do, she is shut into the temple with the God on these nights."

Strabo mentions that among the ancient Armenians it was the custom for virgin girls to be dedicated to the goddess Anaitis, which meant that they must serve as prostitutes attached to her temple for a period preceding their marriage.

In India the ancient practice of marrying girls to deities to promote fertility, survives, says Crooke, "in the form of the

[1] John Graham Dalyell, *The Darker Superstitions of Scotland*, 1835, p. 600.

preliminary marriage of dancing-girls or prostitutes at a temple where, under the title of Devadāsi (slaves of the deity), they cohabit both with the priests and with visitors."[1]   In Bombay, as well as in Madras, such girls are to be found.

III

The Levirate

This law of the ancient Hebrews, and of certain other nations, ordained that in the event of a married man dying without issue, his next surviving brother should marry the widow. The express object of this law was the provision, if humanly possible, of a son and heir.

The Levirate dates back to a period preceding the time of Moses.   There are indications that it was in existence in Palestine among the Canaanites.   Apart from Asia there are traces of its observance in places as far apart as Africa and Mexico.

In the ordinary course, a man was forbidden to marry his brother's wife, as stated in Leviticus xviii. 16, thus : " Thou shalt not uncover the nakedness of thy brother's wife : it is thy brother's nakedness " ; but, where no child had resulted from the union an exception was made.   The precise wording of the passage in Deuteronomy, allowing this exception, is as follows :—

> " If brethren dwell together and one of them die, and
> have no child, the wife of the dead shall not marry without
> unto a stranger ; her husband's brother shall go in unto her,
> and take her to him to wife, and perform the duty of an
> husband's brother unto her.   And it shall be, that the firstborn
> which she beareth shall succeed in the name of his brother
> which is dead, that his name be not put out of Israel."

In other words, when a woman became a widow, her deceased husband's brother usually filled the role of husband : no marriage ceremony of any kind was necessary.   This automatic marriage therefore must be annulled by the ceremony which permitted the widow to marry another man, if either party was disinclined to carry out its provisions.

[1] William Crooke, *Religion & Folklore of Northern India*, 1926, p. 247.

PUBLIC PROCESSION OF THE KING'S WOMEN, DAHOMY

From Archibald Dalzel's *The History of Dahomy*, 1793

A HAREM WINDOW, SIDI-BOU-SAID

From *Picturesque North Africa*, 1925

Apropos of this, Gardner says : " The law, as it previously existed, was not changed by Moses, but simply modified in various respects. Thus he expressly prohibited the marriage of a brother's widow, if there were children of his own alive. He no doubt, allowed, and, indeed, enjoined the brother to marry the widow of his childless brother, but if he was disinclined to take such a step, he was not to be compelled to do so, but had only to declare in court that he had no inclination to marry his brother's widow, and then he was at liberty. But if the brother did not choose to marry her, she was not allowed to marry another man until he had first set her at liberty."[1]

The act of giving a brother's widow permission to marry another man is called Caliza or the ceremony of " loosing the shoe." It is described by Leo of Modena in the following words : " Three rabbins and two other witnesses, the evening before, choose a place where the ceremony may be performed ; the next day, when they come from morning prayers, they all follow the rabbins and witnesses, who in the appointed place sit down, and order the widow and her brother-in-law to appear before them, who declare that they there present themselves in order to be free. The principal rabbin proposes several questions to the man, and exhorts him to marry the widow ; then, seeing him persist in his refusal, after some other interrogatories, the man puts on one of the rabbin's shoes which is fit for any foot, and the woman in the meantime draws near to him, and assisted by the rabbin, says to him in Hebrew, ' My husband's brother will not continue the posterity of his brother in Israel, and refuses to marry me, as being my brother-in-law.' The brother-in-law answers, ' I have no mind to take her.' Hereupon the woman stoops down, loosens and pulls off the shoe, throws it upon the ground, spits before him, and says in Hebrew to him, with the help of the rabbin, ' So shall it be done unto that man who will not build up his brother's house ; and his name shall be called in Israel, the house of him that hath his shoe loosed.' These words she repeats three times, and they who are present answer as often, ' He that hath his shoe loosed.' Hereupon the rabbin immediately tells her, that she may marry again ; and if she requires any certificate of what is done, the rabbins shall deliver one to her."[2]

---

[1] James Gardner, *Faiths of the World*, Vol. II, p. 313.
[2] Quoted by Samuel Burder in *Oriental Customs*, p. 280.

In those early days there would appear to have been no reason why a married man should not marry his brother's widow if he wished, and there are grounds for assuming that polygynous unions of this character were by no means uncommon.

Should there be several surviving brothers, the eldest had the privilege of becoming the widow's second husband; but should he decline each of the other brothers was asked in turn. If all of them refused, once again was the eldest appealed to, this time with the condition, whether expressed or implied, that refusal entailed submission to the indignity of going through the ceremony of the Caliza.

Based upon this old Hebrew law was that of the Athenians, which ordained that no heiress should marry out of her kindred, her nearest relation being compelled to marry her. The Book of Manus states that in the event of a marriage producing no children, it is right and proper for the desired offspring to be secured by a union between the wife and the husband's brother; or, failing this, another near male relative. Of the Circassians Olearius says : " When a man dies without issue, his brother is obliged to marry the widow, to raise up seed to him."[1] The Syrians and the Arabians adopted similar methods to ensure the preservation of the families. Of the last-named Burder observes that " if a father left one or more widows, the sons often married them, provided they were not their own mothers. This usage was suppressed by Mohammed; and before his time it was marked with a degree of detestation."[2]

The only reference to such a custom ever existing in Britain appears to be that of Lord Hailes who says it was in vogue in Scotland down to the eleventh century.

The practice would now appear to be extinct in a universal sense. Even among the modern Jews, says Gardner, " the rabbis invariably enjoin their disciples to refuse compliance with the precept, and nothing remains of the original institution except the ceremony of releasing both parties from a connexion which is never permitted to be formed."[3]

---

[1] Adam Olearius, *Voyages and Travels of Ambassadors into Persia*, 1669, p. 417.
[2] Samuel Burder, *Oriental Customs*, p. 280.
[3] James Gardner, *Faiths of the World*, Vol. II, p. 312.

IV

Spiritual Wives

From the ascetic doctrine of St. Paul may be said to have originated the idea of spiritual marriage in its primitive form; for although the concept as it existed in the early days of Christianity had not the metaphysical trimmings of that promulgated by Swedenborg, and later by such exponents as Brigham Young and John Humphrey Noyes, basically and practically the differences were so slight as to be unnoticeable.

Men whose lives were dedicated to religion, in the days when the clergy were not allowed to marry; women who, as nuns or the brides of God, were reputed to remain virginal; one and all were addicted to spiritual alliances. On the authority of Tertullian, we find that Apelles had two spiritual wives. The Origenists and the Eucratites advocated and practised spiritual marriage; so did Alexander, the Montanist martyr; so, too, Hermas and Irenæus. Then came the revolt against these practices.

The eighteenth century recrudescence of the idea of spiritual marriage, as a result of the spiritualistic teaching of Swedenborg, was followed by an eruption of decorated variants of one theme, as seen in the rise of the Konigsberg Pietists, the Pauline Sociologists, the Latter Day Saints, the Perfectionists, *et al.*, while the doctrine of Free Love emerged as a justificatory concept in cases where no religious foundation was claimed or claimable.

Spiritual marriage was eulogized by its protagonists as being infinitely superior to any other form of marital union, inasmuch that it was based upon the existence of a special affinity between the man and woman concerned. The till-death-doth-us-part alliance of orthodox legal marriage, it was contended, was little more than a business arrangement, in many cases constituting a union of convenience rather than of love, and in all cases implying no survival element, but being terminable at the death of one of the bodies concerned. In any such marriage there is not and there cannot be such a thing as eternal love, which is implicit in the spiritual union between two soul mates. The Swedenborgian belief in the eventual finding in heaven of one's soul mate, was paralleled in the practical ideas of Mormonism and Perfectionism as revealed in the search for and finding of one's true affinity on earth. The difficulties inherent in and the disturbances resultant from the putting into effect of such a philosophy were majestically ignored by its propounders and practitioners. The transcendent morality involved was thought to justify the believer and practitioner intolerantly and tyrannously riding roughshod over conventional beliefs, by giving one, under the banner of a neo-religious-ethical concept, the right to pursue one's search for a soul mate by methods involving and going far beyond those of the practitioners of hedonistic free-love. As one's affinity might prove to be among the legally married, the claim to have the society of one's soul mate now, had to justify and did justify the ignoring of the bonds of earthly marriage, as being, in such circumstances, unworthy of any consideration whatsoever.

v

Concubinage

In the early days there was little basic difference between a wife and a concubine. Particularly was this the case where wife-selling was customary. In fact, among the ancient Hebrews, the act of living continuously for three years in a man's house automatically altered the status of a concubine to that of a wife. Nor was she a creature to be despised and detested in the way which a study of the more modern reaction to a woman of her class would suggest. Until the Middle Ages her position was one verging upon respectability. According to the treatise written by Thomasius, for many centuries of the Christian dispensation, the concubine was not without honour; but with the coming of the Reformation, the whole concept of concubinage took on an entirely different aspect. From that time the concubine was looked upon as a woman of debased morals, not to be tolerated in any decent or respectable society.

The Old Testament contains many references to concubines. Thus we read that Solomon had no fewer than three hundred, Rehoboam had sixty, and David ten.

Among the ancient Romans concubines were the customary

companions of the priests ; so, too, in the centuries that followed, throughout Europe. Gerson recommended the institution of concubinage, in the way that others recommended prostitution, as a means of preventing greater evils. In Germany a form of union termed morganatic marriage was instituted, which in the last analysis was indistinguishable from concubinage.

In China the concubine has always been recognized as a necessity, even by the respectably married woman, who sees no reason why her husband should not have another woman as part of his household. Marco Polo, in his description of the court of the greatest King of the Tartars, named Kublai, or lord of lords, who reigned in the latter half of the thirteenth century, says : " He has four ladies, who always rank as his wives ; and the eldest son, born to him by one of them, succeeds as the rightful heir of the empire. They are named empresses ; each bears his name, and holds a court of her own ; there is not one who has not 300 beautiful maidens, with eunuchs, and many other male and female attendants, so that some of the courts of these ladies contain 10,000 persons ; and when he wishes to visit any one, he makes her come to his apartment, or sometimes goes to hers. He maintains also a number of concubines. There is a race of Tartars who are called Migrat or Ungrat, and are a very handsome people. From them are selected 100 girls, the most beautiful in all their country, who are conducted to court. He makes them be guarded by the ladies of the palace ; and they are examined if they have a sweet breath, and be sound in all their limbs. Those that are approved in every respect wait upon their great lord in the following order : six of them attend every three days, then another six come in their place, and so on throughout the year. It may be asked, if the people of this province do not feel aggrieved by having their children thus forcibly taken away. Assuredly not : on the contrary, they regard it as a favour and an honour ; and the fathers feel highly gratified when their daughters are thus selected. If, says one, my daughter is born under an auspicious planet, his majesty can best fulfil her destiny by marrying her more nobly than I can do. On the contrary, if the young lady, by bad conduct or any misfortune, be found disqualified, he attributes the disappointment to her malignant stars."[1]

---

[1] *The Travels of Marco Polo*, with copious notes by Hugh Murray ; Oliver & Boyd, Edinburgh, third edition, 1845, pp. 115–116.

In Morocco concubinage and polygamy flourished for centuries. The following observations of M. Lampriere, a famous eighteenth century surgeon, who, being admitted to the emperor's harem, to give medical treatment, had a unique opportunity to observe the manners and behaviour of the inmates, are of particular interest. The harem, he tells us, formed part of the palace, and consisted of a number of apartments, with a fountain-equipped central court, all on the ground floor. The furniture, carpetry and hangings were costly and elegant. Each concubine was allowed a single room, and had a separate daily allowance of money from the emperor. The ladies were allowed to hire their own domestics, and indeed could do pretty well what they pleased inside the harem ; but they were not allowed to leave the building without the express permission of the emperor, who, however, except for walks in the grounds for exercise, very rarely granted this favour. When any of the ladies was removed from one palace to another, the lower part of her face was covered with a piece of linen cloth, and she was transported, with a guard of eunuchs, in a lattice-work litter or carriage. The late emperor's harem, according to this observer, consisted of from 60 to 100 females, besides the domestics and slaves. Many of these concubines were Moorish women who had been presented to the emperor by their parents, who considered it an honour to have their daughters in the harem. The eunuchs, who were in charge of the women, and who, in fact, lived always among them, were the children of negro slaves : they were generally either very short and fat, or else very tall, deformed, and lame. Referring in particular to the women, M. Lampriere observes : "After passing the gate of the harem, which is always kept locked, and under the care of a guard of eunuchs, we entered a narrow and dark passage, which brought us to the court into which the women's chambers open. We here saw a great number of black and white women and children, some of them were concubines, some were slaves, and others hired domestics. Upon their observing the unusual figure of a European, the whole multitude in a body surrounded me. Some stood motionless in the usual attitudes of wonder and surprise, with their hands lifted up, their eyes fixed, and their mouths extended ; others burst into immoderate fits of laughter ; while again, others came up close, and viewed me with uncommon attention from head to foot. The parts of my dress which

seemed most to attract their notice were my buckles, buttons
and stockings ; neither men nor women in this country wearing
anything of the kind.   Most of the children, when they saw me,
ran away in the most perfect consternation ; and on the whole,
I appeared as singular an animal, and I dare say had the honour
of exciting as much curiosity and attention, as a lion or man-tiger
just imported from abroad, and introduced into a country town
in England on a market-day.   Every time I visited the harem
I was surrounded and laughed at by this curious mob, who,
on my entering the gate, followed me close to the very chamber
to which I was proceeding, and on my return universally escorted
me out.   The greater part of the women were uncommonly fat
and unwieldy ; had very black and full eyes, with round faces,
and small noses.   They were of various complexions ; some
very fair, some sallow, and others were perfect negroes.   One
of my new patients being ready to receive me, I was desired
to walk into the room ; where, to my great surprise, I saw
nothing but a curtain drawn quite across the apartment, similar
to that of a theatre which separates the stage from the audience.
A female domestic brought me a very low stool, placed it near
the curtain, and told me I was to sit down there and feel her
mistress's pulse.   The lady, who had by this time summoned
up courage to speak, introduced her hand from the bottom of
the curtain, and desired me to inform her of all her complaints,
which she conceived I might perfectly do by merely feeling her
pulse.   It was in vain to ask her where the pain was seated ;
whether in her stomach, head, or back ; the only answer I could
procure was a request to feel the pulse of her other hand, and
then point out the seat of the disease, and the nature of the pain.
Having neither satisfied my curiosity by exhibiting her face, nor
made me acquainted with the nature of the complaint, I was
under the necessity of informing her, in positive terms, that
to understand the disease, it was absolutely necessary to see the
tongue as well as feel the pulse ; without which I could do
nothing for her.   My eloquence, or rather that of my Jewish
interpreter, was, however, for a long time exerted in vain : and
I am persuaded, she would have dismissed me without any
further enquiry, had not her invention supplied her with a happy
expedient to remove her embarrassment.   She contrived at last
to cut a hole through the curtain, through which she extended
her tongue, and thus complied with my injunction, as far as was

necessary in a medical point of view ; but most effectually dis-appointed my curiosity. I was afterwards ordered to look at another of the Prince's wives, who was affected with a scrofulous swelling in her neck. The lady was in the same manner as the other excluded from my sight ; but she was obliged to show me her complaint, by which means I had an opportunity of seeing her face, which I observed to be very handsome."

No account of concubinage would be complete without some reference to the seraglio of the Turkish Grand Signior at Constantinople in the days of its greatest glory. The following description is culled partly from the pages of Moore's *Marriage Customs*, and partly from Little's *Beauty of the Sexes* : " It is a triangle about three Italian miles round, wholly within the city, at the end of the promontory Chrysorecas, now called the Seraglio Point. The buildings run back to the top of the hill, and from thence there are gardens which reach to the edge of the sea. It is enclosed with a very high and strong wall, upon which there are several watch towers ; it has many gates, some of which open towards the sea side, and others into the city, but the chief gate is one of the latter, which is constantly guarded by a company of *capochees* or porters ; in the night it is very strongly guarded towards the sea. The ladies of the seraglio are a collection of beautiful young women, chiefly sent as presents from the provinces and the Greek islands, most of them being children of Christian parents. The brave Prince Heraclius abolished the infamous tribute of children of both sexes, which Georgia formerly paid to the Porte yearly. The number of women in the harem depends on the taste of the reigning Sultan : Selim had two thousand, Achmet had but three hundred, and the late sultan had nearly sixteen hundred. The chief governess is called Kiayah Kadun, or governess of the noble ladies. She is an aged female, whose duty is to inspect their virginity, on their first admittance ; to see that their future education is suited to the character of princesses ; and that the black eunuchs appointed to be their guards, are duly qualified for their stations. They all sleep in separate beds, and between every fifth is a preceptress. They are taught sewing and embroidery, music, dancing, and other accomplishments, and furnished with the richest clothes and ornaments. There is not one servant among them, for they are obliged to wait on one another by rotation ; the last that is entered serves the one who preceded herself. These ladies are

IN THE IMPERIAL HAREM: THE SULTAN'S FAVOURITE
From William J. J. Spry's Life on the Bosphorus, 1895

never suffered to go abroad, except when the Grand Signior removes from one place to another, when a troop of black eunuchs conveys them to the boats, which are enclosed with lattices and linen curtains ; and when they travel by land, are put into close chariots, and signals are made at certain distances to give notice that none approach the roads through which they pass. The boats of the harem, which carry the Signior's wives, are manned with twenty-four rowers, and have white covered tilts, shut alternately by venetian blinds. Among the Sultan's attendants are a number of mutes, who act and converse by signs with great quickness ; also some dwarfs, who are exhibited for the diversion of his majesty. When he permits the women to walk in the garden of the seraglio, all the people are ordered to retire, and on every side there is placed a guard of black eunuchs, with drawn sabres in their hands, while others go round in order to see that no person is near who is not belonging to the seraglio. Should any man be found in the garden, even though it be through ignorance or inadvertence, he is undoubtedly killed, and his head brought and laid at the feet of the Grand Signior, who gives a great reward to the guard who brought it. Sometimes the Grand Signior goes into the garden to amuse himself while the women are there ; and it is then and there that they use their utmost efforts to please and captivate his majesty, by dancing, singing, seducing gestures, and amorous blandishments, by which they endeavour to ensnare the heart of the monarch. The ceremony of throwing the handkerchief, as related of the Sultan, to the girl he likes best, is an idle tale without any foundation. As soon as the Grand Signior has chosen the girl that he has destined to be his companion for the night, all the others follow her to the bath, washing and perfuming her ; she is then dressed superbly, and conducted to the Sultan's chamber with singing, dancing, and rejoicing.

" The title of *Bache-kadun*, principal woman, is the highest dignity of the Grand Signior's harem ; and she has a larger allowance than those who have the title of second, third, or fourth, which are the four free women allowed by the Koran. Lady Wortley Montagu says that, at the time she visited Turkey (1717), the widow of the late Sultan was obliged by the reigning Sultan to quit the seraglio, and choose a husband from among those who were her subjects. She used every argument and intreaty to avoid the disgrace, as it is looked upon ; but nothing could prevail with the sovereign to change his determination, and she actually fixed upon a man, upwards of four-score years of age, though she was little more than twenty herself. On the Sultan announcing his intention to bestow a princess on one of his courtiers, he must repudiate all his wives, dismiss his concubines, and provide for her a magnificent establishment. She has absolute authority over her husband, and wears a diamond-hilted dagger, the only dowry given to the bridegroom by the Sultan, as a badge of her superiority. The bridegroom approaches the apartment of the bride, who is reclining on her sofa. He makes one low bow on entering, another half way, and again at her feet, where he professes his love and hopes. She rises disdainfully and seizes the dagger as if to punish his temerity, when he produces, from his bosom, the Sultan's order which he kisses, applies to his forehead, and presents to her, who exclaims—' The Sultan's will be done.' She is then ushered to his palace with every splendour of cavalcade. Should he be guilty of any infidelity, he is privately strangled; or, on any complaint of her to the Sultan, stripped of his wealth."

"Dr. Clarke relates, that, in 1808, the gardener of the Grand Signior was a German, and that, while the Secretary to the Swedish mission was in conversation with him, it was announced that the Sultan-mother and four Sultanas were about to take the air in the gardens—they instantly closed the shutters, and locked the doors of the lodge. Through two gimlet holes bored for the purpose, they beheld the features of the Sultanas, one of whom was very fair, and all possessed extraordinary beauty. Their dresses were rich beyond all description. Long spangled robes open in front, with pantaloons embroidered in gold and silver, and studded with a profusion of pearls and diamonds, displayed their persons to the greatest advantage. Their hair hung in loose tresses, powdered carelessly, with clusters of jewels; a little on one side of the head they wore small diadems, and their faces, necks, and breasts were quite uncovered. The gardens and the baths of these Sultanas presented every degree of luxury and magnificence which Eastern taste has been able to invent."

VI

Pseudo-Marriages

Strange as the statement may appear to those with little or no knowledge of bisexuality, there have in the past been many cases where both parties to a marriage have been of the same sex. In some of these cases one of the partners has been afflicted with hermaphroditism or pseudo-hermaphroditism and a genuine error has been made; in other instances a deliberate deception has been practised by one party or the other.

Of the last-mentioned type was a case mentioned by Tegg, in which a woman successfully assumed the male role and married in succession three women, deserting each after robbing her: in 1777 she served six months' imprisonment after being placed in the Cheapside pillory.   The same authority gives another case which occurred a few years earlier than the one just recorded (to be precise, in 1773), of a woman who donned male attire for the purpose of courting a woman much older than herself. The attraction was the possession of the sum of one hundred pounds. "But," writes Tegg, "the intended treachery was discovered; and, as the original chronicler of the story says, 'the old lady proved too knowing.'"[1]

According to Burn, the Fleet Registers contain records of marriages numbering at least three, in which both parties were suspected to be of the female sex. In one instance, the parson, under date October 1, 1747, made an entry reading: "John Ferren, gent., sen., of St. Andrew's, Holborn, br., and Deborah Nolan, ditto, spr. The supposed John Ferren was discovered after the ceremony was over to be in person a woman."[2]

Both Tegg and Jeaffreson mention a case of a woman posing as a man, where both "husband" and "wife" were willing parties to the deception. The imposture was disclosed following the death of the supposed "wife," after the two had lived together for thirty-six years as landlord and landlady of a prosperous public-house in Poplar. On her death, the woman left a will bequeathing to her "husband" one-half of the sum of £3,000 which constituted their joint possessions. The dead

---

[1] William Tegg, *The Knot Tied*, 1877, p. 251.
[2] This trick, it was stated, was frequently played.

woman's relatives determined to contest the will, and faced with
the prospect of litigation, the "husband" confessed to the
imposture.   It appeared that as a result of suffering disappoint-
ments in connexion with their love-affairs, while still young,
states Jeaffreson, "they had vowed to live together in celibacy;
and to defend themselves against the addresses of masculine
deceivers they had agreed to enact the part of a married couple.
Having thus acknowledged her confederate's competency to
make a will, the personator satisfied the claims of the legatees,
and continued to carry on the business of the tavern.   A writer
in the *Gentleman's Magazine* (1766) says that, after surrendering
her confederate's share of their savings, the spurious ' husband '
resumed the feminine garb and ' appeared to be a sensible well-
bred woman, though in her male character she had always
affected the plain, plodding alehouse-keeper.'   On this point,
however, the writer in the *Gentleman's Magazine* appears to have
been mistaken.   For at a date considerably subsequent to her
confederate's death she prosecuted at the Old Bailey a person
who had attempted to extort money from her by threatening
to expose the falsity of her masculine appearance.   Perhaps she
resumed her proper style and attire for a short time, and again
relinquished them for the character and garb which had served
her purpose for more than thirty-six years."[1]

---

[1] John Cordy Jeaffreson, *Brides and Bridals*, 1872, p. 100.

PART THREE

CURIOUS FERTILITY RITES AND OTHER CUSTOMS CONNECTED WITH MARRIAGE

CHAPTER XI

MAGICAL RITES RELATING TO MARRIAGE

I

The Cult of Fertility

THERE is nothing to be marvelled at in primitive and savage peoples being mightily concerned with the promotion of fertility in all its forms. It was as inevitable as it was natural for man to become aware of the importance of the reproductive forces. The development from one another of plants, animals, birds, and human beings was not dissociated from a similar process in regard to inanimate objects. All were attributed to magical forces within the universe. In consequence every possible means was adopted to propitiate the gods who were thought to wield the magical power of turning inanimate objects into animate ones, or of creating life in other ways.

This is not the place to go into the phallicism inherent in early religious belief. Suffice it to say that the idea that it was possible for the virgin female of the species to give birth to young by magical means was universally admitted. The gods were believed to possess destructive as well as creative powers, and because of this it was of paramount importance that everything should be done to please these deities, and their representatives. Thus the worship of animals, birds, *et al.* as the personifications of gods; and later the propitiation of idols, saints and priests, as the representatives of deities.

Prominent among the mystic rites of many nations were appeals and prayers directed to phallic deities by women afflicted with sterility. Sometimes saints or holy men were induced to pray on behalf of these females. The Fakirs of the Hindus were notorious for their reputed power of enlisting the services of the gods in this direction, and thus removing the sterility of women. These men practised austerities and mortifications of an extreme nature. They abjured the pleasures and amenities of life. All were partially and many completely nude : their hair uncut and uncombed ; their faces and bodies besmeared with dirt. Alexander says " barren women constantly apply to them for assistance ; which when the good-natured Fakir has an inclination to grant, he leaves his slipper, or his staff, at the door of the apartment of the lady with whom he is praying ; a symbol so sacred that it effectually prevents anyone violating the secrecy of their devotion : but, should he forget this signal, and at the same time be distant from the protection of his brethren, a sound drubbing is frequently the reward of his pious endeavours. But though they will venture sometimes, in Hindustan, to treat a Fakir in this unholy manner, in other parts of Asia and Africa, such is the veneration in which these lusty saints are held, that they not only have access when they please, to perform private devotions with barren women, but are accounted so holy that they may at any time, in public or in private, confer a personal favour upon a woman, without bringing upon her either shame or guilt ; and no woman dare refuse to gratify their passion. Nor, indeed, has anyone an inclination of this kind ; because she, upon whom this personal favour has been conferred, is considered by herself, and by all the people, as having been sanctified and made holy by the action."[1]

Images representing the god *Gopalsami* were worshipped by barren Hindu women. In the town of Ganjam, says Hamilton, there was a pagoda dedicated to this god. Sometimes the idol was taken from the temple, placed in a coach and carried through the streets, while all the virgins and married women who were childless worshipped the god, while the priests taking part in the procession bestowed blessings on them to make them fruitful.[2] And in some form or other these practices have persisted through the years.

Among the Chinese the most elaborate propitiatory rites are carried out. " Every year, between the 11th and the 15th of the first and of the eighth Chinese months," says Doolittle, " several of the most popular temples devoted to the worship of a goddess of children, commonly called 'Mother', are frequented by married and childless women, for the purpose of procuring one of a kind of shoe belonging to her. They are not such

---

[1] William Alexander, *The History of Women*, 1779. Vol. I, pp. 338–339.
[2] Alexander Hamilton, *A New Account of the East Indies*, 1744, p. 382.

as are worn on her own feet. The shoes sought for are generally those which have been presented to the goddess as a thank-offering. Those who come for a shoe burn incense and candles before the image of 'Mother', and vow to render a thanksgiving if she will aid them in bearing a male child. The shoe is taken home and placed in a niche or by the niche which holds the family image of the goddess, where it is worshipped in connexion with 'Mother', though not separately, on the 1st and 15th of each month, with the burning of incense, candles, and mock-money, and fresh flowers. Now this shoe, representing the goddess, is believed by a very large proportion of married women to be quite efficacious in gaining the object sought. When a child thus prayed for is born, should such a fortunate event take place, the happy mother causes, according to her vow, two shoes like the one obtained from the temple, to be made. These two, and the original one, she returns to the temple with her thank-offering, which consists generally in part of several plates of food. Some women get shoes from several different temples, in their eagerness to have offspring. Should they become mothers after this, the goddess in each of these temples must be thanked—the one from whom the last shoe was obtained with the most offerings. Some women, instead of asking for a shoe of the goddess, ask for one of the flowers which she usually has in her hands, or in a flower-vase near by. The shoe is *lent*; the flower is *given*. On reaching home, the woman wears the flower thus obtained in the hair of her head, or it is placed in a flower-vase near by the niche which contains the household goddess 'Mother'. No worship is paid to it. In case several different flowers are obtained at different times from various temples where 'Mother' is worshipped, on the event of the birth of a child, the image of 'Mother' in all these temples must be 'thanked' with meats. Should the supplicant not become a mother, no thanksgiving would be expected by the goddess whose aid she had invoked. After she has gone about five months, the husband of the woman frequently returns thanks to the goddess 'Mother' or some other divinity whom he pleases to worship on this occasion, and begs in the following manner a continuance of favours. A table is arranged in some convenient place near the open heavens. On it are placed ten plates of meats, fish, fowl, rice, etc., a vase of flowers, five kinds of seeds or dried fruits, a lantern, three sticks of incense, two candles, and ten cups of wine.   A priest now begins to recite his formulas.   At the customary period of the performance, he remarks, in substance, as if addressing the divinity worshipped, that such a man has begotten by his wife a child for these five months.   He now presents these offerings as an expression of his gratitude, and begs that she may be protected during the rest of her time in good health, and give birth to the child without detriment, on which event taking place he will present another thanksgiving."[1]

Sometimes the services of a sorcerer or sorceress are procured in an endeavour to bring about the birth of a male child.   The ceremony employed on any such occasion is termed " changing the flower-vase ", as the bearing of children is thought by the Chinese to resemble in some respects the growing of flowers in vases, insomuch as a great deal depends upon the earth contained in these vases.   Says Doolittle : " If no child is born or if it dies, it is supposed to be like producing sickly flowers, *the earth being bad*.   The person employed, as some explain, is expected to go to the other world, and change the earth in the vase which has the flower-tree which represents the particular wife in question, or, as it is briefly called, change her flower-vase ; or she hires someone to make a quantity of artificial flowers, which are then placed in two paper flower-vases.   The sorceress or sorcerer first performs certain ceremonies over these vases, and then changes their relative positions.   Afterward, the paper vases and paper flowers are burned.   Changing their relative positions is thought to indicate something like changing the earth in the flower-vases in the unseen world.   The object of all this is to obtain male and healthy children."[2]

In ancient Rome the goddess Lucina was thought to preside over childbirth and for that reason every pregnant woman did her utmost to propitiate the goddess, and as the palm-tree was thought to have the power of easing pain and facilitating labour, branches of this tree were held in the hands while in the act of supplication.

At weddings in Morocco, according to Westermarck,[3] dates

---

[1] Rev. Justus Doolittle, *Social Life of the Chinese*, Sampson Low, London, Vol. I, pp. 114–116.

[2] Doolittle, op. cit., p. 114.

[3] Edward Westermarck, *Marriage Ceremonies in Morocco*, Macmillan, London. 1914, p. 199.

which have been blessed by being spit upon by the scribes, are eagerly eaten by women anxious to give birth to children.

In ancient Germany and in other parts of Europe, according to Alexander, magical girdles were used to promote speedy and easy deliveries. " But the power of these girdles did not terminate here," says this authority, " it extended even to the child as well as to the mother; and a son born by their assistance, was undoubtedly to be brave, and a daughter to be chaste; hence such girdles were carefully kept in the repositories of kings and of other great personages. Till within these few years, some of them were to be met with in the families of the Chieftains of Scotland. They were marked with many mystical figures, and the ceremony of binding them about the women in labour, attended with certain mystical words and gestures, which only some particular women were supposed to understand; a circumstance by which it appeared that their pretended utility depended more upon magic than on their intrinsic virtues."[1]

Analogous practices, based on superstition, were concerned with the avoidance of evil spells, influences, and the like which might cause barrenness. Hector Boethius, the Scottish historian, mentions the sepulchre of Vanora, the sterile queen, being shunned by women who feared they too might be condemned to sterility should they tread on it.

A curious and disgusting practice adopted by Egyptian women as a means of preventing barrenness, is mentioned by Lane (*An Account of the Manners and Customs of the Modern Egyptians*). At the time of which he writes (the early decades of the nineteenth century), criminals were executed by decapitation in a part of the city of Cairo termed the Rumeyleh. Previous to burial the corpse was placed upon a table of stone and there washed, the water used for this purpose, together with the blood from the dismembered cadaver, entering a trough placed there to serve as a receptacle. The blood-stained liquid was never removed, but allowed to remain there in its stagnancy and stink to high heaven. It was customary for a woman desirous of children, or wishing to expedite delivery, to visit this place, passing under the stone table and then over it, seven successive times; and finally washing her face in the polluted water contained in the trough.

Witches and wizards were thought to possess the power of

[1] William Alexander, *The History of Women*, 1779. Vol. I, p. 437.

rendering women sterile. They were reputed to be capable of effecting this by various means. The tying of a knot, on a cord, in some particular manner was supposed to be extremely efficacious. Bodin says that while at Pictou, in 1567, his hostess " being well skilled in the matter, explained to him that there were about fifty modes of casting the knot, so as to affect either spouse : that it might be devised, so as to operate for a day, for a year—for ever."[1] It was due to this superstition that arose the practice, immediately before the marriage ceremony, of untying all knots on the attire of both bride and bridegroom (see page 9). Pennant affirms that in some parts of Scotland the bridegroom was accustomed to seek protection by standing with the latchet of his shoe loose and a coin under his foot.[2]

The avoidance of evil influences was and is sometimes extended to food. Thompson says in reference to the Bechuanas that " none who eat the kidneys of the ox, will have any offspring. On this account, no one except the aged, will take them."[3]

II

Warding off the Attacks of Evil Spirits

At no time in the life of primitive man can he be free from fear of the machinations of demons or evil spirits, and therefore is he forever busy preventing their approach or neutralizing the effects of their activities. But at no time does this fear show itself more prominently than at the time when the ceremony of marriage is in operation.

The methods employed were either propitiative or truculent. Of the first-named the throwing of rice[4] was intended to propitiate any evil spirits present and induce them either to go away or to refrain from interfering with the marriage celebration. In Morocco the bride's hands and feet are daubed with henna to afford protection against evil influences.[5]

---

[1] Quoted by Dalyell in *The Darker Superstitions of Scotland*, p. 306.
[2] Pennant, *Tour of Scotland*, 1769, p. 187 ; *Voyage of the Hebrides*, 1772, p. 282.
[3] George Thompson, *Travels, etc., in South Africa*, 1827. Vol. I, p. 188.
[4] Until comparatively recently the throwing of rice was a feature of British weddings, being one of the customs which have survived long after their original purposes have been forgotten. To-day confetti has been substituted for rice.
[5] Edward Westermarck, *Marriage Ceremonies in Morocco*, 1914, p. 160.

PUNI GOLLA MUGGU

Part of the ceremonial on the occasion of a marriage
in the Puni Golla tribe of India is the drawing on the
courtyard of nine devices (muggu) of which the one
depicted is the most elaborate

From Edgar Thurston's *Ethnographic Notes in
Southern India*, 1906

The Chinese, who believed that a bride was extremely likely to be attacked by evil spirits while travelling to the house of the bridegroom, and when returning to her parents' house after the marriage, adopted an intimidating method. On the front part of the sedan-chair in which the girl made the journey, there was depicted the figure of a man, mounted upon a tiger, and armed with a formidable-looking sword, which was held aloft in his right hand suggestive of the act of striking. According to Doolittle, " It is said that, in former times, whenever a new bride in her chair passed by a certain place, evil spirits would invariably approach and injure her, causing her to be sick. The great magician (represented by the individual on the tiger, and brandishing a sword), who is the head of a class of Tauist priests, on being invited to destroy these evil spirits, or counteract their pernicious influences, exerted his great powers, and actually accomplished the object. In commemoration of this signal blessing to brides in particular and to mankind in general, and in order to secure immunity from these depraved spirits to future brides in other parts of the empire, the happy device of making a picture of this magician, and of placing it on the screen of the sedans they occupy on going to see their mothers on the third day after the marriage, was adopted. Judging from the universality of the use of this screen on such an occasion at the present time in this part of China, such an expedient to ward off unpropitious influences must be immensely advantageous ! Such a charm is also sometimes found on the red bridal sedans used on the day of the wedding."[1]

Somewhat similar precautions are taken in Manchuria. In front of the sedan chair go two men carrying a red cloth spread out as a means of keeping away demons, while the chair itself " is ' disinfected ' with incense to drive away evil spirits, and in it is put a calendar containing names of idols who control the demoniacal hosts."[2] On arrival at the bridegroom's house, crackers are fired, and before the bride vacates the chair, three arrows are fired at its blinds by the bridegroom.[3]

The Chinese extend these fears at the time of marriage connected with the malevolent intentions of the evil spirits that permeate the atmosphere, to other periods of married life, and

---

[1] Rev. J. Doolittle, *Social Life of the Chinese*, 1866. Vol. I, p. 95.
[2] E. Crawley, *The Mystic Rose*, 1907. Vol. II, p. 37.
[3] Crawley, op. cit., p. 37.

in particular to the time of childbirth. At the time of parturition it is believed that two female demons appear with the specific intention of destroying the mother's life, and that even if her life is spared she will be seriously injured. With the object of frightening and driving away these evil beings the following ceremony, says Doolittle, is observed. I give the description in the author's own words : "A table is spread with eight or ten plates of food, with incense, candles, flowers and mock-money. A priest recites the classics appropriate to the occasion. Ten or twenty pieces of a kind of grass cut up about an inch long, and several likenesses of the crab, cut out of common paper, are put into the censer and burned. Or sometimes several live crabs, after being used in the ceremony, are taken and turned out into the street. It is thought that these will greatly aid in frightening these bad spirits or propitiate their goodwill, so that they will not dare to come into the room at the time of childbirth. The reason why crabs are used is that the name of one of these demons sounds like the name for ' crab ' in the dialect of this place. After the conclusion of this ceremony, the meats and other eatables are removed, and another quantity of incense, candles, seeds, wine, and a cup of clear water, are brought and placed on the table, but *no meats*. The ruler of the Bloody Pond in hell, and various evil spirits in the other world, are then invited by the priest to come and receive the worship of the husband of the woman. The priest performs certain ceremonies ; the object is to gain the goodwill and protection of the ruler of the Bloody Pond in regard to the approaching case of childbirth. A part of the ashes of the incense used at this time is enveloped in a piece of red paper, and suspended near the censer belonging to the family, where it remains until thirty days after childbirth ; it is then taken and put into the censer and burned during a thanksgiving ceremony made in honour of the ruler of the Bloody Pond. Twice every day, previous to the period of childbirth, one stick of incense and one pair of candles are burned before this parcel."[1]

Nor were these views respecting the danger encompassing a woman during her period of parturition restricted to China. In many parts of Europe the belief was prevalent that at this time a woman was more subject to the malicious powers and influences of demons and witches than at any other time of her

[1] Rev. J. Doolittle, *Social Life of the Chinese*, 1866, pp. 116–117.

life. Moreover the new-born infant shared this danger, and there was, too, an ever-present risk that if it were permitted to live, it might at any moment be spirited away. To avoid these dangers and risks many charms, spells and ceremonies were employed. A favourite method was to nail a horseshoe on the door of the house occupied by the lying-in woman. In other cases the evil spirits were driven away by a tremendous noise produced by the beating of pans and kettles outside the door.

It was at one time believed that the evil designs of the malevolent could be eluded by celebrating the marriage secretly before dawn. This and other precautions were commonly observed in many countries. A method considered to be especially effective was the employment of a sorcerer or sorceress to negate the forces of evil or the spells of the malevolent, by the use of counter-agents. Another method, enthusiastically advocated by Brognoli, was the exorcism of evil spirits by prayer and fasting.

Alexander tells us that the Livonians made the sign of the cross with a naked sword on the door of the bridegroom's house, and then stuck the sword in a beam directly above his head, with the express object of protecting him from the influence of malignant spirits. To the same end, says this authority, the bride scattered red rags along the roads, and upon the graves of unbaptized infants.

In the marriage ceremony of the Bonthuk Caste in India, a pig, the legs of which are tied together, is present, and the squealing of this animal added to the music, makes an infernal cacophony. "The more noise the better," says Miles, "as this drives away any evil spirits who might attach themselves to the newly-married pair."[1]

III

Other Curious Superstitions

In Scotland the inhabitants of the Orkney Islands preferred to marry at the increase of the moon; but in certain other parts a full moon was considered the most favourable of all times.

[1] Arthur Miles, *The Land of the Lingam*, Hurst & Blackett, 1933, p. 162.

In the days of the ancients and in some places even to-day, there is a marked disinclination to celebrate a marriage in the month of May (see page 165). Plutarch, two thousand years ago, wrote : " Why do not women marry in May ? Is it from being intermediate between April and June—the one sacred to Venus and the latter to Juno ? " The belief long persisted in Scotland, as we find Forsyth mentions that the month of May is considered unlucky for the solemnization of marriage.[1]

The origin of the practice of carrying the bride over the threshold was due entirely to the superstition current in the early days of civilization to the effect that contact with the earth at such a time would involve the abstraction of some essential virtue or other. " The acquisition, retention, or preservation of certain qualities," says Dalyell, " was ascribed to interception from the earth of the body or substance wherein they were inherent. If reaching it in its fall, they were lost."[2]

In the Scottish Highlands it was customary, as comparatively recently as the beginning of the nineteenth century, for the bride to be conducted to her future spouse in the presence of the minister, in the same way as one went to bathe, that is, by going round in the right or *lucky way*, which was in imitation of the apparent diurnal motion of the sun.[3]

Among the rustics of Scotland, whether Highlanders or Lowlanders, the choice of a propitious day was a matter of some importance. January was considered to be an unlucky month ; so, too, as already mentioned, May. The favoured days in the week were Tuesdays, Thursdays, and Saturdays. In some parts of England it has always been considered unlucky to marry during the period of Lent.

A curious procedure, the avowed object of which was to thwart the power of witchcraft, was observed in the parish of Avoch whenever a fisherman's wedding took place. According to Guthrie : " when the bridegroom's party arrived at the church door, the best man untied the shoe upon the left foot of the bridegroom, and formed a cross with a nail or a knife

---

[1] R. Forsyth, *The Beauties of Scotland*, 1806. Vol. IV, p. 333.

[2] John Graham Dalyell, *The Darker Superstitions of Scotland*, 1835, p. 292.

[3] In ancient days sun worship was widespread in the Highlands, and on Beltan day (the first day of May) a person selected by the drawing of lots, was sacrificed to Baal. The custom persisted through the centuries, except that the sacrifice was dispensed with later, the selected person leaping three times through the flames of a fire kindled for the purpose.

upon the right hand side of the door—the shoe remaining untied."[1]

It was thought that a marriage would prove unhappy if the bridal party, on the way to church, met a monk, a priest, a serpent, a lizard, a cat, or a dog; on the other hand a meeting with a toad, a spider, or a wolf indicated success and happiness.

A strange superstition prevailed at one time in East Anglia to the effect that if a woman married a man with a surname beginning with the same letter as her own, bad luck would dog their steps from the moment the marriage was solemnized. The belief is expressed in the following couplet :—

" To change the name, and not the letter,
Is a change for the worse, and not for the better."

A North of England custom formerly much practised was known as " keeping the doorstep warm." Immediately after the departure of the married couple, one of the guests or an attendant would pour boiling water over the doorstep. This was thought to bring good luck and to indicate that another wedding would soon be celebrated at the same house.

The burning of nuts was at one time considered to be a sure method of looking into the future so far as lovers were concerned. The procedure was simplicity itself. A pair of nuts were selected, to one of which the male's name was given, and to the other the female's name. Bearing distinguishing marks, they were then placed in the fire, and carefully watched. If they burned in a normal manner, a happy marriage was indicated; if the male nut exploded with a crack, or if they flew out of the fire or apart, an unhappy courtship and much misery were sure to be in store; but if the nuts remained motionless and burned to cinders side by side, the couple might rest assured that happiness was to be their lot. There is a reference to the custom by John Gay, thus :—

" Two hazel nuts I threw into the flame,
And to each nut I gave a sweetheart's name ;
This with the loudest bounce me sore amazed,
That in a flame of brightest colour blazed.
As blazed the nut, so may thy passion grow,
For 'twas thy nut that did so brightly glow."

The Arabs, according to Burckhardt, have certain strange

[1] E. J. Guthrie, *Old Scottish Customs*, 1885, p. 95.

superstitions in relation to widows and marriage. No guest at the wedding of a widow will partake of the nuptial bread, should any be provided; for everything connected with the nuptials of a widow is regarded as ill-omened. The husband, for a month after the wedding, will not eat any provisions provided or prepared by his wife, nor even use any crockery or other table utensils with which she has been in contact. All guests bring with them their own cups, and refuse to drink out of those belonging to the newly-married widow.[1]

In India the exposure of young infants is a crime of great frequency among the natives, and seems to be of very ancient origin. Tavernier writes: " When a woman is brought to bed, and the child will not take the teat, they carry it out of the village, and putting it in a linen cloth, which they fasten by the four corners to the boughs of a tree, they there leave it, from morning till evening. By this means, the poor infant is exposed to be tormented by the crows, insomuch that there are some who have their eyes picked out of their heads, which is the reason that, in Bengala you shall see so many of these idolaters that have but one eye, and some that have lost both. In the evening, they fetch the child away, to try whether he will suck the next night; and, if he still refuse the teat, they carry him to the same place next morning, which they do for three days together; after which, if the infant after that refuses to suck, they believe him to be a devil, and throw him into the Ganges. . . . "[2]

In Burma, it was considered, says Father Sangermano,[3] that if the wind happened to carry away any of the betel leaves, which, according to custom, were being carried into the house of a newly-wedded woman, it portended an unhappy marriage and a subsequent separation. A strange Burmese custom observed in the nineteenth century in connexion with childbirth is described by this same authority. The moment the infant was born, a huge fire was made in the apartment. The heat from this fire was of such a degree of intensity that any close approach was impossible without some injury being experienced. Yet the woman was " stretched out before it," and in this position

---

[1] John Lewis Burckhardt, *Notes on the Bedouins and Wahabys*, 1831. Vol. I, p. 267.
[2] Quoted in *Report on Medical Jurisprudence in the Bengal Presidency*, by Norman Chevers, Calcutta, 1857, pp. 167–8.
[3] John Jardine (edited by), *The Burmese Empire a Hundred Years Ago*, as described by Father Sangermano, 1893, p. 144.

received the brunt of the heat " on her naked skin," which, as a result was often badly blistered.   This treatment continued " for ten or fifteen days without intermission, at the end of which time, as it will easily be supposed, the poor woman was quite scorched and blackened."[1] Father Sangermano gives no indication as to the origin of this presumably superstitious practice ; nor have I been able to find an explanation from any other source.

The old superstition connected with " throwing a shoe " lived through many centuries, and even to-day an old shoe is usually fixed to the back of the conveyance which takes the bride and bridegroom on the first stage of their honeymoon journey. For some reason which seems to be unknown the left shoe was always considered to be more lucky than the right, and even more important was the age of the shoe. As Tennyson expresses it :—

> " From this thou shalt from all things seek
>   Murrow and mirth and laughter ;
> And whereso-er thou move, good luck
>   Shall throw her old shoe after."

A belief current at one time was that in the event of a younger daughter marrying before her elder sister or sisters, the unmarried, whether one or several, must dance without shoes at the wedding of their younger sister, failing which terpsichorean display the older member or members of the sisterhood would be doomed to spinsterhood.

---

[1] Ibid., p. 165.

CHAPTER XII

CHASTITY IN THE MARRIED STATE
AND ITS ENFORCEMENT

I

The Emergence of Chastity as a Treasured Possession

CHASTITY is not and never can be an unchanging concept. The meaning given to it depends wholly upon the regulations and orthodox ideas regarding sex and morals that are in existence at any given time in a specific place. Thus chastity in one century or one generation may differ materially from chastity in another century or another generation. More and further, chastity in one country may be something entirely different from chastity in another country. In any place and at any time therefore, if chastity is to have any meaning at all, there must be formulated a set of rules regarding what constitutes immorality otherwise no one can be unchaste.

The question of what is immoral and what is moral in regard to sexual conduct having been established, any departure from this standard constitutes immorality. The chaste person observes these rules, or rather the very fact of observing them constitutes chastity. In the Mormon community at the time of Brigham Young, neither he nor his polygynous associates were guilty, from a Mormonistic concept, of unchastity.

There is a wealth of evidence that at one time little regard was paid to sexual continence. We have seen that for religious and other reasons, in some races, virginity was dreaded or despised. It is true that in the majority of instances this applied so far as the female was concerned in certain circumstances only, and usually before marriage. In the majority of primitive tribes, and in all the higher civilized races, at any rate, extra-marital intercourse was tabooed. True, there were marked exceptions, mostly it must be observed where religious connotations entered into the picture. Thus, in the ancient city of Babylon, capital of Assyria, every woman was compelled to visit the temple of

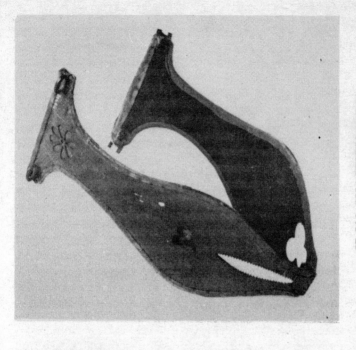

IRON CHASTITY BELT
Waist-belt missing
15th-16th century

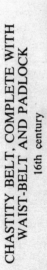

CHASTITY BELT, COMPLETE WITH
WAIST-BELT AND PADLOCK
16th century

Venus once in the course of her lifetime, and there perform an act of prostitution with a stranger. It was alleged that this extraordinary law was promulgated by an oracle. The woman, whatever her rank or position, had no choice as regards who her partner was to be, and she must accept whatever fee he might tender. Similar practices were in vogue in other countries, where, according to Alexander, a number of young women were selected to fill the role of prostitutes in the service of the goddess of debauchery, and in this way save the rest of the female populace from a similar fate.

For other reasons than the propitiation of the deity has, on occasion, it been deemed necessary to sacrifice the continency of the country's women, even where sexual modesty was valued. One such occasion occurred in Iceland, when, in 1707 the country was ravaged by a contagious disease. So heavy was the death-rate that a serious danger of depopulation arose. To meet and overcome this, the King of Denmark decided on a heroic and, in the country of Iceland at any rate, a hitherto unconceived measure. He made it lawful for every young woman to give birth to six illegitimate children, and further he ordained that so far from this act being one of shame or involving degradation or loss of reputation, it should rank as something to be praised in the name of patriotism. So well did the plan succeed that, we are told, in the course of a few years it was found necessary to rescind the law, as the country was in danger of becoming overcrowded, and the women becoming hopelessly promiscuous.

While pre-marital continence has usually been demanded of females, it has never been demanded of males. In other words the standard of chastity has been on quite a different footing as regards the sexes. The reasons for this are many, but the most important one of the lot is concerned with the risk of pregnancy following any departure from chastity on the part of the female, a reason which ranked even higher in importance as property rights loomed larger with the march of civilization. Gradually, therefore, women began to realize that their virginity was an asset of considerable value.

So far as the married state is concerned, chastity means, and has always meant, in all civilized countries, the restriction of intercourse to one's legal partner. Here the taboo applies equally to husband and wife. Any departure from this rule is sufficient to bring the alliance to a termination.

II

Methods of Securing Chastity

Man's wish to feel that his wife was his exclusive property and his desire to make certain that he was not called upon to be responsible for any children of whom he was not the father, have at one time and another led him to take elaborate precautions to ensure the chastity of his wife during periods when he was compelled, or found it necessary, to be away from home.

The oldest methods adopted to this end were naturally the most obvious and simplest available, to wit, restriction of liberty by confinement, and placing under the constant surveillance of trusted guards. Apropos of this, Alexander says : " The rapes of Io, and of Proserpine, gave birth perhaps to the confinement of women among the Greeks, and similar misfortunes might be followed by similar consequences among other nations. But whether the confinement of women originated from the rape of Dinah, we pretend not to determine ; of this, however, we are certain, that in length of time it became a custom among the Jews as well as among their neighbours. King David had his wives confined, for we are told that they went up to the house-top to see him march out against his son Absalom, which at this day is all the liberty allowed the women of the East, when they wish to be indulged with the sight of any public procession or show. But though the women of kings were at this period generally shut up, it would seem that those of private persons enjoyed more liberty, for the same David sent and brought the wife of Uriah to his house, which all the authority with which he was invested could not have done without a tumult, had she been as strictly guarded, and the persons of women as sacred and inviolable as they are now in the East. When we come to the history of Solomon, we have plain accounts of a seraglio for the confinement of his women ; and in that of Ahasuerus, King of Persia, we learn that his seraglio was constituted not only on a plan of the severest confinement, but also of the most voluptuous sensuality. It would be needless to trace this custom downwards to later periods, as it is well known that it became the common practice of almost all nations to the time of the Romans, who perhaps, were the first people who totally discarded it."[1]

In many cases confinement in the seraglios was not in itself deemed to afford a sufficient means of protection, hence the use of guards. Here again human passions and appetites being what they are, men who were likely to have such appetites aroused and who were capable of gratifying them, were considered unsuitable for employment in this capacity. To overcome the difficulty, the services of eunuchs were enlisted. It would appear that in the days of Samuel, it was customary for the kings of the nations in the neighbourhood of the district inhabited by the Israelites to employ eunuchs as guards for their wives : Samuel himself implies as much when, as one of the reasons which he brought forward against his people choosing a king was the fact that any such leader " would take their eunuchs to guard his women."

In practice, however, despite its widespread employment, the custom of using eunuchs in this way was by no means so effective as was at one time thought. In the first place, contrary to popular belief, emasculation does not always or necessarily destroy sexual appetite or power, and there are on record many instances where these mutilated men have successfully engaged in sexual intercourse. Moreover, there was always the possibility of a guard accepting a bribe. It was for these reasons that in Spain, at one time, it was the practice to employ as guards vindictive old women, who, it was contended, would be more likely to prove incorruptible " as envy would stimulate them to prevent the young from enjoying those pleasures which they themselves had no longer any chance for," but here again the lure of gold proved too much for their resistive powers, and the method had to be abandoned.

Perhaps the most curious of all methods of preserving female chastity is that employed by the natives in the interior of Africa. A grotesque hollow figure made of bark and straw, inside which is a man, walks through the village in the night, emitting frightful noises. This figure, which is called Mumbo Jumbo, is reputed to possess universal knowledge and is called upon to settle disputes, and to decide what punishment is to be inflicted upon offenders. In particular the wrath of Mumbo Jumbo is said to be aroused through any violations by the females of their

---

[1] William Alexander, *The History of Women*, 1779.   Vol. II, p. 20.

chastity, and wives are led to believe that such offences will inevitably be discovered and punished.

The practice of infibulation among many savage races as a means of preserving the virginity of unmarried girls, and the use of the Herculean Knot by the ancient Greeks for the same purpose, no doubt suggested the girdle of chastity of the Middle Ages.

It has been said that the first to compel his wives to wear this singular contrivance was Francesco da Carrara, the fourteenth century ruler of Padua. How true this statement may be it is impossible to discover, as accounts of the career, trial and subsequent execution of the tyrant vary so tremendously in detail as to leave one bewildered, but certain it is that girdles of chastity were employed in Europe about that time. Moreover there is some dispute as to the country of origin. Like the condom, the girdle of chastity is something of which no country is anxious to claim the credit for its introduction or invention. But the consensus of opinion seems to favour Italy. In the sixteenth century King Henry the Second of France had an instrument of this nature specially made for Catherine de Medici.

The appliance was constructed in many forms ; some as simple as others were elaborate. One of the least intricate models used to be on exhibition in the Musée de Cluny, Paris. It consists of a velvet-covered steel hoop-like girdle, with a curved ivory centre-piece for covering the vulva, and is fitted with a lock. Another type of girdle, formerly to be found in the same museum, consists of two engraved steel plates, hinged together.

There are numerous references in literature to the use of these girdles, but to what extent the accounts are apocryphal it is difficult to judge. Rabelais, Brantôme, Guillaume de Marchault, Tallemant des Réaux, Voltaire, and others, referred to their use. Perhaps the most important reference, however, is that contained in the speech of the French lawyer Freydier in the case of Mademoiselle Marie Layon v. Sieur Pierre Berlhe. The girl, who was the mistress of Sieur Berlhe, was compelled by him to wear a girdle of chastity. This appliance was described by Freydier as being made of woven brass wire ; it was secured in front with a padlock, the key of which remained in the possession of the defendant. The contrivance was designed to leave only a narrow space open, and around this opening were sharp spikes.

Since those days the use of the girdle spread to most parts of the civilized world, though from the evidence available it would appear that only men of a degree of jealousy bordering on the pathological have gone to such extreme lengths in their efforts to ensure the chastity of their wives or mistresses. In Ploss and Bartels' *Woman*, we read that the Pennsylvanian Dutch settlers used something of this nature, called ' Day Belts ' : they were made of leather, " studded with rivets and padlocked."[1] The same authoritative work gives several recent cases : a case at Batavia, N.Y., in 1931, of a man compelling his wife to wear a belt of leather and steel, fastened with padlocks ;[2] another case a year later, in Paris this time, of a woman who had been forced by her husband to wear a girdle for three months.[3] As recently as 1946, according to a report published in the *News of the World* (June 16, 1946) a case occurred at Atlantic City, in which " the allegation that he locked a steel chastity belt of mediæval design on his wife formed the basis of a charge of ' atrocious assault and battery ' brought against a 39-year-old wood worker." The report goes on : " He is William Truaz, whose wife, Mrs. Rose L. Truaz, was quoted by Police-Captain Edward Webb as having declared that he padlocked the belt about her before he left to go to work. Mrs. Truaz was brought to police headquarters, where a locksmith removed the belt by cutting one of the one-inch steel links in the chain. The police stated that Truaz, when arrested, said he manufactured the belt during his spare time, and applied it to his wife to ' keep her from running around.' "

Before leaving the subject of the various means adopted to ensure chastity, it is well to mention a curious method mentioned by Alexander as being practised in Poland. " Most of the young women belonging to the peasants," he said, " have little bells fastened to various parts of their clothes, to give notice to their mothers and other female guardians where they go, that those may always have it in their power to detect them should they attempt to intrigue or secrete themselves from their view."[4]

[1] Ploss and Bartels, *Woman : An Historical Gynaecological and Anthropological Compendium* (edited by E. J. Dingwall), Heinemann (Medical Books), 1935. Vol. II, p. 27.
[2] Ibid., pp. 26–27.
[3] Ibid., p. 27.
[4] William Alexander, *The History of Women*, 1779. Vol. II, p. 34.

CHAPTER XIII

SELLING, LOANING, AND EXCHANGING WIVES

I

The Sale of Wives

WE have seen that in many races it is customary to sell young girls at all ages from childhood to maturity to men in search of wives. It is now necessary to turn to another practice, that of the selling of women after marriage by husbands who have become tired of their partners. Pericles sold his wife; so, too, Cato. And in many savage and primitive tribes even to-day the practice is common. There is evidence of its incidence in Tibet and neighbouring territories.

Various reasons have been put forward for the origin of the practice in England, but the one suggested by the writer of the article entitled 'Wife-selling' in the magazine *All the Year Round* (December 20, 1884) appears to be an eminently credible one. This writer says the practice was probably based upon old Anglo-Saxon law, which ordained that if a freeman took away another freeman's wife, "he was to pay his full weregild, to buy another wife for the injured husband, and deliver her at his home." The law then existing regarding the purchase of a bride from a parent or guardian was modified in the reign of Canute so that the girl could not be compelled to marry against her will, and any sum of money which exchanged hands at the time of marriage must no longer constitute a compulsory payment but be a voluntary gift. "It is not unnatural to suppose," continues this writer, "that the commodity thus obtained by money was transferable to another for a similar consideration, whenever it may have become useless or disagreeable to its original purchaser. It seems, however, not impossible that the commencement of the custom would be found even in times antecedent, when women, guilty of unfaithfulness, were either put to death or sold as slaves."

From such information as is available it would appear that the earliest instance in Great Britain of such a transaction was the sale of Margaret de Camoys, in the year 1302. In the deed recording this transfer, the husband, John de Camoys, " delivered and yielded up, of his own free will, to Sir William de Paynel, his wife, Margaret de Camoys, and likewise gave and granted to the said Sir William all goods and chattels of which the said Margaret was possessed, and consented and granted that the said Margaret should abide and remain with the said Sir William, during his pleasure." This remarkable document was completed in the presence of several witnesses.

Now there was nothing in the law of the land, either at the time of the afore-mentioned transaction, or subsequently, which gave a husband the right to sell his wife to another party ; but, willy-nilly, the belief in the legality of such a procedure persisted through the centuries, and we find many records of these sales in Great Britain and Ireland.

In 1553 a clergyman named Thomas Snowdel, who also enjoyed the somewhat curious nickname of " Parson Chicken ", sold his wife to a butcher, in an effort to retain his benefice when Queen Mary announced that all priests who had married would be turned out of their livings.

So far as can be ascertained, however, the sale of a wife continued to be a somewhat rare occurrence until well into the eighteenth century, when the practice became far more widespread. " On the 31st August 1773," runs a paragraph in *The Annual Register*, " three men and three women went to the Bell Inn, in Edgbaston Street, Birmingham, and made the following entry in the toll-book, which is kept there : ' Samuel Whitehouse, of the parish of Willenhall, in the county of Stafford, this day sold his wife, Mary Whitehouse, in open market, to Thomas Griffiths, of Birmingham, value one shilling. To take her with all faults '."

The sum of one shilling seems a ridiculously low price, even in those days, for a wife, but this did not by any means constitute a record so far as cheapness was concerned. *The Times* (March 30, 1796) mentions the sale by John Lees of his wife for sixpence. At a sale attended by hundreds of people at Dudley in 1859, the highest bid was sixpence. Three years later, at Selby, Yorkshire, the price of a pint of beer was the best offer made ; and there was another sale at Sheffield, in 1881, for the price of a quart of the same liquor. Even these prices, low though they were in all conscience, did not touch rock bottom, for at Alfreton, in 1882, the price of a glass of common ale was accepted, so eager apparently was the husband to get rid of his spouse. In Ireland things were no better, as a case reported by *The Pall Mall Gazette* (October 20, 1882) shows : Patrick O'Neill purchased the wife of a man named George Drennan for the sum of one penny and a dinner !

Doubtless the age and appearance of the woman had a good deal to do with the price realized. In some cases, apparently, the husbands regaled the onlookers with accounts of the domestic and other capabilities of their wives, avoiding any reference to defects or bad points, but there were exceptions, as instanced in the following case culled from the pages of the periodical, *All the Year Round* :—

" The *Annual Register* for 1832 gave an account of a singular wife sale. Joseph Thomson, a farmer, after a brief married life of three years, finding that the union was irksome, agreed with his wife to separate. Acting upon the prevalent notion that by putting his spouse up to auction, and so parting with her, the marriage bonds were legally unloosed, he came to Carlisle with her, and by the bellman announced the sale. At noon the auction commenced in the presence of a large number of persons ; the wife, a spruce, lively damsel of about two-and-twenty years of age, being placed on a large oak chair, with a halter of straw round her neck. Thomson then spoke as follows : ' Gentlemen, I have to offer to your notice my wife, Mary Anne Thomson, otherwise Williams, whom I mean to sell to the highest and fairest bidder. Gentleman, it is her wish as well as mine, to part for ever. She has been to me only a born serpent. I took her for my comfort and the good of my home, but she became my tormenter, a domestic curse, a night invasion, and a daily devil. Gentlemen, I speak with truth from my heart, when I say God deliver us from troublesome wives and frolicsome women ! Avoid them as you would a mad dog, a roaring lion, a loaded pistol, *cholera morbus*, Mount Etna, or any other pestilential thing in Nature. Now, I have shown you the dark side of my wife, and told you of her faults and failings ; I will introduce the bright and sunny side of her, and explain her qualifications and goodness. She can read novels and milk cows ; she can laugh and weep with the same ease

that you could take a glass of ale when thirsty.   She can make
butter, and scold the maid ; she can sing Moore's melodies, and
plait her frills and caps ; she cannot make rum, gin, or whisky,
but she is a good judge of the quality from long experience in
tasting them.   I therefore offer her with all her perfections and
imperfections for the sum of fifty shillings."   After such a frank
harangue the marvel of it is that there was any bid at all.
However, the account goes on to say that " after waiting about
an hour, Thomson knocked down the ' lot ' to one Henry Mears,
for twenty shillings and a Newfoundland dog, and the parties
separated, being mutually pleased with their bargain."

Occasionally recourse was had to barter, as in a case mentioned
in the *Gentleman's Magazine* : in 1764, a Norfolk farmer offered
to exchange his wife for an ox, the only stipulation being
that he should be allowed to select the ox himself.   A more
curious instance of wife-barter was recorded, says *All the Year
Round*, in the columns of the *Public Advertiser* (September 19,
1768).   This newspaper says : " On Thursday last a publican
in Shoreditch sold his wife for a ticket in the present lottery,
on condition that if the ticket be drawn a blank, he is to have
his wife again as soon as the drawing of the lottery is
over."

Although in many instances the prices realized were extremely
small, and in other cases the seller had to be content with
something offered in exchange, there are for the finding plenty
of instances where wives brought their husbands much more
satisfactory sums, as the following paragraph in *The Times*
July 22, 1797) seems to indicate : " The increasing value of
the fair sex is esteemed by several eminent writers, the certain
criterion of increasing civilization.   Smithfield has, on this
ground, strong pretensions to refined improvement, as the price
of wives has risen in that market from half a guinea to three
guineas and a half."

As might be expected there were occasions in plenty when
no one could be induced to purchase the woman, thus creating
a state of affairs which must have increased considerably the
potentialities for unhappiness between the couple.   Such an
instance is humorously described in the following old
ballad :—

" A jolly shoemaker, John Hobbs, John Hobbs;
A jolly shoemaker, John Hobbs.
>   He married Jane Carter,
>   No damsel look'd smarter;
>   But he caught a tartar,
>   John Hobbs, John Hobbs;
Yes, he caught a tartar, John Hobbs.

He tied a rope to her, John Hobbs, John Hobbs;
He tied a rope to her, John Hobbs!
>   To 'scape from hot-water
>   To Smithfield he brought her;
>   But nobody bought her,
>   Jane Hobbs, Jane Hobbs;
They all were afraid of Jane Hobbs.

Oh, who'll buy a wife? says Hobbs, John Hobbs;
A sweet, pretty wife, says Hobbs;
>   But somehow, they tell us,
>   The wife-dealing fellows
>   Were all of them sellers,
>   John Hobbs, John Hobbs,
And none of them wanted Jane Hobbs.

The rope it was ready, John Hobbs, John Hobbs.
Come, give me the rope, says Hobbs;
>   I won't stand to wrangle,
>   Myself I will strangle,
>   And hang dingle-dangle,
>   John Hobbs, John Hobbs;
He hung dingle-dangle, John Hobbs.

But down his wife cut him, John Hobbs, John Hobbs;
But down his wife cut him, John Hobbs.
>   With a few hubble-bubbles,
>   They settled their troubles
>   Like most married couples,
>   John Hobbs, John Hobbs;
Oh, happy shoemaker, John Hobbs.

The custom was by no means restricted to the United Kingdom.
Marchant instances the following curious case in the American
State of Pennsylvania : " There is a good deal of romance to
the acre in the farming lands near Wilkesbarre. A middle-aged
rustic, who had been smitten with the charms of a saloon-keeper's
wife, recently bought out the husband's rights for 75 dollars,
receiving a bill of sale and a quit-claim deed. Hot drinks were
ordered all round, dinner was served, and the farmer drove the

whole party home. Not long afterwards the woman who had been sold went riding three times with a physician, and the farmer demanded back his money. She had no money in her house, but there was a two-year-old colt in the barn, and so she told the farmer to take the colt and ' call it square '. The farmer tied the colt to his sleigh and drove briskly to his lonesome hearth. Meanwhile, the husband who had sold his wife had made love to a neighbour's daughter, and run away with her to New York. The doctor now goes out riding with the former owner of the colt; the farmer wears his old clothes, and never shaves; and the saloon-keeper and his fugitive bride have vanished from the sight of all the gossips."[1]

Despite the fact that wife-selling was illegal, the practice was widespread; and the belief persisted among the unlettered that so long as the deal took place in public and the sale was by auction, everything was all right. To some extent this idea continued and in some places even gained ground in consequence of the reluctance on the part of local authorities to prosecute the offenders. Sometimes, however, the husband got into trouble, as in a Yorkshire case, where, on June 28, 1837, at the West Riding Sessions, a man named Joshua Jackson was sentenced to one month's imprisonment with hard labour for selling his wife. But punishment of so severe a character was exceptional; for the most part, the culprits were reprimanded. And then, towards the close of the nineteenth century, the practice gradually fell into disuse.

II

The Loan and Exchange of Wives

In many savage tribes it is customary to loan wives to strangers for hire, especially where the need is great. But not always is any fee accepted or offered. Among the Natches, for instance, husbands lend their wives to each other.

In some races the need for offspring induced the borrowing of women, and there have been occasions when such a practice was the law of the land. Thus Solon, the ancient Athenian sage, promulgated an edict to the effect that in the interests of the

[1] W. T. Marchant, *Betrothals and Bridals*, London, 1879, p. 139.

State, which required strong and vigorous children, any young man was empowered, when he pleased, to demand permission to cohabit with the wife of a less robust fellow-citizen.

But in most instances, other than where promiscuity was rampant, the need for money was the motive. Thus when the Babylonians fell upon poor times, wives were compelled by their husbands to offer themselves to strangers as temporary wives in return for money.

The provision of temporary wives for their guests is looked upon as mere hospitality by some savage tribes. Lord Avebury, quoting Lafitau, says that among certain Brazilian tribes, where it is customary to fatten and eventually to eat prisoners of war, even these men who are destined to satisfy an anthropophagous appetite, are usually provided with temporary wives during their last days on earth.[1]

The exchange of wives is sometimes an act of friendship. The practice is an ancient one : Socrates lent Xantippe to Alcibiades. In certain instances, it is a religious rite. In some parts of Australia, the natives exchange wives as a means of escaping or avoiding impending evil. In Fiji an exchange of wives is a reputed cure for illness ; similarly with the Eskimos. Wood says : " The Keiaz, of the Paropamisan mountains, in India, lend their wives to their guests, as do also the people of Kamul. The Munniepores pawn their wives ; the Ansarians have their wives in common ; and the people of Martawan, of the tribe of Ansarians, let out their wives and daughters."[2]

[1] Lord Avebury, *The Origin of Civilization*, sixth edition, Longmans, Green & Co., 1902, p. 140.
[2] E. J. Wood, *The Wedding Day in all Ages and Countries*. Vol. I, p. 151.

Chapter XIV

THE COUVADE AND OTHER CURIOUS PRACTICES

I

The Couvade

THE strange practice for which the name couvade was coined by Sir E. B. Tylor has been observed in many parts of the world. It really amounts to a simulated reversal of the roles of husband and wife during the process of childbirth. The moment the woman starts with labour pains the husband goes to bed and remains there until after the child is born, affecting to experience the pains associated with parturition, and receiving the watchful care and attention which is usually accorded to the woman.

There are considerable variations in actual practice. Sir E. F. Im Thurn says that the woman continues with her usual work until the actual time of birth, which takes place in the forest, and in the course of a few hours is again at work. But not the father. He takes to his hammock the moment the child is born; he "abstains from work, from meat and all food but weak gruel of *cassava* meal, from smoking, from washing himself, and above all from touching weapons of any sort, and is nursed and cared for by all the women of the place. . . . This goes on for days, sometimes weeks."[1] In some cases the husband dons clothes belonging to his wife before lying down on the bed.

It should be borne in mind that in all primitive races there is a strongly developed belief that the food eaten by a pregnant woman will have considerable effects or influence upon the characteristics of the child, just as it is universally believed that consumption of the flesh of animals, etc., imparts to adults the peculiarities or characteristics of such animals ; e.g. the courage and ferocity of the lion, tiger, *et al*. Thus among the Hottentots, it is held that the eating of a leopard's flesh by a pregnant woman will result in the child having the characteristics of the leopard. These beliefs are extended to the father of the child as well.

[1] Sir E. F. Im Thurn, *Among the Indians of Guiana*, 1883, p. 218.

Crawley[1] gives a number of instances : in New Guinea, should the father eat the flesh of the *water-haas*, one of the characteristics of which is the protruding nature of its teeth, the child will have protruding teeth too ; if the father partakes of the spotted *labba*, a spotted child will be born. Lord Avebury[2] instances the refusal of the Caribs to eat the flesh of pigs or tortoises, because of its supposed stunting effects ; and the practice, indulged in by the Maoris, of causing their children at the time of baptism to swallow pebbles, in order to ensure hard-heartedness and lack of pity in adulthood. Where the custom of couvade is practised it is not to be wondered at that the husband, while filling the place of the mother, should take the greatest care as regards the food he eats.

In view of all this one is not surprised that the couvade is still to be found among many savage tribes, but it is strange reading that as comparatively recently as sixty years ago the custom, in an attenuated form, still lingered in one part of the United Kingdom. For Black, writing in 1883, says : " In Ireland a tradition remains. The husband does not indeed pretend to suffer the pains of labour, but the nurses boast that they possess the power of transferring the sufferings to him or to any other person they please. Literally, in earlier times when the nurse announced to the husband that he was about to be a father she brought the pretended pains, for her appearance was tantamount to a declaration that his confinement and restricted living must commence. Now the nurse threatens a real transfer, and, not understanding why the husband should be the only sufferer, she boasts of being able to give the mother's pain to any man, particularly, my informant says, to old bachelors."[3]

Numerous are the explanations that from time to time have been formulated for this curious custom, but each one, in the last analysis, is at best a hypothesis which brims with dubiousness. It may however be well to glance at the most important of these explanations. Tylor and Westermarck are of opinion that it represents a symbolic form of expressing the relationship between father and child, the very fact that those practising it believe in the influence of the food eaten and the acts done by

---

[1] Ernest Crawley, *The Mystic Rose*, 1927.   Vol. II, p. 178.
[2] Lord Avebury, *The Origin of Civilization*, Longmans, Green, 1902, p. 20.
[3] William George Black, *Folk-Medicine*, 1883.

the father at the time of the infant's birth, sustaining this explanation.   In further support of this hypothesis is the point to which Dawson draws attention, that the practice apparently has not been noticed " amongst the various peoples who do not understand the function of the male element in procreation, as for instance various Australian tribes."[1]

Féré is of opinion that the cases of what he terms " sympathetic " couvade supply the solution of the problem.   He avers that it is by no means " uncommon for husbands to share the vomitings that occur in pregnancy."   He gives particulars of one of the cases that have come within his own experience, that relating to a man aged thirty-two years, after eighteen months of marriage.   " He complained of vomiting, which had begun ten days before and occurred either in the morning a short time after waking or after the midday meal. . . . The morning sickness had occurred every day with wonderful regularity, and he brought up what seemed to him about a quarter of a pint of clear, viscous liquid.   In each case the vomiting was preceded by a nausea that came on suddenly. He gave of his own accord an explanation of his sickness ; his wife had been *enciente* two months and a half.   In the evening of the day on which he had been attacked, his wife, who up to that time had shown no signs of any particular disorder, told him on her return from a walk that she had had nausea and had brought up some glair."   As the gestation developed his wife complained of kidney pains.   "At the end of two days it became very difficult for him to walk ; he had an intense and continuous cephalea, sleep almost disappeared, and it used to be interrupted by violent cephalic pains that caused him to cry out.   It is further noteworthy that when his wife, two years later, was again pregnant, this state of affairs was duplicated.[2]

II

Jus Primæ Noctis

Much dispute exists in regard to the origin of the custom known as *jus primæ noctis*, and indeed the assertion has been

[1] Warren R. Dawson, *The Custom of Couvade*, 1929.
[2] Ch. Féré, *The Sexual Instinct : Its Evolution and Dissolution*, pp. 101–102.

repeatedly made that it never even existed. By this custom a king, a chief, a lord, or a priest had the right, if he should wish to exercise it, of demanding that every bride should spend the first night with him.

So far as savage tribes are concerned there is evidence that such a right does exist, and that it is exercised. In many instances the practice is mixed up with religious rites, as in those cases where the right is deemed to belong to a deity, or a priest acting as a representative of the god. Hamilton, in his book on the East Indies, says that when a *Samorin* marries, he must not cohabit with his bride until she has visited the Nambourie or chief priest, who " if he pleases, may have three nights of her company, because the first fruits of her nuptials must be a holy oblation to the god she worships."[1] Reports of the existence of the custom in Malabar, Teneriffe, Cambodia, Greenland, and Nicaragua are available.

As regards civilized countries much of the material which has been brought forward at one time and another in support of the existence of the right in past ages has since been proved to be legendary. But for all that the whole of the evidence cannot be so lightly dismissed. In the days of absolute monarchy the rulers of Turkey, Persia and other countries were prone to take such women as they wished for their seraglios, and it is not unlikely that they had no scruples in adopting the custom.

There is, too, some evidence of the practice being current in Scotland at one time. It appears, from the accounts of many historians, that Evenus III, the sixteenth king of Scotland, made a law by which the king had the right to demand the first night after marriage of all noblemen's daughters ; while noblemen themselves and heritors of lands had the same privilege in regard to the daughters of their tenants and vassals. Further, this law enacted that the wives and daughters of every subject should be common to the king and his nobles. The law giving the first night after marriage to the landlord remained in force, we are told, until the reign of Malcolm III, whose queen, St. Margaret, demanded and secured its abolition : instead a mark of silver was given in each case as the price of the redemption of the girl's chastity.

The historian Bœce says : "Ane othir law he maid, that wiffis of the commonis sall be fre to the nobillis ; and the lord of the

---

[1] Alexander Hamilton, *A New Account of the East Indies*, 1744, p. 310.

MANNERS AND CUSTOMS OF THE
MIAOTZU: THE COUVADE

From a Chinese manuscript album of the late 18th century,
the property of Dr. S. W. Bushell, C.M.G., in the Victoria
and Albert Museum, London. Reproduced by permission
of the Director of the Museum

ground sall have the maidenheid of all virginis dwelling on the same. And thocht the first two lawis was revokit efter he counsall, yit this last law wes sa pleasand to the young nobillis, that it couth nevir be abrogat, quhill the time of King Malcolme Cammore, and his blist quene sanct Margaret, quhilkis thocht the samin sa injurus baith to God and man, that they solistit the nobillis to revok the said law, takand thairfore ane goldin penny, callit the marchetis : quhilk is yit payit to the lord of the ground, quhen virginis ar to be maryit, in redemption of thair honour and chaistite."[1]

III

Infanticide

From the beginning of time it has been customary among most savage tribes and primitive races to destroy unwanted children at birth.   There was and is no law against the practice and in numerous instances it was and is countenanced by custom. Religion also enters into the matter, as where the child slaughter is a form of sacrifice to the gods. Far more rarely it is a cannibalistic practice, not merely because of a shortage of food, but owing to the fact that in some tribes the flesh of infants is esteemed to be a delicacy.   Howitt says that " in hard summers the new-born children were all eaten by the Kaura tribe in the neighbourhood of Adelaide."[2] Where not openly encouraged or approved by religion or law, it is often practised secretly, especially in families where frequent births are bringing about an intolerable economic situation.

In ancient Greece and Rome infanticide was practised as a eugenic measure, and it was along these lines that Aristotle and Plato advocated it, the first-named holding that any child who was not a perfect specimen should be put to death immediately. Plato was of opinion that the children of parents who had passed beyond the virile period of life (women older than 40, and men over 55) were not worth rearing. The Spartans dealt summarily with these undesirable youngsters, especially those of the male

[1] Henry Bœce, The History and Chronicles of Scotland, Edinburgh, 1821,   Vol. I. pp. 83–84.
[2] A. W. Howitt, The Native Tribes of South-East Australia, Macmillan, 1904.

sex. The moment a boy was born, a deputation of elders visited the house, and if in their opinion he was not likely to grow up into a strong, healthy citizen, they held that he did not merit the expenditure of any more trouble and expense, and that he should be thrown into the quagmire at the bottom of the mountain named Taygeta.

From the earliest periods of which information is available, the Chinese practised infanticide. Barrow stated that no fewer than nine thousand children a year were exposed in the streets of Pekin alone, until death came. Every morning the police of the city carted away those that had been exposed during the night, some of them still breathing, to be buried in a large pit outside the city walls. Doolittle, writing in the middle of the nineteenth century, said it was openly admitted that female infants were often put to death soon after being born : for religious and other reasons male children were prized while girls were unwanted. In many cases, the parents did not actually kill the children by drowning, suffocation, et al., but abandoned them, either by placing them in the streets as mentioned by Barrow, or carrying them to one of the " dying lots " where old, disabled and starving people were accustomed to congregate and there await the inevitable. Not all these infants died however. Some were carried off and sold into slavery or prostitution ; others, more lucky, were taken away by missionaries. Again, some were destined to suffer what was perhaps the worst fate of all, slaughter for human consumption, should the time of their abandonment happen to be coincident with one of those famines which, in the past at any rate, have so frequently prevailed in China. The discarded infants were seized greedily by the starving. Often, of course, the parents sold the infants as prospective wives, slaves, or prostitutes ; in time of famine they sold them to the butchers. But whatever the reason, and whatever the method, the fact remains that in many parts of China female infanticide was common.

Doolittle writes : " In the spring of 1861, a female servant employed in a missionary's family confessed that her husband destroyed one of her two little girls at birth. A servant in another family was herself doomed to death by her father soon after birth, but escaped that fate in consequence of his meeting with an accident which the neighbours interpreted as an omen against killing her. Another servant, in another family, has a

relative who destroyed seven girls out of a family of eight
children ; the remaining one, being a boy, was permitted to live.
A woman employed as a nurse in an American missionary's
family has repeatedly said, in answer to inquiries, that, out of
eleven girls born to her mother, her father allowed only four
to survive."[1] The same authority affirmed that infanticide was
practised on occasion by wealthy families. A female servant
stated " that in the native wealthy family where she was employed
before she came to labour in the missionary's family, one girl
had been already destroyed, two had been kept alive, and it was
understood that if the last child had been a girl it would also
have been destroyed, for the simple reason *that more girls in the
family were not desired*! " Boys were invariably looked upon as assets.

India for centuries was one of the countries in which infanticide
was rife. Gardner, who says this crime was at one time extremely
often practised in Benares and adjoining districts, quotes a
remarkable statement by " one who was long resident in India."[2]
The statement reads : " The great supporters of this iniquitous
practice were formerly the Rajhpoots, the Rajhkomars, and the
Rajhvansis, among whom a single female infant was never
permitted to exist, nor did they consider their destruction as
an act of sin or cruelty, though I am unable to believe, as many
have affirmed, that they regarded the sacrifice as an acceptable
offering to the gods. It appears rather to have originated in
convenience, on account of the ruinous expense attending their
marriage, and to have been practised without fear of offence
to the deities, for their belief is, that the souls of those daughters
who were thus destroyed were eventually returned to them in
the persons of sons ; and when this did not appear to be borne
out by the birth of a male child, it only followed that Siva was
displeased, and conciliation was resorted to, until a son should
really be born to them. In these cases it was usual to seek
propitiation by placing the next female infant in the hands of
the Brahmins, to be solemnly sacrificed in the temple of Ganesa,
whereby that god might be moved to compassion for the babe,
and be induced to intercede with Siva for the future birth of
male children to the parents. It is easy to perceive whence
this delusion had its commencement, since a handsome douceur
to the immolating priests was an indispensable part of the

---

[1] Rev. J. Doolittle, *Social Life of the Chinese*, 1866.   Vol. II, p. 205.
[2] James Gardner, *Faiths of the World*, 1858.   Vol. II, p. 133.

ceremony, which in all respects differed from the method of destruction privately used. In the latter place the operation was performed with very little form or expense, by what the Hindoos call *drinking milk*. No sooner had the sex of the infant been ascertained, than a cauldron of warm milk was brought into the apartment where the mother lay, and after prayers for the child's return in the form of a son, the little innocent was immersed in the milk, and held down until life became extinct, and then it was carried to the Ganges and thrown into the stream. When, however, the deed was committed to the Brahmins to be executed by way of sacrifice to Ganesa, the poor babe was carried to the temple, and, being laid upon its back, was, after certain diabolical ceremonies, destroyed by the club of the inhuman *fakhir*."

Where superstition reigns supreme, strange things have a habit of happening, and one's life may depend upon an omen. Thus in Madagascar, according to Gardner, " the fate of the infant depends on the calculation of lucky and unlucky days. Should the destiny of the child be declared by the astrologer to be evil, the poor helpless babe is doomed to destruction."[1]

In India, China, and other civilized countries the practice of infanticide no longer receives the support of authority, and instances that still occur are of a secret or surreptitious nature. But in savage tribes in various parts of the world the crime has always been and still is, in many cases, perpetrated. Foremost among these are the native tribes of South-East Australia, where limitation of food supplies is given as the main reason. In the old days, however, according to Howitt, the misfortune of being born a sturdy member of a tribe might well be the means of sealing the child's doom. For, says this authority, " in all the tribes of the Wotjo nation, and also the Tatathi and other tribes on the Murray River frontage, when a child was weak and sickly they used to kill its infant brother or sister, and feed it with the flesh to make it strong."[2] Among the American Indians, says Alexander, when twins were born to a woman of the Moxes tribe, it was the custom to bury one of the infants alive, owing to the firmly-held belief that a mother could not nurse two children at the same time.[3]

[1] Gardner, op. cit., p. 133.
[2] A. W. Howitt, *The Native Tribes of South-East Australia*, Macmillan, 1904, p. 750.
[3] William Alexander, *The History of Women*, 1779.   Vol. I, p. 446.

Of infanticide among the South Sea Islanders, the Rev. John Williams writes : " Generally, I may state that, in the Society Islands, I never conversed with a female that had borne children prior to the introduction of Christianity, who had not destroyed some of them, and frequently as many as from five to ten. During the visit of the Deputation, our respected friend, G. Bennett, Esq., was our guest for three or four months ; and, on one occasion, while conversing on the subject, he expressed a wish to obtain accurate knowledge of the extent to which this cruel system had prevailed. Three women were sitting in the room at the time, making European garments, under Mrs. W's direction ; and after replying to Mr. Bennett's inquiries, I said, ' I have no doubt but that each of these women has destroyed some of her children.' Looking at them with an expression of surprise and incredulity, Mr. B. exclaimed, ' Impossible ! such motherly, respectable women could never have been guilty of so great an atrocity.' ' Well,' I added, ' we'll ask them.' Addressing the first, I said to her, ' Friend, how many children have you destroyed ? ' She was startled at my question, and at first charged me with unkindness, in harrowing up her feelings by bringing the destruction of her babes to her remembrance ; but, upon hearing the object of my inquiry, she replied, with a faltering voice, ' I have destroyed *nine*.' The second, with eyes suffused with tears, said, ' I have destroyed *seven* ' ; and the third informed us that she had destroyed *five*. Thus three individuals, casually selected, had killed one-and-twenty children !—but I am happy to add that these mothers were, at the time of this conversation, and continued to be so long as I knew them, consistent members of my church."

" On another occasion, I was called to visit the wife of a chief in dying circumstances. . . . In the prospect of death, she sent a pressing request that I would visit her immediately ; and, on entering her apartment, she exclaimed, ' O, servant of God ! come and tell me what I must do.' Perceiving that she was suffering great mental distress, I inquired the cause of it ; when she replied, ' I am about to die.' ' Well,' I rejoined, ' if it be so, what creates this agony of mind ? ' ' Oh ! my sins, my sins,' she cried ; ' I am about to die.' I then inquired what the particular sins were which so greatly distressed her, when she exclaimed, ' Oh, my children, my murdered children ! I am about to die and I shall meet them all at the judgment-seat of Christ.' Upon this I inquired how many children she had destroyed ; and, to my astonishment, she replied, ' I have destroyed *sixteen* ! ' "[1]

It is a mistake to think that infanticide is one of the practices which is now restricted to a few savage tribes existing in out of the way corners of the world, and so far as civilized countries are concerned has long since vanished with the bad old days. There are many children killed at birth to-day in the most highly civilized countries, although to a very large extent abortion has now superseded infanticide. So far as English law is concerned both practices are of a criminal nature and punishable with imprisonment. With the passing of the Infanticide Acts of 1922 and 1938 the distinction between infanticide and murder is clear. The destruction of an infant which has not reached the age of twelve months by a mother who is not fully recovered from childbirth ranks as infanticide and is not a capital crime.

IV

Wife-Beating

At the time when a husband considered his wife to be as much a piece of property as was his horse or his dog, the right to inflict corporal punishment for a variety of offences and misdemeanours was rarely, if ever, questioned. The law, even in the States which, in those days, ranked as among the highly civilized, admitted and upheld this right : only in flagrant cases, where the husband administered punishment which was thought to be of an unjustifiably severe character, such, for instance, as to endanger life, or for trivial offences, could the woman, with the smallest chance of success, lodge any protest.

Among primitive races, where it is usual for women to do all the laborious, humdrum, menial labour, not unnaturally the husband often finds it necessary to drive his wife to her tasks by the use or threat of blows. In the Fiji Islands, wife-beating is recognized as a husband's prerogative, and as being a necessary means of ensuring the carrying out of his wishes. Williams says : " Near to the King of Lakemba, and afterwards to the

[1] John Williams, *A Narrative of Missionary Enterprises in the South Sea Islands*, London, 1837, pp. 558–560.

King of Mbua, I saw lying a stick of heavy wood about the size of a broom-handle. On enquiry I found that the free use of this truncheon was very effective in subduing the wayward wills of the women when they became disorderly. Tanoe's staff used for this purpose was inlaid with ivory, but did not on this account give less pain."[1] Mungo Park, writing of the Mandingo negroes of the African interior, says that a husband sometimes has occasion to resort to corporal punishment, in order to keep peace among his various wives. And one can well understand that this applies in all cases where polygyny is practised.

In Great Britain the right of the husband to chastise his wife was generally recognized for many centuries, indeed until as comparatively recently as the eighteen hundreds. It would appear that in this, as in so many other things, the opinion of the public was in advance of legislation, for before the law stepped in to bring to an end so despicable, arbitrary, unfair, and tyrannous a state of affairs, the neighbours often expressed their resentment at a husband's treatment of his wife. In Scotland this resentment sometimes expressed itself in a strange practice known as "*Riding the Stang.*" It is described by Forsyth thus : " When any husband is known to treat his wife extremely ill, by beating her, and when the offence is long and unreasonably continued, while the wife's character is unexceptionable, the indignation of the neighbourhood, becoming gradually vehement, at last breaks out into action in the following manner : All the women enter into a conspiracy to execute vengeance upon the culprit. Having fixed upon the time when their design is to be put into effect, they suddenly assemble in a great crowd, and seize the offending party. They take care at the same time to provide a stout beam of wood, upon which they set him astride, and, hoisting him aloft, tie his legs beneath. He is thus carried in derision round the village, attended by the hootings, scoffs, and hisses of his numerous attendants, who pull down his legs, so as to render his seat in other respects abundantly uneasy. The grown-up men, in the meanwhile, remain at a distance, and avoid interfering in the ceremony. And it is well if the culprit, at the conclusion of the business, has not a ducking added to the rest of the punishment. This, however, forms no essential part of the ceremony. Of the origin of this custom we know nothing. It is well known, however, over the country ;

[1] Quoted by James Greenwood in *Curiosities of Savage Life*, 1865. Vol. I, p. 224.

and within these six years, it was with great ceremony performed upon a weaver in the Canongate of Edinburgh."[1]

In Wales, wife-beating was anciently allowed. If a wife called her husband opprobrious names, squandered his money, got into debt, pulled his beard in rage or anger, or was discovered making love to another man, the injured spouse was justified in giving her as many as three blows with a stick on any part of her head. Apparently no restrictions were made as to the size or nature of the stick, or the severity of the blows, but it was stated that if he should inflict more blows, or punish her in this way for a less cause, he was liable to pay a considerable fine.[2]

In connexion with a case in India, in 1936, it was contended by the Sessions Judge of Madura district that every husband had the right to inflict corporal punishment on his wife for impudence or impertinence, but according to *The Indian Social Reformer* (August 29, 1936), no such right is recognized by the Indian Penal Code. This journal stated : " The learned Sessions Judge's declaration of the rights of husbands in this regard has no foundation, so that no one may rely upon that in future as any justification or excuse for beating wives."

Wife-beating is now a punishable offence in civilized countries. In the State of Maryland the punishment is made to fit the crime in every sense of the word, the penalty being a whipping with the cat-o'-nine-tails. In March, 1938, at Baltimore, a man named Clyde Miller, aged 37 years, for beating his wife, aged 33, was given twenty strokes by the sheriff in the presence of sixty official witnesses, before serving a sentence of six months' imprisonment. The British United Press report, from which these particulars are taken, says that " Mrs. Miller was beaten into insensibility, by her husband after a quarrel. Her screams roused the neighbourhood, and people who ran to their flat found her unconscious."

V

Other Curious Practices

In ancient Greece, the Athenians had a law by which women and slaves were debarred from practising midwifery. One consequence of this was that many women of refinement refused

---

[1] R. Forsyth, *The Beauties of Scotland*, 1806. Vol. III, p. 157.
[2] J. S. Forsyth, *The Antiquary's Portfolio*, 1825. Vol. I, p. 14.

INFANTICIDE IN INDIA, AS PRACTISED IN
THE TEMPLES OF GANESA, AT BENARES

From James Gardner's *The Faiths of the World*, 1858

to submit to the attentions of a male at the time of delivery, with the result that there were numerous deaths. To remedy this distressing state of affairs, a woman named Agnodice, who was skilled in the art of midwifery, donned the attire of a man for the purpose of attending women in labour. As the news leaked out and was whispered here and there, the services of Agnodice were in great demand. " The rest of the physicians," says Alexander, " enraged that she should monopolise all the business, arraigned her before the Court of Areopagus as having only obtained the preference to them by corrupting the chastity of the wives whom she delivered. This obliging her to reveal her sex, the physicians then prosecuted her for violating the laws of her country. The principal matrons of the city, now finding her in such danger, assembled together, came into the court, and petitioned the judges in her favour. The petition of the matrons was so powerful, and the reasons which they urged for having employed her, so conducive to the preservation of female delicacy, that a law was made, allowing women to practise midwifery."[1]

The Moravians of North America at one time had a peculiar method of arranging the marriages of their adherents. Captain Anburey, writing in Connecticut on September 2, 1781, had this to say : " The Moravians are not only very assiduous, but ingenious too. They have adopted a sort of marriage, but from the manner of its celebration you cannot suppose that mutual tender endearments and happiness subsist between the parties united, as with us. A young man feels an inclination to marry, which does not proceed from any object he is enamoured with, for he never sees his wife but once before the ceremony takes place ; it being contrary to the principles of their religion to suppose it is from the passions of nature, but merely to uphold the society, that it may not sink into oblivion. The young man communicates his inclination to their priest, asking of him a girl to make his wife, who, consulting with the superintendent of the young women, she produces her who is next in rotation for marriage. The priest presents her to the young man, and leaves them together for an hour, when he returns. If they both consent, they are married the next day. If there is any objection, both their cases are very pitiable, but especially the woman's, as she is put at the end of the list, which amounts to near sixty

[1] William Alexander, *The History of Women*, 1779.   Vol. I, p. 435.

or seventy; nor does the poor girl stand the least chance of a husband till she arrives again at the top, unless the man feels a second inclination for marriage, for he never can obtain any other woman than the one with whom he had the first interview. This, I am induced to think, was the reason of there being such a number of old women among the single ones. Thus you see, my friend, that marriage in its inexpressible enjoyments, is not the result of the passions, but a mere piece of mechanism, set to work by chance, and stopt alone by necessity."[1]

According to the accounts of various eighteenth and early nineteenth century travellers and explorers, among several tribes of Canadian Indians it was customary for the men to acquire their wives by the exhibition of skill in wrestling. Indeed, in this respect, mastery of the art was often even more valuable than the possession of wealth : as an instance among the Kutchin tribe a good wrestler could always secure a wife.[2] The rival suitors engaged in a struggle for supremacy and the girl, who often was an onlooker, became the wife of the victor. This practice, although not devoid of novelty, did not call for condemnation, seeing that apparently it met with the approval of the females concerned; but the taking, by one of superior strength or skill, of another man's wife, which was tolerated in some tribes, was not only a strange practice, but, by every standard of equity and justice, it was a reprehensible and a criminal act. Moreover it showed beyond any doubt or question how low and ignominious was the position of woman among many sections of North American aboriginal society at that time. For in cases where a married woman was taken from her husband in this manner, she had no voice whatever in the matter. Hearne points out that in some instances her reluctance to become the wife of the victor was so great that she resisted strongly, and the incident often degenerated into a scene of the greatest brutality. He writes : "I have seen the poor girls stripped quite naked, and carried by main force to their new lodgings."[3] In another case, of course, the woman might be delighted to be rid of her husband, or for any one of many

<hr />

[1] Captain T. A. Anburey, *Travels Through the Interior Parts of America, in a Series of Letters*, new edition, London, 1791.   Vol. II, pp. 455-456.
[2] Sir John Richardson, *Arctic Searching Expedition : A Journal of a Boat-Voyage Through Rupert's Land to the Arctic Sea*, Longmans, Brown, Green and Longmans, London, 1851.   Vol. I, p. 383.
[3] Samuel Hearne, *A Journey from Prince of Wales's Fort*, Dublin, 1796, p. 107.

reasons, might consider without dismay the prospect of a fresh marital partner.

A curious marital custom practised by the Hindus is known as " tree marriage ". There are several reasons assigned for its existence. The state of being unmarried is an obnoxious and in some cases an ostracized one, thus marriage to a tree or rather to the spirit which is supposed to be incorporated in and to animate the tree, overcomes the drawbacks incidental to celibacy and at the same time avoids the disadvantages of a union with a member of the female sex. Similarly, the state of being a widower is to be avoided at all costs, and here again " tree marriage " is an easy way of overcoming such disadvantages. But perhaps the main reason for such " marriages " is the means they provide of overcoming the evils reputed to be inseparable from the taking of a third human wife : marriage to a tree has none of these evils, and a fourth wife can be taken with impunity.

One of the strangest of all forms of marriage is what may be described as a part-time marital union. It is practised by the Hassaniyeh Arabs, according to Lord Avebury, who says : " the woman is legally married for three days out of four, remaining perfectly free for the fourth."[1]

A queer custom, which is of very ancient origin, is that of dressing the bridegroom in female clothing for the marriage ceremony, presumably as a form of disguise. Whether or not the reason for this precautionary measure was with the object of avoiding or diminishing the sexual danger supposed to be inseparable from the marriage union, as Crawley maintains ; or as a protection against evil spirits, as other authorities aver, is by no means certain. Plutarch refers to the practice in connexion with the Spartans, and there are references to its observance by several native tribes. In Morocco, says Westermarck, the young man is dressed as a bride ; also in some rural districts of this same country " the bride on her part imitates the appearance of a man by wearing her shawl thrown over her left shoulder, or leaving her old home clad in a man's cloak, or having designs resembling whiskers painted on her face."[2]

A popular belief was at one time current that in the event of a woman offering to marry a man under the gallows, and the offer being accepted, the condemned criminal could not be

[1] Lord Avebury, *The Origin of Civilization*, sixth edition, p. 78.
[2] Edward Westermarck, *Marriage Ceremonies in Morocco*, Macmillan, London, 1914, p. 27.

executed. Similarly, where a woman was condemned to death, an offer of marriage and its acceptance, would save her life. It has been said that the idea originated from the act of a woman who forgave the murderer of her husband and in making an appeal for his life to be spared expressed her willingness to marry him. At any rate whatever the origin of the belief, it never had any foundation in fact. Brand, in commenting on the fallacy, says : " In Warning for Servants, or the case of Margaret Clark, lately executed for firing her master's house in Southwark, 1680, p. 31, we read : ' Since this poor maid was executed, there has been a false and malicious story published concerning her in the True Domestick Intelligence of Tuesday, the 30th of March : ' Kingstone, March the 21. There was omitted in the Protestant Domestick Intelligence in relating the last words and confession of *Mary* Clark (so he falsely calls her), who was executed for firing the house of M. De La Noy, dyer in Southwark : viz. that at her execution there was a fellow who designed to marry her under the gallows (according to the ancient laudable custome), but she, being in hopes of a reprieve, seemed unwilling ; but when the rope was about her neck, she cryed she was willing, and then the fellow's friends disswaded him from marrying her, and so she lost her husband and her life together.' There is added : ' We know of no such custome allowed by law, that any man's offering at a place of execution to marry a woman condemned shall save her.' "[1]

Apparently, however, the belief was not altogether devoid of legal backing in eighteenth-century New York, for, according to the traveller, Gustavus Vassa, a man on the point of being executed was reprieved and given his liberty following his marriage on the scaffold to a woman whose only clothing was a shift.[2]

A popular fallacy which persists to this day is that the captain of a ship is authorized to marry couples at sea, and that such a marriage is just as legally binding as one solemnized in a church or a register office. The truth is that no ship's captain has the right to perform any such ceremony. A marriage at sea must be performed by an ordained clergyman, and by no other person. The ship's captain acts as the registrar, entering the details in the log of the vessel on which the ceremony is performed.

[1] John Brand, *Observations on the Popular Antiquities of Great Britain.* Vol. III, p. 380.
[2] Alice Morse Earle, *Customs and Fashions in Old New England*, p. 79.

PART FOUR

CURIOUS RITES IN CONNEXION WITH THE CELEBRATION OF MARRIAGE.

CHAPTER XV

MARRIAGE RITES OF THE HEBREWS AND THEIR CONTEMPORARIES

I

Ceremonies of the Jews

THE ancient Jews had an elaborate wedding ceremony. If the woman was a virgin she was married on the fourth day of the week; if a widow, on the fifth day. On the day fixed for the ceremony, whether it was the fourth or the fifth in the week, the bride was arrayed as elegantly as her circumstances permitted; and, attended by young women who sang as they walked, was conducted into a room, where her head was dressed in ringlets and ornamented with ribbons. Now all was in readiness, so far as the girl was concerned, for the marriage ceremony.

With a nuptial crown on her head, the bride was now escorted to the house of the bridegroom's father. " The procession," says Dr. Nevin (*Biblical Antiquities*), " generally set off in the evening, with much ceremony and pomp. The bridegroom was richly clothed with a marriage robe and crown, and the bride was covered with a veil from head to foot. The companions of each attended them with songs and the music of instruments; not in promiscuous assemblage, but each company by itself; while the virgins, according to the custom of the times, were all provided with veils, not indeed so large and thick as that which hung over the bride, but abundantly sufficient to conceal their faces from all around. The way, as they went along, was lighted with numerous torches. In the meantime, another company was waiting at the bridegroom's house, ready, at the first notice of their approach, to go forth and meet them. These seem generally to have been young female relations or friends of the bridegroom's family, called in at this time, by a particular invitation, to grace the occasion with their presence. Adorned with robes of gladness and joy, they went forth with lamps or torches in their hands, and welcomed the procession with the customary salutations. They then joined themselves to the marriage train, and the whole company moved forward to the house. There an entertainment was provided for their reception, and the remainder of the evening was spent in a joyful participation of the marriage supper, with such social merriment as suited the joyous occasion. None was admitted to this entertainment beside the particular number who were selected to attend the wedding; and as the regular and proper time for their entrance into the house was when the bridegroom went in with his bride, the doors were then closed, and no other guest was expected to come in."

It would appear that at one time, the announcement in the presence of witnesses, by the two parties, of their intention to live together as husband and wife, and the pronouncement of a solemn blessing by the relatives present, constituted all that were necessary. Says Dr. James Gardner : " Thus Boaz merely declared in the presence of the elders assembled at the gate of the city, that he had resolved to take the daughter of Naomi to be his wife."[1] And all the people that were in the gate, and the elders, said, " We are witnesses. The Lord make the woman that is come into thine house like Rachel and like Leah, which two did build the house of Israel : and do thou worthily in Ephratah, and be famous in Bethlehem. So Boaz took Ruth, and she was his wife : and when he went in unto her, the Lord gave her conception, and she bare a son."

A modern Jewish ceremony was on quite different lines, however. Accompanied by four friends, bearing a velvet canopy on four poles, the bridegroom marched to the place where the service was to take place. As this procession approached, the bride's attendants and friends, who were awaiting the arrival of the bridegroom and his party, cried out in unison " Blessed be he that cometh." Then the bridegroom walked around the bride three times in succession, and took her by the hand. This was a signal for corn to be thrown on them by the attendants and guests, accompanied by the chanting of the words " Increase and multiply." Sometimes along with the corn money was thrown. And all this time the bride held the bridegroom by the right hand, with her face turned to the south.

The bridal couple were then stationed opposite each other

[1] James Gardner, *Faiths of the World*, 1858. Vol. II, p. 378.

under the canopy. The priest took a glass of consecrated wine in his hand, and said : " Blessed art thou, O Lord our God, King of the universe, the Creator of the fruit of the vine. Blessed art thou, O Lord our God, King of the universe, who hath sanctified us with thy commandments, and hath forbidden us fornication, and hath forbidden to us the betrothed, but hath allowed unto us those that are married unto us by the means of the canopy and of the wedding-ring." Then bride and bridegroom in turn tasted the wine, and the latter placed a gold ring upon the bride's second finger, saying, in the presence of those who stood around the canopy : " Behold, thou art married unto me with this ring, according to the rites of Moses and of Israel." Then came the reading of the contract, which specified that the bridegroom A agreed to take the bride B as his lawful wife, according to the laws of Moses and of Israel ; and that he undertook to keep, maintain, honour, and cherish her, according to the manner of all the Jews, who honour, maintain, and cherish their wives ; that he also undertook to keep her in clothing, according to the custom of the world.

The priest and the reader each drank a glass of wine ; and, following a prayer, the bride drank a glass of the wine, and finally the bridegroom repeated the performance, but on emptying the glass, he threw it on the floor or against a wall so that it flew into many pieces. The object of this was to remind them of death, to whose power mortals must yield sooner or later, and therefore to induce them to live in such a manner as not to fear its approach. The ceremony was concluded as all the persons present cried out *mozul tour*, i.e. may it turn out happily. It is worthy of mention that, because a Jew must have his head covered while praying, a hat is worn by the bridegroom during the nuptial proceedings.

Mention has been made of the bride wearing a crown at the wedding. Gardner says : "Among the early Christians the act of crowning the parties was the commencing part of the marriage ceremony. After the 128th Psalm had been sung, with the responses and doxologies, and an appropriate discourse had been delivered, and after some preliminary rites, the priest lifted the nuptial crowns which had been laid upon the altar, and placing one upon the head of the bridegroom, and the other upon the head of the bride, he pronounced these words, ' This servant of the Lord hereby crowns this handmaid of the Lord in the name of the Father, and of the Son, and of the Holy Ghost, world without end.   Amen.'   This ceremony was followed by prayers, doxologies, and the reading of the Scriptures, particularly Eph. v. 20–33, and John ii. 1–11, at the close of which the assembly repeated the Lord's Prayer, with the customary responses, and the usual form of benediction.   On the eighth day the married pair presented themselves again in the church, when the minister, after an appropriate prayer, took off the nuptial crown, and dismissed them with his solemn benediction.   This ceremony, however, was not uniformly observed."[1]

For many centuries the custom was universally observed by the Jews ; indeed it appears that the crowning of the bridegroom continued until its abolition by Vespasian, and the crowning of the bride until the time of Titus.   Crowns were used in other countries, notably in Greece.   The materials of which they were constructed varied considerably.   Thus in Greece, olive branches entwined with white and purple ribbon were used ; in Russia, the crowns were made of gold, silver, and sometimes tin.

II

Rites of Contemporary Races

The ceremony employed by the ancient Babylonians was of an exceedingly curious nature.   It is well described by Layard, thus : " The parties entered into the contract in the presence of witnesses, amid dancing and rejoicing.   The next day, the bride, covered from head to foot with a thick veil, was led to the bridegroom's house, surrounded by her friends decked out in the gayest attire, and accompanied by musicians.   She was kept behind the corner of a darkened room for three days, during which the guests fasted ; afterwards the bridegroom was allowed to approach her.   The courtyard of the house was filled with dancers and players on the fife and drum during the day and great part of the night.   The bridegroom, on the third day, was led from house to house, by his friends, receiving at each a trifling present.   He was then placed within a circle of dancers, and the guests and bystanders stuck small coins on his forehead. As the money fell, it was caught in an open kerchief held under

[1] James Gardner, *Fathers of the World*, 1858.   Vol. I, p. 644.

his chin.   After this ceremony, a party of young men rushing into the crowd, carried off the most wealthy guests, and locked them up in a dark room until they paid a ransom to be released. All the money collected was added to the dowry. The remainder of the day was spent in feasting, raki drinking and dancing."[1]

A curious custom was observed in Chaldea. On the occasion of a marriage the priest made new fires in the house, and these were not to be extinguished during the lifetime of the couple. If by any mischance these fires were allowed to go out the marriage was thereby annulled.   It was owing to this belief that the proverb originated " Provoke me not too much, that I throw water into the fire."[2]

III

Rites of the Ancient Greeks and Romans

The superstition rampant among the ancient Greeks induced them to pay much attention to the choice of a month and a particular day in that month on which to celebrate a marriage. January was the most favoured month, Euripides recommended the time of the full moon, but the most favoured time of all was considered to be when the sun and moon happened to be in conjunction, which was when they held the festival known as the " marriage of the gods."

Immediately before the wedding ceremony both bride and bridegroom bathed in water obtained from some specified fountain. This procedure having been completed they walked to the temple where the ceremony was to take place, friends accompanying them and singing their praises all the way.   On arrival at the temple both bride and bridegroom were presented with ivy branches, which were looked upon as symbolic of the indissolvable bond of matrimony.   Sacrifices were next offered on the altar, the animals being disembowelled and their entrails scrutinized for auguries of a favourable nature.

Usually the bride was not conducted to her husband's house until evening came, as it was thought the darkness would conceal her blushes. The journey was made in an oxen-drawn chariot,

[1] Sir A. H. Layard, *Discoveries in the Ruins of Ninevah and Babylon*, 1853.
[2] W. T. Marchant, *Betrothals and Bridals*, 1879, p. 113.

attended by singers and dancers.   Such a scene is well-described by Homer, thus :—

> The sacred pomp and genial feast delight,
> And solemn dance, and hymeneal rite ;
> Along the streets the new-made brides are led,
> With torches flaming, to the nuptial bed :
> The youthful dancers in a circle bound
> To the soft flute and cithern's silver sound ;
> Through the fair streets the matrons in a row
> Stand in their porches, and enjoy the show.

On arrival, the axle-tree of the conveyance was burnt, as an indication that the bride would never return.   The house was decorated with garlands, a pestle was tied to the door, a sieve was carried by a servant, and a vessel containing parched barley by the bride, to indicate her eagerness and ability to attend to household duties.   All the members of the party went inside, where a sumptuous meal and entertainment had been prepared. During this banquet a boy, covered with thorn boughs and acorns, brought a basket of bread, and exclaimed, " I have left the worst and found the better," which intimated that the married state was much preferable to the single.

This feast had a degree of importance unconnected with its social or entertainment value.   It really served to provide the only tangible proof that a marriage had taken place at all.   In one of these ancient Greek marriages, there was no record in writing of its celebration ; it was because of this that guests were invited to attend the wedding feast, and they constituted the witnesses should proof be necessary.

After the dancing and merriment had come to an end, the husband and his bride were escorted to the marriage bed by the light of torches, around one of which was tied the bride's hair-lace.   With the departure of relatives and friends the couple were obliged, in accordance with the laws of Athens, to eat a quince between them, thereby intimating that their conversation ought to be pleasant and agreeable.

The ancient Athenians had a peculiar ceremony which was performed immediately before a wedding, involving the cutting of the girl's hair as an offering to one of the deities having the care of marriage.

Before a marriage was solemnized, too, the assistance of the gods had to be obtained in other ways, mainly by human and animal sacrifices. Agamemnon in Euripides refers to the custom thus :—

> " Send now thy daughter to her father's charge
> Committed ; for the lavers ready stand,
> The salted cakes which o'er the lustral fire
> The hand must cast, the heifers too, whose blood
> Must in black streams before the nuptials flow
> To the chaste queen Diana, are prepared."

In ancient Rome three kinds of marriages were recognized : (a) *confarreatio*, (b) *coemptio*, and (c) *usus*. The first-named of these forms called for a ceremony, which was of a religious nature ; the *coemptio* consisted of a form of purchase, in which the contracting parties, in the presence of five witnesses, solemnly bound themselves to live together in marriage, sealing the contract by each giving to the other a piece of money ; while in the case of *usus* the mere fact of continuous (i.e. without the woman being absent for more than two nights) cohabitation for a period of not less than one year constituted marriage.

In common with the widespread superstition of the age, it was the firm belief of the Romans that certain specific days were favourable to marriage while others were distinctly unfavourable. Thus the entire months of February and May were inauspicious, particularly the last-named, which was thought to be under the influence of spirits inimical to happiness in the married state. Also the Calends, Nones, and Ides of each month in which they occurred were unfavourable, as were certain festivals.

The wedding day having been selected with due care, on this important occasion the bride was adorned with a long purple-fringed white robe, with a girdle at the waist, which in the evening following the marriage celebration, was untied by her husband. Her hair, the locks of which were divided with the point of a spear, was decorated with flowers, and she was closely veiled.

If the marriage was by *confarreatio* an animal, usually a sheep, was sacrificed to the gods, its gall having been discarded to signify the removal from marriage of any bitterness. A prayer was then offered by the Pontifex Maximus, who conducted the ceremony, and yet another sacrifice, after which a cake made of flour, salt, and water was consumed. The whole of the procedure was in the presence of ten witnesses. By this form of marriage the wife was brought into the power of her husband and became his property.

Wood says that " a Roman marriage by *confarreatio* is denoted, in many antiquities, by a man and woman standing; she gives her right hand to the man, and in her left holds three wheat ears. The man wears a toga, the woman a stola and peplum, thrown over her shoulders. Her hair is rolled and raised round her head, as in Diana and Victory, a fashion usual with virgins and brides. Hands touching each other, with wheat ears, are also emblems of marriage by *confarreatio*. There are many bas-reliefs of marriages in Montfaucon. In one of the Villa Borghese, and another of the Justiniani Palace, the bride is veiled, and an old woman by her side is probably the nurse, the constant attendant of young girls."[1]

In the evening the bride was escorted by several friends and three boys, one of whom carried a torch of pinewood, to her husband's house, the door of which was decorated with garlands and flowers. On arrival the bride was lifted bodily across the threshold by men who had been married once only. As regards the origin of this practice, Wood writes: "It is said by some that this custom was a relic of the usage of capture or force in marriage, and by others that it was to indicate that the bride lost her virginity unwillingly; while others say that it was followed so that the bride might not strike her foot against the threshold, and thus cause an evil omen."[2] Previous to her entry, the bride smeared the doorposts with fat, and wrapped wool around them, as a means of averting enchantments and any evil machinations of practitioners of the black art.

When installed in her husband's home, the keys of the house were handed to her. All the persons who had been present at the wedding now joined in a meal given by the husband. This brought the celebrations to an end.

---

[1] Edward J. Wood, *The Wedding Day in All Ages and Countries*, 1869. Vol. I, p. 61.
[2] Wood, op. cit., p. 63 (cf., p. 124).

CHAPTER XVI

MARRIAGE RITES OF OTHER RACES AND IN VARIOUS COUNTRIES

I

Ceremonial Marriage in India, Persia, etc.

ALWAYS have the marriage ceremonies of the Hindus been of a most elaborate nature. Like the members of so many other races the people of India exercise the greatest care in the choice of a day which is favourable. For instance a rainy day is considered to be extremely unlucky. The day having been decided upon and the time for the ceremony having arrived, a sacred fire, called *Homam*, is made of the wood of the *rawasittow*, a consecrated tree, and the priest recites a number of prayers. The bridegroom then throws three handfuls of rice on the head of his bride, and she does the same to him. The next step consists of the washing of the bridegroom's feet by the bride's father. Having done this he takes his daughter by the hand, and directs her to put her feet into the water in which have just been washed the bridegroom's feet. Then, handing to the bridegroom a sum of money, he says: " I have no longer anything to do with you, and I hereby give you up to the power of another." At the same time he produces a jewel called *tali*, consisting of the golden head of an idol, to which a string is attached. This jewel is inspected by all who are present, prayers are said, and finally the jewel is knotted around the bride's neck by the bridegroom. Apropos of this *tali*, Little states that it is the knot which symbolizes possession, for without it the ceremony might be a futile procedure : it has occasionally happened that when the bridegroom was about to fix the *tali* in position, the bride's father, not being satisfied with the bridegroom's gift, or having received a higher offer for the bride, decided to go no further with the ceremony. " When once the *tali* is put on, the marriage is indissoluble ; and on the death of the husband, the *tali* is burnt along with him, to show that the marriage bands are broken."[1] The ceremony thus concluded, an entertainment is given by the bride's father. This feast continues for five days, during which time the sacred fire is kept alight. On the seventh day the married couple are carried in a sedan to the bridegroom's house.

The procedure in other parts of India is described by Ward, who says : " During the night preceding the wedding, the most hideous noises are made at the houses of the two parents, with instruments whose noise resembles that of a kettledrum. In the beginning of the night, the women leave four pots containing lamps at each of the two houses, expressing their wishes for the long life of the bride and bridegroom. They also place at each house two balls of rice flour in the form of sugar loaves, which they call Shree, and towards the close of the night, they eat rice with the girl and boy. These customs are accompanied with much hilarity. Early in the morning, the women and female neighbours again assemble, and taking with them a pan of water, the pots which contain the oil-lights, the balls of rice flour, and some betel-nut, go round to the neighbours, and give to each a morsel of the betel-nut. On returning home, in some towns, they place the boy and girl, at different houses, on a bamboo door, when the mother, as an expression of her joy and goodwill, lights some straw from the thatch, and turns it round the right foot of the boy, or girl, three several times ; after which the persons present lift up the door, with the boy or girl placed on it, three, five, or seven times ; the women then, taking some thread, and stretching it, walk round them four times, and then tie this thread with some blades of doorvu grass, round the right arm of the boy, and the left arm of the girl. They prepare also a kind of ointment with oil and spices fried together, and rub it on the head and all over the bodies of the young couple. All these actions have no other meaning, than that they are tokens of joy. In the forenoon, at both houses, to secure the happiness of the boy and girl, they present offerings to deceased ancestors. The bridegroom, as a mark of affection, sends to the bride a present of fish, betel, sweetmeats, plantains, sour milk, and cloth ; in some cases, the bride makes a similar present to the bridegroom. In the course of the afternoon, the

---

[1] Thomas Little, *The Beauty, Marriage Ceremonies and Intercourse of the Sexes in all Nations*, 1824. Vol. III, p. 69.

heads of the young couple are shaved ; and while the bridegroom
stands upon a stone placed in the middle of a small artificial pool
of water, round which trees are planted, and lamps placed, the
wicks of which are made of the fruit of the thornapple plant,
the women bring the pot containing the lamp, the ball of paste
called Shree, and a number of other precious things, and going
up one by one to the bridegroom, with these things touch his
forehead. If the person has the means, the rest of the time
till night is occupied in feasting relations, bramhuns, neighbours,
etc. The bride, bridegroom, and the person who gives the
bride in marriage, all fast till the wedding is over."[1]

Among the wealthier sections of the community, a much more
elaborate ceremony is customary, and the guests invited make
a huge total. According to this same authority, the affair
presents a magnificent spectacle. The procession to the bride's
home is a long one : in front of the palanquin of the bridegroom,
his father's servants, carrying silver staves, walk slowly ; then
follow open carriages containing dancing women and singers ;
and an elephant bearing a metal instrument which is beaten at
intervals. As the procession is in the night, the streets through
which it passes are illuminated with flambeaux, while fireworks
are discharged at intervals along the route. In describing one
of these costly and elaborate weddings, Ward says : "After
entering the house, the bridegroom is led to the place where
the marriage rites are to be performed, and where the father-
in-law, taking off the old garments and poita of the boy, arrays
him in new clothes, and takes him into an inner apartment,
where they make him stand on a stool placed on the cow's head
and certain other things buried in the earth, adding a number
of female superstitious practices, to induce the bridegroom to
behave well to the bride. They next bring the bride on a stool
covered with the bridegroom's old garments, and carry the girl
round the bridegroom seven times ; they then permit the bride
and bridegroom fairly to look at each other for the first time.
The happy pair are then brought to the former place, and made
to sit near each other, when the father-in-law puts into the hands
of the bridegroom fourteen blades of kooshu grass, tied in two
separate parts, which the boy ties under his feet. The father-
in-law now pours some water into the right hand of the

[1] William Ward, *A View of the History, Literature, and Mythology of the Hindoos*,
1820, third edition, Vol. III, pp. 168–170.

bridegroom, and while the latter holds it there, the former reads
an incantation, at the close of which the bridegroom lets it fall
on his feet; rice, flowers and doorva grass are next given, which
he lays on his head; water is presented as at first with a prayer;
and then sour milk; then again water. The officiating brahmun
now directs the boy to put his hand on a pan of water, and then
places the hand of the bride on that of the bridegroom, and ties
them together with a garland of flowers." The bride is then
given, to the accompaniment of an elaborate flow of words,
to the bridegroom; the presents are given, and then the garland
of flowers is removed. Now let Ward take up the tale: "A
cloth is now drawn over the heads of the couple, while they
again look at each other; and this part of the marriage ceremony
here closes, after the boy and the girl have been directed to bow
to the shalugramu and to the company, that they may receive
the blessing of the gods and of the brahmuns. A brahmun, or
a female whose husband and son are living, then fastens the
bride and bridegroom together by their garments with the above
piece of cloth, as a token of their union; and they are thus led
back into the midst of the family."[1]

Many of the rites that to the Englishman or American appear
unnecessary, grotesque, or nonsensical, are performed with the
specific intention of propitiating the gods, or they have other
magical properties. Many are fertility rites pure and simple,
as in the pouring of water on the head of the bride, and the use
of turmeric in unguents for anointing purposes.[2]

In one form of Hindu marriage, according to Wood,[3] after
the bride's father has tied the mantles of bride and bridegroom
together in a knot, the bridegroom pours on the hands of the
bride a quantity of clarified butter, while someone else gives her
rice, which she receives in her cupped hands, after which butter
is poured over the rice. She then opens her hands to allow
the rice to fall on a fire which has been kindled in readiness.
After several peregrinations around the fire have been performed,
more oblations made, and prayers recited, the bridegroom pours
rice out of a basket into the fire, to the accompaniment of a
prayer. The bride is then directed by the bridegroom to step
successively into seven circles, while appropriate texts are recited:

[1] Ward, op. cit., pp. 172–173.
[2] William Crooke, *Religion and Folklore of Northern India*, 1926, p. 245.
[3] Edward J. Wood, *The Wedding Day in All Ages and Countries*, 1869. Vol. I,
p. 128.

the completion of the seventh step ends the ceremony and the marriage is now irrevocable.

To the number seven arcane qualities were attributed by the ancient Hebrews and contemporary races, and traces of the superstition have survived through the ages. As is indicated in the aforementioned Hindu rites, considerable importance was attached to this number; also in the marriage ceremonies performed in other parts of India it was customary for both bride and bridegroom to walk seven times around the sacred fire.

In some districts of India the marriage ceremony is prolonged and tedious. Thus in Southern India, writes Miles, the bridegroom "must go all through the recitation of the religious ceremony. He is helped through this tiresome performance by his spiritual teacher, or by his father. Ghi, by being poured on the fire, is offered to the gods, and after that the service to ancestors is performed."[1] All these procedures, and many others, are mere preliminaries to the actual ceremony of marriage, which includes two curious features. The first of these is the seedpan rite. Four earthen pans, representing the gods Indra, Varuna, Yama, and Soman, are arranged in the form of a square, and a fifth pan is placed so as to occupy a central position in this square. The second rite is known as the tying of the wrist-thread. On the pan representing Varuna two threads are laid, one of which the bridegroom, after smearing it with a paste containing turmeric, ties around the bride's left wrist. The other thread is tied by the priest to the bridegroom's right wrist. After this, the bride's father, says Miles, to whom I am indebted for these particulars, " washes the feet of the bridegroom " in milk and water.

Another strange marriage custom, practised by a tribe in Neilgherry, is described by Wood. Around a hut a fence is constructed of such a degree of thickness that the sight cannot penetrate it. The single girls and young men who are desirous of getting married then take their places, the females inside the hut, and the males outside the fence, through which they proceed to thrust long sticks. The girls then troop out of the hut, each catching hold of a protruding end. The young man holding one end of the stick becomes the husband of the girl who seizes its other end.

Describing a Mahometan marriage, of which she was an

[1] Arthur Miles, *The Land of the Lingam*, Hurst & Blackett, 1933.

eye-witness, celebrated in Calcutta, Ida Pfeiffer says: "On the day appointed for the ceremony, the nuptial bed, elegantly ornamented, is carried, with music and festivity, to the house of the bridegroom, and late in the evening, the bride herself is conveyed there in a close palanquin, with music and torches, and a large crowd of friends, many of whom carry regular pyramids of tapers; that well-known kind of firework, the Bengal-fire, with its beautiful light-blue flame, is also in requisition for the evening's proceedings. On arrival at the bridegroom's house, the newly-married couple alone are admitted; the rest remain outside playing, singing, and hallooing until broad day."[1]

A strange Burmese custom is mentioned by Father Sangermano as being observed at the time he wrote his interesting book. On the night of a marriage, a party of lads gathered around the house of the newly-married couple. They were armed with stones and other objects suitable for use as missiles, which they hurled upon the roof and through the windows, inflicting much damage to the building and its contents, and sometimes injuring the inmates. All through the night the bombardment went on, and apparently there was no way of escaping the ordeal, once news of the marriage leaked out. "It is difficult to conceive," says Father Sangermano, "any reason for this extraordinary practice."[2]

In ancient Persia, the inhabitants firmly believed that any person who was married or had at any time been married held a superior position in the future state. Because of this they were accustomed, when a person died in a state of celibacy, to hire someone to marry the corpse.

The Persian wedding contract is witnessed by the cadi, or magistrate. On the wedding night the bride, covered from head to foot in a veil of red silk or painted muslin, is mounted upon a horse sent by the bridegroom for this purpose. All along the route to the bridegroom's house a mirror is held before her face by one of the bridesmaids, as an admonition to her that this is the last time she will look therein as a virgin. The festivities last for eight or ten days.

An interesting description of a royal Persian wedding is given by Wood. It reads: "In October, 1867, the heir to the throne

---

[1] Ida Pfeiffer, *A Woman's Journey Round the World*, c. 1852, p. 154
[2] John Jardine (edited by), *The Burmese Empire a Hundred Years Ago as Described by Father Sangermano*, 1893, p. 166.

of Persia was married to his cousin, both of them being only sixteen years of age. The ceremony was conducted with great pomp. The cavalcade in which the bride left her home was preceded by about one hundred horses, mules and camels, carrying servants, carpets, tents, and her outfit; then followed many led horses covered with rich housings; and next came the carriage containing the princess, who was concealed behind wooden blinds. The vehicle was drawn by six horses. It was followed by mules carrying palanquins closed with curtains, and containing the women of the bride's suite. The procession was closed by a large number of officers and dignitaries on beautifully caparisoned horses; and it was accompanied by violin, trumpet, and tamborine players. The princess was thirty-three days upon her journey; and having arrived at the city of her intended husband, she was provisionally lodged in a palace there. Public rejoicings preceded the marriage; and on the day fixed for the ceremony, three hours after sunset, the princess was conducted in a litter with torches, to her lord's palace, where the marital rites took place."[1]

Fullom gives an interesting account of the marriage customs observed by the nomadic tent-dwelling tribes of Persia, who celebrate their nuptials in the dreary solitudes of the desert. He says: "As the bride is being conducted in solemn silence from the tent of her mother to her future home, she is met about midway by the bridegroom, who carries in his hand an orange or an apple, and, when sufficiently near to make sure of his aim, throws it at the veiled maiden with all his force, as the harder he hits her, the more fortunate she will be esteemed. Instantly the lady's friends raise a great outcry, and make a rush at the ungallant bridegroom, who spurs off, and, being mounted on the fleetest horse of his tribe, generally contrives to outstrip his pursuers, and arrive first at the tent. Should he, however, be overtaken, his horse becomes the prize of his captor, though, if he is in poor circumstances, it may be redeemed for two or three pieces of silver. When the bride reaches the tent of the sham recreant, the girls and women of her party, clinging round her horse, implore her not to alight, while the friends of the bridegroom are equally importunate on the other side, though they blend their invitations with urgent entreaties that she will

[1] Edward J. Wood, *The Wedding Day in all Ages and Countries*, 1869. Vol. I, pp. 95-6.

relinquish a portion of her dower.   To this she seldom consents, as it is her only safeguard from ill-usage ; but sometimes, with the confiding weakness of her sex, she readily complies.   Then she descends from her horse, and, amid the renewed opposition of her friends, takes the fatal step of entering the tent—to her indeed the house of bondage."[1]

No banns of marriage are ever published in connexion with marriage celebrated in the Armenian churches.   All arrangements are made by the parents.   On the day appointed, the bridegroom, mounted on horseback, heads a procession to the church.   His head is decorated with a network of gold and silver or a flesh-coloured veil (according to his rank), which hangs down to his waist.   Immediately behind him rides the bride, covered from head to foot with a white veil.   She holds in her right hand one end of a girdle, the bridegroom holding the other end.   Two unmounted attendants, on each side of her horse, hold the reins. On some occasions horses are dispensed with, the bride being escorted on foot between two matrons, and the bridegroom being accompanied by a friend.   Behind the bride and bridegroom are relations and friends, carrying wax tapers.   Usually there is a band of music.   Dismounting at the church, and still holding the girdle, the bride and bridegroom proceed to the altar, before which they stand side by side.   The priest places a Bible in their hands, and proceeds to perform the ceremony of the ring, on the conclusion of which he celebrates Mass.

Before leaving the subject of Armenian marriages it seems fitting to reproduce a description given by Pouqueville of a curious ceremony held at Pera during his residence there.   Here it is in the author's own words : " I once saw a strange procession pass by, which they informed me was an Armenian wedding, and I took care to have the characters explained to me as they passed by, so sorrowful and grave did they appear.   The march commenced by fiddlers and flute-players (who made a most dreadful and unharmonious squeaking), with dancers, who sang and tripped it at the same time ; they were followed by a group of relations ; next to them a body of men, with torches of yellow wax, who seemed as if escorting a funeral ; immediately afterwards the bride was seen, supported by two of her nearest relations ; a sack was drawn over her head down to her feet ; but, in order that her respiration should not be checked, they

[1] S. W. Fullom, *The History of Woman*, 1855, pp. 115-116.

put a wooden platter or tea-board upon her head, by which the sack was kept from her mouth and nostrils. She was separated from the bridegroom by a party of guests. He then came alone, enveloped in napkins, with his arms crossed and placed on his breast; his head was covered with a silk shawl, and inclined on the left shoulder; while his long whiskers and lamentable appearance gave rather the idea of a criminal about to receive punishment, than a bridegroom about to receive the hymeneal crown. Behind him, I know not for what reason, came two Armenians, holding in their hands two rusty sabres, of which they appeared to be in dread, and raising them from time to time in a menacing attitude towards heaven; the rest of the relations followed at a melancholy and slow pace. As the ceremony took place in my neighbourhood, I had an opportunity of observing that the good Armenians did not lose their time in vague ceremonies; for the banquet degenerated into a most scandalous orgie, which lasted without interruption for three days and three nights."[1]

In the island of Java, the Mahometans are polygynists and concubinists to boot. The anonymous author of a book[2] dealing with marriage ceremonies, in regard to the conditions prevailing in the eighteenth century, observes that on the day fixed for the wedding, the relations and friends of both bridegroom and bride, as well as the servants of their respective families attend the ceremony. Soon after midday the bridegroom sets forth with his retinue: four men, forming the van of the procession, carry a contrivance consisting of sticks attached to a pole, which is continually struck with small sticks carried by others marching alongside. Next are several men with drums, which are beaten with sticks mostly, but sometimes with the hands; then come others carrying sticks in their hands which they strike against other sticks fixed about their necks. Following these musicians, if one may correctly describe them by this name, are men varying in number from sixty to one hundred, according to the wealth and rank of the bridegroom: many are decorated with the feathers of peacocks, the skins of animals, etc.; others are armed with swords, knives, and darts, and these warriors occasionally give demonstrations, for the

---

[1] Quoted by Theophilus Moore in *Marriage Customs and Modes of Courtship*, 1820, pp. 168–9.
[2] *Marriage Ceremonies as now Used in all Parts of the World*, London, 1744.

entertainment of the onlookers, of their skill and prowess with the weapons they carry. Next are a number of young women, elegantly attired and carrying flowers, pictures and other articles for presenting to the bridegroom and his bride : these women are followed by others bearing articles of furniture, provisions, and household goods of every description. The procession ends with the bridegroom, richly upholstered for the occasion, and mounted on a splendid horse : on each side of him rides a personal friend. When the van of the procession arrives at the bride's home, the drummers take up positions near the door to await the coming of the bridegroom ; the other men make a lane for the women bearing the gifts and furniture. On arrival at the door, the bridegroom dismounts, and immediately there appears his bride, carrying a vessel containing water : going down on her knees there and then, she washes his feet, then leads him by the hand inside the house, where they sit and talk. After some little time has elapsed, the bridegroom and the bride reappear ; the procession is reformed in the same order as before, and a triumphal return march is made to the bridegroom's house, where for three successive days entertainments and feasts are held in celebration of the marriage.

II

Marriage Rites of Egypt, Morocco, etc.

Little information appears to be available respecting marriage ceremonies of ancient Egypt, but as regards modern Egypt an excellent description of a wedding is given by Edward William Lane, in *An Account of the Manners and Customs of the Modern Egyptians*. As, in the main, it cannot be bettered I am reproducing the text, with some omissions and emendations.

The bridegroom should receive his bride on the eve of Friday, or that of Monday, but the former is generally esteemed the more fortunate period. Let us say, for instance, that the bride is to be conducted to him on the eve of Friday. During two or three or more preceding nights, the street or quarter in which the bridegroom lives is illuminated with chandeliers and lanterns, or with lanterns and small lamps, suspended from

EGYPTIAN BRIDAL PROCESSION — I

EGYPTIAN BRIDAL PROCESSION — II

From Edward William Lane's *An Account of the Manners and Customs of the Modern Egyptians*, 1836

cords drawn across from the bridegroom's and several other houses on each side to the houses opposite ; and several small silk flags, each of two colours, generally red and green, are attached to other cords. An entertainment is also given on each of these nights, particularly on the *last* night before that on which the wedding is concluded, at the bridegroom's house. On these occasions, it is customary for the persons invited, and for all intimate friends, to send presents to his house, a day or two before the feast which they purpose or expect to attend ; they generally send sugar, coffee, rice, wax candles, or a lamb : the former articles are usually placed upon a tray of copper or wood, and covered with a silk or embroidered handkerchief. The guests are entertained on these occasions by musicians and male or female singers, or by dancing girls.

On the preceding Wednesday (or Saturday, if the wedding be to conclude on the eve of Monday), at about the hour of noon, or a little later, the bride goes in state to the bath. The procession is headed by a party of musicians with a hautboy or two, and drums of different kinds. Frequently, some person avails himself of this opportunity to parade his young son previously to circumcision : the child and his attendants, in this case, follow next after the musicians. Sometimes, at the head of the bride's party are two men who carry the utensils and linen used in the bath, upon two round trays, each of which is covered with a silk handkerchief. In general, the first persons among the bride's party are several of her married female relations and friends, walking in pairs ; and next, a number of young virgins. Then follows the bride, walking under a canopy of silk, of some gay colour, as pink, rose-colour or yellow, or of two colours, in the form of wide stripes, often rose-colour and yellow. It is carried by four men, by means of a pole at each corner, and is open only in front ; and at the top of each of the four poles is attached an embroidered handkerchief. The dress of the bride entirely conceals her person. Upon her head is placed a small pasteboard cap, or crown. A red Kashmeer shawl is placed over this, and conceals from the view of the public the richer articles of her dress, her face, and her jewels, excepting one or two ornaments, generally of diamonds and emeralds, attached to that part of the shawl which covers her forehead. She is accompanied by two or three of her female relations within the canopy ; and often, when in hot weather, a woman walking backwards before

her, is constantly employed in fanning her, with a large fan of
black ostrich feathers, the lower part of the front of which is
usually ornamented with a piece of looking-glass. The procession
moves very slowly : it is closed by a second party of musicians,
similar to the first, or by two or three drummers. The whole
bath is sometimes hired for the bride and her party exclusively.
They pass several hours in washing, sporting, and feasting ;
and frequently female singers are hired to amuse them. Having
returned from the bath to the house of her family, the bride
and her companions sup together. If hired female singers have
contributed to the festivity of the bath, they, also, return with
the bride, to renew their concert. Their songs are always on
the subject of love, and of the joyous event which occasions
their presence. After the company has been thus entertained,
a large quantity of henna having been prepared in the form
of a paste, the bride takes a lump of it in her hand, and receives
contributions from her guests : each of them sticks a coin
(usually of gold) in the henna which she holds upon her hand,
and when the lump of paste is closely stuck with these coins,
she scrapes it off her hand upon the edge of a basin of water.
Having collected in this manner from all her guests, some more
henna is applied to her hands and feet, which are then bound
with pieces of linen, and in this state they remain until the next
morning, when they are found to be sufficiently dyed with its
deep orange-red tint. Her guests make use of the remainder
of the dye for their own hands. This night is known as ' The
Night of the Henna.' It is on this same night, and sometimes
also during the latter half of the preceding day, that the
bridegroom gives his chief entertainment.

On the following day the bride goes in procession to the house
of the bridegroom, generally setting out a little after midday.
They proceed in the same order, and at the same slow pace,
as has already been described in the march to the bath. If
the bridegroom's house is near, the procession follows a
circuitous route, through the principal streets, for the sake of
display.

Sometimes these bridal celebrations are enlivened by entertainments provided on the way and usually preceding the procession
itself. Two swordsmen, clad in nothing but their drawers, will
engage each other in a mock combat ; or two fellaheen will
cudgel each other with long staves. In the procession of a bride

of a wealthy family, any person capable of performing some extraordinary feat to amuse the spectators is almost sure of being a welcome assistant, and of receiving a handsome present. Among the most common of the feats witnessed on such an occasion is the performance of a laborious task by a water-carrier ; who, for the sake of a present, carries a water-skin filled with sand and water, of greater weight and for a longer period than any of his brethren will venture to do, and this he must accomplish without ever sitting down, except in a crouching position, to rest. In the case of one important marriage there walked before a procession a young man who had made an incision in his abdomen, and drawn out a large portion of his intestines, which he carried before him on a silver tray. After the procession, he restored them to their former place, and remained in bed many days before he recovered from the effects of this foolish and disgusting act. Another man, on the same occasion, ran a sword through his arm, before the spectators, and then bound over the wound, without withdrawing the sword, several handkerchiefs, which were soaked with blood. These facts were described to me, says Lane, by an eye witness.

Apropos of this custom, Burckhardt says : " I have seen many nuptial processions of persons high in office at the court of Mohammed Aly ; the bride was seated in a carriage, and all the different trades and professions of the town appeared personified upon richly decorated open waggons drawn by horses; in these waggons the tradesmen and artists had established their shops, and sat working in the same manner as in their own regular abodes : sixty or seventy of those waggons followed the carriage of the bride. Before them went rope-dancers, harlequins, etc., and at their head was a masked figure that is frequently seen parading in front of nuptial processions of an inferior order, and conducted with much less pomp and splendour ; this figure is a young man whose head, arms, legs, and entire body are patched over with white cotton, so that no part of the skin can be perceived, his person appearing as if completely powdered over. He exhibits, in the natural position, that object which constituted the distinguishing attribute of the ancient Roman god of the gardens, during the whole time of the procession. How this custom, which is not known in other places, began among the Egyptians, I am unable to ascertain ; but it seems not improbably some remnant of the worship paid by their forefathers to that god, whose temple at Karnak is the most considerable now existing in Egypt."[1]

And now let Lane again take up the tale : " The bride and her party having arrived at the bridegroom's house, sit down to a repast. Her friends, shortly after, take their departure ; leaving with her only her mother and sister, or other near female relations, and one or two other women. The ensuing night is called ' The Night of the Entrance '.

"The bridegroom sits below. Before sunset, he goes to the bath, and there changes his clothes ; and, after having supped with a party of friends, waits till a little before the time of the night-prayer, and then, according to general custom, repairs to some celebrated mosque and there says his prayers. If young, he is generally honoured with a *zeffeh* on this occasion : he goes to the mosque preceded by musicians with drums and one or more hautboys, and accompanied by a number of friends, and by several men bearing *meshals*. The *meshal* is a staff with a cylindrical frame of iron at the top filled with blazing wood, or having two, three, four, or five of these receptacles for fire. The party usually proceeds to the mosque at a quick pace, and without much order. A second group of musicians, with the same instruments, or with drums only, closes the procession. After prayers have been said, the procession returns from the mosque with more order and display, and very slowly, perhaps because it would be considered unbecoming in the bridegroom to hasten home to take possession of his bride. It is headed, as before, by musicians, and two or more bearers of *meshals*. These are generally followed by two men bearing, by means of a pole resting horizontally upon their shoulders, a hanging frame, to which are attached about sixty small lamps, in four circles, one above another ; the uppermost of which circles is made to revolve, being turned round occasionally by one of the two bearers. These numerous lamps, and several *meshals* besides those before-mentioned, brilliantly illumine the streets through which the procession passes, and produce a remarkably picturesque effect. The bridegroom and his friends and other attendants follow, advancing in the form of an oblong ring, all facing the interior of the ring, and each bearing in his hand one or more wax candles, and sometimes a sprig of henna or some other flower, excepting the bridegroom and the friend on either

[1] John Lewis Burckhardt, *Arabic Proverbs*, 1875, p. 137.

side of him.   These three form the latter part of the ring, which
generally consists of twenty or more persons.   At frequent
intervals the party stops for a few minutes ; and during each of
these pauses, a boy or man, one of the persons who compose the
ring, sings a few words of an epithalamium.   The sounds of the
drums, and the shrill notes of the hautboy cease during the rendering of these songs.   The train is closed, as in the former case,
by a second group of musicians.

"Soon after his return from the mosque, the bridegroom leaves
his friends in a lower apartment, enjoying their pipes, coffee,
and sherbet.   The bride's mother and sister, or whatever other
female relations were left with her, are above ; the bride herself,
and the *bellaneh*, in a separate apartment.   If the bridegroom be
a young man, it is considered proper that he, as well as the bride,
should exhibit some degree of bashfulness : one of his friends,
therefore, carries him a part of the way up to the harem.   On
entering the bride's apartment, he gives a present to the *bellaneh*,
and she retires.   The bride has a shawl thrown over her head,
and the bridegroom must give her a present of money, which
is called ' the price of the uncovering of the face ', before he
attempts to remove this, which she does not allow him to do
without some apparent reluctance, if not violent resistance, in
order to show her maidenly modesty.   On removing the covering,
he says, ' In the name of God the Compassionate, the Merciful,'
and then greets her with this compliment : ' The night be
blessed,' or ' is blessed,' to which she replies, if timidity does
not choke her utterance, ' God bless thee.'   The bridegroom
now sees the face of his bride for the first time, and generally
finds her nearly what he has been led to expect.   Often, but not
always, a curious ceremony is then performed.   The bridegroom
takes off every article of the bride's clothing excepting her shirt ;
seats her upon a mattress or bed, the head of which is turned
towards the direction of Mecca, placing her so that her back
is also turned in that direction ; and draws forward, and spreads
upon the bed, the lower part of the front of her shirt : having
done this, he stands at a distance of rather less than a yard before
her, and performs the prayers of two *rek'ahs* ; laying his head
and hands, in prostration, upon the part of her shirt that is
extended before her lap.   He remains with her but a few minutes
longer : having satisfied his curiosity respecting her personal
charms, he calls to the women (who generally collect at the door,

where they wait in anxious suspense) to raise their cries of joy ; and the shrill sounds acquaint the persons below and in the neighbourhood, and often, responded to by other women, spread still further the news that he has acknowledged himself satisfied with his bride. He soon after descends to rejoin his friends, and remains with them an hour or more, before he returns to his wife. It very seldom happens that the husband, if disappointed in his bride, immediately disgraces and divorces her : in general he retains her, in this case, a week or more."

In Morocco, marriages have always been elaborate and expensive affairs. At one time it was customary for the bride and her female relatives to paint their faces red and white, and their hands and feet yellow. The bride usually makes a journey through the principal streets of the city. She is mounted on a mule, equipped with an ornamental tower-like structure, in which she sits, thinly veiled. The people following behind sing, howl and bang drums, making a hideous clamour. A wealthy or an important bride rides a camel instead of a mule. No fewer than three feasts are held in connexion with the marriage ; the first on the occasion of the bride being brought home ; the second, restricted to females, on the day following the ceremony ; and, on the seventh day after the wedding, the third, at which the bride's father and mother as well as her other relatives are present.

The Abyssinians, at one time, had nothing in the form of a marriage contract or ceremony. No witnesses were necessary. Marriage was purely a matter of mutual agreement and terminable at pleasure. In short what it amounted to was little more than a decision to live together until one or other was tired of the arrangement.

Later in the history of the country and in the more civilized parts, according to Moore, all marriages were confirmed before a priest. The Jesuit Alvarez, who was present at a ceremony where the patriarch officiated, says, the bride and bridegroom were waiting at the church door ; where a couch was prepared for them ; and on which they were ordered to sit. With a cross in one hand and a censer in the other, the patriarch made a kind of processional march round them. Then, laying his hands on their heads, he told them as they became one flesh, so they ought to have one heart and mind. He then went into the church and performed divine service, when, giving them his

ARRIVAL OF MARRIAGE PRESENTS AT THE BRIDAL RESIDENCE

From Rev. G. N. Wright's *China: In a Series of Views*, 1843

blessing, the ceremony was ended.   After consummation, the husband and wife sat at separate tables ; or, if they agreed to eat together, brought their victuals ready dressed, or sent them in by their slaves or attendants.

Apparently the ceremony varied in different places and in different circumstances.   Gaia gives one of the most remarkable of these ceremonies, thus : " The celebrant, after he has cut a lock of hair from the heads of the bridegroom and the bride, and dipped them into wine mingled with honey, exchanges the locks, and places that which belonged to the former on the head of the latter, and so *vice versa*, in the very same place from whence they were taken, sprinkling them at the same time with holy water.   After this ceremony is over, the newly-married couple, attended by their friends, go home, and never stir abroad for a month.   When the bride goes out, she wears a black veil over her face, which she never turns up till after the expiration of six months, except she proves with child."[1]

An extremely curious custom is mentioned by Louise Jordan Miln[2] as being practised in Tunis and in some parts of Algeria. After the marriage ceremony, the husband walks backwards as he crosses the threshold of the house, holding in front of him a knife, while the bride, following him into her new home, places her fingers on the blade in the act of entering.

III

Marriage Rites of China and Japan

In China the most appropriate and felicitous time for marriage, says Davis, is considered to be in spring, and the first moon of the year (February) is looked upon with most favour.   It is in this month that the peach-tree blossoms, and there are many allusions to this particular tree in connexion with marriage.   In the Chinese *Book of Odes* are some relevant verses, of which a paraphrase of a literal translation made by Sir William Jones, is as follows :—

[1] Quoted by William Tegg, *The Knot Tied*, 1877, pp. 172–3.
[2] Louise Jordan Miln, *Wooing and Weddings in Many Climes*, T. Arthur Pearson, 1900, p. 117.

" Sweet child of spring, the garden's queen,
    Yon peach-tree charms the roving sight ;
Its fragrant leaves how richly green,
    Its blossoms how divinely bright !
So softly shines the beauteous bride,
    By love and conscious virtue led,
O'er her new mansion to preside,
    And placid joys around her spread."

Before the day fixed for the wedding, " the bridegroom," says
Davis, " is invested ceremoniously with a dress-cap or bonnet,
and takes an additional name. The bride at the same time,
whose hair had until this hung down in long tresses, has it
turned up in the manner of married women, and fastened with
bodkins."[1]

Early on the wedding day the bride arises, bathes and dresses.
While she is bathing the musicians are required to play. Her
breakfast consists theoretically of the fowl, the vermicelli, etc.,
sent by the family of her affianced husband, but she eats very
sparingly. When the precise time, previously fixed by the
fortune-teller, approaches for taking her seat in the sedan, her
toilet is completed by one of her parents taking the thick veil
provided by her fiancé and placing it over her head, completely
covering her face. She is now led out of the room by one
of her female assistants, and takes her seat in the sedan, which
has been brought into the reception-room of the house. The
floor from her own room to the sedan is covered for the occasion
with a kind of red carpeting, so that her feet may not touch
the ground. She takes her place in the sedan amid the sound
of fire-crackers and music. The bride, her mother, and the
various members of the family, are required by custom to indulge
during the morning in hearty and protracted crying.

The sedan is adorned in the most elaborate and magnificent
manner possible with festoons of flowers and other ornaments.
As soon as the bride is seated, and before the procession starts,
her parents or some members of her family, take a bed-quilt
by its four corners, and, while holding it thus before the bridal
chair, one of the bride's assistants tosses into the air, one by one,
four bread-cakes, in such a manner that they fall into the quilt.
These cakes were sent by the fiancé at the same time as the cock

[1] John Francis Davis, *The Chinese*, 1845, p. 266. For the main points in the
description that follows of Chinese marriage rites I am indebted to this book
by Davis, and also to Doolittle's *Social Life of the Chinese*.

and vermicelli.   The woman, during this procedure, is constantly
repeating solicitous phrases, which are assented to by others of
the company.   The quilt containing these cakes is then gathered
up and carried into an adjoining room.   The object of this rite
is to profit the family of the bride's parents, which is in some
manner indicated by the quilt and cakes being retained in the
house.   Soon after this the sedan is locked and the bridal
procession starts *en route* for the residence of the bridegroom,
amid explosions of fire-crackers and the music of the band.

Leading this procession are two men carrying large lighted
lanterns, bearing the ancestral name of the groom cut in large
characters out of red paper, and pasted on them.   Then come
two men carrying similar lanterns, having the family name of
the bride pasted on them in a similar way.   These belong to her
family and accompany her only a part of the way.   Next comes
a large red umbrella followed by men carrying lighted torches,
and by the musicians.   Near the bridal chair are several brothers
of the bride or friends of her family, and several relatives and
friends of the groom.   These latter are despatched from the
house of the groom early in the morning, for the purpose of
meeting the procession and escorting the bride to her new home.
This deputation sometimes arrives at the house of the bride
before she sets out on her journey, and, if so, accompanies the
procession all the way.   About midway between the homes of
the bride and the groom, the procession stops in the street and
the important ceremony of "*receiving the bride*" is formally
transacted.   The friends of the bride stand near each other, and
at a little distance away are the friends of the groom.   The former
produce a large red card, having the ancestral name of the bride's
family written on it ; the latter produce a similar card bearing
the ancestral name of the groom.   These they exchange, and
each, seizing in his own hands *à la Chinois*, bows towards the
members of the other party.   The two men in the front of the
procession who carry the lanterns bearing the ancestral name
of the groom now turn about, and, going between the sedan
chair and the two men who carry the lanterns bearing the
ancestral name of the bride, come back to their former position
in the procession, having gone around the party which has the
lanterns with the bride's ancestral name attached.   This latter
party, while the other is thus encircling it, turns around in an
opposite direction, and starts for the residence of the bride's

family, accompanied by that part of the escort which consisted of her relatives or the friends of her family. The rest of the procession now proceeds on its way to the residence of the bridegroom, the band playing a lively air. At intervals along the street fire-crackers are exploded. It is said that, from the precise time when the two parties carrying lanterns bearing the ancestral names of the two families separate from each other in the street, the name of the bride is changed into the name of her betrothed.

On arrival at the groom's house, of the carefully closed and locked sedan, the bride's nearest male relative, who has charge of the key, hands it to the bridegroom who is standing at the door awaiting the coming of the bridal party. For he alone has the privilege of opening the door of the sedan, and his eagerness for a sight of the woman he intends to marry can well be imagined, as it must be remembered they have never met before. In most cases he is well pleased, but sometimes it happens that disappointment is to be his lot, in which case he shuts and relocks the door of the sedan immediately, and orders the procession to retrace its steps. If, however, all is well, the bride steps out of her chair, and is led by the groom into the hall. A woman who is the mother of male children welcomes the bride with felicitous greetings.

At one time, says Wood, it was customary, immediately after the entry into the bridegroom's house of the bride, for a priest to sacrifice a cock by decapitation, and then sprinkle the couple with some of its blood.

The ceremonies enacted after the bride had entered the house of the bridegroom varied somewhat in different parts of China, and as time went on some of the more ancient ones were either abandoned or modified. One of the most important of these old ceremonies and one which in some form or other seems to have been universally observed was that known as " worshipping the temple." The description of it which follows is culled from the pages of Doolittle's invaluable book on China :—

"A table is placed in the front part of the reception room. The table is said to be placed ' before heaven.' Two candlesticks, containing two large lighted candles, and a censer containing lighted incense, are put upon this table, the censer between the candlesticks. Among other things, there are also placed on it two miniature white cocks, made of sugar, five kinds of dried

MARRIAGE PROCESSION AT THE BLUE CLOUD CREEK,
CHIN-KEANG-FOO

From Rev. G. N. Wright's China: *In a Series of Views*, 1843

fruit, a bundle of chopsticks, a foot-measure, a mirror, a pair of shears, and a case containing money-scales. Some or all of these are frequently placed on a platter made out of the wood of the willow tree. Two singularly-shaped goblets, sometimes connected by a red silk or red cotton cord several feet long, are also put upon the table. When everything is ready, the bride is led out of her room, and takes her place by the table on the right side of the groom. *The faces of both parties are turned toward the table*—that is, toward the open light of the heavens. At certain signals from one of the female assistants of the bride, who is aided to do her part by these women, both parties kneel down four times, each time bowing their heads toward the earth once in profound silence. They then rise to their feet and change places, the bride standing on the left of the bridegroom. They now kneel down four times, bowing their heads as before. This portion of the ceremony is called '*worshipping heaven and earth*'. They then turn around so that their faces are *toward the inner or back side of the room*, instead of toward the front or outside, as before, the bride being on the right side of her husband. The ancestral tablet having been previously placed on a table in the back side of the room, and candles and incense having been lighted and arranged near them in the customary way, the bridegroom and bride now bow down and worship these tablets eight times, according to the manner after which they have just ' worshipped heaven and earth '. They again resume their original relative positions, differing only in that *they face each other*, and do not stand side by side. Separated from each other by only a few feet, they now kneel down four times again, and bow their heads once each time toward the ground. After this they rise to their feet, and remain standing in silence, while they are helped to the wedding wine. One of the female assistants takes the two goblets, which sometimes are said to be tied together by a red cord, from the table, and, having partially filled them with a mixture of wine and honey, she pours some of their contents from one into the other, back and forth several times. She then holds one to the mouth of the groom, and the other to the mouth of the bride, who continue to face each other, and who then sip a little of the wine. She then changes the goblets, and the bride sips out of the one just used by the groom, and the groom sips out of the one just used by the bride, the goblets oftentimes remaining tied together. Sometimes she uses only one goblet in giving the wine. She then places the goblets on the table, and proceeds to break off a bit of the sugar cocks and give to the bridegroom and to the bride ; perhaps also a few of the five kinds of fruit which have been provided are handed to them. After this the groom usually takes a bunch of chopsticks in one hand and the long case which contains the money-scales in the other, and makes a pretence of raising up by their means the thick covering which conceals the head and face of his bride from his view. It is only a pretence, and he returns the chopsticks and the money-scales to the place whence he took them. This usually concludes the ceremony. The lighted candles are taken by the married woman who addressed the bride with propitious language on her arrival, and carried into the bride's room, whither the groom accompanies his bride, but immediately returns to the public room, while she remains attended by her assistants to dress for dinner."[1]

In past ages it was customary for the bridegroom, after dressing himself in his most magnificent attire, to go through what was termed the sixth rite of marriage. The procedure is described by Huc as follows : " When the family has assembled in the domestic sanctuary, the bridegroom kneels down, and prostrates his face to the ground. Perfumes are then burnt before the tablets of ancestors, and the important event is announced to them. The master of the ceremonies then invites the father to take a place on the seat prepared for him. As soon as he is seated, the bridegroom receives on his knees a cup of wine, of which he first pours a few drops on the earth by way of libation, and before drinking makes four genuflexions before his father. Afterwards he advances towards the seat and in a kneeling posture receives the commands of his father. The father says : ' Go, my son, go and seek your wife, and behave in all things with prudence and wisdom.' The son prostrating himself four times before his father, replies that he will obey, after which he enters a palanquin that is already waiting at the door. His friends, and a numerous array of attendants, march before him, bearing lanterns of the most brilliant colours, a custom that arose at a time when it was usual to celebrate marriages in the night. When he has reached the house of the bride, the bride-groom waits at the gate of the second court until his father-in-law

[1] Rev. J. Doolittle, *Social Life of the Chinese*, 1866. Vol. I, pp. 79–87.

comes to introduce him."[1] At the time when the rite was in vogue, it was applicable to every man irrespective of wealth or rank : the Emperor himself observed it. The custom fell into disuse, however, and was replaced by the one already described in which the bridegroom sent a sedan chair for his bride to make the journey in.

From an English point of view one of the most extraordinary of the many strange customs connected with marriage in China is the practice of allowing three days of mourning to precede a wedding, the reason for this being that the marriage of their children is considered by Chinese parents to presage their own deaths. Further, no congratulations are offered or expected. White dresses or other white clothes are never worn at weddings : mourning is always in white.

In eighteenth-century Japan, a marriage was not so long or so elaborate an affair as in China, according to the reports of observers. The bride's dress was white, signifying that from the time of her marriage, so far as her parents were concerned, she was dead, and, as being emblematic of the same thing, the pillow of her bridal bed was placed toward the north, this being the position in which the dead were placed. The bride-groom and bride, with their relations and friends, went to the place appointed (usually the summit of a hill) for the wedding, by separate routes. The ceremony was performed in a small tent, the sole contents of which were an altar, and, surmounting it, a representation of the god of marriage. The couple, on entering, seated themselves facing each other. Behind the bride, but outside the tent, stood her parents and those of the bride-groom ; behind the bridegroom, and similarly without the tent, were the musicians. The ceremony then commenced. The bride lighted the flambeau, which she carried in her hand, at one of a number of lamps stationed just outside the tent, and at the same time recited certain phrases after the priest. Then the bridegroom secured a light from the blazing flambeau of his bride for the one he carried. This procedure was carried out to the accompaniment of joyous shouts and congratulations from all the relatives and friends present, and the priest then pronounced the couple man and wife, and dismissed them with his benediction. A large bonfire was next made, and on it were pitched the toys and playthings which had amused the bride

[1] M. Huc, *Chinese Empire*, 1855.

in her childhood days. The sacrifice of two oxen to the dog-headed god completed the rites. Then the bride was escorted to her husband's house, which had been gaily decorated for the occasion, and where for eight successive days feasts in celebration of the marriage were held.

In modern Japan the ceremony is more elaborate and is celebrated in the bridegroom's house. The bride is taken into a room, and seated with two young female attendants. She is then joined by the bridegroom. The only other persons present are the mediator, who has carried out the negotiations for the marriage, and his wife. All is now ready for the *sake*-drinking procedure, known as the three-times-three ceremony, which really constitutes the marriage rites. Three lacquer wine-cups of graduated sizes, so that they fit inside each other, are placed on a table. A butterfly-decorated vessel containing the consecrated wine or *sake*, and an identical vessel that is empty, are next placed on the table. One of the girl attendants, representing the male butterfly, pours wine from the full vessel into the empty one, held by the other girl representing the female butterfly, and she in turn pours some of the wine back again, this procedure being symbolical of union. Next the first girl pours a little *sake* into the smallest and uppermost of the three cups, and the bride sips from it three separate times. Now it is the bridegroom's turn : he goes through the same performance. Then, placing the used cup beneath the other two, he takes up the second and medium-sized one, holds this while it is filled, sips three times, and then hands this cup to the bride. Finally, comes the third and last re-arrangement of the cups, the bride once again having the initiatory role : she takes the largest cup and after having it filled with wine, drinks three successive times from it, a procedure which the bridegroom repeats, and then places the cup under the other two, the three cups now being in their original positions. And in this manner is the marriage ceremony completed.

The need to perpetuate the family name has always been a matter of paramount importance, and is no less so in the Japan of to-day. It is this need which creates the peculiar state of affairs in which a man " is married after the fashion of a woman," being chosen to carry on the family name where "a family has daughters and no sons."[1] Such a man is called an " adopted husband."

[1] Ruth Benedict, *The Chrysanthemum and the Sword*, Secker & Warburg, 1947.

JAPANESE WEDDING CEREMONY

From *Hildreth's "Japan as It Was and Is"*, 1907

IV

Marriage Rites in Other Countries

As in England, it was long customary for the wedding ceremony in France to be performed outside the church. And this applied without exception to persons of all ranks or stations in life. When the daughter of King Henry the Second of France was married to Philip the Second of Spain by the Bishop of Paris, the ceremony was conducted at the church door of Notre Dame. At that time, too, the newly-married couple were not allowed to enter the bedchamber until the bed had been blessed by the priest.

In seventeenth-century France the bride was escorted to the church by the bridegroom and his cortege, consisting of his relations and friends. They all walked in procession, the bridegroom taking the lead with his two nearest relations. Immediately following were the married men, then the single men, all arranged in couples : in each case those of nearest kinship going first. Next came the bride, sometimes wearing a coronet of white flowers or pearls ; in other instances having her head bare of decoration. She, too, was accompanied by two of her nearest relatives, one on each side. Then came other relations and friends of the female sex, walking in couples, the single ones after the married, and in each case arranged in order of kinship, exactly as the men were. If the bride wore a coronet, each of these females was decorated with one as well. Finally, came an attendant laden with bread and wine for use in the church. The return journey, after the ceremony, was made in similar fashion. At that time it was customary for favours, or knots of ribbon, to decorate the arms of wedding-guests, though eventually, according to Misson, the practice became restricted to the peasantry.

A peculiar custom at one time observed in France is described by the seventeenth-century writer Vaughan, thus : " The antient Frenchmen had a ceremonie, that when they would marrie, the bridegrome should pare his nayles and send them unto his new wife ; which done, they lived together afterwards as man and wife."

Another strange old custom was that of marriage by proxy.

Wood refers to it as being prevalent in Auvergne, " where also the lord of the soil had the privilege of attending at the ' bedding ' of a bride, and of putting one leg in her bed." This last-named vulgar and distasteful practice could in most cases be avoided by payment of a sum of money, which varied considerably, but, according to Wood, " ultimately the amount was fixed at one crown." In the year 1491, continues this authority, the Arch-duke Maximilian married by proxy the Duchess of Bretagne, " and he consummated the union by his ambassador attending with a train of lords and ladies, baring his leg to the knee, and putting it into the bed of the duchess, thereby taking possession of her bed and body."[1] Later, following the annulment of the union, the Duchess married Charles VIII of France. In Spain, during the reign of Charles the Fifth, marriages by proxy were celebrated at Valladolid ; in England, too, the custom had a limited vogue (see page 235), as also did that of the proxy putting his leg in the bride's bed.

In Spain at one time it was singularly easy for a girl to entrap a man into marriage. According to Bourgoing, when a girl had attained the age of twelve years, she could compel a youth to marry her provided he had reached the age of fourteen, and she could prove that he had promised marriage or given her to understand that he wished her to become his wife, and that he had " anticipated the rights of a husband with her." If the charges were denied, the girl must submit proof to an ecclesiastical vicar. Not that much in the way of proof was called for. The giving of presents ; the writing of a love-letter, even though it contained no actual offer or mention of marriage ; the evidence of neighbours to the effect that the couple had been seen together at an unseasonable hour : any of these was sufficient. The defendant was imprisoned while the inquiry was being held, and should the vicar decide that the marriage must take place the prisoner was not liberated until the ceremony had been held.

Among the gipsies of Spain, the betrothed girl, before the celebration of the marriage, is subjected to a scrutiny by four matrons appointed specifically for the purpose ; two of these matrons being relatives of the bridegroom and the other two relatives of the bride. Says George Borrow, " a rigorous examination ensues, in which a handkerchief of finest French

[1] Edward J. Wood, *The Wedding Day in all Ages and Countries*, 1869. Vol. II, p. 24.

cambric takes a leading part.   Should the bride be pronounced blameless by these female inquisitors, the bridal takes place the next day ; but should they discover that she has proved frail, the chances are that she will be made away with privately, and in a manner which will leave no trace behind."[1]   The main feature of the bridal is the feasting associated with it.   Eating, drinking, singing and dancing continue all through the day and night.   Borrow, describing one such bridal at which he was present, mentions as the most " singular part of the festival," the spreading of sweetmeats to the depth of several inches on the floor of one room.   Then the bride and bridegroom, and all the other gipsies present, entered this room and commenced dancing.   " In a few minutes," writes Borrow, " the sweetmeats were reduced to powder, or rather to mud, and the dancers were soiled to the knees with sugar, fruits, and yolks of eggs. Still more terrific became the lunatic merriment."   And so, to the accompaniment of braying, crowing, finger-snapping, and shouted obscenities, the dance continued riotously to its end. These festivals last for days, and often the cost is so excessive that the bridegroom finds himself beggared as a result.

A seventeenth-century German custom, also practised in France and Holland, was the presentation to the guests of engraved medals : this was however restricted to the aristocratic classes.

For the following account of a singular marriage ceremony formerly in vogue at Mouchgut, on Rugen Island, I am indebted to Moore's *Marriage Customs* (1820) : " Neither man nor woman ever thinks of matrimony till they are in possession of a kath or cottage ; and as soon as the parties are agreed, the consent of their ground landlord is requested.   In the afternoon of the wedding-day, the relations and friends of the bridegroom repair to his house, and *vice versa* with the bride, each inviting their friends separately.   The two parties proceed toward the church-yard, where they unite ; the bridegroom then salutes his intended by pressing her hand.   If the bride belong to another village, she takes leave of her relations with tears, as if she were never more to behold them.   After the ceremony in the church is over, both sexes separate, and the females retire to the warm beerhouse, where one of them presents the bride with some warm beer, and desires her in a verse to drink beer with all her friends, and make herself happy till they meet in heaven.   The warm

---

[1] George Borrow, *The Zincali*, 1843.   Vol. I, pp. 327–328.

beer, plentifully studded with large raisins, is circulated briskly till towards evening, when the discharge of a pistol summons them to the bridegroom's dwelling, where an immense dish of rice constitutes the first course which is succeeded by a variety of others ; during which time, the cup-bearer is actively employed. The dress of the bride is little more ornamental than usual, excepting a wreath she wears on her head, above which is a kind of crown made of box twigs, having the leaves gilt or silvered ; her hair is dressed for the purpose, stiffened and glossed with the whites of eggs.   The bridegroom is distinguished by a large white handkerchief, a present from the bride, the corners of which hang down low in front."

In ancient Poland the marriage was performed in a church, the bride wearing a towering silver-gilt crown, and attended by girl friends decorated with long red veils.   The actual ceremony was followed by practices of a most unusual nature, based probably on long-held superstitions.   The bride was compelled to walk round the fire three times, then to sit down in front of it, wash her feet in a bowl of water, and sprinkle the liquid on the bed and furniture.   Blindfolded, with her mouth filled with honey, and her face veiled, she was conducted to each door of the house in turn, which she had to kick with her right foot.   Wheat, rye, oats, barley, rice and beans were all thrown at the doors ; the throwers reciting words to the effect that the bride should never want for any of these foodstuffs as long as she remained true to her religion and performed her domestic duties.   These antics concluded, her veil was removed. After the evening banquet in celebration of the wedding, the bride's hair was cut off, and her head wrapped in a white linen cloth.   This covering was worn until she gave birth to a son. Finally, she was escorted to her chamber, and the bed sprinkled with water.

In the days of the old Czarist Russia, before the dawn of the eighteenth century, the nuptial ceremonies had many peculiar features.   The wedding day was not fixed until a fortune-teller had been consulted, and had given a pronouncement to the effect that the day proposed would prove a favourable one.   It was then customary for the bride to be examined by a number of women with a view to discovering and, if possible, remedying any bodily defect.   On the day ultimately appointed the bridegroom, his friends, and the priest, went to the bride's house, where a feast had been prepared for them. The bride, veiled, and wearing a crown of gold or silver-gilt, was seated at a table opposite the bridegroom, a curtain separating the two. The women who were present sang and scattered hops on the heads of the assembled guests. The parents of the bride and bridegroom exchanged rings. The whole party now repaired to the church, where the ceremony was to be celebrated. A piece of crimson taffeta was spread on the floor for the couple to stand upon. The priest, after asking for and receiving oblations of bread and other foodstuffs, gave the pair his benediction. Then taking the right hand of the bridegroom and the left hand of the bride, he asked them three times in succession whether they were prepared to marry and continue to love and be faithful to each other. After receiving their affirmations to this effect, the priest sang a psalm, while the guests held hands and danced with much solemnity. A garland of wormwood or rue was then placed by the priest on the heads of the couple, with the object of implying, it was said, that the marital state was to be expected to contain much bitterness. Then followed the drinking of the health of both bride and bridegroom by the priest out of a gilded wooden cup or a glass; they too drank thrice from the same vessel, which was then thrown on the floor, broken, and trampled upon, while the bridegroom pronounced as follows : ' Let them be so trampled upon and confounded who maliciously endeavour to create ill-will between us.' Linseed and hempseed were next scattered by the female guests over the heads of the bride and bridegroom. Finally the clerk threw a handful of hops over the bride's head, as a symbol of fertility. The church ceremony thus completed, the bride, still veiled, was escorted home ; the procession being led by the priest carrying a cross, accompanied by the female guests and a man wearing a goatskin coat, who recited prayers, the import of which was to wish that the bride might have as many children as there were hairs on the skin of the coat he wore. Arriving at their destination, the newly-married couple seated themselves at a table, where they were presented with bread and salt ; while, says Moore, a chorus of boys and girls sang the epithalamium, which was always grossly obscene. And, states the same authority, according to some writers, the bride presented her husband with a whip of her own making, in token of submission to his commands.

In the seventeenth century all Turkish marriages were arranged by a close friend of the bridegroom, called the Sagois. For the eight days immediately preceding the wedding no one was allowed to see the bride unless she was closely veiled. On the day before that fixed for the ceremony, accompanied by her nearest relations, who carried torches, she was taken to a bath and washed thoroughly by women attendants. Her hair, her nails, the palms of her hands, and her heels were all dyed red. Next day, being the wedding-day, a banquet was held at the bride's house. Her father then and there formally delivered her over to the Sagois, who escorted her, on horseback, to the bridegroom's residence. The relations and other guests followed, as well as carts laden with furniture and other possessions. The bride, closely veiled, with an umbrella over her head, bowed to all whom she met on the way, irrespective of their rank or position. At the house, where she was received by the bridegroom, a feast was held, at the conclusion of which the Sagois conducted her to her husband's chamber, where, pending his arrival, she was placed in charge of the eunuchs attached to the establishment. Only on the husband's arrival did she discard her veil, albeit with some show of resistance or disinclination.

The Germans had a ceremony in which the husband was called on to make a present to his wife on the morning after the wedding, which present was to remain her sole and absolute property. It was known as the Morgengale, or morning gift, and was supposed to recompense her for her lost virginity. Among the wealthier classes it was the bride's privilege to name the present she desired : it might be a sum of money ; more often it took the form of a piece of jewellery. Naturally and inevitably such a custom was abused, the requests being often of an exorbitant nature, so much so indeed that they had to be limited by the State : in some parts of Germany the sum was a fixed one. The practice was abolished by law in 1839.

It was at one time usual in Germany for an extraordinary feast to be held on the evening preceding the marriage. It was styled the *Polter-Abend*, which means a " noisy evening." At this feast it was customary for the bridesmaids to bring the myrtle wreath, which they had collectively purchased, and present it to the bride. While the feast was proceeding inside the house, in the street the " noisy evening ", in the true sense of the term, was celebrated. " For," said Mayhew, whose interesting work,

German Life and Manners (page 126), provides these particulars, "soon after midnight it is the custom of the town's folk on these *Polter-Abends* to bring out all the old broken crockery, pots and pans, they can collect, and to throw them one after another at the door. The noise thus made by the smashing of the several articles, is considered to be prophetic as well as symbolical of the disturbances likely to ensue between the couple in after-life. So general is this practice on the nuptial eve, that the heap of broken crockery often extends half across the street before the morning, and two or three wagons are sometimes required to carry away the fragments. Indeed, on one occasion, when a drunken sadler-master, who bore one of the worst characters in the city, was about to be united, the whole of the citizens turned out, each with something to cast against the door of the bride—for we should mention that such feasts are always given by the relatives of the girl. Nor did the citizens cease until the portals were broken open, and the thoroughfare completely blocked up with the shattered missiles."

Another old German custom in connexion with the feast held in the house of the bride's father on the night of the wedding had features of so unusual a character as to merit mention here. An excellent descriptive account of one of these celebrations is given by Mayhew, who writes : "As the clock strikes twelve at midnight, the most peculiar part of the entertainment takes place. Then two of the bridesmaids take the wreath from the bride's head, and the sprig of myrtle from the buttonhole of the bridegroom ; after which a handkerchief is tied over the eyes of the newly-married lady, and when her own myrtle wreath has been placed in her hand, the unmarried girls proceed to dance round her in a circle, while she tries to place the garland upon the head of one of the damsels skipping about her. Whoever may happen to have the wreath placed on her head is, as the belief runs, certain to be married within a year from that date. The same kind of ceremony goes on with the bridegroom, and while the single folk are dancing, the rest of the party sing certain verses to the air of the ' Bridesmaid's Chorus ', in *'Der Freischutz'*. When the dance and song are finished, a white muslin cap, which has been made by the bridesmaids expressly for the occasion, is placed upon the newly-married lady's head as a sign that she is now a dame ; while the gentlemen proceed to cover the head of the bridegroom with an ordinary white

cotton nightcap that has a tassel at the crown of it. This part
of the ceremony being ended, the company all seat themselves
again, and the drinking and jesting go on as before. In a few
minutes, however, one of the gentlemen disappears quietly under
the table and removes a garter from the leg of every one of the
ladies present, it being the custom with the damsels on such
occasions to wear bright ribbons expressly for this part of the
ceremony. The ribbon garters are then handed up above the
table and cut into small pieces for each of the gentlemen to wear
at his button-hole, like the decoration of the ' Legion of Honour '.
Nor must English people, who would hardly believe that such
a custom could exist among civilized folk at the present day,
imagine that this part of the bridal festivities prevails only among
the coarser grades of people. On the contrary, it is practised
at the entertainments even of the wealthier classes, and indeed
the ancient custom is not omitted at the wedding of royal
personages in Germany."[1]

Formerly pay weddings were very common in Germany.
They bore some resemblance to the penny weddings of Scotland.
After the German wedding, a feast was given, and on the table
at which the bride was seated, was a large basin or other receptacle
into which each guest placed either a sum of money, or an article
of value, as jewellery, gold, silver, etc. An alternative method
was for each guest to pay a fixed fee for the refreshments provided.

---

[1] Henry Mayhew, *German Life and Manners*, 1865, pp. 128–129. Apparently
Mayhew was unaware that a similar custom was at one time prevalent in England
(see page 227).

CHAPTER XVII

MARRIAGE RITES OF PRIMITIVE AND SAVAGE TRIBES

I

Curious Ceremonies Practised in the Old World

In savage and primitive society the marriage contract is really no more than the employment of magic ceremonies to render the union of the two parties unharmful to each other; or in other words to neutralize the injurious effects supposed to be inherent in contact between the two sexes. It is imperative that the ceremony should make it safe for the couple who are to be united in matrimony to live together. The male gives a portion of himself to the female, and vice versa; thus performing a magic rite exemplified in the use of a charm, which consists of something that has been in close personal contact with one party or the other. In the actual marriage ceremony this idea of union is expressed in the joining of hands. In many tribes nothing more than this is required to effect the marital union; though in certain cases there is some elaboration of the basic idea, as in the tying of one hand or one thumb of the bridegroom to one hand or one thumb of the bride. The giving of food may constitute a proposal of marriage and the taking of such a gift an acceptance of the proposal, as among the natives of Borneo.[1]

In most cases the actual ceremony of marriage is a simple enough affair, often the mere offer of presents to the girl's father and their acceptance concludes the matter, there being no religious rites of any kind. In other cases the mere fact of consummation constitutes marriage. Apropos of this, among the Hottentots, strangely enough, the marriage ceremony in some cases follows consummation. Moore says: " Hottentot marriages are made by the parents or nearest relations; and if the

[1] S. St. John, *Life in the Forests of the Far East*, 1862. Vol. I, p. 54.

female disapprove of the match, she is nevertheless compelled to pass the night with the man whom her friends have chosen. If he force her to consummation, she is constrained to become his wife ; but, on the contrary, if she preserves herself un-contaminated, she is ever after free from him. Should the nuptials take place, the day after an ox is killed to feast the company, who not only eat the flesh, but also besmear themselves with the blood and fat, powder themselves with a stuff they call *bucku*, and paint their cheeks with red chalk."[1] The same authority goes on to describe the actual wedding rites : " The marriage ceremony is thus performed : the men squat in a circle as, indeed, they do on most occasions, and the bridegroom is placed in the centre ; the women also, in the same manner, form another circle to surround the bride. The priest then goes from one circle to the other, and alternately urines on the bride and bridegroom, who make furrows with their nails in the grease with which they are plastered, in order to rub in the precious libation ; he then pronounces the nuptial benediction in the following words : ' May you live happily together ! May you have a son before a year is expired ! May he be a good hunts-man and a great warrior ! ' When they have dined, a pipe is filled with tobacco, which each successively smokes from, taking two or three whiffs, when they hand it to their neighbour. It is singular that, though the Hottentots are immoderately fond of spirituous liquors, music, and dancing, yet they use neither at their weddings."[2]

In Africa, at Sierra Leone, a curious custom was at one time observed. The girls of marriageable age, dressed in their best apparel, were assembled in the presence of their parents and the public generally, before whom they danced and in other ways displayed their charms and accomplishments. The young men of the village chose partners for themselves, and after giving presents to the respective fathers, led the girls away and married them.

In many African tribes we find the strange practice of the bridegroom donning female clothes before or at the time of marriage, in some cases the garments being the property of the girl he is going to marry. Crawley[3] cites several instances of

[1] Theophilus Moore, *Marriage Customs*, 1820, p. 218.
[2] Moore, op. cit., p. 219.
[3] See Ernest Crawley, *The Mystic Rose*. Vol. II, p. 116.

this custom, which would appear to be of very ancient origin and by no means restricted to any particular race or country.

The Kaffirs celebrate their marriages in a rather more elaborate manner than is usual among African tribes, and the following description given by Mr. Fynn, and quoted by the Rev. Joseph Shooter, is of interest : " Without entering into unimportant particulars, the general custom is that the bride, attended by all the young women in her neighbourhood, proceeds to the kraal of the bridegroom, escorted by her male relatives and friends bearing their assagais and shields. She is also attended by her mother, and other married women. The ceremony may commence immediately on the arrival of the bride, or on the following day, as may be arranged. When it commences, the bridegroom and his companions seat themselves on the ground, while the bride and her attendants approach within a short distance, dancing in a semicircle. The young men connected with the bridegroom soon unite in the dance ; the old women, who are related to the latter, dance around at a distance, addressing the bride in songs of a depressing nature, that she may not feel too highly elated, or assume too much importance in her new position. On the other hand, the old women who accompany her boast of her beauty and chastity, extolling her goodness of heart, and proclaiming how carefully she has been reared by her parents. The dance having continued for some time, the bride leaves her position and dances by herself in front of her companions. She then proceeds, accompanied by two of her bridesmaids, towards the bridegroom who is surrounded by his nearest relatives, and dances directly in front of him. It most frequently happens that the bride will take some liberty with the bridegroom just at this time, such as addressing him by some opprobrious term, or kicking dust in his face—thus intimating that the moment of her submission has not yet arrived. Her attendants then come forward with the unshafted assagais, beads, and picks, which are distributed by one of the bridesmaids to the nearest relatives of the bridegroom. An ox is slaughtered by the bridegroom, and feasting commences. This appears to be the fixing point of the ceremony. An ox or a cow is then given for slaughter to the bride's mother. Although dancing and other amusements be continued, the bridegroom and bride may from that moment be regarded as man and wife (so long as the relations of the bride remain at the bridegroom's kraal, the bride remains with her relatives), but she is not designated a wife until she has borne a child or has a house under her charge."[1]

In some tribes there are modifications of these rites. Shooter mentions one such, where the bridegroom, when he has decided on the time for the marriage to be celebrated, sends a cow to the girl's mother. When this occurs, the head of the bride is shaved, after which she goes to the kraal of the bridegroom, accompanied by relatives of both sexes. On arrival, presents are exchanged, and a hut is placed at the disposal of the various members of the party, in which they pass the night. Next morning they leave the kraal, camping outside in the grass, gipsy-fashion. The male friends of the bride then return to the bridegroom's kraal for the purpose of claiming the ox, which represents the crux of the ceremonial procedure.

A strange custom of the tribe of Moors at Benowm, in the interior of Africa, is described by Mungo Park, the explorer. He writes : " In the evening (April 10th) the Tabala, or large drum was beat to announce a wedding, which was held at one of the neighbouring tents. A great number of people of both sexes assembled, but without that mirth and hilarity which take place at a Negro wedding : here was neither singing, nor dancing; nor any other amusement that I could perceive. A woman was beating the drum, and the other women joining at times like a chorus, by setting up a shrill scream, and at the same time, moving their tongues from one side of the mouth to the other with great celerity. I was soon tired, and had returned into my hut, where I was sitting, almost asleep, when an old woman entered, with a wooden bowl in her hand, and signified that she had brought me a present from the bride. Before I could recover from the surprise which this message created, the woman discharged the contents of the bowl full in my face. Finding it was the same sort of holy water, with which, among the Hottentots, a priest is said to sprinkle a new-married couple,[2] I began to suspect that the old lady was actuated by mischief, or malice ; but she gave me seriously to understand, that it was a nuptial benediction from the bride's own person ; and which, on such occasions, is always received by the young unmarried

---

[1] Joseph Shooter, *The Kaffirs of Natal and the Zulu Country*, London, 1857, pp. 72–74.
[2] The liquid used was obviously urine. For a description of the rite practised by the Hottentots, see page 200.

THE PARADE OF UNMARRIED GIRLS, ONTONG JAVA

From H. Ian Hogbin's *Law and Order in Polynesia*, 1934

A MALAY BRIDE: THE HONEYMOON

The ornaments are suspended to the bridal
bedstead for a month

From Carl Bock's *The Head-Hunters of Borneo*, 1881

Moors as a mark of distinguished favour. This being the case, I wiped my face, and sent my acknowledgments to the lady. The wedding drum continued to beat, and the women to sing, or rather to whistle, all night. About nine in the morning, the bride was brought in state from her mother's tent, attended by a number of women who carried her tent (a present from her husband), some bearing up the poles, others holding by the strings, and in this manner they marched, whistling as formerly, until they came to the places appointed for her residence, where they pitched the tent. The husband followed, with a number of men leading four bullocks, which they tied to the tent strings : and having killed another and distributed the beef among the people, the ceremony was concluded."[1]

The marriage ceremony of the Mandingo negroes inhabiting the interior of Africa, is described by this same author, who witnessed a wedding at Kamalia, thus : " When the day for celebrating the nuptials is fixed on, a select number of people are invited to be present at the wedding : a bullock or goat is killed, and great plenty of victuals dressed for the occasion. As soon as it is dark, the bride is conducted into a hut, where a company of matrons assist in arranging the wedding dress, which is always white cotton, and is put on in such a manner as to conceal the bride from head to foot. Thus arrayed, she is seated upon a mat, in the middle of the floor, and the old women place themselves in a circle round her. They then give her a series of instructions, and point out, with great propriety, what ought to be her future conduct in life. This scene of instruction, however, is frequently interrupted by girls, who amuse the company with songs and dances, which are rather more remarkable for their gaiety than delicacy. While the bride remains within the hut with the women, the bridegroom devotes his attention to the guests of both sexes, who assemble without doors, and by distributing among them small presents of kolla-nuts, and seeing that everyone partakes of the good cheer which is provided, he contributes much to the general hilarity of the evening. When supper is ended, the company spend the remainder of the night in singing and dancing, and seldom separate until daybreak. About midnight, the bride is privately conducted by the women into the hut which is to be her future residence, and the bridegroom, upon a signal given, retires from

[1] Mungo Park, *Travels in the Interior Districts of Africa*, 1816. Vol. I, pp. 133–134

his company. The new married couple, however, are always disturbed towards morning by the women, who assemble to inspect the nuptial sheet (according to the manners of the ancient Hebrews, as recorded in Scripture[1]), and dance round it. This ceremony is thought indispensably necessary, nor is the marriage considered as valid without it."[2]

The South Sea Islands missionary, John Williams, describes a wedding witnessed in the Island of Savaii, the largest of the Navigator group. A chief named Malietoa, who was about to marry a handsome girl whom he had purchased, sent a message to the missionary, inviting him and his party to attend the ceremony. The following account of the proceedings, because of its exceptional interest, is given as written by Williams nearly a century and a half ago : "A group of women, seated under the shade of a noble tree, which stood at a short distance from the house, chaunted, in a pleasing and lively air, the heroic deeds of the old chieftain and his ancestors, and opposite to them, beneath the spreading branches of a bread-fruit tree sat the newly-purchased bride, a tall and beautiful young woman, about 18 years of age. Her dress was a fine mat, fastened round the waist, reaching nearly to her ankles ; while a wreath of leaves and flowers, ingeniously and tastefully entwined, decorated her brow. The upper part of her person was anointed with sweet-scented coco-nut oil, and tinged partially with a rouge prepared from the turmeric root, and round her neck were two rows of large blue beads. Her whole deportment was pleasingly modest. While listening to the chaunters, and looking upon the novel scene before us, our attention was attracted by another company of women, who were following each other in single file, and chaunting as they came the praises of their chief. Sitting down with the company who had preceded them, they united in one general chorus, which appeared to be a recital of the valorous deeds of Malietoa and his progenitors. This ended, a dance in honour of the marriage was commenced, which was considered one of their grandest exhibitions, and held in high estimation by the people. The performers were four young women, all daughters of chiefs, of the highest rank, who took their stations at right angles, on the fine mats with which the dancing-house was spread for the occasion, and they interchanged

[1] See page 33.
[2] Mungo Park, op. cit. Vol. I, pp. 260–261.

positions with slow and graceful movements both of their hands and feet, while the bride recited some of the mighty doings of her forefathers.   To the motions of the dancers, and to the recital of the bride, three or four elderly women were beating time upon the mat with short sticks, and occasionally joining in chorus with the recitative.   We saw nothing in the performance worthy of admiration, except the absence of everything indelicate —a rare omission in heathen amusements.   We were informed that most of the wives of the principal chiefs were purchased ; and that if a sufficient price is paid to the relative, the young woman seldom refuses to go, though the purchaser be ever so old and unlovely."[1]

The members of one of the tribes of Borneo, the Bindjoos, according to the anonymous author of *Marriage Ceremonies*, were addicted to curious practices in connexion with their weddings. To be eligible for marriage the young man must have killed a member of an enemy tribe, and in the event of his wife dying, a second marriage depended upon a second killing.   On the wedding day, says this writer, after feasts had been given, the bridegroom washed his hands in the blood of a freshly-killed cock, while the bride washed hers in that of a hen.   They then presented to each other their blood-dripping hands, after which another feast closed the ceremony.

II

Curious Ceremonies Practised in the New World

Among the North American Indians marriages have always been simple affairs.   In fact, because of their inherent simplicity, Little went so far as to suggest that they hardly deserved the name of marriages at all.   There were, however, variations in respect of different tribes, in some cases a rather peculiar cere- mony being observed.   When the wedding had been announced, all the relatives and friends of both sides assembled in the cabin of the oldest branch of the families, irrespective of nearness of kindred, and there danced and feasted for a time.   This part of

---

[1] John Williams, *A Narrative of Missionary Enterprises in the South Sea Islands*, 1837, pp. 348–349.

the ceremony being ended, all those present, with the exception of four of the oldest relatives of the bridegroom and a similar number of the oldest relatives of the bride, retired. The bridegroom and bride then stood upon a large mat, holding a wooden rod in a horizontal position between them, while the eldest of the males delivered a short address on conjugal duties, etc. The sermon concluded, the couple, after singing and dancing together, broke the rod into as many pieces as there were persons present, and to each of these witnesses one of the pieces was presented : it was their duty to preserve the fragments as evidence of the marriage having taken place. An entertainment followed, after which the bride was escorted to her parents' home, where she was visited occasionally by her husband until she gave birth to her first child. If in due course no issue was forthcoming, or if for any reason the couple wished to separate, an assembly was again called and the various witnesses of the wedding were requested to produce the fragments of the rod in their possession. These fragments were reassembled, in the presence of the husband and wife, and then cast into a fire, thus dissolving the marriage.

Carver, to whom we are indebted for much information respecting the customs of the North American Indians, says that although in the main the tribes differ very little from each other as regards their marriage rites, there are some exceptions. "The Naudowesses," he writes, "have a singular method of celebrating their marriages, which seems to bear no resemblance to those made use of by any other nation I passed through. When one of their young men has fixed on a young woman he approves of, he discovers his passion to her parents, who give him an invitation to come and live with them in their tent. He accordingly accepts the offer, and by so doing engages to reside in it for a whole year in the character of a menial servant. During this time he hunts, and brings all the game he kills to the family, by which means the father has an opportunity of seeing whether he is able to provide for the support of his daughter and the children that might be the consequence of their union. This however is only done while they are young men, and for their first wife, and not repeated like Jacob's servitude. When this period is expired, the marriage is solemnized after the custom of the country, in the following manner : three or four of the oldest male relations of the bridegroom, and as many of the bride's, accompany the young couple from their respective tents to an open part in the centre of the camp. The chiefs and warriors being here assembled to receive them, a party of the latter are drawn up in two ranks on each side of the bride and bridegroom immediately on their arrival. The principal chief then acquaints the whole assembly with the design of their meeting, and tells them that the couple before them, mentioning at the same time their names, are come to avow publicly their intentions of living together as man and wife. He then asks the two young people alternately, whether they desire that the union might take place. Having declared in an audible voice that they do so, the warriors fix their arrows, and discharge them over the heads of the pair; this done, the chief pronounces them man and wife. The bridegroom then turns round, and bending his body, takes his wife on his back, in which manner he carries her, amid the acclamations of the spectators, to his tent. This ceremony is succeeded by the most plentiful feast the new married man can afford, and songs and dances, according to the usual custom, conclude the festival."[1]

A marriage rite peculiar to the Elk nation, is described by Tegg. The Elks, he says, raised vast mounds. Five of these were used in connexion with matrimonial ceremonies. " The prophets, perceiving that compulsory matrimonial unions engendered strife, instituted a ceremony by which females might have power to escape unwilling thraldom, without infringing on the right of the parent to bestow the child. The ceremonial consisted in running the ring or circular trail around the matrimonial mounds, that were slightly elevated, and made level and smooth. During the annual feasts, the resident prophet occupied the summit of the prophet's matrimonial altar, dedicated to the nation of which they were members. On the appearance of a male at the base of the altar, the prophet ascended it, and the suitor took a position east of the altar and at its centre, the female taking hers on the west. All being now ready, the prophet commands the man to pursue his bride. They both start at full speed ; and if she is overtaken before she makes three circuits of the altar, she is his bride ; otherwise, he may not receive her in marriage."[2]

In seventeenth-century Mexico there were many elaborate observances before a marriage was celebrated and these were

[1] J. Carver, *Travels Through the Interior Parts of North America in the years* 1766, 1767, *and* 1768, London, 1781, pp. 372–374.
[2] Wm. Tegg, *The Knot Tied*, 1877, p. 268.

carried out for the most part by the man's parents. After a girl had been chosen as potentially suitable, a sorcerer was consulted, and if the projected alliance was deemed to be inauspicious, further search was made until the right female was hit upon. The girl's parents were then approached, and, usually after considerable delay and feigned reluctance, the wedding was arranged. On the day appointed, the bride, accompanied by relatives, friends and musicians, visited the bridegroom's house, where they were received by his parents and the priest who was to officiate. The couple then seated themselves on a mat spread in the centre of a room containing a fire, which was regarded as a mediator in all disputes between husband and wife. The priest then tied one corner of the bride's veil or of her gown to the bridegroom's mantle, a procedure of special importance as it signified the wish of the couple to be inseparable. Thus joined, for seven successive times they marched behind the priest around the fire, then they again seated themselves on the mat at equal distances from the fire, so as to share its warmth equally. In this position they offered copal to the gods and exchanged presents. This completed the marriage ceremony. In the evening the wedding was celebrated with a feast. In some cases, instead of going to the bridegroom's home for this ceremony, the couple went to a temple, where the tying process was carried out by the priest, after which, still tied together, they, with the cleric, walked to the house of the bridegroom, where the circumnavigation of the fire was enacted. When night came, the bride, escorted by several female friends, each of whom held a lighted torch, walked to the bridegroom's house.

A peculiar rite at one time observed in some parts of Mexico, was the cutting away, by the priest, of part of the bride's hair ; also, the bridegroom carried the bride for a little while upon his back as part of the ritual. In another part, any man desirous of taking a wife presented himself at the nearest temple. On learning his wish the priests, placing him in front of the idol, and in full view of the congregation, cut off part of his hair, and announced that here was a man who required a wife. It was the rule that on leaving the temple he must accept as wife the first unmarried female he encountered.

Turning to South America we find among the most singular marriage rites those observed in Peru. The ancient inhabitants of this country were sun-worshippers and the chief priest of the

HOW THE KING OF FIJI
RULED HIS WIVES

A MEMBER OF THE FAN TRIBE
OF WEST AFRICA BARGAINING
FOR A BRIDE

From James Greenwood's *Curiosities
of Savage Life*, 1863

sun, termed the Inca, who was the highest and most powerful personage in the State, once every year, in the town of Cusco, caused all the young men who had that year attained the age of 24 years and the young women who had reached 18 years, to assemble. These were the earliest ages at which marriage was permitted. The young men and girls formed a circle around the seated Inca. He called them by name in turn, presenting one to the other, and exacted from each pair a promise of mutual fidelity. They were then free to marry.

The Indians visited by Depons had a very simple marriage ceremony. The relations, friends, and neighbours of both bridegroom and bride were invited. The male brought wood and other materials for the building of a hut ; while the females provided meat, fish, fruit and bread for a feast in celebration of the wedding. The men sang an epithalamium to the bridegroom and the women sang one to the bride. Dancing, singing and feasting continued until darkness came, when the bride was presented to the bridegroom, and this terminated the ceremony.[1]

Among the natives of Darien (Central America), a strange marriage ceremony was formerly in vogue. On announcing their wish to be married, the young couple, with their respective fathers, were taken into a cabin, where the bridegroom's father delivered a harangue. Holding in his hands a bow and arrows, the point of one arrow being directed towards the young man and the point of the other arrow towards the girl, he danced around them until he had to stop from sheer exhaustion ; then, after resting a while, he adopted a kneeling posture, and presented his son to the bride, whose father also went through a similar performance. At the conclusion of the ceremony, affirms Moore, " a party of men begin to cut down trees and clear a spot of ground, on which they plant Indian corn for the future support of the young couple."[2]

In the South Seas, notably at Otaheite, one of the Society Islands, according to the accounts of missionaries, curious rites were practised. A rude altar was first erected in the house of either the bridegroom or the bride. It was covered with a white cloth, and on this cloth were placed the clothes that had enclosed the tomb of the bride's father. The couple, their relatives and friends, now repaired to the family burial place, where a large

---

[1] F. Depons, *Travels in South America*, 1807, p. 208.
[2] Theophilus Moore, *Marriage Customs*, 1820, p. 261.

sheet of white cloth was spread on the ground. The bridegroom and bride then changed into their wedding apparel, and all was ready for the most important part of the ceremony. The bride's mother, assisted by two or three of her female relations, proceeded to break a sugar-cane into small pieces ; these were laid upon the leaves of a tree called *amai* ; then, causing the blood to flow from their own arms or bodies with incisions made by shark's teeth, they allowed this blood to fall on the sugar-cane and leaves, which were then presented to the bridegroom and bride. These leaves, with the blood and sugar-cane upon them, were then offered to the supposed god of the family. In one instance, says Moore, " the mother of the bride, who was advanced in years, appeared thoughtful, and produced the skulls of her deceased husband and elder brother, which, according to the custom of the country, she had preserved and anointed with coco-nut oil. The skulls were held before the leaves, sugar-cane, and blood, at the time of presentation to the parties. After these ceremonies, the cloth spread upon the *morai* (burying-place) was taken up and sent as a present to the chief. The clothes put on by the couple at the *morai* are considered as sacred, and not to be worn in common. There are also various forms that succeed marriage. If the woman be a virgin, the father and mother perform an *amooa*, or offering, of a hog or fowl, and a plantain tree to their son-in-law, before they may eat of his provisions ; but not if she be a widow, or have been repudiated. The bride's relations make presents of cloth, hogs, etc., to the new-married pair."[1]

[1] Moore, op. cit., pp. 330–331.

CHAPTER XVIII

MARRIAGE CUSTOMS OF GREAT BRITAIN AND AMERICA IN OLDEN TIMES

I

Curious Old Wedding Customs

BEFORE Christianity was introduced to Britain marriage was a very simple affair, into which religious observances did not enter. It was a civil institution amounting to nothing more than an arrangement between the father of the female and the male who wished to marry her.

And for a long time marriage continued to be free from ecclesiastical domination. Polygyny and polyandry were both frowned upon by the early Anglo-Saxons. Every girl was in the custody of her father or other near male relative.

The marriage itself, if history does not lie, was devoid of the ostentation which was so marked a feature, even in those times, of the ceremonies observed in so many other lands. The day previous to the wedding was, for the bridegroom and his friends, a day of feasting. Next morning a party of these friends rode over to the bride's house and escorted her to her lover. With the bride, on this for her momentous journey, went a matron, called a brideswoman, a number of bridesmaids, the bride's guardian and several male relatives. The entire company, bride, bridegroom and their respective attendants, then went to the church. The presence of the bride's guardian was essential. A veil or piece of cloth was held over the heads of the bride and bridegroom, and the priest then gave the nuptial benediction, after which both parties to the contract were crowned with flowers. This custom is referred to in the " Clerk of Oxenford's Tale " by Chaucer, who says that at her marriage Grisild had " a coronne on hire hed."

In the early days of Christianity it was not essential that the marriage knot should be tied by a priest or that a religious ceremony of any kind should be performed ; though it is true that most couples did approach the priest with the object of securing his blessing and thus giving to the union a more favourable and propitious aspect. It was not until well into the sixteenth century, in 1563 to be precise, that the Council of Trent, by a ruling which enacted that the validity of a Catholic marriage depended upon its consecration by a priest, altered radically the position. In the reign of the first Henry an Act was passed making the validity of a marriage dependent upon the contract being made in the presence of witnesses.

One of the regulations imposed by the Church was the publication of the banns, by which was meant the proclamation to the church congregation of the intention of the man and woman named to be joined together in holy matrimony. The aim of this regulation was to prevent clandestine marriages, and it may be said to have succeeded to the extent that it was within the power of the church to do this. According to Tertullian, every marriage that was not previously announced to the congregation of the church ranked as a clandestine union, and might even be considered to constitute in its consummation an act of fornication. The aim of the Church was to discover whether there existed any just cause why the parties should not be joined in wedlock, and to this end it was ordained that the publication should be made on three several Sundays preceding the day fixed for the solemnization of the marriage during divine service in the church of the parish in which the parties dwelt, or if the man and woman lived in different parishes the banns should be read in the churches of both. To-day the banns of marriage are read in English churches in accordance with the expressed object of discovering if there be any just cause why the ceremony should not take place. But in its early conception, at any rate, the regulation went much farther than anything conceivable nowadays : its main aim was to discover whether either party, by some secret act of promiscuity, was already married or had been guilty of some immorality which would render the proposed alliance a breach of the laws concerning consanguinity. According to the Church, the mere fact of intercourse, irrespective of any matrimonial intention or promise, resulted in the near relatives of the person with whom secret intercourse had been committed ranking as within the prohibited degrees of consanguinity just as though a marriage, celebrated in an ecclesiastical manner, had taken place. Apropos of this, Jeaffreson mentions the case of Janet Betoun, the Lady Buccleugh of Scott's *Lay of the Last Minstrel*, who, in order to be released from her marriage to Simon Preston of Craigmillar, confessed in a spiritual court " that before her marriage she had been guilty of a particular offence with Walter Scott of Buccleugh, who was her husband's cousin within the prohibited degrees."[1] The marriage, which it was held had never been a true marriage, was annulled.

A curious sixteenth century custom was the carrying of a knife by the bride during the wedding ceremony. This knife, the hilt of which was usually jewelled, was encased in an ornamented and engraved sheath of gold, and hung from a girdle. Contemporary literature contains several references to the practice. Thus Dekker (*Match Me in London*) has the following :—

> " See at my girdle hang my wedding-knives."

Then there is the passage from Davison (*Poetical Rhapsody*, 1601):—

> " Fortune doth give these paire of knives to you,
> To cut the thred of love if't be not true."

And in *The Witch of Edmonton*, we read :—

> " But see, the bridegroom and bride come ; the new pair of Sheffield knives fitted both to one sheath."

At one time, too, the bride was accustomed to allow her hair, which it was fashionable in those days to wear long, to hang loosely behind in a dishevelled manner. In this way did Anne Boleyn go to the altar with King Henry the Eighth.[2] In his play, *The White Devil*, John Webster mentions this custom :—

> "And let them dangle loose as a bride's hair."

Another practice which formerly was seldom omitted from an English wedding was the strewing of herbs and flowers along the path leading from the church, immediately before the bride and bridegroom trod it. Braithwaite refers to the custom in his *Straffado for the Divell* (1615) thus :

> "All haile to Hymen and his marriage day.
> Strew rushes, and quickly come away ;
> Strew rushes, maides ; and even as you strew,
> Think one day, maides, like will be done for you."

---

[1] John Cordy Jeaffreson, *Brides and Bridals*, 1872, p. 117.
[2] England Howlett in the chapter entitled " Marriage Customs " in *Curious Church Customs*, edited by William Andrews, Hull, 1895, p. 105.

George Smith, writing in 1770, says of a bride :

"Now, like the gather'd flow'rs that strew'd her way,
    Forc'd from my love, untimely I decay."

Brooke (*England's Helicon*) has this reference :
    "Now busie maydens strew sweet flowres."

And finally from Rowe (*Happy Village*, 1796) :
    "The wheaten ear was scatter'd near the porch,
    The green bloom blossom'd strew'd the way to church."

At one time it was customary for the guests to throw money over the heads of the bride and bridegroom. Apropos of this, Wood gives several references to the practice, taken from the Wardrobe Accounts of Edward II. "Thus, on the 26th of June, in the tenth year of that king's reign, money to the value of £2.10.0. was 'thrown over the heads of Oliver de Bourdeaux and the Lady Maud Trussel during the solemnization of their nuptials, at the door of the chapel within the park of Woodstock, by the King's order.' Again, on the 9th of February, 1321, money to the amount of £2 was 'thrown by the King's order at the door of the King's Chapel, within the manor of Havering-atte-Boure, during the solemnization of the marriage between Richard, son of Edmund, Earl of Arundel, and Isabella, daughter of Sir Hugh Le de Spenser, junior.' "[1]

The custom of handing out wedding favours, consisting of rosettes, to the guests, has gone out of fashion, though the wearing of white carnations still continues. The men wore favours of various coloured ribbons, in accord with the bride's selection or wishes, on their arms, breasts, or hats. Ben Jonson refers to this practice thus :

"Let us know your bride's colours and yours at least ", and in *The Collier's Wedding* there are the following revealing lines :

"The blithsome, bucksome country maids,
    With knots of ribbands at their heads,
    And pinners flutt'ring in the wind,
    That fan before and toss behind."

These ribbons were in the form of true-love knots ; from time immemorial the knot having been an emblem of the ties of duty and fidelity between lovers. The custom came to us from the Danes.

Wine-drinking in the church was formerly a common practice

[1] Edward J. Wood, *The Wedding Day in All Ages and Countries*, 1869. Vol. II, p. 176.

at English weddings. It was essential that the wine, and any cakes which were soaked in it, as well as the wine-cup, should first receive the priest's blessing. The bride-cup, as it was called, was carried before the bride, and from it, all the persons present, as well as the newly-married couple, were expected to drink in the church. " This custom was prevalent, in Shakespeare's time, among every description of people, from the regal head to the thoroughpaced rustic; accordingly, we are informed, on the testimony of an assisting witness, that the same ceremony took place at the marriage of the Elector Palatine to King James's daughter, on the 14th day of February, 1612–13 : there was ' in conclusion ', he relates, ' a joy pronounced by the King and Queen and seconded with congratulations of the lords there present, which crowned with draughts of *Ippocras* out of a *great golden bowle*, as a health to the prosperity of the marriage (began by the prince Palatine and answered by the princess). After which were served up by six or seven barons so many bowles filled with wafers, so much of that work was consummate."[1]

Another notable wedding where the custom was observed, was that of Queen Mary and Philip of Spain in 1554. There are many references to it in contemporary literature. Beaumont and Fletcher's play, *Scornful Lady*, contains the passage :

> " If my wedding-smock were on,
> Were the gloves bought and given, the licence come,
> Were the rosemary[2] branches dipp'd, and all
> The hippocras and cakes eat and drunk off;
> Were these two arms encompass'd with the hands
> Of bachelors to lead me to the church."

In Shakespeare's *Taming of the Shrew*, Petruchio drinks wine and throws sops in the sexton's face :

> " He calls for wine :—A health, quoth he ; as if
> He had been aboard, carousing to his mates
> After a storm :—Quaff'd off the muscadel,
> And threw the sops all in the sexton's face ;—
> This done, he took the bride about the neck ;
> And kiss'd her lips with such a clamorous smack,
> That, at the parting, all the church did echo."

[1] Quoted by Nathan Drake from Reeds's Shakespeare, Vol. IX, p. 115 *n*. (a quotation from Finet's Philoxenis, 1656).

[2] Rosemary, supposed to have a stimulating effect on the memory, gained a reputation as a symbol of fidelity, hence its popularity in connexion with weddings : a sprig was often dipped in the bride-cup, also it was used in ornamenting the bridal-bed. Ophelia says : " There's rosemary, that's for remembrance ; pray you, love, remember."

Again, in Armin's *History of the Two Maids of Moreclacke* (1609) a servant refers to the practice in the words : " The muscadine stays for the bride at church" ; and Dekker (*Satirio-Mastix,* 1602) has the passage : "And when we are at church bring the wine and cakes."

Other names were sometimes given to the bride-cup or bride-bowl, notably the knitting-cup and contracting-cup. In Ben Jonson's *Magnetick Lady* appear the lines :

> " Mind
> The Parson's pint t'engage him—
> A knitting-cup there must be."

And in Middleton's *No Wit, no Help like a Woman's,* we read :

> " Even when my lip touch'd the contracting cup."

At that time an English rustic wedding was termed a bride-ale. Of this curious ceremony an excellent description is available in Robert Laneham's *Letter on the Queen's Entertainment at Kenelworth Castle,* in the year 1575, this entertainment including a representation of a country Bride-ale exhibited in the great court of the castle. The description is as follows : " Thus were they marshalled. First, all the lustie lads and bold bachelors of the parish, suitably every wight with his blue buckram bridelace upon a branch of green broom (cause rosemary is scant there) tied on his left arm (for a that side lies the heart), and his alder poll for a spear in his right hand, in martial order ranged on afore, two and two in a rank : Some with a hat, some in a cap, some a coat, some a jerkin, some for lightness in his doublet and his hose, clean trust with a point afore : Some boots and no spurs, he spurs and no boots, and he neither one nor t'other : One a saddle, another a pad or a pannel fastened with a cord, for girts wear geazon : and these to the number of sixteen wight riding men and well beseem : But the bridegroom foremost, in his father's tawny worsted jacket (for his friends were fain that he should be a bridegroom before the *Queen*), a fair straw hat with a capital crown, steeplewise on his head : a pair of harvest gloves on his hands, as a sign of good husbandry ; a pen and inkhorn at his back, for he would be known to be bookish ; lame of a leg that in his youth was broken at football : Well beloved yet of his mother, that lent him a new mufflar for a napkin that was tied to his girdle for losing. I was no small sport to mark this minion in his full appointment, that through good schoolation

became as formal in his action, as had he been a bridegroom
indeed ; with this special grace by the way that ever as he would
have framed him the better countenance, with the worse face
he looked.

"Well, Sir, after these horsemen, a lively morrice-dance,
according to the ancient manner ; six dancers, maid-marian, and
the fool. Then three pretty puzels (maids or damsels from
pucelle), as bright as a breast of bacon, of a thirty year old a piece,
that carried three special spice-cakes of a bushel of wheat (they
had it by measure out of my *Lords* backhouse), before the bride:
Cicely with set countenance, and lips so demurely simpering, as
it had been a mare cropping of a thistle. After these, a lovely
lubber woorts,[1] freckle-faced, red-headed, clean-trussed in his
doublet and his hose taken up now indeed by commission, for
that he was so loth to come forward, for reverence belike of his
new cut canvass doublet ; and would by his good will have been
but a gazer, but found to be a meet actor for his office : That
was to bear the bride-cup, formed of a sweet sucket barrel, a
faire-turned foot set to it, all seemly besilvered and parcel gilt,
adorned with a beautiful branch of broom, gayly begilded for
rosemary ; from which, two broad bride laces of red and yellow
buckram begilded, and gallantly streaming by such wind as there
was, for he carried it aloft : This gentle cup-bearer, yet had his
freckled physiognomy somewhat unhappily infested as he went,
by the busy flies, that flocked about the bride-cup for the sweet-
ness of the sucket that it savoured on ; but he, like a tall fellow,
withstood their malice stoutly (see what manhood may do), beat
them away, killed them by scores, stood to his charge, and marched
on in good order. Then followed the worshipful bride, led (after
the country manner) between two ancient parishioners, honest
townsmen. But a stale stallion, and a well spred (hot as the
weather was) God wot, and ill smelling was she ; a thirty-five
year old, of colour brown-bay not very beautiful indeed, but
ugly, foul, ill-favoured ; yet marvellous vain of the office, because she heard say she should dance before the *Queen*, in which
feat she thought she would foot it as finely as the best : Well,
after this bride, came three by two and two, a dozen damsels for
bride-maids ; that for favor, attyre, for fashion and cleanliness,
were as meet for such a bride as a treen ladle for a porridge-pot ;

---

[1] *Woorts* : of this word I know not the precise meaning ; but suppose it is
meant to imply *plodded* or *stumbled on*.

more (but for fear of carrying all clean) had been appointed, but these few were enow."[1]

It has been suggested that the custom of holding the marriage service at the church porch instead of within the church itself, arose from a desire to give to the ceremony the greatest possible degree of publicity.   In support of this contention is the fact that an important feature of the church porch marriage was the disclosure in the presence of the assembled guests and onlookers of the amount of the bride's dower, which became the property of the husband immediately the marriage was completed, and according to Selden the assignment of the dower could be made at the church door only.   Another suggested reason for the practice was the firm opinion of the theologians that to hold a marriage ceremony within the church was a sacrilegious procedure.   In view of the denunciation of all forms of sexual expression by the early Christians, and their undiluted approval of asceticism generally, I am inclined to think that the reluctance of ecclesiastical authority to adopt a measure which seemed to favour the departure in any way from the ideological concept of rigid asceticism may have had a good deal to do with the origin and continuation of the custom.

There is some dispute as to when exactly the practice arose, many historians appearing to think it started in England about the time of the Norman Conquest ; but Jeaffreson, whose views are certainly worthy of respect, is of opinion that this statement is based on the most dubious evidence, and says " it seems probable that the custom of the porch which existed in Norman England may have been general, if not universal, before the Conquest."[2]

In Chaucer's story of " The Wife of Bath " is the boast "Husbands at churche doore have I had five."   In 1299, Edward the First was married to Marguerite of France at the door of Canterbury Cathedral.   When Henry the Second's daughter, Elizabeth of France, was married to Philip the Second of Spain, Eustache de Bellay, Bishop of Paris, performed the ceremony at the door of Notre Dame ; and in 1579, at the door of this same church, Henrietta Maria was married to King Charles by proxy.

In the reign of Edward the Sixth, however, the ban on the bride and bridegroom being united in the church itself was lifted,

---

[1] Quoted by Nathan Drake from Nichols's *Queen Elizabeth's Progresses*. Vol. 1 —Laneham's Letter, pp. 18–20.

[2] John Cordy Jeaffreson, *Brides and Bridals*, 1872, p. 49.

and in consequence church porch marriages became noticeably fewer. Queen Mary reintroduced the ban, but it was finally rescinded when domination by the Protestant religion became complete.

One result of the custom was that the weather loomed large in importance on the wedding day, and it was customary to celebrate most unions in summer : a rainy day, in an era when the umbrella was unknown, and it was usual for the principals, attendants, and guests at weddings to make the journey on foot, meant prolonged inconvenience and unpleasantness. This anxiety about the elements is well expressed in the following lines, which Marchant, to whom I am indebted for the quotation, reproduces :

" Ring out the merry bell ; the bride approaches :
The blush upon her cheeks hath shamed the morning,
For that is dawning palely. Grant, good saints,
These clouds betoken naught of evil omen ! "[1]

Ranking among the most extraordinary of marriage ceremonies, is that of the Scottish Gipsies. The following account is from Simson's valuable historical work : "A marriage cup, or bowl, made out of solid wood, and of a capacity to contain about two Scotch pints, or about one gallon, is made use of at the ceremony. After the wedding-party is assembled, and everything prepared for the occasion, the priest takes the bowl and gives it to the bride, who passes urine into it ; it is then handed, for a similar purpose, to the bridegroom. After this, the priest takes a quantity of earth from the ground, and throws it into the bowl, adding sometimes a quantity of brandy to the mixture. He then stirs the whole together, with a spoon made of a ram's horn, and sometimes with a large ram's horn itself, which he wears suspended from his neck by a string. He then presents the bowl, with its contents, first to the bride, and then to the bridegroom ; calling at the same time upon each to separate the mixture in the bowl, if they can. The young couple are then ordered to join hands over the bowl containing the earth, urine, and spirits ; when the priest, in an audible voice, and in the Gipsy language, pronounces the parties to be husband and wife ; and as none can separate the mixture in the bowl, so they, in their persons, cannot be separated till death dissolves their union. As soon as that part of the ceremony is performed, the couple undress, and repair to their nuptial couch. After remaining there for a considerable time, some of the most

---

[1] Marchant does not give the source of this quotation.

confidential relatives of the married couple are admitted to the apartment, as witnesses to the virginity of the bride; certain tokens being produced to the examining friends, at this stage of the ceremony. If all the parties concerned are satisfied, the bride receives a handsome present from the friends, as a mark of their respect for her remaining chaste till the hour of her marriage. This present is, in some instances, a box of a particular construction. These matters being settled on the spot, the wedded pair rise from the marriage-bed, again dress themselves in their finest apparel, and again join the wedding-party. The joy and happiness on all sides is now excessive. There is nothing to be heard or seen but fiddling and piping, dancing, feasting, and drinking, which are kept up, with the utmost spirit and hilarity imaginable, for many hours together. The nuptial mixture is carefully bottled up, and the bottle marked with the Roman character, M. In this state, it is buried in the earth, or kept in their houses or tents, and is carefully preserved, as evidence of the marriage of the parties. When it is buried in the fields, the husband and wife to whom it belongs frequently repair to the spot, and look at it, for the purpose of keeping them in remembrance of their nuptial vows. Small quantities of the compound are also given to individuals of the tribe, to be used for certain rare purposes, such, perhaps, as pieces of the bride's cake are used for dreaming-bread, among the natives of Scotland, at the present day."[1]

A curious custom common among the poorer classes in Scotland during the seventeenth century was for the guests to provide the money to pay for the wedding feast and to give the couple a start in their life together. These "Penny Weddings", as they were called, were the scenes of much merriment and rejoicing. In an amusing song,[2] Francis Semple has described such an occasion, thus :—

> " Fy let us a' to the bridal,
>   For there'll be liltin' there,
> For Jock's to be married to Maggie,
>   The lass wi' the gowden hair ;
> And there'll be lang-kale with pottage,
>   And bannocks o' barley meal ;
> And there'll be good saut herrin',
>   To relish a cogue o' gude yill.

[1] Walter Simson, A History of the Gipsies, London, 1865, pp. 261–263.
[2] Quoted by Charles Rogers in Scotland, Social and Domestic, 1869, pp. 113–114.

> And there'll be Sandie the souter,
>   And Will wi' the mickle mou',
> And there'll be Tam the plouter,
>   And Andrew the tinkler, I trow;
> And there'll be bow-leggit Robbie,
>   Wi' thoomless Katie's gudeman,
> And there'll be blue-cheekit Dallie,
>   An' Laurie, the laird o' the lan'.
>
> And there'll be girnagain Gibbie,
>   And his glaikit wife, Jennie Bell,
> And mizly-chinned flytin' Geordie,
>   The lad that was skipper himsel';
> There'll be a' the lads wi' the lasses,
>   Sit down in the mids o' the ha',
> Wi' sybows and reefarts and carlins,
>   That are baith sodden an' raw.
>
> And there'll be badges an' brachen,
>   And fouth o' gude gabbocks o' skate,
> Powsoudie and drummock an' crowdie,
>   And caller nouts put on a plate.
> And there'll be meal-kail an' castocks,
>   Wi' skink to sup till ye rive;
> And roasts to roast on a brander
>   An' flouks that were taken alive.
>
> Scraped haddocks, wilks, dulse an' tangle,
>   And a mill o' gude sneeshin' to pree;
> When weary wi' eatin' an' drinkin',
>   We'll sup and dance till we dee.
> Fy, let us a' to the bridal,
>   For there'll be liltin' there,
> For Jock's to be married to Maggie,
>   The lass wi' the gowden hair."

Rogers, the historian, says the Penny Bridals had, in the seventeenth century, degenerated into scenes of social disorder. "In 1645," he writes, "they were condemned by the General Assembly, and in 1647 the Presbyteries of Haddington and Dunbar insisted on their suppression as 'the seminaries of all profanation.' By these courts it was ordained that not more than twenty persons should assemble at weddings, and that piping and dancing should cease. Kirksessions subjected pipers and fiddlers to their severest censures for discoursing music at bridals. Persons who were convicted of 'promiscuous dancing' were mulct in considerable penalties and placed on the stool of repentance.   Ecclesiastical tribunals subsequently discovered that the irregularities at the penny wedding did not arise from the arts of the musician or of the dancing master, but were owing to the quantity of liquor which was consumed.   They passed regulations to check the extent of the potations.   It was provided that the festivities should not be prolonged beyond a single day.   The presence of strangers from neighbouring parishes was prohibited, except when a considerable payment was made to the Kirksession for the privilege of receiving them. When marriage feasts were furnished by publicans, Kirksessions ruled that the *lawin* should not exceed a certain amount.   A *lawin* of six shillings of Scottish money, was commonly allowed."

Other measures were enacted by the Church with a view to checking the scale of these marriage feasts, and further of creating or extending difficulties in the way of getting married at all. Thus the Kirksessions limited the cost of the feast and the number of persons attending it.   The Glasgow Kirksession in 1583 enacted that the cost of the marriage feast should not exceed eighteen pennies Scots ; while that of Stirling, in 1599, in a more generous mood, allowed the cost to reach five shillings, but decreed that no marriage should take place in the Church unless the parties deposited the sum of four pounds as a guarantee that it should not exceed that amount.   Delays and difficulties were caused by irksome regulations, such as the allowance of an interval of forty days between the publication of the banns, and the celebration of the marriage.   Then there were the obligations imposed upon the couple, to wit, that they must make " a pecuniary consignment in the hands of the session-clerk that their union would certainly be solemnized," and they must " procure a cautioner, who became bound that they would not cohabit before receiving the nuptial benediction."[1]   In many cases ecclesiastical regulations were set at nought by holding the wedding feasts in tents pitched in open fields.   In other ways, too, the rules of the Church were broken, even, it was said, by elders themselves.   Thus in 1703, says Rogers, John Hart, elder of Hawick, acknowledged " upon his knees," before his brethren, that he had made a penny bryddal at his daughter's marriage.   " Prayer was offered to God to grant him repentance, and he was suspended from office."[1]

---

[1] Charles Rogers, *Scotland, Social and Domestic*, p. 368.
[2] Ibid., p. 370.

AS we intend to enter the *Matrimonial State*, on *Tuesday*, the 7th Day of *December* next, we are encouraged by our Friends to make a BIDDING on the occasion, the same Day, at the Sign of the *Three Salmons, Water Street;* when and where the favour of your good company is humbly solicited, and whatever donation you may be pleased to bestow on us then, will be received with gratitude, and repaid with punctuality, whenever called for on a similar occasion,

By your humble Servants,

**ROGER HANCOCK,
JANE DAVIES.**

The young Man's Father and Mother (Edward and Jane Hancock,) Brother and Sister (Joseph and Charlotte Hancock,) desire that all Gifts of the above Nature due to them, be returned to the young Man on the said day, and will be thankful together with his Uncle and Aunt (Thomas and Mary Hancock, Three Salmons,) for all favours granted.

Also, the young Woman's Father and Mother (Daniel and Mary Davies,) and Brothers (Thomas, David, and John,) desire that all Gifts of the above Nature due to them, be returned to the young Woman on the above day, and will be thankful for all favours granted.

J. EVANS, PRINTER, CARMARTHEN.

A WELSH "BIDDING". 1830

An old custom, known as "thrigging", which bears some analogy to the Penny Wedding, is mentioned by Guthrie[1] as being practised by the fishing people of Ardersier in Scotland. Usually the men there marry while very young, and in consequence, have little money for furnishing a house. A few days after the wedding, the young wife calls on her friends and neighbours, and at each house visited, she is presented with some article suitable for household use.

Of a somewhat similar character were the "biddings" at one time prevalent in Wales, where the guests were invited by a hired "bidder", or by means of a public notice; strangers as well as friends being at liberty to attend, provided they made some contribution either in goods or money.

Wood says that "a custom similar to the Welsh biddings prevailed in Cumberland, Westmoreland, and other parts of the North of England at the end of the last [eighteenth] century."[2] Such marriages were termed "bidden weddings" and were public affairs. The same authority gives two quotations which throw considerable light on the custom. The first of these is from Vaughan's *Golden Grove* (1608) and reads : "The marriage day being come (in some shires of England), the invited guests do assemble together, and at the very instant of the marriage doe cast their presents (which they bestowe upon the new-married folkes) into a bason, dish, or cup which standeth upon the table in the church, ready prepared for that purpose. But this custome is onely put in use amongst them which stand in need." The second is from the *History of Sr. Billy of Billericay and his Squire Ricardo* : "In most parts of Essex it is a common custom, when poor people marry, to make a kind of dog-hanging, or money-gathering, which they call a wedding-dinner, to which they invite tag and rag, all that will come ; where, after dinner, upon summons of the fiddler, who setteth forth his voice like a town-crier, a table being set forth, and the bride set simpering at the upper end of it, the bridegroom standing by with a white sheet athwart his shoulders, while the people march up to the bride, present their money and wheel about. After this offering is over, then is a pair of gloves laid upon the table, most monstrously bedaubed about with ribbon, which by way of auction is set to sale at

[1] E. J. Guthrie, *Old Scottish Customs, Local and General*, 1885, p. 122.
[2] Edward J. Wood, *The Wedding Day in All Ages and Countries*, 1869. Vol. II, p. 86.

who gives most, and he whose hap it is to have them, shall withall have a kiss of the bride."

Because of the low fees charged, the Manchester Parish Church was an exceedingly popular venue for marriages in the first half of the nineteenth century, and for this reason it was often necessary for a number of couples to be married at the same time, especially on Easter Monday. These were called multiple or wholesale weddings. Sir George Head describes one such affair which came under his own observation, thus : " I attended the Old Church at Manchester one Monday morning, in order to witness the solemnization of several marriages I had reason to suppose were then and there to take place. I had heard on the preceding Sunday the banns proclaimed as follows : ' For the first time of asking, 65 ; for the second time, 72 ; for the third time, 60.—Total, 197.' Having been advised to be on the spot at eight in the morning, I repaired thither at that hour ; Operations, however, did not commence before ten ; that latter is the usual time of proceeding to business, although in cases of persons married by licence, eight o'clock is the hour. A full quarter of an hour before the striking of the clock, two beadles in parish liveries had taken ground opposite the church-door, and a sufficient number of persons, chiefly young women, had assembled, whose curious and anxious looks testified that something extraordinary was about to take place. By this time, also, suspicious-looking persons in pairs were beginning to arrive on foot, whose countenances were accordingly scrutinized without mercy by the crowd of loiterers, and as the church-door was not open, every matrimonial candidate who waited to be let in was subjected to the same ordeal. The couples were all poor people, and as to the brides and bridegrooms, as few were dressed in special *costume*, and all were very generally attended by friends and relatives, it was not easy to say which was which. One party arrived at the church-door evidently wishing to belong (as everything in this world goes by comparison) to the higher classes, and though dragged by one solitary horse, made a strenuous effort to outshine. Their carriage, a narrow vis-à-vis fly, intended for two persons, now contained four, besides a fat man with bushy whiskers, probably the bride's brother, who occupied the box with the coachman. Within, packed as close as they could possibly sit, on one side were two bridesmaids ; opposite to these the bride and bridegroom ; the latter a spruce sandy-haired young man, looking flushed and eager. One of his arms encircled the waist of the young lady, on whose blooming countenance he bestowed glances of the very tenderest description—in fact, his looks were so peculiarly expressive, that, attitude and all considered, I hardly knew whether to compare him, in my mind, to the statue of Cupid regarding his Psyche, or a Scotch terrier watching at a rat-hole . . . The Coachman and his companion wore white favours; the former meditating effect, inflicted some smart strokes of the whip on the horse, intending to bring him on his haunches with a jerk; but the poor jaded animal, evidently over-driven, had sense enough to anticipate the object proposed, and stopped dead short a few paces before, by which both men on the box were very nearly pitched over his head. The people sat in the fly till the church-door was opened, and then the ladies got out and tripped across the pavement into the church. They wore short petticoats and white satin bonnets scooped out in the hind part, with sugar-loaf crowns, and their back hair underneath combed upwards. When all was ready, and the church-doors opened, the clergyman and clerk betook themselves to the vestry, and the people who were about to be married and their friends seated themselves in the body of the church opposite the communion-table, on benches placed there for the purpose. Not less than fifty people were assembled, among whom I took my seat quietly without being noticed. The party who had arrived upon wheels, most exclusively paraded, in the meantime, up and down, as if unwilling to identify themselves with the humbler candidates for matrimony, in another part of the church. The latter at first took their seats in solemn formality, each one at the same time rather inquisitively surveying his neighbour; but as the clergyman and clerk were some time in preparation, the men first broke silence by whispering one to another, which caused the women to titter, till by degrees they all threw off their reserve, and made audible remarks on the newcomers. There was little *mauvaise honte* among the women, but of the men, poor fellows! some were seriously abashed; while among the hymeneal throng there seemed to prevail a sentiment that obtains pretty generally among their betters, namely, the inclination to put shy people out of conceit with themselves. Thus at the advance of a sheepish-looking bridegroom, he was immediately assailed on all sides with ' Come in, man; what art afraid of? Nobody'll hurt thee.' And then a general laugh went round in a repressed tone, but quite sufficient to confound and subdue the newcomer. At last a sudden buzz broke out—'the clergyman's coming!' and all then was perfectly silent. About twelve couples were there to be married; the rest were friends and attendants. The clerk, who was an adept in his business, and performed the duties of his office in a mode admirably calculated to set the people at their ease, and direct the proceedings, now called upon the former to arrange themselves altogether round the altar. In appointing them to their proper places, he addressed each in an intonation of voice particularly soft and soothing, and which carried with it the more of encouragement as he made use of no appellative but the Christian name of the person spoken to. Thus he proceeded: 'Daniel and Phœbe; this way, Daniel; take off your gloves, Daniel.—William and Anne; no, Anne; here, Anne; t'other side, William.—John and Mary; here, John; oh, John; gently, John.' And then addressing them all together:] 'Now all of you give your hats to some person to hold.' Although the marriage service was generally addressed to the whole party, the clergyman was scrupulously exact in obtaining the accurate responses from each individual. No difference was shown towards the exclusive party, other than by being placed on the extreme left."[1]

Of the Rev. Joshua Brookes, who also officiated at this church, the story is told that on one occasion it was pointed out to him that he had accidentally joined in wedlock the wrong parties. His reply was: "Pair as you go out; you're all married; pair as you go out."

Multiple marriages have also been performed in the poorer parts of London. The Rev. Arthur W. Jephson, of St. John's, Walworth, performed many such weddings, sometimes uniting forty or more couples at the same time: in such circumstances one marriage service only was read, but in each case the words of bondage were spoken. Another church where these multiple weddings were performed was St. John's, Hoxton.[2]

A peculiar old custom, at one time much practised in the North of England, is referred to by Brand, who says it was usual for the young men who were present at a wedding " to strive,

---

[1] Sir George Head, *A Home Tour through the Manufacturing Districts and other parts of England, Scotland, and Ireland*, John Murray, London, 1840. Vol. I, pp. 70–73.
[2] George R. Sims, *Living London*, Cassell, 1903, p. 20. From the article " Marrying London " by Mrs. Belloc-Lowndes.

WEDDING IN LONDON, ABOUT 1900,
ON A SOCIABLE, OR "BICYCLE
MADE FOR TWO"

A WEDDING OF FIVE COUPLES AT HOXTON
From *Living London*, Cassell, 1903

immediately after the ceremony, who could first pluck off the bride's garters from her legs. This was done before the very altar. The bride was generally gartered with ribands for the occasion. Whoever were so fortunate as to be victors in this singular species of contest, during which the bride was often obliged to scream out, and was very frequently thrown down, bore them about the church in triumph." Sometimes the young men decorated their hats with the bride's garters, as mentioned by Butler (*Hudibras*) in the couplet :

> " Which all the saints, and some since martyrs,
> Wore in their hats like wedding garters."

Herrick, too, refers to this custom, in *Hesperides* :

> " Quickly, quickly, then prepare,
> And let the young men and the bride-maids share
> Your garters ; and their joyntts
> Encircle with the bridegroom's points."

Occasionally the practice resulted in a scuffle ; and, as mentioned by Brand, it sometimes ended with the bride landing on the floor. In view of these risks there is little wonder that many brides, to avoid any such happenings, took care that their garters were easily reached and detached, or even went so far as to hand them to the contestants. Not always was the practice carried out in the church, according to an entry by Pepys in his *Diary*, where he says, following a dinner, " there was pulling off Mrs. Bride's and Mr. Bridegroom's ribbons."

Among the most curious of the practices carried out when, after the ceremony, the newly-married couple had repaired to their home, was the custom known as " bedding " the bride and bridegroom, performed by the female and male attendants respectively. In reference to this practice, Misson says : " The bridesmaids carry the bride into the bedchamber, where they undress her, and lay her in bed. The bridegroom, who by the help of his friends, is undress'd in some other room, comes in his nightgown, as soon as possible, to his spouse, who is surrounded by mother, aunt, sister, and friends, and without any further ceremony gets into bed. Some of the women run away, others remain, and the moment afterwards they are all got together again."[1] Presumably, no embarrassment was experienced by the

[1] M. Misson, *Memoirs and Observations on Travels over England*, 1719, p. 352.

newly-married couple in having their privacy thus invaded, which is understandable in regard to any practice which is well nigh universal in its observance. And this is what " bedding " in those remote days would appear to have been if contemporary records have any evidential value. Even in connexion with the marriage, during the reign of George the Second, of the Princess Royal to the Prince of Orange, in a description appearing in the *Stamford Mercury* (March, 1733), there is a reference to the custom in the following excerpt, lifted from the columns of the newspaper by Marchant :[1] "About twelve, the royal family supped in the great state ballroom : their majesties were placed at the upper end of the table, under a canopy ; on the right hand sat the Prince of Wales, the Duke and the Prince of Orange, and on the left the Princesses. The Countess of Hertford carved. About two the bride and bridegroom retired, and were afterwards seen by the nobility, sitting up in their bedchamber in rich undresses. The counterpane of the bed was of lace of exceeding great value. The fashions worn were, for ladies, fine laced heads dressed English ; their hair curled down on the sides, powdered behind and before, with trebled ruffles, one tucked up to their shifts in quilled plaits and two hanging down ; the newest silks were Padriasoys, with large flowers of tulips, peonies, anemones, carnations, &c., in their proper colours, some wove in the silk and some embroidered."

Another bedchamber rite was the strange custom of " flinging the stocking ", which occurred immediately after the aforedescribed " bedding ". Misson describes the procedure thus : " The Bridesmen take the Bride's Stockings, and the Bridesmaids the Bridegroom's ; Both sit down at the Bed's Feet, and fling the Stockings over their Heads, endeavouring to direct them so as that they may fall upon the marry'd couple. If the Man's Stockings, thrown by the Maid, fall upon the Bridegroom's Head, it is a Sign she will quickly be marry'd herself ; and the same Prognostick holds good of the Woman's Stockings, thrown by the Man. Oftentimes these young People engage with one another upon the Success of the Stockings, tho' they themselves look upon it to be nothing but Sport."[2] Pepys mentions the practice ; so, too, does Sir Walter Scott. Allan Ramsay, the poet, says :

[1] W. T. Marchant, *Betrothals and Bridals*, 1879, p. 103.
[2] M. Misson, *Memoirs and Observations in Travels over England*, 1719, p. 352.

> " The bride was now laid in her bed,
>   Her left leg ho was flung;
>   And Geordy Gib was fidgen glad,
>   Because it hit Jean Gun."

And in the *Gentleman's Magazine* are these lines :

> " Bid the lasses and lads to the merry brown bowl,
>   While rashers of bacon shall smoke on the coal ;
>   Then Roger and Bridget, and Robin and Nan,
>   Hit 'em each on the nose with the hose if you can."

In eighteenth-century London there was often to be observed at wedding celebrations the presence of a party of musicians consisting of butchers flourishing marrowbones and cleavers. A pictorial delineation of such a band is given by Hogarth. For the following descriptive account I am indebted to Chambers's *Book of Days* (Vol. I., p. 360) : " The performers were the butchers' men—' the bonny boys that wear the sleeves of blue.' A set of these lads, having duly accomplished themselves for the purpose, made a point of attending in front of a house containing a marriage party, with their cleavers, and each provided with a marrowbone, wherewith to perform a sort of rude serenade, of course with the expectation of a fee in requital of their music. Sometimes, the group would consist of four, the cleaver of each ground to the production of a certain note ; but a full band —one entitled to the highest grade of reward—would be not less than eight, producing a complete octave ; and, where there was a fair skill, this series of notes would have all the fine effect of a peal of bells. When this serenade happened in the evening, the men would be dressed neatly in clean blue aprons, each with a portentous wedding favour of white paper in his breast or hat. It was wonderful with what quickness and certainty, under the enticing presentiment of beer, the serenaders got wind of a coming marriage, and with what tenacity of purpose they would go on with their performance until the expected crown or half-crown was forthcoming. The men of Clare Market were reputed to be the best performers, and their *guerdon* was always on the highest scale accordingly. A merry rough affair it was ; troublesome somewhat to the police and not always relished by the party for whose honour it was designed ; and sometimes, when a musical band came upon the ground at the same time, or a set of boys would please to interfere with pebbles rattling in tin canisters, thus throwing a sort of burlesque on the performance, a few blows would be interchanged. Yet the Marrowbone-and-Cleaver epithalamium seldom failed to diffuse a good humour throughout the neighbourhood; and one cannot but regret that it is rapidly passing among the things that were."

The rewards of the butchers were at times considerable. An examination of the books of the Marrowbone-and-Cleavers Society of the parish of St. George, Hanover Square, reveals that in the year 1745, the sum received in connexion with weddings at the fashionable St. George's Church amounted to no less than £380. Apropos of this custom, William Connor Sydney says: "That which was at first regarded as a gratuity, came, in process of time, to be recognized as a right, and such proportions did the burden assume, that the aid of Parliament was at last invoked for its removal."[1]

It was at one time believed that if a man married a woman while she was wearing nothing but a chemise, he was not responsible for her debts. There is an entry in one of the Fleet registers referring to a bride who ran across Ludgate Hill in her shift; and the *Daily Journal* (November 8, 1725) mentions an exhibition of the same character at Ulcomb, in Kent. At Grimsby, on August 23, 1815, a widow, in order that her second husband should not be burdened with any debts left by her first "proceeded out of the window, in a state of nudity, where she was received into the arms of her *intended*, in the presence of two substantial witnesses."[2] And there were other cases: at Whitehaven, in 1766, when a woman, who divested herself of everything except her shift, was actually married inside the church; in a Wiltshire village, in 1714, a marriage took place where the bride wore nothing but a smock.

The practice was not confined to Britain: it was current in North America. In some parts of New England, in the eighteenth century, the marriage of a woman " in her shift on the king's highway" was held to constitute a repudiation of any debts she might have. Peter Kalm, writing in 1772, says:

[1] William Connor Sydney, *England and the English in the Eighteenth Century*, Edinburgh, 1891, second edition. Vol. I, p. 69.
[2] John Ashton, *Social Life Under the Regency*, Chatto & Windus, London, 1899, p. 390. In reference to the belief that marriage by a woman in a state of nudity, or wearing a shift only, exempted the husband from payment of her debts, Ashton says: "This error seems to have been founded on a misconception of the law, because it is laid down (*Bacon's Abridgement*, Tit. Baron and Feme) that ' the husband is liable for the wife's debts, because he acquires an absolute interest in the personal estate of the wife, etc.' An unlearned person, from this, might conclude, and not unreasonably, that, if his wife *had no estate whatever*, he could not incur any liability.'

DRUMMERS AND BUTCHERS WITH MARROW-BONES
AND CLEAVERS ATTENDING AFTER A WEDDING
From William Hogarth's *"Industry and Idleness"* Series

" There is a very peculiar diverting custom here, in regard to marrying. When a man dies, and leaves his widow in great poverty, or so that she cannot pay all the debts with what little she has left : and that, notwithstanding all that, there is a person who will marry her, she must be married in no other habit than her shift. By that means, she leaves to the creditors of her deceased husband her clothes, and everything which they find in the house. But she is not obliged to pay them anything more, because she has left them all she was worth, even her clothes, keeping only a shift to cover her, which the laws of the country cannot refuse her. As soon as she is married, and no longer belongs to the deceased husband, she puts on the clothes which the second has given her. The Swedish clergymen here have often been obliged to marry a woman in a dress which is so little expensive, and so light. This appears from the registers kept in the churches, and from the accounts given by the clergymen themselves. I have likewise often seen accounts of such marriages in the English gazettes, which are printed in these colonies ; and I particularly remember the following relation : A woman went, with no other dress than her shift, out of the house of her deceased husband to that of her bridegroom, who met her halfway with fine new clothes, and said, before all who were present, that he lent them to his bride ; and put them on her with his own hands. It seems he said that he lent the clothes, lest, if he had said he gave them, the creditors of the first husband should come and take them from her ; pretending, that she was looked upon as the relict of her first husband, before she was married to the second."[1]

Many of these marriages were celebrated in the evening and sometimes when the bride discarded all her clothes, she stood in a closet, or was otherwise partially or wholly concealed. There are various references to the practice (in addition to the account given by Peter Kalm) for the finding in contemporary literature. Thus, in *Along New England Roads*, William C. Prime says that when, in February, 1789, Major Moses Joy married a widow named Hannah Ward, the bride occupied a closet, where she stood in a state of nudity, holding out her hand to the Major through a hole in the closet door. There is mention in Hall's *History of Eastern Vermont*, of a nude bride hidden in a recess behind a curtain during the wedding ceremony. Alice

[1] Peter Kalm, *Travels into North America*, London, 1772. Vol. I, pp. 334-335.

Morse Earle, who gives these references, also mentions, in relation to smock-marriages on the public highway in York, Me., in 1774, one case where it was said " the pitying minister threw his coat over the shivering bride, widow Mary Bradley, who in February, clad only in a shift, met the bridegroom half way from her home to his."[1]

A contributor to Chambers's *Book of Days* (Vol. I, p. 723), mentions a curious East Anglian custom which existed about the time of writing (1863). "At any rate," he said " I knew of its being observed a few years ago ; it is that if a younger sister marries before the elder one, the elder must *dance the hog's trough*. In the case to which I refer, a brother went through the ceremony also, and the dancers performed their part so well, that they danced both the ends off the trough, and the trough itself into two pieces. In the West of England it is a fixed rule that the lady should dance in *green stockings* ; but I am not aware of any peculiar stockings being required on the occasion in East Anglia."

Yet another strange custom was the practice of sewing-up in a sheet the bride, mentioned by Herrick, thus :—

" But since it must be done, despatch and sowe
Up in a sheet your bride and what if so ? "

At the marriage of Sir Philip Herbert and Lady Susan in the reign of James the First, this custom was observed.[2]

A practice peculiar to Ayrshire and some of the border villages was known as " creeling the bridegroom," which took place on the morning following the wedding. On the bridegroom's back was fixed a creel, or wicker basket ; and a long pole to which a broom was attached was placed over his left shoulder. Carrying this equipment, he was compelled to run a sort of race in which his bride was expected to join, endeavouring to free him from his burden. The readiness and swiftness she displayed in taking up and pursuing the chase were supposed to indicate the degree of her satisfaction with the marriage.

A variant of this custom is mentioned by Dalyell. " On the morning after marriage, the youth of both sexes, or perhaps females were the principal participators, assembled along with the new married pair. A basket was transmitted among them,

---

[1] Alice Morse Earle, *Customs and Fashions in Old New England*, 1893, p. 79.
[2] C. J. S. Thompson, *Love, Marriage and Romance in Old London*, Heath Cranton, 1936.

and gradually filled with stones, until reaching the bridegroom, when it was suspended from his neck. Then receiving some additional load, his affectionate helpmate, to testify her sense of the caresses he had lavished on her, cut the cord and relieved him of this oppressive burden. Such has been the later practice ; whence those declining to submit, awaken suspicions that their love has already cooled ; that they had insinuated themselves into affections which they did not requite, and so they are held unworthy of public esteem."[1]   In some parts of Scotland the custom was rigidly enforced, particularly as the man in charge of the proceedings was invariably the one who had himself been the previous victim. In Galashiels, the practice came to an end when " one Robert Young, who, on the ostensible plea of a ' sore back,' lay a-bed all the day after his marriage, and obstinately refused to get up and be ' creeled ' ; he had been twice married before, and no doubt felt that he had had enough of ' creeling.' "[2]

Another quaint custom at one time practised at Pettie, is mentioned by Guthrie.[3] It appears that in former times it was usual, whenever a wedding was solemnized in the church of Pettie, for the youngsters who attended the parish school to congregate in front of the door, and prevent any member of the bridal party entering the church until the bridegroom agreed to contribute a small sum towards the cost of a new football, or alternately secured exemption from payment of this fine by kicking the ball at present in use over the church. This was not a feat within the power of everyone, and if the bridegroom refused to make the attempt or, after trying and failing, still obstinately declined to pay, one of the boys would remove the bride's shoes, after which the confused and embarrassed bridegroom, together with the wedding guests, were permitted to enter the church.

A somewhat similar " blackmailing " custom was formerly practised by the boys of Burnley Grammar School, who levied a fine on persons married at St. Peter's Church in the same town. On the wedding day, two of the boys deputed for the purpose, interviewed the best man and demanded a fee. Apparently this fee was unspecified, the precise amount being left to the

---

[1] John Graham Dalyell, *The Darker Superstitions of Scotland*, 1835, p. 296.
[2] Chambers's *Book of Days*.   Vol. I, p. 722.
[3] E. J. Guthrie, *Old Scottish Customs*, 1885, p. 120.

generosity of the groomsman. The money received was used for the maintenance of the school's library.[1]

In this same connexion the ancient Welsh practice of " chaining " deserves mention. As they were leaving the church door the bride and bridegroom were stopped by a number of rustics who stretched a band of twisted straw or hay, decorated with flowers, across their path or wound it around them in the manner of a chain, and demanded the payment of a toll as a condition of release.[2]

A curious ceremony, reeking with superstition, was formerly practised in the Orkney Isles, near the Loch of Stennis, where stand a number of stones arranged in circular formations, one of which is known as the Circle of the Sun and the other as the Circle of the Moon. The procedure was for the bride to walk around the Moon circle while the bridegroom walked around the Sun circle. This done the two came together near the stone of Odin, in the centre of which was a large perforation. Taking up positions on either side of this stone, they clasped hands through the opening, and in this manner became man and wife, no other ceremony being necessary.

Little mentions a queer custom prevalent in the Isle of Man during the sixteenth century, whereby should " any man take a woman by constraint, or force her against her will ; if she be a maid or single woman, the deemster shall give her a rope, a sword, and a ring ; and she shall have her choice either to hang him with the rope, cut off his head with the sword, or marry him with the ring. Report says that every complainant has been lenient except one, who presented the rope ; but relented on the prisoner being tucked up, and desired he might be let down. She then presented the ring ; but the man replied that one punishment was enough for one crime : therefore he should keep the ring for some future occasion."[3]

A curious eighteenth-century custom in Maryland, is referred to by Peter Kalm. At that time many Europeans who had emigrated to the New World were practically destitute and there were cases where, after being married, the bridegroom stated

---

[1] John Harland and T. T. Wilkinson, *Lancashire Folk-Lore*, 1882, p. 265.
[2] A somewhat similar custom is practised in Burma. A string is tied across the road leading to the bride's house, and the bridegroom and his friends are halted and forced to part with a sum of money before proceeding on their way (see *The Burman*, by Sir J. G. Scott, Macmillan, 1910, p. 58).
[3] Thomas Little, *The Beauty, Marriage Ceremonies and Intercourse of the Sexes, in all Nations*, 1824. Vol. III, p. 35.

his inability to pay the clergyman's fee, and promised to do so at the first opportunity. With rare exceptions this was the end of the matter, the clergyman never seeing the man again. To avoid this, the clergy of Maryland concocted an ingenious and effective plan. Its simplicity is apparent from Kalm's description : " When the clergyman marries a very poor couple, he breaks off in the middle of the Liturgy, and cries out, *Where is my fee ?* The man must then give the money, and the clergyman proceeds ; but if the bridegroom has no money, the clergyman defers the marriage till another time, when the man is better provided. People of fortune, of whom the clergyman is sure to get his due, need not fear this disagreeable question, when they are married."[1]

According to this same authority restrictions as regards marriage were placed on certain of these indigent immigrants from Europe. Many of them landed in America owing their passage money from Europe, and no clergyman was permitted to marry such as had bound themselves to serve a number of years in order to pay off this debt, without the consent of their employers. Also, says Kalm : " No clergyman is allowed to marry a negro with one of European extraction, or he must pay a penalty of one hundred pounds, according to the laws of Pennsylvania."[2]

At one time royalty and certain privileged members of the aristocracy were permitted to practise marriage by proxy. For instance, Henry the Eighth married Anne of Cleves in this manner ; so, too, did James the Second, before he became king, marry Mary of Modena. But such marriages were few and far between, and even when a case did occur there was often a supplementary marriage along orthodox lines at a later date. "The Church," says Howlett, "always looked with great disfavour on this form of marriage."[3]

It would be unfitting not to include among these curious marriage practices the custom, peculiar to England, of rewarding with a flitch of bacon the couple who, during the first " year and a day " of their life together could swear that they had never regretted getting married. This unique presentation was made in the Essex town of Dunmow. The custom originated

---

[1] Peter Kalm, *Travels into North America*, second edition, 1772. Vol. I, p. 333.
[2] Ibid., p. 334.
[3] *Curious Church Customs*, edited by William Andrews (from an article by E. Howlett entitled " Marriage Customs "), p. 106.

as long ago as the year 1104, and was founded by the Lady Juga, sister of Ralph Baynard, holder of the manor at the time when the Domesday Book was compiled. To the married couple who claimed the bacon the oath was administered by the steward in these words :—

> " You shall swear by custom of confession,
> That you ne'er made nuptial transgression ;
> Nor since you were married man and wife,
> By household brawls or contentious strife,
> Or otherwise at bed or at board,
> Offended each other in deed or word ;
> Or in a twelvemonth and a day,
> Repented not in thought any way ;
> Or since the parish clerk said ' Amen ',
> Wished yourselves unmarried again,
> But continued true, and in desire
> As when you joined hands in holy quire."

After expressing this oath and thereby claiming the prize, the court pronounces :—

> " Since to these conditions without any fear,
> Of your own accord you do freely swear ;
> A whole gammon of bacon you shall receive,
> And bear it away with love and good leave ;
> For this is the custom of Dunmow well known—
> Tho' the pleasure be ours, the bacon's your own."

Whether the married couples who could conscientiously take the oath were so few as to justify the belief of those responsible for the origination of the custom, whether few cared for the inevitable attendant publicity, or whether those living in the immediate vicinity, and those only, thought the prize worth the effort or expense of fetching, is not clear ; but the fact remains that in pretty nearly three centuries, the number of claimants, even allowing that the records may not be complete, seems to have been a singularly small one. Tegg says : " From the Chartulary of the Priory, which is deposited in the British Museum, it appears that only three couples obtained the bacon previous to the suppression of the religious houses. These were respectively on the 27th April 1445, in the year 1467, and on the 8th of September 1510."[1] Again, in subsequent centuries, extremely long periods elapsed between the presentations : thus between the successful claim of William and Jane Parsley in 1701, there appears to have been none until 1751, when John

---

[1] William Tegg, *The Knot Tied*, 1877, p. 228.

THE DUNMOW FLITCH

From William Harrison Ainsworth's *The Flitch
of Bacon*, 1879, after a drawing by
Sir John Gilbert, R.A.

Shakesshaft and his wife were presented with a flitch. And then, a matter of twenty years later, when the next claim was made, the couple and their friends were grievously disappointed : the priory of Dunmow was closed, there was no one to carry out the ceremonial procedure. Decade after decade went to glory and no one seemed interested in the old Dunmow custom as anything other than a matter for historical comment, until, in 1851 (just one hundred years after the last presentation), Mr. and Mrs. Hurrell of Felstead, Essex, applied for the prize. "As the custom had been so long dormant," says Tegg, "the Lord of the Manor of Dunmow Priory did not entertain the application. When the public heard of the refusal on the part of the Lord of the Manor to reward the happy couple for their matrimonial felicity, the inhabitants of Dunmow and district resolved to entertain the claim, and a committee being formed, they invited Mr. and Mrs. Hurrell, on the 16th July, 1851, to a public fete at Easton Park, where the loving pair, after the oath had been administered to them by Mr. Pavey, received a gammon of bacon amid the tremendous cheering of the gathering."[1]

Four years later, interest having been aroused, partly by the presentation to Mr. and Mrs. Hurrell, and partly by the appearance of Harrison Ainsworth's novel, entitled *A Flitch of Bacon*, at a meeting of the Dunmow residents, it was decided that an attempt should be made to revive the old custom, and to invite Mr. Harrison Ainsworth to present the bacon to any successful applicant. As a result, awards were made, in the presence of seven thousand people, to the Chevalier de Chatelain and his wife, and to Mr. and Mrs. Barlow, the claimants on this occasion. It is true the old ceremonial procedure in all its details was not adhered to, but the applications were heard by a mixed jury in Dunmow town-hall, Mr. Ainsworth officiating as judge. Since that date claims were made in 1857, 1869, 1874 and 1876.[2]

It appears to be still possible to claim and win the award. As recently as 1951, Mr. and Mrs. White, says Mr. Richard Dimbleby (*Sunday Chronicle*, May 20, 1951) were awarded the prize. There was, however, a notable feature connected with this particular contest. "The 'Flitch'," writes Mr. Dimbleby, "was cash, instead of bacon, but otherwise the trial of the candidates was conducted with all solemnity before the eminent Mr. Crocker."

[1] Tegg, op. cit., p. 233.
[2] Tegg, op. cit., p. 240.

II

Customs Connected with the Wedding Cake, Ring, etc.

Some authorities there are who contend that the modern wedding cake owes its origin to the ancient Roman custom, in connexion with marriage by *confarreatio*, of a cake being broken into pieces over the head of the bride, who held in her left hand three wheat-ears. According to Lord Avebury, however, the custom of providing cake in some form or other at weddings was not restricted, even in the days of antiquity, to any one country or race. He says : "Among the Iroquois, the bride and bridegroom used to partake together of a cake of sagamite. The Fiji Islanders have a similar custom, which also prevails among most of the hill tribes of India."[1] At most ancient British marriages cakes or biscuits were broken over the bride's head, or grains of wheat, barley, or oats were dropped on her head, as she left the church. In Herrick's *Hesperides* we read :

"While some repeat
Your praise, and bless you, sprinkling you with wheat."

Thomas Moffet, in *Health's Improvement*, writes : " The English, when the bride comes from church, are wont to cast wheat upon her head ; and when the bride and bridegroom return home, one presents them with a pot of butter, as presaging plenty, and abundance of all good things." Jeaffreson, writing in 1872, says : " My friend, Mr. Moncure Conway, tells me that it is not long since he was present at a wedding in London, where rice was poured over the head of the bride. The groom and bride of this wedding were English people, moving in the middle rank of prosperous Londoners."[2] There is little doubt these and analogous practices were relics of the ancient fertility cults connected with marriage.

In those long distant days when cakes and biscuits were first broken over the bride's head, it was customary for the guests to eat the fragments. There was nothing about them to tempt the appetite in any way, but there was a good deal of superstition attached to the effect upon the consumer, and the manner in which the bits of cake fell. Thus Smollett in *Humphrey Clinker* : "A cake being broken over the head of Mrs. Tabitha Lismahago,

---

[1] Lord Avebury, *The Origin of Civilization*, sixth edition, 1902.
[2] John Cordy Jeaffreson, *Brides and Bridals*, 1872, p. 320.

the fragments were distributed among the bystanders, according to the custom of the ancient Britons, on the supposition that every person who ate of this hallowed cake should that night have a vision of the man or woman whom heaven designed should be his or her wedded mate." In a slightly different form the belief persists to this day, the piece of cake being placed under the pillow of the person who wishes to peep into the future. Apropos of these and analogous superstitions connected with the wedding cake, Wood writes : " In the East Riding of Yorkshire, on a bride alighting from her carriage at her father's door, a plate covered with morsels of bride-cake is flung from a window upon the heads of the crowds congregated in the street below ; and the divination consists in observing the fate which attends its downfall. If it reach the ground in safety without being broken, the omen is a most unfavourable one ; but if, on the other hand, the plate be shattered to pieces—and the more the better—the auspices are looked upon as most happy."[1]

It was not unnatural that something of a more palatable nature should be substituted for these dry, unappetising cakes and biscuits, and in the time of Elizabeth small currant cakes made with eggs, butter, sugar and spice became fashionable ; it was not long before the idea occurred to some enterprising confectioner to top these cakes with almond paste. Thus Herrick :

> " This day, my Julia, thou must make,
> For mistresse bride, the wedding-cake ;
> Knead but the dow, and it will be
> To paste of almonds turn'd by thee ;
> Or kisse it thous, but once or twice
> And for the bride-cake there'll be spice."

The next step was the substitution of one large cake for the collection of small ones, plain to start with, but at last, in the reign of Charles the Second, the sugar-topped and decorated cake was evolved. True to the old custom, this large cake was still broken over the bride's head. Gradually this practice, too, was discontinued, and the cake was cut into pieces and distributed to the guests in the way we are familiar with to-day.

Sometimes the bridecake was of huge dimensions, in keeping with the gargantuan wedding feasts usual when food was both plentiful and cheap. The following description of such a wedding is given by John Sykes, the Newcastle-on-Tyne bookseller and

---

[1] Edward J. Wood, *The Wedding Day in All Ages and Countries*, 1869. Vol. II, p. 225.

historian. The wedding was at the little town of Bishopwear-mouth on May 21, 1753. The young couple, who set out for the church at about half past seven, were preceded, says Sykes, " by three violins and a bagpipe. Seventy people went hand in hand, all distinguished by blue cockades, besides an innumerable multitude which did not observe such just regularity. The bill of fare for dinner was as follows : five bushels of malt brewed for table-beer, ten bushels for ale, sixteen quarters of lamb, eight turkeys, ten green geese, eight hams, four dozen hens, twelve ducks, twenty quarters of mutton, ten quarters of veal, sixteen neat's tongues, a quarter of beef roasted whole, twenty stones of beef boiled, six bushels of white peas, eighty pounds of butter, sixteen pies ; the bride's pie was carried between two persons on a hand-barrow to the bakehouse ; twenty gallons of brandy, eight dozen lemons, seven stones of double refined sugar, ten bushels of wheat, a hundredweight of tobacco, six gross of pipes; tarts, whip-possets, cheese-cakes and jellies innumerable."

Another account, given by the same authority, reads : " Was married at Rothbury, in Northumberland [on June 7, 1750], Mr. William Donkin, a considerable farmer of Tossin, in the same county, to Miss Eleanor Shotton, of the same place. The entertainment on this occasion was very grand, there being provided no less than 120 quarters of lamb, 44 quarters of veal, 20 quarters of mutton, a great quantity of beef, 12 hams, with a suitable number of chickens, &c., which was concluded with 8 half-ankers of brandy made into punch, 12 dozens of cider, a great many gallons of wine, and 90 bushels of malt made into beer. The company consisted of 550 ladies and gentlemen, who were diverted with the music of 25 fiddlers and pipers, and the whole was concluded with the utmost order and equanimity."[1]

The origin of the wedding ring is lost in the realms of antiquity. In many cases there has been confusion between betrothal and wedding rings, and it is certain that among the ancient Romans and contemporary races the use of rings for betrothals preceded their use at weddings.

The earliest ring of which there is any record was made of iron, and was probably of Egyptian manufacture. According to Josephus, the Jewish historian, gold rings were used by the Israelites. Moses and Aaron both wore finger rings. The

---

[1] John Sykes, *Local Records, or Historical Register of Remarkable Events*, new edition, Newcastle, 1833. Vol. I, p. 194.

Lacedemonians, we are told, used rings of iron only. It would appear, however, that almost every kind of metal has at one time or another been used for making rings.

In these early days a circle was held in veneration, as it was thought to be imbued with magical properties and virtues. For this reason, the ring was used in marriage. That the ring must be perfectly round was therefore essential ; and in the early days any interruption of its circularity was held to be an augury of evil befalling the marital union, hence the diamond ring or indeed any ring decorated with stones in a way which affected its roundness was taboo. Some of these beliefs persisted through many centuries, particularly that concerned with the ring symbolising union. The remark of Queen Elizabeth to Secretary Maitland was significant : "I am marryed alreddy to the realme of England, when I wes crownit with the ring quhilk I beir continawallie in taikin thairof."[1]

In England, in the thirteenth century, rings made of rush were used : Shakespeare for one, Fletcher for another, and Spenser for a third, refer to them. In *The Rivals* of Sir William D'Avenant appear the lines :—

> "I'll crown thee with a garland of straw then,
> And I'll marry thee with a rush ring."

Apparently these rush rings were used for pretended or fake marriages, for on the authority of Du Cangue, we learn that the Bishop of Salisbury, in 1217, in giving a warning in this connexion, said : "Let no man put a ring of rush, or of any other material, upon the hands of young girls, by way of mock celebration, for the purpose of more easily seducing them, that, while believing he is only perpetrating a jest, he may not in reality find himself bound irrevocably to the connubial yoke."

Occasionally rings other than those designed expressly for use at weddings were, in cases of emergency, pressed into use, as in connexion with Fleet marriages, in the records of which curtain rings are mentioned. In many parts of Ireland, however, it was held that for a marriage to be valid a gold ring must be used, and so firmly were people of this opinion, that those who could not afford to buy such a ring borrowed one for the occasion. Quakers looked upon the ring with aversion because of its heathenish origin, and until comparatively recently dispensed with it altogether. In the wedding ceremony of the Latter Day Saints, too, the ring had no part.

---

[1] James Graham Dalyell, *The Darker Superstitions of Scotland*, 1835, p. 289.

The Puritans, during Cromwell's time, like the Quakers at a later date, looked upon the wedding ring as of pagan origin, and attempted to bring about its abolition. Apropos of this, Samuel Butler says:

> " Others were for abolishing
> That tool of matrimony, a ring,
> With which the unsanctify'd bridegroom
> Is marry'd only to a thumb
> (As wise as ringing of a pig
> That's used to break up ground and dig),
> The bride to nothing but her will,
> That nulls the after-marriage still."

Originally the ring was placed on the fourth finger, owing to the contention of the early anatomists that a vein in that digit was in direct communication with the heart. Apparently changes in the particular digit were frequent : in the latter part of the eighteenth century the ring was sometimes placed on the thumb.

Nowadays the placing of a ring on the hand of the bride is an essential part of the Church of England marriage service. There is, however, no stipulation as regards it being of gold or indeed of any particular metal. And so long as it will go over the finger it is of no moment whether or not it is too large. As already mentioned curtain rings were sometimes used in the Fleet marriages, and though it may be objected that these ceremonies were unorthodox and surreptitious affairs at best, there have been occasions when no less strange rings have figured in marriages performed in churches. For instance, the church key has been used on occasion.

In the sixteenth century, inscribed rings became fashionable. The inscription was placed inside the hoop of the ring, and consisted of a motto or posy, usually a single line. The wedding ring of Anne of Cleves bore the inscription " God send me well to Kepe " ; Lady Cathcart's, on the occasion of her fourth marriage, " If I survive I will have five " ; that of the wife of Dr. George Bell, Bishop of St. David's, " God make me a good mother, and an obedient housewife " ; while the ring given to his wife on their wedding-day by Bishop Cokes, bearing representations of a hand, a heart, a mitre, and a death's head, was inscribed " These three I give thee, till the fourth set me free ", The practice was abandoned towards the end of the eighteenth century. Apparently the only form of inscription to be used in modern times is that comprising the initials of both bride and bridegroom.

CHAPTER XIX

CLANDESTINE MARRIAGES

I

The Notorious Fleet Marriages

IT has already been mentioned that in Europe until the Council of Trent, in the middle of the sixteenth century, ordained that every marital union should be made by a priest or other ecclesiastic in the presence of two or more witnesses, marriage was purely a civil affair. This decree did not, however, apply to Britain, where the Council of Trent had no power, marriages still continuing to be regulated by Common Law; and although as Burn puts it, in virtue of domestic institutions, a form was enjoined for the more solemn celebration of matrimony, and persons departing from these regulations were liable to ecclesiastical censure, still other and more private modes of contracting a marriage were tolerated and acknowledged by law.

The position in England at that time was simply that any two persons were at liberty to have their marriage solemnized by a priest if they so wished; but they could enter into an equally binding marital contract without the aid of the Church. The civil contracts were of two kinds. Of these Burn says: " a contract *per verba de præsenti*, that is to say, between persons entering into a present engagement to become man and wife, or a promise *per verba de futuro*, which was an agreement to become husband and wife at some future time, if the promise were followed by consummation, constituted marriage without the intervention of a priest; for the contract *per verba de præsenti* was held to be a marriage complete in substance, but deficient in ceremony. Although the promise *per verba de futuro* in itself was incomplete in both points, yet the cohabitation of the parties after exchanging the mutual promise, implied such a present consent at the time of the sexual intercourse, as to perfect the marriage in substance and give it equal validity with the contract *de præsenti*, that is to say, the validity of an irregular marriage, which could not be annulled by the Ecclesiastical Court, though it might be censured for its informality, nor could the *vinculum* be affected by a subsequent regular marriage. Certain privileges have been allowed to those who solemnized their marriage according to the form prescribed by the ecclesiastical law, which were denied to those who refused to comply ; yet the marriage, although celebrated in a different manner, was indissoluble, it being considered a divine institution, to which only a full and free consent of the parties was necessary. Before the time of Pope Innocent the Third (1198) there was no solemnization of marriage in the church, but the man came to the house where the woman resided and led her home to his own house, which was all the ceremony then used : hence the expression ' *uxorem ducere et capere in virum*.' "[1]

For five years, from 1653 to 1658, the ecclesiastical court was shorn of all its power as regards marriage, which was purely a civil contract. But with the dissolution of the Little Parliament marriages again could be celebrated in accordance with ecclesiastical law at the desire of the parties concerned.

It is true that at all times the church did its utmost to get marriage under its control. In 1200 the Synod of Westminster ordered that no marriage should be celebrated without banns having been published in the church on three successive occasions, unless by the special authority of the bishop. The object of banns was the prevention of irregular marriages, but such unions continued to take place despite all the theologians were able to do. Thus the Constitution of William la Zouch (1347) noticed the performance of clandestine marriages, and that "some contriving unlawful marriages, and affecting the dark, lest their deeds should be reproved, procure every day, in a shameful manner, marriages to be celebrated without publication of banns duly and lawfully made, by means of chaplains that have no regard to the fear of God and the prohibition of the laws."

One of, if not, the earliest of the churches where couples were married without banns or licence was in Duke's Place. There are grounds for supposing such marriages were taking place towards the close of the sixteenth century, and thenceforward for at least a century the church was kept busy. As was to be

---

[1] John Southerden Burn, *The Fleet Register Comprising the History of Fleet Marriages*, London, 1833, p. 2.

expected, attempts were made to stop the practice. Thus, according to an entry in the Bishop of London's Registry (1 Compton 95), it appears that the Commissioners for Ecclesiastical Causes, on the 17th February, 1686, suspended for three years (*ab officio et beneficio*), Adam Elliott, Rector of St. James, Duke's Place, "for having married or suffered persons to be married at his church without banns or licence." This suspension was rescinded a few months later, however, as a result of a petition to the Commissioners, claiming that the Church of St. James, Duke's Place, did not come under the jurisdiction of the Bishop of London in matters ecclesiastical. Another securing exemption was the Trinity Minories : this church, it was claimed, was " in the gift of the Crown, and the incumbent or Curate thereof (for it is neither rectory nor vicarage institutive) holds the same by an instrument of donation, under the Great Seal of England." The curates, it was said, claimed that they were not " subject to the Bishop of London as Ordinary, on purpose to defend their marrying without banns or licence." Here the marriages, according to the registers, covering a period of well over a hundred years, numbered many thousands.

The publicity connected with the suspension of Elliott, Rector of St. James, drew the attention of the public to these clandestine unions and the discovery that a legal union could be performed in an unconsecrated building at any hour of the day or night, at small cost, led to an increased demand for such marriages. Moreover, they appealed to all classes. They appealed to the poor on economical grounds ; they appealed to many of the wealthy because of their novelty and notoriety. The popularity of the Trinity Minories and Duke's Place as venues for what were popularly known as " lawless marriages " was soon to be eclipsed by that of the Fleet Prison.[1] To understand how this came about, it will be necessary to take a glance at the constitution of this infamous place of incarceration.

On the east side of what is now known as Farringdon Street, where it joins Ludgate Hill, in the year 1290, a building was erected for use as a prison. It was demolished by fire during the Wat Tyler rebellion, and re-erected as a place of confinement for those convicted by the notorious Star Chamber. Once again, in the Great Fire of London, was the prison to be a victim of the

[1] So-called from the Fleet ditch adjoining, which got the name "fleet" from the swift running of the water.

flames ; and once again was it to re-emerge, phœnix-like, this time specifically as a prison for debtors, and for those guilty of contempt of the Courts of Chancery, the Exchequer and the Common Pleas.

The lot of many of these debtors was not so terrible as one is wont to associate with imprisonment in those bad old days : they were allowed a good deal of liberty, and any one of them who was able to pay for the privilege could not only live outside the confines of the prison proper, but could, subject to certain rules, move about the adjacent parts of London pretty much at will. Now invariably among the many hundreds of men housed in " the Fleet " and its environs, were a number of parsons, and it was to these clerics that occurred the idea of joining in wedlock those couples who, for any one of a number of possible reasons, wished to be married without the publishing of banns and the other delays inseparable from an orthodox ceremony carried out in accordance with ecclesiastical law and regulations. The imprisoned clergymen, free from the scruples which might retard their respectable confreres, caring not one jot for any censorious criticism from the church dignitaries, were prepared to marry on any day and at any time within the canonical hours, any couple willing to pay the fees.

In that rare publication *The Humours of the Fleet*, we read : " The immediate origin of the Fleet marriages appears to have been as follows : a set of imprudent, extravagant, or vicious clergymen, confined in the Fleet for debt, and therefore in no condition to be deterred by the penalty of £100 inflicted by the law on clergymen convicted of solemnizing clandestine marriages, tempted also by the opening made through Elliott's suspension, conceived the brilliant idea of making a kind of marriage-shop, open at all times, of their rooms in the prison, and most probably under still more *liberal* arrangements than Elliott had permitted : there was but one difficulty—the suspension from ecclesiastical functions, which was pretty sure to follow—but they knew well the state of the law ; their marriages would be legal even after suspension : so, casting aside every other consideration but the gain that would accrue, they commenced marrying on the easiest terms, and, as they made a habit of proclaiming, without hindrance of business or the knowledge of friends. Their marriage soon became highly popular among certain classes of the community, and a fearful nuisance to others. By the beginning of the eighteenth century we find the parsons here carrying on an immense trade. In 1705, on the petition of a Mr. Ashton, complaining of divers ill practices in the Fleet, a committee examined into the subject of the famous marriages and reported the existence of many gross abuses in the Fleet, under the sanction of the Warden. From this time some little check appears to have been placed on the latter, but, on the whole, the evils went on steadily increasing up to the period of their sudden abolition."

At first these marriages were performed in the prison chapel itself, but there were drawbacks and difficulties in connexion with this practice which soon led the parsons to make arrangements for the use of other places, notably the taverns which abounded within the rules of the Fleet prison, for their purpose. In some cases a partnership or other arrangement existed between the parson and the publican, and one room was fitted up as a chapel, not that this was essential, but because many clients preferred the ceremony of marriage to have some sort of religious background. Occasionally a resident parson was paid a weekly salary of twenty shillings by the tavern-keeper; in other instances one was sent for as the need arose and the fee divided between the parson and the publican. Many parsons, however, preferred to rent houses of their own and perform the ceremonies in private rooms fitted up as chapels. Naturally, competition was keen, and because of this, all, parsons and tavern-keepers alike, found it expedient to employ touts or " plyers ", as they were usually termed. Pennant refers to these gentry as follows : " In walking along the street, in my youth, on the side next to the prison, I have often been tempted by the question, ' *Sir, will you be pleased to walk in and be married?* ' Along this most lawless space was hung up the frequent sign of a male and female hand conjoined, with, '*Marriages performed within*' written beneath. A dirty fellow invited you in. The parson was seen walking before his shop; a squalid profligate figure, clad in a tattered plaid nightgown, with a fiery face, and ready to couple you for a dram of gin, or roll of tobacco. One great chancellor, Lord Hardwick, put these demons to flight, and saved thousands from the misery and disgrace which would be entailed by these extemporary thoughtless unions."[1]

So far as is ascertainable from the earliest existent registers, the first Fleet marriage appears to have been that mentioned in

[1] Thomas Pennant, *Of London*, 1790, pp. 208–209.

a letter from Alderman Lowe to Lady Hickes in the September of 1613 (Lansd. MSS. 93–17), which reads: " Now I am to inform you that an ancyentt acquayntance of yrs and myne is yesterday maryed in the Fleette, one Mr. Gorge Lestor, and hath maryed Mris Babbington Mr. Thomas Fanshame mother in lawe. Itt is sayed she is a woman of good wealthe so as nowe the man wylle able to lyve and mayntain hymself in prison, for hether unto he hath byne in poor estate. I praye God he be nott encoryged by his marige to do as Becher doth, but I hope he wyll have a better conscyence and more honestye than the other men hathe."

It would appear that these marriages did not become numerous until the aforementioned suspension of the Duke's Place rector, which, while it did not and could not stop clandestine unions, caused most clergymen to be chary of incurring the displeasure and denunciation of the Ecclesiastical Commissioners.

From the end of the seventeenth century, however, the Fleet was a highly popular rendezvous for those wishing to marry quickly and secretly. The procedure was extremely simple. All the couple had to do was to hie them to Ludgate Hill, and there avail themselves of the services of a " plyer ". Apropos of this, Burn refers to an engraving of 'A Fleet Wedding (published about 1747) between a brisk young sailor and his landlady's daughter at Rederiff ', which represents the old Fleet market and prison, with the sailor, landlady, and daughter just stepping from a hackney-coach, while two Fleet parsons in canonicals are offering their services. The verses below the print are as follows:

> " Scarce had the coach discharg'd its trusty fare,
> But gaping crowds surround th' amorous pair ;
> The busy Plyers make a mighty stir,
> And whisp'ring cry, D'ye want the Parson, Sir ?
> Pray step this way—just to the Pen in Hand,
> The Doctor's ready there at your command :
> This way (another cries) Sir, I declare,
> The true and ancient Register is here :
> Th' alarmed Parsons quickly hear the din,
> And haste with soothing words t' invite 'em in :
> In this confusion jostled to and fro,
> Th' inamour'd couple know not where to go ;
> Till slow advancing from the coaches side,
> Th' experienced matron came (an artful guide),
> She led the way without regarding either
> And the first Parson splic'd 'em both together."[1]

John Southerden Burn, The Fleet Registers, 1833, p. 9.

Not all those engaged in the matrimonial business were clergymen. The disreputable character of the parsons and their associates, and the disgraceful and vulgar carryings-on observable in the Fleet and vicinity are well illustrated in a letter published in *The Grub Street Journal*, June 10, 1736, which reads : " Gentlemen—Having frequently heard of the many abominable practices in the Fleet, I had the curiosity on Sunday, May 23, to take a view of the place as I accidentally was walking by. The first thing observable was one J—— L——, by trade a carpenter (whose brother, it is said, keeps the sign of the B—— and G——), cursing, swearing, and raving in the street in the time of divine service, with a mob of people about him, calling one of his fraternity, (J. E.) a Plyer for Weddings, an informing rogue, for informing against one of their Ministers for profane cursing and swearing, for which offence he paid three pounds odd money : the hearing of which pleased me very well, since I could find one in that notorious place, which had some spark of grace left ; as was manifested by the dislike he shewed to the person that was guilty of the profanation of God's sacred name. When the mob was dispersed, I walked about some small time, and saw a person exceeding well-dress'd in a flower'd morning gown, a band, hat and wig, who appeared so clean that I took him for some worthy divine, who must have accidentally come out of the country by coach, and as accidentally be making the same remarks as myself ; but upon enquiry was surpris'd at being assured, that he was one T—— C——,[1] a watchmaker, who goes in a minister's dress, personating a clergyman, and taking upon him the name of Doctor, to the scandal of the sacred function. He may be seen at any time at the Bull and Garter, or the Great Hand and Pen and Star, with these words underwritten—' The old and true Register ' near the Rainbow Coffee-House.—T. S. "

Entries giving particulars of the marriages were made by the parsons concerned, in books kept for the purpose, and from these registers, as well as from the reports of various trials arising out of the activities of the Fleet parsons, much valuable information is gleanable.

At the trial for bigamy of Edmund Dangerfield, in 1736, the following particulars were elicited in the course of the examination of one of the most notorious of the Fleet parsons, a Dr. John Gainham (or Gaynam) :—

[1] Thomas Crawford.

Dr. Gainham—I don't know the prisoner.   I did marry a man and woman of these names.   Here, this is a true register. ' Edmd. Dangerfield, of St. Mary Newington Butts, bachelor to Arabella Fast '.   When I marry at any house I always set it down, for I carry one of the books in my pocket, and when I go home I put it in my great book.

Court—Do you never make any alteration ?

Dr. Gainham—Never, my Lord.   These two were married at Mrs. Ball's at the Hand and Pen, by the Fleet Prison, and my name is to her book.

Counsel—'Tis strange you should not remember the prisoner.

Dr. Gainham—Can I remember persons ?   I have married 2,000 since that time.

Prisoner's defence—Arabella Fast said to me, ' There is a minister (naming his name) who often lies with me, and if you'll say you are my husband we may get some money out of him.' I took a room for her, within a fortnight after ;   she told me the parson was come to London and now was the time to make him our prize.   ' Come into our room (says she) about 10 o'clock at night '—I did, and found Arabella and he a-bed.   ' Hey ! (says I) how come you a-bed with my spouse ? '   ' Sir, (says he) I only lay with her to keep my back warm.' . . .   In the morning the gentleman said, ' I must make you a present if you can produce a certificate.' I knew not what to say.   ' Sir, (says Arabella) we were married at the Fleet,' and says she, ' For a crown I can get a certificate from the Fleet.'   I gave her a crown, and in half an hour she brings me a certificate.—The prisoner was acquitted."

No inquiries were made or questions asked.   For the couple to say they wished to be married, or for one of them to make this assertion, was enough :   the affair was quickly hurried through, the necessary entry made in the register, and the pocketing of the fee ended the matter.   It was no unusual thing for the man or the woman to be drunk.   The possibilities inherent in such a state of affairs ranked as one of the most pernicious evils connected with the Fleet marriages, as M. l'Abbe le Blanc in his *Letters of a Frenchman*, pointed out in these words : "As the wedding ceremony may here be transacted in any place whatever, I have heard that a clergyman who was in prison, to get a more tolerable subsistence, hung an advertisement at his window with these words, '*Weddings performed cheap here*'. They authorize all the acts of the common prostitute—their most common way is to intoxicate the man they have a design upon and then such a creature who wants to be the *wife* of a man who would perhaps be ashamed to own her for a mistress, prevails upon him by her dangerous caresses, to own before witnesses that he takes her for his wife . . . whence it frequently happens that a man who went to bed very easy and very drunk, finds himself at waking, married to a creature whom he most heartily despises and abhors. The other day a gentleman of Lincoln who had been unfortunate in this respect, shot himself through the head the next day, as soon as he understood the foolish step he had taken."

That these remarks were not exaggerated is indicated in evidence given in court when Richard Leaver was indicted for bigamy in 1737.

Alice Allington. " On January 18, 1733, I was married to the prisoner, at the Hand and Pen, in Fleet Lane, by the famous Doctor Gainham.

Prisoner. " I don't know that woman for my wife. I know nothing about the wedding. I was fuddled overnight, and next morning I found myself a-bed with a strange woman —'And who are you? how came you here?' says I. 'O my dear, says she, we were marry'd last night at the Fleet.' (*Sessions Papers*)

Even these practices did not, however, represent the extent of the unscrupulousness and depravity to which the Fleet parsons were capable of descending. Entries in the registers were often faked, witness the evidence given at the trial of John Miller for bigamy :—

Ann Hodgkins. " On the 11th March, 1724, in the evening, the prisoner and this woman Mary Moore were married at my house in Fleet Lane, by James Starkey, a minister that lodged with me nine years. Mr. Ballantine gave her away, and his wife was present at the same time.

Ballantine. " I never gave away Mary Moore to the prisoner, nor ever so much as saw them together at Mrs. Hodgkins' house in my life; but anybody may have a certificate at her house for half-a-crown, and have their names entered in her book, for as long time past as they please.

Mrs. Ballantine. " I never saw the prisoner and Mary Moore married at Mrs. Hodgkins' house, though I lodged there, nor ever knew of their being married at all.

Ann Glover. " Mary Moore says she'll do my business for me. I went with her to prove her marriage at Mrs. Hodgkins', and Mrs. Hodgkins said, for half-a-guinea she'd enter her name in the Register, for a certificate would not do if the marriage was not registered : her name was not in the book, and I saw Starkey the parson underline her name in the book five years backwards. The parson is now run away into Scotland, and Mary Moore begg'd me not to appear at this trial.

Andrew Montgomery. " Mrs. Hodgkins offered me a marriage certificate for a young woman that happened to be with child, and was hunted by the parish officers, and she said, for half-a-guinea it might be entered backwards in the book and would screen her from the anger of her friends.

Prisoner acquitted, and allowed a copy of his indictment."

Nor did these parsons and their minions display any reluctance to adopt, or squeamishness in the application of, other questionable, dubious or illegal measures. There was a case reported in the *Grub Street Journal*, where a " plyer " employed by the Bull and Garter, induced John Funnel, a fruit-seller, for the sum of half-a-guinea, to impersonate a man named John Todd and marry a woman in his name, the ceremony being performed by a blind parson hired for the purpose. In another instance, according to the *Weekly Journal* (June 29, 1723), sailors were inveigled into matrimony every day in the week, and clocks were kept " standing at the canonical hour, though perhaps the time of day be six or seven in the afternoon." On some occasions women were married against their will. There was the case of Ann Leigh, an heiress, who was decoyed away from her friends and married against her consent. Indeed so rife was this practice that it was not safe for a respectable female to venture alone into the vicinity of the prison. The following letter from the pages of the *Grub Street Journal* (January 15, 1735) is revealing :—

Sir.—There is a very great evil in this town, and of dangerous consequence to our sex, that has never been suppressed, to the great prejudice and ruin of many hundreds of young people every year; which I beg some of your learned heads to consider, and consult of proper ways and means to prevent for the future. I mean the ruinous marriages that are practised in the liberty of the Fleet, and thereabouts, by a set of drunken swearing persons, with their myrmidons, that wear black coats and pretend to be clerks and registrars to the Fleet. These ministers of wickedness ply about Ludgate Hill pulling and forcing people to some peddling alehouse or brandy-shop to be married, even on a Sunday stopping them as they go to church and almost tearing their clothes off their backs. To confirm the truth of these facts, I will give you a case or two which lately happened.

Since Midsummer last a young lady of birth and fortune was deluded and forced from her friends, and by the assistance of a wry-necked swearing parson married to an atheistical wretch, whose life is a continued practice of all manner of vice and debauchery. And since the ruin of my relation, another lady of my acquaintance had like to have been trepanned in the following manner. This lady had appointed to meet a gentle-woman at the old Playhouse in Drury-lane: but extraordinary business prevented her coming. Being alone when the play was done, she bade a boy call a coach for the city. One dressed like a gentleman helps her into it, and jumps in after her. 'Madam,' says he, 'this coach was called for me, and since the weather is so bad and there is no other, I beg leave to bear you company: I am going into the city and will set you down wherever you please.' The lady begged to be excused; but he bade the coachman drive on. Being come to Ludgate Hill, he told her his sister who waited his coming, but five doors up the Court, would go with her in two minutes. He went, and returned with his pretended sister, who asked her to step in one minute, and she would wait upon her in the coach. Deluded with the assurance of having his sister's company, the poor lady foolishly followed her into the house, when instantly the sister vanished, and a tawny fellow in a black coat and black wig appeared. 'Madam, you are come in good time, the Doctor was just a-going!' 'The Doctor,' says she, horribly frighted, fearing it was a madhouse: 'what has the Doctor to do with me?' 'To marry you to that gentleman: the Doctor has waited for you these three hours, and will be paid by you or that gentleman before you go!' 'That gentleman,' says she, recovering herself, ' is worthy a better fortune than mine,' and begged hard to be gone.   But Doctor Wryneck swore she should be married, or if she would not, he would still have his fee, and register the marriage from that night.   The lady finding she could not escape without money or a pledge, told them she liked the gentleman so well, she would certainly meet him to-morrow night, and gave them a ring as a pledge : which, says she, ' was my mother's gift on her death-bed, injoining that, if ever I married it should be my wedding ring.'   By which cunning contrivance she was delivered from the black Doctor and his tawny crew.   Some time after this I went with this lady and her brother in a coach to Ludgate Hill in the daytime, to see the manner of their picking up people to be married.   As soon as our coach stopped near Fleet Bridge, up comes one of the myrmidons.   ' Madam,' says he, ' you want a parson ? '   ' Who are you ? ' says I.   ' I am the clerk and registrar of the Fleet.'   ' Show me the chapel.'   At which comes a second desiring me to go along with him.   Says he, ' That fellow will carry you to a peddling alehouse.'   Says a third, ' Go with me ; he will carry you to a brandy-shop.'   In the interim comes the Doctor. ' Madam,' says he, ' I'll do your job for you presently ! '   ' Well, gentlemen,' says I, ' since you can't agree, and I can't be married quietly, I'll put it off 'till another time,' so drove away.   Learned sirs, I wrote this in regard to the honour and safety of my own sex ; and if for our sakes, you will be so good as to publish it, correcting the errors of a woman's pen, you will oblige our whole sex, and none more than, Sir,

Your constant reader and admirer,

VIRTUOUS.

Various attempts were made to stop these activities of the Fleet parsons, notably in 1712 and 1716, but without any perceptible success.   The reasons for their failure were given in a publication issued in 1720, in which the following observations were made :—

1. The penalty on the gaoler (which had ever since deterred the Warden of the Fleet suffering any marriage there) was not extended to the owners of taverns, alehouses, etc.

2. The penalty on the clerk was too small and was not extended to every person present at the marriage.

3. The 10th Anne might be eluded by the offenders removing themselves back to the Fleet by *habeas corpus*.

4. Every indigent clergyman that forfeits £100, depending on the delay of a writ of error, carries on his offences with impunity for a year and a half, in which time his gain amounts to five times the sum of £100, and then he runs away.

Although for one reason or another the Fleet was the most widely known and undoubtedly the most notorious, there were other places in London where it was possible to be married with the same secrecy and just as expeditiously. There was the King's Bench Prison; there was the May Fair; and, later, there was the Savoy. Of these, by far the most celebrated was the May Fair chapel, where the Rev. Alexander Keith joined in matrimony any couple who expressed their mutual desire to become man and wife. His announcement appeared in the advertisement pages of the *Daily Post* (July 20, 1744), thus :—

"To prevent mistakes, the little new chapel in May Fair, near Hyde Park Corner, is in the corner house opposite to the City side of the great chapel, and within ten yards of it, and the minister and clerk live in the same corner house, where the little chapel is, and the license on a crown stamp, minister's and clerk's fees, together with the certificate, amount to one guinea as heretofore, at any hour till four in the afternoon. And that it may be better known, there is a porch at the door like that of a country church."

Horace Walpole, in a letter dated February 27, 1752, to Sir Horace Mann, tells of a wedding celebrated in the Curzon Street chapel. Apropos of the marriage of the beautiful Miss Elizabeth Gunning, younger of two sisters, after a lightning courtship by the Duke of Hamilton, he says that Lord Coventry has long dangled after the elder sister. About six weeks before, the Duke had fallen in love with Elizabeth Gunning and determined to marry her in the spring, but some two weeks ago, at an assembly held at the house of Lord Chesterfield, he made violent love to her. Two nights later, continues Walpole (and here it is as well to give the story in his own words) : "Being left alone with her, while her mother and sister were at Bedford House, he found himself so impatient that he sent for a parson. The Doctor refused to perform the ceremony without licence or ring; the

Duke swore he would send for the Archbishop; at last they were married with a ring of the bed-curtain, at half-an-hour after twelve at night, at May Fair chapel. The Scotch are enraged; the women mad that so much beauty has had its effect; and, what is more silly, my Lord Coventry declares that now he will marry the other."

In another letter, this time addressed to George Montagu, dated September 3, 1748, Walpole referred to a wedding equally strange. He wrote: "Did you know a young fellow that was called handsome Tracy? He was walking in the Park with some of his acquaintances, and overtook three girls; one was very pretty: they followed them, but the girls ran away, and the company grew tired of pursuing them, all but Tracy. He followed them to Whitehall-gate, where he gave the porter a crown to dog them: the porter hunted them, he the porter. The girls ran all round Westminster and back to the Hay-market, where the porter came up with them. He told the pretty one she must go with him, and kept her talking till Tracy arrived quite out of breath, and exceedingly in love. He insisted on knowing where she lived, which she refused to tell him; and after much disputing, went to the house of one of her companions, and Tracy with them. He there made her discover her family, a butterwoman in Craven Street, and engaged her to meet him the next morning in the Park; but before night he wrote her four love-letters, and in the last offered two hundred pounds a year to her, and a hundred a year to Signora la Madre. Griselda made a confidence to a staymaker's wife, who told her the swain was certainly in love enough to marry her if she could determine to be virtuous and refuse his offers. 'Ay,' says she, ' but if I should, and should lose him by it.' However, the measures of the cabinet council were decided for virtue; and when she met Tracy the next morning in the Park, she was convoyed by her sister and brother-in-law, and stuck close to the letter of her reputation. She would do nothing, she would go nowhere. At last, as an instance of prodigious compliance, she told him that if he would accept such a dinner as a butter-woman's daughter could give him he should be welcome. Away they walked to Craven Street; the mother borrowed some silver to buy a leg of mutton, and they kept the eager lover drinking till twelve at night, when, with a chosen committee the faithful pair waited on the minister of May Fair. The Doctor

FLEET MARRIAGE CERTIFICATE
1727

A FLEET WEDDING
From a drawing by "Phiz"

was in bed, and swore he would not get up to marry the king, but that he had a brother over the way who perhaps would, and who did. The mother borrowed a pair of sheets, and they consummated at her house; and the next day they went to their own palace."[1]

Owing to the situation of the King's Bench prison, it was not popular as a place for solemnizing marriages, although occasional clandestine unions were celebrated there until the time when, early in the eighteenth century, it lost its privileges. Tegg says: "In the neighbourhood of the King's Bench was a part of the Borough called 'The Mint', a place of refuge for thieves and malefactors of the worst description; which, with White Friars, the Savoy, and other places about London, claimed certain privileges, and held out the advantages of a sanctuary to all debtors, thieves, and malefactors. At this place marriages were performed, and amongst the Fleet Registers are three Registers of King's Bench and Mint marriages."[2]

The old Savoy Chapel, which, being extra parochial, was not subject to ecclesiastical law, was also utilized for the purpose of solemnizing clandestine marriages. It was to John Wilkinson, the popular chaplain of the Savoy, that occurred the idea of using the chapel for this purpose.

And so, for their competitors, as well as for the Fleet parsons, all went swimmingly until the Marriage Act became law. In 1753, Lord Hardwicke introduced a Bill which enacted that any person solemnizing a marriage in any other than a church or public chapel, without banns or licence, should on conviction be adjudged guilty of felony, and be transported for fourteen years, and that all such marriages should be void. The provisions of this Bill, despite the most determined opposition, including that of the redoubtable Mr. Fox, eventually became the law of the land on March 25, 1754.

During the protracted period which, in consequence of fierce and prolonged controversy, elapsed before Lord Hardwicke's Bill became law, the parsons of the Fleet, May Fair, and the Savoy worked overtime. On the day before the Act came into force 217 couples were married at the Fleet and 61 at May Fair; and so far as these two venues were concerned these marriages

---

[1] Quoted by J. Heneage Jesse, in *Literary and Historical Memorials of London*, Bentley, 1847. Vol. I, p. 59.
[2] William Tegg, *The Knot Tied*, 1877, p. 209.

were the last. The Savoy, it is true, continued until John Wilkinson was prosecuted and sentenced to fourteen years' transportation.

II

The Marriages of Gretna Green

So far as those belonging to the poorer sections of the population of England were concerned, the Marriage Act of 1754 put an end to clandestine unions. But as regards the wealthy, the position was a very different one indeed. It was still possible to be married secretly and hurriedly, and without ecclesiastic rubric or ceremony. All that one need do was travel to Scotland, to the little village of Springfield, near Gretna Green, just across the border, in the county of Dumfriesshire.

According to the law relating to marriage then applying in Scotland, a union was valid if the couple made, before witnesses, a mutual declaration of their desire to live together as man and wife : the ceremony could be performed on the instant and on the spot. Indeed, according to Erskine, even a ceremony was unnecessary, mutual consent being enough to constitute a lawful marriage ; while Edgar affirmed that the mere fact of a man and a woman taking up house together and declaring themselves to be husband and wife was sufficient to make them, in the eyes of the law, married persons.[1] An English couple need stay on the soil of Scotland no longer than the time taken to join them in matrimony, after which they could return immediately to England, and they were married as surely and as durably as if the ceremony had been performed in an English church. In these circumstances, it was not unnatural that, with the abolition of clandestine marriages in England, many couples, especially of the wealthy classes, crossed the border to the nearest spot affording the necessary facilities for marriage according to Scots law.

[1] A former Scots nuptial ceremony is referred to by Constance F. Gordon Cumming, thus : " Sometimes the young couple each took a handful of meal, and kneeling down, with a bowl between them, emptied their hands therein, and mixed the meal ; at the same time taking an oath on the Bible never to sever till death should them part." At a case tried at Dalkeith, in 1872, " this simple marriage ceremony," says this author, " was proved by Scotch law to be legally binding." (From the Hebrides to the Himalayas, Sampson Low, London, 1876. Vol. I, p. 274.)

In this connexion, Forsyth says : "At the southern extremity of the county [Dumfriesshire] Graitney (commonly called *Gretna*) has long been famous, in the annals of matrimonial adventure, for the marriages of fugitive lovers from England, which have been celebrated there. This is never done by the clergyman of the parish. Indeed, although no particular solemnity is necessary to the constitution of the marriage contract any more than to any other lawful engagement in Scotland, and although any person may act as the celebrator of the marriage, to the effect of rendering the engagement completely binding, and the issue of it lawful children, capable of inheriting the property of their parents ; yet severe statutory penalties may be inflicted upon the celebrator and witnesses of any marriage entered into without regular proclamation of banns. Hence irregular, or, as they are called in Scotland, *clandestine* marriages, are only celebrated by persons who have nothing to lose."[1]

Of the village of Springfield, Gretna, Pennant writes : "At a short distance from the bridge is the little village of Gretna, situated in Scotland but within a mile of the English border, the resort of all amorous couples whose union the prudence of parents or guardians prohibits. Here the young pair may be instantly united by a fisherman, a joiner, or a blacksmith, who may marry for a fee varying in value from two guineas to a glass of whisky. But the price is generally adjusted by the information of the postilions from Carlisle (eight miles distant), who are in the pay of one or other of the above worthies ; but even the drivers, in case of necessity, have been known to undertake the sacerdotal office. This place is distinguished from afar by a small plantation of firs, the Cyprian grove of the neighbourhood, a sort of landmark for fugitive lovers. As I had a great desire to see the high priest, by stratagem I succeeded. He appeared in the form of a fisherman, a stout fellow in a blue coat, rolling round his solemn chops a quid of tobacco of no common size. One of our party was supposed to come to explore the coast. He questioned him about the price, which, after eyeing us attentively, he left to our honour. The Church of Scotland does all that it can to prevent these clandestine marriages, but in vain, for these infamous couplers despise the fulminations of the kirk, and excommunication is the only penalty it can inflict."

[1] R. Forsyth, *The Beauties of Scotland.* Vol. II, p. 276.

This marriage-mart, for Gretna was nothing else, did a roaring business in more ways than one. Apart from the fees, which were often handsome ones reaching, on occasion, we are told, as much as one hundred guineas, which changed hands for the actual marriage certificate; the innkeepers and the shops shared in the plunder, as it was customary for the couples to stay at least one night in the village. Apropos of this Hutchinson writes: " There are several marrying-shops in this most remarkable and interesting parish, by the proprietors of which this trade is pretty much monopolized to the exclusion of many others who would set up for themselves in so profitable a line, if they could contrive it; but when strangers rush hastily into the place, they must of necessity repair to some hotel or inn, there to abide whilst the ceremony is being perpetrated; and thus the proprietors of such establishments possess advantages in monopoly which no private persons can cope with, although any inhabitant may have equal right to marry the strangers, just as much as the innkeepers. Thus a kind of understanding has been set up, and entered into between the innkeepers of Carlisle and the innkeepers of Gretna; the former sending customers to the latter, their friends, and the latter playing back into the hands of the former by sharing the rich proceeds; and in this manner they reciprocally carry on a right slashing business."[1]

Sir George Head, in his tour of Scotland in 1835, evinced much interest in (to use the quotation he himself gives) :—

" That mystical bourne,
From whence maidens and bachelors seldom return."

Sir George says: " The old original marrying-house is in the village of Springfield, nearly a mile from Gretna Green, an exceedingly small public house, kept at present by one John Sowerby, as notified by a square sign, nailed against the side of the house, over the door. The house, since the days of old David or Daniel Laing, has undergone no alteration, and the same business as formerly is transacted under its roof; but the matrimonial branch is now confined almost altogether to the poorer classes. . . . Gretna Hall, a very respectable-looking country inn, is immediately contiguous to Gretna Green, which latter is, as many people know, nine miles from Carlisle. At this house all the modern matrimonial affairs, among the higher

---

[1] Peter Orlando Hutchinson, *Chronicles of Gretna Green*, 1844, p. 25.

classes, have of late years been conducted; and hither all inquiring strangers are directed point blank; besides, a painted board points out the way from the Green to lovers and travellers, along a wide, straight drive, leading to the door. The establishment possesses considerable advantages over the old one—indeed the one is a comfortable country residence, whereas the other more resembles a pot-house, such as the ' Jolly Sailor ', or ' The Three Loggerheads ', in a seaport-town. The new clergyman also, who may be said, phœnix-like, to have arisen from the ashes of the old one—for whether or not the ancient Daniel or David departed in a fit of spontaneous combustion, is a point, I believe, hardly determined—exists under terms of comparison with his predecessor equally favourable. He is not only clergyman, but landlord also—both persons in one ; whence it arises, partly proceeding from his own moral qualities, and partly owing to his office of landlord, which confines him to the spot, that he possesses those qualifications that every Gretna Green clergyman ought to have—namely, he is at all times to be found in a hurry ; and, finally, when found, sober, and able to perform his duty. In person he is a slight, fair, good-looking man ; of age about forty, of prepossessing manners, and mild and respectful in his demeanour ; and of him it may be particularly remarked, that without bearing the mien of a dignitary of the church, he seems a person qualified to encourage a timid bride, and allay the scruples of any young lady his customer, provided she chance to bring any so far along with her. On the present occasion, he was dressed in the style of a respectable layman or farmer—altogether in rural costume, namely, a clean, tidy, light-coloured fustian shooting-jacket and shooting etceteras. In case of emergencies a qualified deputy or sub-clergyman resides on the spot, in the person of a slim, civil, harmless-looking lad, his son, who, were it not that youth, where the fair sex are concerned, seldom detracts from personal merit, might be thought too young ; he states his age to be two-and-twenty, though he looks hardly out of his teens. At all events, it is well in matters of love to insure against the possibility of disappointment, and prudent thus to have, in case the old man happen to be out of the way, a young one at hand. No matter by which of the clergymen the everlasting knot be tied, whether the young one or the old one, a regular entry of the marriage is made in a book kept for the purpose ; this entry, after some months, is copied into the register; in the meantime, the register alone is submitted to the inspection of inquisitive strangers."[1]

For many generations it was firmly believed (and the belief survives in some quarters to this day), that the Gretna Green wedding ceremonies were invariably performed by the local blacksmith. With the promulgation of this belief, Sir Walter Scott had a good deal to do. He wrote: "The village of Gretna, towards the termination of the Solway Firth, has been famous in the annals of matrimonial adventure, for the clandestine marriages of fugitive lovers from England, which have been solemnized at this celebrated temple of Hymen. The priest who died lately, a blacksmith by trade, has been known to draw one hundred guineas from one couple for performing the ceremony. Springfield, another flourishing village, is only a short distance from Gretna. At the port of Sarkfoot, there is a considerable importation of wood, tar, slates, and other merchandise."

Now, that a David Laing at one time acted in the capacity of "priest" is quite true. It was David Laing who married Edward Gibbon Wakefield and Miss Turner. But David was no blacksmith. Nor was his son, Simon, who gave up his weaving to take up the trade of marrying, following his father's retirement, and thereafter practised no other. Of others who performed marriage ceremonies, Joseph Paisley was not a blacksmith[2] as repute had it, but a tobacconist;[3] and George

---

[1] Sir George Head, *A Home Tour through the Manufacturing Districts and other parts of England, Scotland, and Ireland*, John Murray, London, 1840. Vol. I, pp. 374–276.

[2] Elliott states that Paisley acquired the name of ' blacksmith ' from his quickness in uniting eloping parties, the common saying being " strike the iron when it is hot, Joseph."

[3] Forsyth gives the following details, culled from the Statistical Account of Graitney: "The persons . . . are priests of their own creation. . . . There are at present more than one of this description in this place : but the greatest part of the trade is monopolized by a man who was originally a tobacconist, and not a blacksmith, as is generally believed. He is a fellow without literature, without principles, without morals, and without manners. His life is a continued scene of drunkenness. His irregular conduct has rendered him an object of detestation to all the sober and virtuous part of the neighbourhood. Such is the man (and the description is not exaggerated) who has had the honour to join, in the sacred bands of wedlock, many people of great rank and fortune from all parts of England. It is forty years and upwards since marriages of this kind began to be celebrated here. At the lowest computation about sixty are supposed to be solemnized annually in this place. Taken at an average through the year, they may be estimated at 15 guineas each ; consequently this traffic brings in about £945 a year. The form of ceremony, when any ceremony is used, is that of the Church of England. On some occasions, particularly when the parson is intoxicated, which is often the case, a certificate is given. The certificate is signed by the parson himself and two witnesses under fictitious signatures." (R. Forsyth, *The Beauties of Scotland*. Vol. II, pp. 276–277.)

Gordon a former soldier. A contemporary fallacy, asserts Hutchinson, was that the blacksmith requested his clients, as an essential part of the marriage ceremony, to jump over a broomstick.

The blacksmith legend was given much publicity by the enterprising proprietor of a beershop in the village. This man, by name Thomas Little, erected a sign over the doorway depicting a marriage ceremony being performed in a smithy, with an anvil acting as an altar, and a blacksmith officiating. But Hutchinson, author of an authoritative book on Gretna Green marriages, says: " In spite of all our inquiries, and searching, and scrutiny, we could not discover that a blacksmith had of late years performed the ceremony, nor indeed, that a blacksmith had *ever* done it at any period *whatever*."[1] But what did transpire, from the investigations of this authority, was the reason why a native artist should place the venue of the wedding in a blacksmith's shop when every Scotsman was fully aware of the fact that such a ceremony had never been celebrated in such a place. In all its ingenuousness I give the explanation here; it is taken from Hutchinson's interesting book: " To this the answer was, ' Oh, why, we know it's wrong, strictly speaking; but then we know that our best customers the English, whom we wish to attract and please, have taken such a notion into their heads; and the fact of its popularity is quite recommendation enough for us to adopt it as a sign. Never mind strict truth in this matter; when a party of runaways from the south come over the Moss into the village, they immediately see a sign that coincides with the favourite idea, and the pleasure derived from this concordance from seeing their cherished fancy revealed to them here in bright colours, is a thing not to be passed by or withstood. The truth therefore, is nothing; you perceive the policy of the sign."[2]

Robert Elliott, according to his own confession, in the period from 1811 to 1839, married no fewer than 7,744 persons. In his book, *The Gretna Green Memoirs*, he described the marriage ceremony as he and his predecessors performed it, thus: " The parties are first asked their names and places of abode; they are then asked to stand up, and enquired of if they are both single persons; if the answer be in the affirmative, the ceremony proceeds. Each is next asked, ' Did you come here of your

[1] Hutchinson, op. cit., p. 176.
[2] Hutchinson, op. cit., p. 188.

own free will and accord?' Upon receiving an affirmative answer the priest commences filling in the printed form of the certificate. The man is then asked, 'Do you take this woman to be your lawful wedded wife, forsaking all others, and keep to her as long as you both shall live?' He answers, 'I will.' The woman is asked the same question, which being answered the same, the woman then produces a ring, which she gives to the man, who hands it to the priest; the priest then returns it to the man, and orders him to put it on the fourth finger of the woman's left hand, and repeat these words, 'With this ring I thee wed, with my body I thee worship, with all my goods I thee endow, in the name of the Father, Son, and Holy Ghost, Amen.' They then take hold of each other's right hands, and the woman says, 'What God joins together let no man put asunder.' Then the priest says, 'Forasmuch as this man and this woman have consented to go together by giving and receiving a ring, I, therefore declare them to be man and wife before God and these witnesses, in the name of the Father, Son, and Holy Ghost, Amen.'"

This prolonged service described by Elliott was not essential however. Presumably it was employed in cases where the couple expressed a desire for a ceremony of a type bearing some resemblance to orthodox ecclesiastical usage. The majority were concerned with getting the job completed in the quickest possible time and with the least ceremony; and in most instances the filling in of the printed certificate of marriage which was available, constituted the major part of the proceedings. Hutchinson says: "The spaces left blank in the paper are filled up with the names and places of abode of the parties; and then they subscribe their names at the right hand lower corner, whilst two witnesses (who may be the innkeeper and the postilion) do the same on the other side of the document. This is all that is necessary to constitute a legal and binding marriage, and the certificate is always a sufficient voucher that it has taken place."[1]

The Act passed in the reign of Queen Victoria, although it did not stop the Gretna Green weddings, had a curbing effect. The Act contained the following clause: "After the thirty-first of December, one thousand eight hundred and fifty-six, no irregular marriage contracted in Scotland, by declaration, acknowledgment, or ceremony, shall be valid, unless one of the parties has at the

---

[1] Hutchinson, op. cit., p. 212.

date thereof his or her usual residence there, or has lived in Scotland for twenty-one days next preceding such marriage ; any law, custom, or usage to the contrary notwithstanding."

Another form of clandestine marriage is described by Rogers : " In the burgh of Rutherglen, Lanarkshire," he writes, " till within the last twenty years, persons were married, without proclamation of banns, by a peculiar arrangement on the part of the authorities. A friend of the parties was sent to the Procurator-Fiscal, to lodge information that they had been married without legal banns. The Fiscal summoned the delinquents before the sheriff, who, on their admitting the charge, imposed a fine of five shillings. The Fiscal took the penalty, and handed to the parties a printed form, duly filled up, which by discharging the fine, certified the marriage. Ruglen or Rutherglen marriages have passed into a proverb."[1]

[1] Charles Rogers, *Scotland, Social and Domestic*, 1869, p. 118.

PART FIVE

PROHIBITIONS AND TABOOS RELATING TO MARRIAGE

CHAPTER XX

TABOOS IN CONNEXION WITH MARRIAGE

I

The Emergence and Development of the Incest Taboo

INCEST is the sexual union of a man and a woman who are related to each other by blood in any one of the degrees which are prohibited by law. These degrees of kinship vary in different countries and they vary in the same country at different times in its history. A marriage within any one of these prohibited degrees of relationship is an incestuous union. It is important to note that there must be consanguinity. A prohibited marriage which is not consanguineous is not incestuous; it is merely unlawful.

In some primitive tribes there is much confusion respecting the matter of consanguinity, which leads to marriage being prohibited where the relationship in reality is of the slightest, and in many cases where there is no relationship at all. Writing of the Kaffirs, Thompson says : " In their connubial connexions they observe with great strictness certain rules of consanguinity, and are particularly scrupulous never to intermarry with persons descended from the same ancestors as themselves, although related only in the ninth or tenth degree. If they are able to trace their descent from the same progenitor, however remote, they are always called brothers and sisters."[1] Such a state of affairs may easily lead to the practice of exogamy.

Many savage and primitive races have always been either wholly or partially incestuous. Thus there are Indians living in Central and South America who regularly commit incest with their daughters ; according to Mantegazza, in Cambodia fathers marry their daughters, mothers their sons, and brothers their sisters ; Junker says the chiefs of Niam Niam marry their

---

[1] George Thompson, *Travels and Adventures in Southern Africa*, 1827, second edition. Vol. II, p. 356.

daughters; in Madagascar, brother and sister marriages are common; Langsdorff states that at the beginning of the nineteenth century, the Aleuts were cohabiting incestuously, fathers with their daughters, sons with their mothers, and brothers with sisters.[1]   So, too, among the aborigines of New Zealand.

Consanguinity in the civilized state has not always been prohibited or condemned universally as it is to-day.   Ancient Egypt is regarded as its classical home, the kings, encouraged by the example of their deities, Isis and Osiris, married their own daughters and sisters with reckless abandon.   Ahmose I married his sister, so did Amenhotep I.   Queen Hatshepsut married her half-brother.   The laws of the ancient Phœnicians allowed the union in marriage of a son with his mother, or a father with his daughter.   Abraham took as wife his half-sister; Nahor took the daughter of his brother; Lot committed incest with his own daughters.   Likewise, in ancient Greece, under Solon, a man and a girl sired by the same father could marry with impunity, such a union not being recognized as consanguinous.   Turning to Rome, Attila married his daughter; Claudius, his niece.   The Persians of old similarly, according to Tertullian, encouraged unions between sons and mothers; among the Medes and the Scythians brother and sister marriages were everyday affairs.   In ancient Arabia the son was compelled by law to marry his widowed mother.   In Peru, the old Incas married their eldest sisters; in Teneriffe, the ancient kings did the same.

The restriction of marriage to certain families, classes, or circles, which Dr. W. M. Thomson well describes as a " system of *matrimonial* clanism,"[2] the principal object of which appears to be the retention of property within a family or clan, tends to encourage close and often incestuous unions.   It was a basic principle of many forms of Mosaic sociology, and has figured in the laws affecting marriage in many races since.

In modern civilization, however, the marriage of near blood relations is everywhere prohibited.   Incest, while it does occur, is practically restricted to extra-marital intercourse, and in most countries is a criminal act.   In Scotland, after the Reformation, incest was punishable by the Ecclesiastical Courts.   In 1611 the

---

[1] W. G. Sumner, *Folkways*, 1907, p. 485.   This work is a mine of information on the subject of incest in savage society.

[2] W. M. Thomson, *The Land and the Book*, 1862, p. 292.

Synod of Fife, dealing with a case, ordained Laurence Ferguson, in the parish of Kirkcaldy, who had been guilty of incest, to "pass ilk Saboth day from kirk to kirk *per circulum*, throughout the haill kirkes in the boundis of the Exerceis of Kirkaldie, according as he salbe injoyned be the brethren of the samine, and that in sackcloth, for the space of ane yeir compleitt, without any intermissionne of dayes, vntil the next diocesian Assemblie to be holdin (God willing) in St. Androis, in the moneth of Apryl, 1612."

In England incest became a punishable offence with the passing of the Punishment of Incest Act, 1908, which provides that intercourse by any male person with his mother, sister, daughter or granddaughter is punishable with imprisonment. For the purpose of the Act a half-brother or a half-sister ranks the same as a brother or sister. The fact that the female was a willing party is no defence. If she does consent, and is over the age of sixteen years, she is as guilty of a criminal act as is the male.

The causes of the rigid taboo imposed upon the marriage of blood relations, not only throughout the civilized world since the dawn of Christianity, but among many savage and primitive races, is obscure. It is true many ingenious attempts at an explanation have from time to time been propounded, but they are little more than guesswork. The generally accepted view that the observed ill-effects of breeding from blood relations led to the prohibition of consanguinity in marriage is somewhat strained, and certainly could not apply in regard to many savage tribes in which the taboo was in operation long before its adoption by civilized nations. As an explanation, therefore, of the first conception of the incest taboo I find myself unable to accept it. Apropos of this argument I wrote some years ago, in my *Encyclopædia of Sex*, the following comments : " It seems to me to be full of flaws. It predicates, in the first place, a knowledge of the principles governing procreation which only came many centuries later. In the second place, it is doubtful if inbreeding, because of the survival of the fittest which was the primary law of nature in those days, would have the harmful effects which in certain circumstances it has to-day."

It has been said that individuals who grow up together have no sexual attraction for each other, a point to which both Westermarck and Havelock Ellis have drawn attention. But admirable and sanity-brimming as is this as a reason why members of the same family, in normal circumstances, and particularly in present-day conditions in civilized states, are seldom drawn to each other in amorous passion; it provides no explanation whatever for the taboo of consanguinity and the need for society to invoke the aid of the law to prevent incest.

To quote once more from one of my previously-published books : " My own hypothesis, which I present not dogmatically, but as a guess with as much chance of hitting the truth as any other guess, is that the horror of incest was of gradual growth, eventually coming to fruition simultaneously with the development of property rights and the end of polyandry. Incest and polyandry are bedmates. Wherever women are scarce, and the males, through isolation, danger, or other causes, are prevented from seeking women of other races or families, polyandry is common ; and for precisely the same reasons, incest is common, too. Man is not inclined to turn up his nose at any particular woman, however ugly and unappetising she may be, if there is no other female for the choosing. . . . In modern civilization, poverty, by limiting man's opportunities, acts analogously. The case-histories given by Krafft-Ebing are mostly concerned with peasants and debauchees. Zola in *La Terre* and Sue in *The Mysteries of Paris* refer to the widespread practice of incest among the lower orders. Anyone who keeps his ears open knows that in every village and town carefully hushed-up instances of incest are of common occurrence."[1]

In modern civilized countries, apart from the horror associated with any form of incestuous intercourse, the disadvantages and dangers inseparable from careless inbreeding are sufficient to lead the State, in the interests of health and vigour, to exercise a rigid taboo on consanguinity. There is abundant evidence that inbreeding in very many cases has been the cause of progressive degeneration in human beings, as well as in animals and birds. Inbreeding fixes the qualities already possessed by the parent stock, whether these qualities be good or bad. Outbreeding, that is the mating together of unrelated stock, on the other hand, provided the breeding stock is suitably selected, has a tendency to introduce new features or to develop existent ones, but whether the variations thus induced are advantageous or otherwise is a moot point. It is by outbreeding that new breeds or varieties of animals and birds are created. And certainly in

[1] George Ryley Scott, *Marriage in the Melting Pot*, T. Werner Laurie, 1930, p. 205.

most cases outbreeding leads to additional vigour or physical stamina.   At the same time it must be remembered that many other factors besides unintelligent or promiscuous inbreeding figure in the causation of physical and mental degeneration, and sterility.

II

The Condemnation and Punishment of Adultery

Apart from those savage and primitive tribes in which promiscuity, even within the marital state, was uncondemned or encouraged; great value has always, and as regards all races, been placed upon a married woman's fidelity.   In most cases the marital union has been brought to an end by a detected or an admitted act of unchastity.   Adultery was looked upon as a reason for divorce in the early days of Christianity.

Often in savage races the punishment was death, and in some cases death in a most horrible form.   In many instances both parties concerned shared the same fate.   Martins says : "A man found in the harem of Muato-jamvos was cut in pieces and given, raw and warm, to the people to be eaten."[1]

Punishment for the wife caught in adultery there always has been in any State claiming to be civilized.   In the olden days the punishment was severe.   The Mosaic code was especially so : it ordained that both parties to the crime be stoned to death. We see evidence of the views of the Israelites as well as the lawmakers in the way in which the members of the tribe of Benjamin were very nearly annihilated because they would not hand over to justice the wife of Levite and her partner in adultery.

Bizarre methods were often used to prove or disprove the chastity of a woman.   Among the ancient Greeks, for instance, it was customary, when a woman was accused of immorality, for a tablet inscribed with an oath affirming her chastity, to be hung around her neck.   She was then ordered to walk into a river, lake, or other body of water until it reached the calves of her legs, and at this juncture to repeat the oath written on the tablet : in the event of the oath being false, the water, it was believed, would rise up until it submerged the hanging

[1] Quoted by W. G. Sumner in *Folkways*, p. 334.

tablet; if the oath were a true statement, the water would remain calm and at its present level, thus clearing the accused of all suspicion.

These Greeks of olden days had other methods, too, for proving the chasteness of married women who were unjustly suspected or accused by their husbands. It was firmly believed that the gods, in their commiseration for a woman in this plight, were pleased to exempt her from the pain and difficulty attending childbirth, and therefore any woman who went through the ordeal of parturition without a groan, affirming that she was quite free from pain, was declared, whatever evidence to the contrary her husband might bring forth, to be as chaste as Vesta.

The woman accused of unchastity who was lucky enough to bear twins or triplets became cleared of every shadow of suspicion on the instant and on the spot. The ancient Greeks were adamant in the belief that only a wife of unexceptionable virtue and the purest character would be singled out by the gods for so profound a blessing as a multiple birth.

In the Bible of the Hindus the punishment for those guilty of adultery takes many forms. I quote from Alexander's *History of Women*: "If a man commit adultery with a woman of a superior caste, he shall be put to death; if by force he commit adultery with a woman of an equal or inferior caste, the magistrate shall confiscate all his possessions, cut off his genitals, and cause him to be carried round the city mounted on an ass. If by fraud he commit adultery with a woman of an equal or inferior caste, the magistrate shall take his possessions, brand him on the forehead, and banish him the kingdom. Such are the laws of the Shastra, so far as they regard all the superior castes, except the Brahmins; but if any of the most inferior castes commit adultery with a woman of the castes greatly superior, he is not only to be dismembered, but tied to a hot iron plate and burnt to death; whereas the highest caste may commit adultery with the very lowest, for the most trifling fine; and a Brahmin, or priest, can only suffer by having the hair of his head cut off; and, like the clergy of Europe while under the dominion of the Pope, he cannot be put to death for any crime whatever. But the laws, of which he is always the interpreter, are not so favourable to his wife; they inflict a severe disgrace upon her, if she commit adultery with any of the higher castes; but if with the lowest, the magistrate shall cut off her hair, anoint her body with ghee, and cause her to be carried through the whole city, naked, and riding upon an ass; and shall cast her out on the north side of the city, or cause her to be eaten by dogs. If a woman of any of the other castes goes to a man, and entices him to have criminal correspondence with her, the magistrate shall cut off her ears, lips and nose, mount her upon an ass, and drown her, or throw her to the dogs." The Shokas, who inhabit the Himalayas, not only inflict severe corporal punishment on the guilty man but often extend this punishment to his parents. Also their possessions are seized and handed over to the husband of the seduced woman.[1] In some tribes of American Indians the husband bites off his wife's nose.[2]

In ancient Greece adultery was looked upon as a most heinous crime and accordingly considered to call for savage punishment. The exact nature of the punishment however varied in different parts of the country and in different ages. Often the penalty imposed was blinding. Little tells us that Hippomenes sentenced his own daughter, Limone, as well as her partner in crime, " to be yoked to a chariot till the man died; the woman was afterwards shut up with a horse, and they were both starved to death."[3] At Gartyn, in Crete, the law-makers were more merciful, however, as the same authority tells us that adulterers were covered from head to foot with wool, " to denote the effeminacy of their tempers "; and taken through the city to appear before a magistrate, " who deprived them of nearly all their privileges, and rendered them incapable of taking any part in public affairs."[4] At one time, another singularly severe punishment, from the point of view of most women, though not of a capital nature, was that which enacted that anyone detected in the act of adultery should never again be permitted to don elegant attire: if she appeared in public smartly dressed any person was at liberty to tear the clothes from her back and give her a sound thrashing into the bargain.

In Java any of the emperor's women guilty of adultery were put to death either by the sword or a dose of poison. The following description of an execution is from the pen of an

[1] A. Henry Savage Landor, *In the Forbidden Land*, William Heinemann, London, 1898. Vol. I, p. 115.
[2] J. Carver, *Travels Through the Interior Parts of North America*, 1781, p. 375.
[3] Thomas Little, *The Beauty, Marriage-Ceremonies and Intercourse of the Sexes*, second edition, London, 1824. Vol. II, p. 137.
[4] Little, op. cit., Vol. II, p. 137.

eye-witness : " In the forenoon, about eleven o'clock, the fair criminals were led into an open space within the palace. The judge sentenced them to be poisoned with a lance, dipped in *upas*. An Alcoran was then presented to them, and they were forced to confess, according to the Mahometan laws, that the sentence passed upon them was just. This they did by laying the right hand upon the Alcoran, and the left upon their breasts, with their eyes looking towards Heaven : the judge then raised the Alcoran to their lips, and they kissed it. Thirteen posts, each about five feet high, had been previously erected ; to these the delinquents, thirteen in number, were fastened, and their bosoms bared. They continued a short time in prayer, attended by several priests, until the signal was made by the judge, when the executioner produced an instrument like the spring-lances used for bleeding horses. With this instrument, which was poisoned with the gum of the *upas*, the unhappy creatures were pierced in the middle of the breast. The operation was performed on all, in less than two minutes ; and, within five minutes, a violent tremor, attended with a *subsultus tendinum*, seized on them, and in sixteen minutes, they had all expired, in the greatest agonies, calling upon God and Mahomet to have mercy on them."[1]

In Guinea capital punishment was formerly the fate of both man and woman. Two graves were dug first of all. A stake was erected in one of them, and to it was secured the female culprit, so that she could, as the initial part of her punishment, witness the fate of her lover. Iron bars were laid across the top of the second grave, on them the man was laid face downwards, securely fixed in this position, and literally roasted alive over a fire lighted at the bottom of the grave. On the completion of this gruesome programme, a number of women, each carrying a pot of scalding water, arrived on the scene : they poured the hot water over the captive woman's head, after which the bonds were cut away, the stake uprooted, and the woman's body thrown to the bottom of the grave.

The ancient Egyptians did not go so far as to inflict the death penalty, but they took measures which ensured that the man, at any rate, would not repeat his offence, and that, except in abnormal circumstances, the repetition of any such crime on the part of the female was unlikely : they castrated the male,

[1] Little, op. cit., Vol. III, p. 114.

and they cut off the woman's nose.   The injured husband, too, by the laws of Sweden and Denmark, in ancient days, was permitted to kill his wife and to castrate her lover.   In France, Margaret of Burgundy was hanged, while her lovers were flayed alive.

In other parts of the world equally drastic punishments were devised.   In the China of long ago it was customary to sell the offending wife as a slave.   The Grand Seignor, should one of his wives come under suspicion, did not wait for actual proof, but ordered her to be put in a sack, which was then sewed up, and with its human contents, thrown into the nearest river. But even such penalties as these did not mark the limit to which cruelty and tyranny could go.   Pope Sixtux Quintus, not content with the death of the adulterers themselves, had such husbands as lodged no complaints against their erring wives although well aware of their infidelities, put to death as well.

In England, King Edgar stopped short at the death penalty : he ordered the offender, whether male or female, to live three days a week on bread and water for a space of seven years, though, how, short of actual imprisonment, the sentence was enforced, is by no means clear.   King Ethelbert ordained that a man guilty of adultery with another man's wife, should pay a fine to the husband and buy him another wife.   At the time when Canute came to the throne, the punishment then in force was abscission of the nose and ears, but he would have none of this, and replaced it with condemnation to perpetual celibacy.

In other lands, too, the lawmakers devised punishments which were deemed efficacious without having recourse to actual mutilation or death.   A singularly mild punishment was that devised by the Muskhogees, a tribe of North American Indians, the adulterers being forced to remain strictly continent for the space of time covered by four full moons.   In Abyssinia, the punishment meted out to a woman guilty of adultery was the shaving of her head, the confiscation of her possessions, and expulsion from her husband's home.

As might well have been expected in a land where parting with money has always been as painful a process as a major surgical operation, in ancient Wales, according to Alexander, " even the king thought that a full reparation was made for the dishonour of defiling his bed, by obliging the offender to pay a rod of pure gold, of the thickness of the finger of a ploughman, who had ploughed nine years, and which would reach from the ground to the king's mouth when sitting."[1]   In ancient Germany, a woman caught in adultery was stripped naked, deprived of her hair, driven from her husband's house, and whipped through the streets.

In Scotland, at one time, the capital penalty could be the lot of the person convicted of adultery.   In 1585, at Perth, David Gray and Helen Watson were hanged.   But withal, such cases were rare.   Punishment of a degradatory character was more usual.   At Lanark, in the May of 1642, the sentence passed on two adulterers, by the Presbytery was " to go through the whole kirkes of the Presbyterie, and at the kirke-doore of each to stand barefoot and barelegged, from the second bell to the last."[2] On October 15, 1635, the sentence passed by the Kirksession of Dumfries on a couple convicted of adultery was " to sit seven Sundays in sackcloth, and to stand the first and last Sabbath at the church-door, barefooted."[3]   It was decided in 1586, by the Kirksessions of Glasgow, to place such offenders in the pillory for six Sabbaths ; ten years later the same authority made the penalty a ducking in the Clyde.

Punishment was sometimes meted out by the Scots people themselves to anyone guilty of making love to the spouse of a neighbour or friend.   If the culprit were a man he was compelled to run the gauntlet.   For this purpose, at his house, the people of the town or village, at an arranged time, gathered.   Removing everything but his shirt, they tied the man to the back of a cart brought for the purpose, and threw his clothes inside.   In this manner he was dragged along the road, while his tormenters whipped him, beat him with sticks, or hurled missiles at him, to the accompaniment of jeers and insults.   On reaching the outskirts of the town or village, the man was released and allowed to don his clothes.   Should the accused be a member of the female sex, on being found guilty by a jury of matrons, her punishment was that known as " riding the stang."   She was placed astride a pole or stang, and carried at shoulder height through the town or village by a party of men, to the nearest lake or other body of water, into which she was thrown.

---

[1] William Alexander, *The History of Women*, 1779.   Vol. II, p. 302.

[2] Charles Rogers, *Scotland, Social and Domestic*, 1869, p. 365.

Ibid., p. 364.

III

Taboos Concerning Menstruation and Pregnancy

From the beginning of time, through many centuries of civilization, the menstruating woman has been looked upon as an unclean being, and the bloody discharge itself as something evil and dangerous. The laws of Moses made this clear; so did Mohammed's instructions in the Koran. The Zoroastrians, like many of their contemporaries, believed that a woman at such a time was under demoniac influence, especially that of Ahriman. The Laws of Manu stated that the energy, strength, sight and wisdom of any man who approached his wife during the period of menstruation would all be lost or impaired.

Among many savage tribes it is implicitly believed that any contact with menstrual blood will have serious results, and women at their periods are compelled to live apart from their husbands. In some tribes the belief is held that the blood is the result of "the bite of a supernatural animal."[1] According to Powers, the Karoks of California hold the view that the medicine prescribed for a sick man, should it come into contact with a menstruating woman, will cause the man to die.

On a girl's arrival at puberty and following the first signs of menstruation, a curious ceremony is observed by the natives of Chiragua. According to Moore,[2] she is suspended in a hammock from the roof of the cottage in which she lives, and kept there for a full month. At the end of this period the hammock is let down half way, and in this posture the girl is kept for another month; at the termination of which the neighbouring women, armed with clubs and sticks, assemble, and strike with fury and determination at everything in the cottage. The object of this strange procedure is to kill the serpent which, according to popular belief, has stung the girl and caused the bleeding. Only when this has been accomplished is she fit to be married. In Brazil it was customary to segregate women during their menstrual periods.

Pregnancy, like menstruation, is regarded as a state of uncleanness. Among some tribes the husband and wife separate

[1] Ernest Crawley, *The Mystic Rose*, 1927. Vol. I, p. 231.
[2] Theophilus Moore, *Marriage Customs*, 1820, p. 277.

during the time of gestation, which explains why in so many cases the man is never present when parturition occurs. The Ewe-speaking peoples, says Ellis, consider both mother and infant unclean for forty days.[1]

A strange custom practised by the African tribe known as the Ishogos, in connexion with a woman who has given birth to twins, is described by Du Chaillu. These negroes believe that one of the infants is likely to die soon after birth if the mother comes in contact with her neighbours or strangers, and to avert this calamity she is isolated until both the infants have grown up, when apparently the danger is no longer supposed to threaten them. During all this time no one but the woman's father and mother are permitted to enter the habitation assigned to her. The end of this period of isolation is celebrated by a festival in which all the inhabitants of the village take part, " singing, beating the tam-tam, and rattling pieces of wood together " all through the night. In the case described by Du Chaillu, the woman had suffered what virtually amounted to six years' imprisonment. Little wonder that every expectant mother dreads the time of parturition with the possibility of the occurrence of so calamitous an event as a multiple birth. " Nothing," says Du Chaillu, " irritates or annoys an expectant mother so much as to point to her and tell her that she is sure to have twins."[2]

To keep away evil spirits, immediately before the birth of a child, the Hindus place the skull of a dead cow, smeared with red lead, at the door of the hut in which parturition is taking place. The well-to-do Hindus keep a record of the exact time of birth, this information is communicated to an astrologer, who is requested to cast the nativity of the child. The astrologer, says Ward, goes home and draws up a document which prognosticates what will happen to the child year by year, sometimes during every period of its existence. The astrologer's fee varies from one rupee to two hundred rupees, depending upon the good fortune of the infant.

Sympathetic magic is a pronounced feature in the superstitions of the Acawoio and Caribi tribes of Guiana. Thus, when husband and wife have the slightest inclination that the family is on the point of being increased, they both refrain from eating

[1] W. G. Sumner, *Folkways*, p. 512.
[2] Paul B. Du Chaillu, *A Journey to Ashango-Land*, Murray, 1867, p. 274.

A RED INDIAN MENSTRUAL LODGE

From Henry R. Schoolcraft's *Information respecting the History, Condition and Prospects of the Indian Tribes of the United States*, 1856

certain kinds of meat, because of their reputed evil effects on the child. The flesh of the Agouti, because of the smallness of the animal, is avoided for fear the child, too, will be small; while the Labba, because of its protruding mouth, is also tabooed.[1]

Dalyell says " sanctified girdles for relieving the pains of labour, or for accelerating parturition, are said to have been kept by many Scottish families, until nearly the middle of the eighteenth century."[2] The belief is an ancient one, for we find Pliny mentioning that the process of parturition was speeded up by a woman who had children encircling the patient with her own girdle, and then loosening it with these words : " I have bound thee—so do I loose thee." A somewhat similar superstition existed in Spain, where " the church-bell was encircled with the girdle of a woman in labour, and struck thrice to promote parturition."[3]

Unfortunately in those days when superstition held such predominance in all fields, every effort in the direction of easing the suffering or helping the delivery of a parturient woman were in danger of being ranked as witchcraft, and the practitioner being labelled a sorcerer.

The period of pregnancy and the time of parturition were alike considered dangerous. In Germany and in Scotland it was formerly held that every woman experiencing either of these ordeals was in danger of being kidnapped by fairies at noon-day. So prevalent was this belief that charms were invariably used as preventives. Robert Kirk, in his *Essay on Fairies*, says : " The Tramontains to this day put bread, the Bible, or a piece of iron in women's beds when travelling, to save them from being thus stolen." The reason for the kidnapping was that these women were wanted to nurse fairy children.

Children, too, were supposed to be subject to similar risks, especially between birth and baptism, when the power of the fairies was most to be dreaded. It was believed that in some cases these elves, who were supposed to be under the dreadful obligation of sacrificing the tenth individual to the Devil every seventh year, substituted for healthy children, others which were idiots or malformed in some way. In Scott's *Minstrelsy* we read :—

[1] W. H. Brett, *The Indian Tribes of Guiana*, p. 355.
[2] John Graham Dalyell, *The Darker Superstitions of Scotland*, p. 135.
[3] Ibid., p. 136.

"And pleasant is the Fairy land ;
 But, an eiry tale to tell !
Ay, at the end o' seven years,
 We pay the teind to hell."[1]

And again, in a supplemental stanza to Collins's *Ode on the Popular Superstitions of the Highlands of Scotland*, Mr. Erskine writes :—

" Then wake (for well thou can'st) that wond'rous lay,
 How, while around the thoughtless matrons sleep,
 Soft o'er the floor the treacherous fairies creep,
And bear the smiling infant far away :
 How starts the nurse, when, for her lovely child,
She sees at dawn a gaping idiot stare !
 O snatch the innocents from demons vilde,
And save the parents fond from fell despair !
 In a deep cave the trusty menials wait,
When from their hilly dens, at midnight's hour,
 Forth rush the airy elves in mimic state,
And o'er the moon-light heath with swiftness scour :
 In glittering arms the little horsemen shine ;
Last, on a milk-white steed, with targe of gold,
 A fay of might appears, whose arms entwine
The lost, lamented child ! the shepherds bold
The unconscious infant tear from his unhallow'd hold."

All kinds of maladies, as well as imperfections, in both infants and adults, were ascribed to the baneful machinations of the Fairies, who from time to time emerged from their subterraneous retreats to carry out their fell work.

At Ardersier, in the county of Invernessshire, there is evidence that the belief in the evil activities of the Fairies was strongly held. From what Guthrie has to say on this matter, it appears that the tale was told of a man named Munro who was the father of a child which, either owing to its emaciated and ailing state or for some other reason, was thought both by Munro and his neighbours to be a changeling that had been substituted by the Fairies for his own infant. Now in the district where Munro lived was a carse containing a cone-shaped knoll, which, says Guthrie, " was famed as the scene of the moonlight revels of Titania and her Court ; and it was believed that if the changeling were left overnight on the hillock, the real child would be found in its stead in the morning."[2] The father, fully believing in

---

[1] Vol. II, p. 238.
[2] E. J. Guthrie, *Old Scottish Customs*, p. 121.

the truth of this legend, exposed the weakly child to the ordeal, with the result which might well have been anticipated—in the morning he found a corpse.

As was always customary in regard to superstitions of this nature, charms were brought into use to counteract the influence of the Fairies and to recover the children. " One of the most effectual, though the most horrible," says Nathan Drake, " was the assignment to the flames of the supposed changeling, which it was firmly believed would, in consequence of this treatment, disappear, and the real child return to the lap of its mother. 'A beautiful child, of Caerlaveroc, in Nithsdale,' relates Mr. Cromek from tradition, ' on the second day of its birth, and before its baptism, was changed, none knew how, for an antiquated elf of hideous aspect. It kept the family awake with its nightly yells ; biting the mother's breasts, and would neither be cradled nor nursed. The mother, obliged to be from home, left it in charge to the servant girl. The poor lass was sitting bemoaning herself—' Wer't nae for thy girning face I would knock the big, winnow the corn, and grun the meal ! '—' Lowse the cradle band,' quoth the Elf, ' and tent the neighbours, an' I'll work yere wark.' Up started the elf, the wind arose, the corn was chaffed, the outlyers were foddered, the hand mill moved around, as by instinct, and the *knocking mell* did its work with amazing rapidity. The lass, and her elfin servant, rested and diverted themselves, till, on the mistress's approach, it was restored to the cradle, and began to yell anew. The girl took the first opportunity of slyly telling her mistress the adventure. *'What'll we do wi' the wee diel?'* said she. ' I'll wirk it a pirn,' replied the lass. At the middle hour of night the chimney-top was covered up, and every inlet barred and closed. The embers were blown up until glowing hot, and the maid, undressing the elf, tossed it on the fire. It uttered the wildest and most piercing yells, and, in a moment, the Fairies were heard moaning at every wonted avenue, and rattling at the window boards, at the chimney head, and at the door. ' In the name o' God bring back the bairn,' cried the lass. The window flew up ; the earthly child was laid unharmed on the mother's lap, while its grisly substitute flew up the chimney with a loud laugh."

The same belief existed concurrently in Lancashire, and charms were used to prevent fairies from exchanging their own imps for normal infants.

In *Notes and Queries* (Vol. VI, 432) a correspondent refers to a strange old superstition concerning turning a bed after childbirth. It was believed that if the bed were to be turned for the purpose of making it, until a month had elapsed after the confinement, ill-luck for the mother or the child would surely follow.

Pliny was of opinion that coral was a charm against fascination, hence the custom of giving coral-bells, which, particularly if blessed by a priest, would keep evil spirits away from the child.[1]

A curious practice at one time observed in Scotland at the birth of a child, is given by Sir Walter Scott in a note to *Guy Mannering*. He says : " The *groaning malt* was the ale brewed for the purpose of being drunk after the lady, or goodwife's safe delivery. The *ken-no* has a more ancient source, and perhaps the custom may be derived from the secret rites of the *Bona Dea*. A large and rich cheese was made by the women of the family, with great affectation of secrecy, for the refreshment of the gossips who were to attend at the *canny minute*. This was the *ken-no*, so-called because its existence was secret (that is, presumed to be so) from all the males of the family, but especially from the husband and master. He was accordingly expected to conduct himself as if he knew of no such preparation ; to act as if desirous to press the female guests to refreshments, and to seem surprised at their obstinate refusal. But the instant his back was turned, the *ken-no* was produced, and after all had eaten their fill, with a proper accompaniment of the *groaning malt*, the remainder was divided among the gossips, each carrying a large portion home, with the same affectation of great secrecy."

Superstition, rife in Scotland as in most other countries, has always been the cause of strange practices. Thus, immediately after birth, whatever the time of the year, an infant was immersed for a brief period in cold water. A female visitor, before touching a newly-born infant, crossed herself with a burning brand.[2]

There was at one time a widespread belief that to take a baby downstairs before it went up, was unlucky. This belief, in the days when most infants were born and spent their early days in an upstairs bedroom involved difficulties. To avoid this

[1] John Harland and T. T. Wilkinson, *Lancashire Folk-Lore*, John Heywood, Manchester, 1882, p. 262.
[2] Charles Rogers, *Scotland, Social and Domestic*, p. 118.

ill-luck many curious devices were adopted. In the West Riding of Yorkshire, a nurse, says Black, " placed a chair on the dressing-table, and climbed with the baby to the top, exclaiming, ' There, bless its little heart, it shall not go downstairs first.' "[1] Says the same authority, in Scotland a substitute was found " in going up three steps of a ladder " ; a procedure which the mother was sometimes compelled to adopt also.

IV

The Taboo on the Remarriage of Widows

In primitive society, and in the early days of civilization, too, the position of the woman who had the misfortune to lose her husband while she was young or middle-aged was an unfortunate and in many cases a distressing one. In many savage tribes such a woman is held to be a source of danger to others because she is thought to be accompanied always by her deceased husband's ghost. Alexander, writing a century-and-a-half ago, says : "At the Cape of Good Hope, as widows are less esteemed than virgins, in order that they may not impose themselves on the men for such, they are obliged by law to cut off a joint from a finger for every husband that dies ; this joint they present to their new husband on the day of their marriage. In the Isthmus of Darien, both sexes were formerly obliged to observe this custom, that none of them might impose themselves on each other for what they were not ; or according to some authors, which is not less probable, it was their marriage ceremony, by which they were affianced to each other. Widows are in several places neglected, and allowed at least to fall a prey to famine ; but in Darien, the barbarity is carried much farther ; when a widow dies, such of her children as are too young to provide subsistence for themselves are buried with her in the same grave, no one being willing to take the charge of them, and the community not being so far ripened as to discover that the loss of every individual is a loss to the State."[2]

In India, since the abolition of suttee, the remarriage of widows,

[1] William George Black, *Folk-Medicine*, 1883.
[2] William Alexander, *The History of Women*, 1779.   Vol. II, p. 389.

apart from exceptional cases, was prohibited, as stated in the *Adi Purana*, the *Kratu Sanhita*, and the *Aditya* and *Vrihannaradiya Puranas*. These exceptions are set out in the *Parasara Sanhita*, thus : " On receiving no tidings of a husband, on his demise, on his turning an ascetic, on his being found impotent, or on his degradation, under any one of the five calamities, it is canonical for a woman to take another husband." In any other circumstances, very often the lot of the widow became in many respects almost intolerable : her head was shaved, she was half-starved, and ostracized in a way one would expect a criminal to be. And if any man had the hardihood to marry a widow, he, too, shared in this ostracism.

At one time, in China, according to Macartney, on the death of the emperor, all his wives were removed to a building called the Palace of Chastity, in which they were confined for the remainder of their lives. Burder says : "Amongst the Arabians, if a father left one or more widows, the sons often married them, provided they were not their own mothers. This usage was suppressed by Mohammed ; and before his time it was marked with a degree of detestation. Lord Hailes (*Annals of Scotland*, p. 39) informs us, that this custom prevailed in Scotland so late as the eleventh century : and he supposed it might have originated from avarice, in order to relieve the heir from the payment of a jointure."[1] Among the ancient Hebrews, no private person was allowed to marry the king's widow : she belonged to his successor. For this reason God gave all the wives of Saul to David (2 Samuel xii, 8).

In Tartary, in the thirteenth century, wives were purchased, but according to Rubruguis, a widow, however pretty and desirable, could never find anyone willing to marry her. The reason for this was a religious one. " They believe," he says, "that their wives serve them in another world as they do in this ; for which reason a widow has no chance to secure a second husband, whom she cannot serve in the other world."

In early Christianity, when virginity and asceticism were ideological states, to marry once was bad enough and marked the limit of ecclesiastical toleration ; to marry a second time was a sure way of exciting disapproval, if not actual censure. Even a widower was expected to spend the rest of his days in an unmarried state. This attitude towards remarriage

---

[1] Samuel Burder, *Oriental Antiquities*, 1840, p. 280.

persisted through many centuries, and it was not until well into the seventeenth century that widows could take a second husband without being condemned by friends and relatives as well as meeting with the disapprobation of the ecclesiastical authorities.

CHAPTER XXI

THE END OF THE MARITAL CONTRACT

I

Curious Divorce Customs

RULES regulating the termination of marriage, while both partners are living, have in many cases been created and developed coincidentally with the rules regulating marriage. In those races, or at such a period in the history of a nation, when no such thing as divorce was known or recognized, the termination of a marital partnership was possible without recourse to law. The primitive marriage union, where no ceremony, either ecclesiastical or civil, was practised or required, had as its concomitant the breaking up of such a union in an equally simple manner. The husband and wife separated and in this manner the alliance ended. The fact that, in the last analysis, both in its creation and in its destruction, such a marriage was little different from what might well be described as an experiment in " free love " did not make it any the less, to the ancients, and to the members of certain savage tribes, a form of marital union within their particular definition of marriage.

When marriage became an institution, and the parties to it were bound by rules, the lawmakers of ancient Rome and Greece recognized the need at times for the dissolution of the contract. And the reasons for divorce being procurable were often, judged by modern social standards, of a singularly curious nature. According to Plutarch, a man could divorce his wife for adultery or alcoholism, as well as other misdemeanours ; also when she had borne him as many children as he desired. " The Athenians," says Moore, " permitted divorce upon very slight occasions, but it was not permitted without a bill specifying the reason of their separation, which the magistrate must see and approve. The Athenian women were allowed to separate from their husbands upon any just ground of complaint ; but they were under the

necessity of appearing in person and publicly exhibiting their
complaint to the archon, that by so doing their husbands might
have an opportunity of seeing and prevailing on them to return.
Plutarch relates that Hipparete, the wife of Alcibiades, being a
virtuous woman and very fond of her husband, was at last
induced from his debauched life and continual entertainment
of courtezans, to leave him and retire to her brother Callias's
house.   Alcibiades still continued his loose manner of living;
but his wife being obliged, before she could obtain a divorce,
personally to appear before the magistrate, her husband came in,
took her away by force, and carried her home through the forum,
where she remained with him till her death, no one daring to
interfere."[1]

Sometimes the reason given was triviality itself, as where
Sempronius Sophus, because his wife had the temerity to attend
amusements without his consent, divorced her; sometimes it
was to satisfy the hedonism of an autocrat, as where Augustus,
because he was in love with Livia, used his power to force her
husband to get a divorce.[2]   But in those days it was not merely
the men who divorced their wives; women were able, with
almost equal ease, to get rid of their husbands.   Thus Juvenal
gives an instance of a woman who, in the short space of five years,
married eight times; while Jerome refers to one who had
married for the twenty-third time and her husband had himself
been previously married a score times.[3] Herod the Great's
sister, Salome, sent a bill of divorce to her husband Costobarus;
and, according to Josephus, Herodias left her husband for the
purpose of marrying his brother, Herod Antipas.   And, says
Burder: "This seems to have been the case with Josephus
himself, who informs us, in *Vit*. sect. 75, that his wife quitted
him, and that he thereupon married another."[4]

Strabo refers to a strange custom prevalent among the
Tapyrians which obliged the father of two or three children
by one wife, to abandon her, so that she was free to take another
husband, and, according to Lord Avebury, who mentions this,
"there is some reason to suppose that a similar custom once
prevailed among the Romans."[5]

[1] Theophilus Moore, *Marriage Customs*, 1820, pp. 79–80.
[2] William Graham Sumner, *Folkways*, Boston, 1907, p. 378.
[3] Ibid., p. 378.
[4] Samuel Burder, *Oriental Customs*, 1840, p. 279.
[5] Lord Avebury, *The Origin of Civilization*, sixth edition, 1902, p. 139.

Turning to the ancient Hebrews, it would appear, from a reading of Deuteronomy, that a man could get rid of his wife without much difficulty. A bill of divorcement was written and handed to her. It was in this manner that Abraham ended his marriage with Hagar. Not until the coming of Christianity was the position altered, as indicated in the words of Jesus recorded in the book of Matthew :—

> "The Pharisees also came unto him, tempting him, and saying unto him, Is it lawful for a man to put away his wife for every cause? And he answered and said unto them, Have ye not read, that he which made them at the beginning, made them male and female; and said, For this cause shall a man leave father and mother, and shall cleave to his wife: and they twain shall be one flesh. Wherefore they are no more twain, but one flesh. What, therefore, God hath joined together, let not man put asunder. They say unto him, Why did Moses then command to give a writing of divorcement, and to put her away? He saith unto them, Moses, because of the hardness of your hearts, suffered you to put away your wives : but from the beginning it was not so. And say unto you, whosoever shall put away his wife, except it be for fornication, and shall marry another, committeth adultery : and whoso marrieth her which is put away doth commit adultery."

In China divorce is securable by the husband on many grounds, some of which are trivial, as bad temper or poor health. But the main reasons are sterility, theft, and immorality. In India marriage is for life in all circumstances, the contract being endable by the death of one partner and in no other way.

One of the strangest of all divorce ceremonies was that of the ancient Gipsies. The act of separation took place over the cadaver of a horse. The animal, which had to be in perfect health, and free from defects, was killed as near midday as possible, the person who performed the sacrificial act being chosen by casting lots, and then named the 'priest'. First, the horse was let loose and allowed to roam at will, its movements being carefully observed : the behaviour of the horse, and the trouble it gave in the subsequent pursuit and capture, were supposed to indicate the extent of the woman's guilt. The animal was now brought before the 'priest' and charged with the woman's alleged crime. " When this part of the trial is finished," wrote Simson, to whose interesting book I am indebted for these details, " the ' priest ' takes a large knife and thrusts it into the heart of the horse ; and its blood is allowed to flow upon the ground till life is extinct. The dead animal is now stretched out upon the ground. The husband then takes his stand on one side of it, and the wife on the other ; and, holding each other by the hand, repeat certain appropriate sentences in the Gipsy language. They then quit hold of each other, and walk three times round the body of the horse, contrariwise, passing and crossing each other, at certain points, as they proceed in opposite directions. At certain parts of the animal (the *corners* of the horse, was the Gipsy's expression), such as the hind and fore feet, the shoulders and haunches, the head and tail, the parties halt, and face each other ; and again repeat sentences, in their own speech, at each time they halt. The two last stops they make, in their circuit round the sacrifice, are at the head and tail. At the head, they again face each other, and speak ; and lastly, at the tail, they again confront each other, utter some more Gipsy expressions, shake hands, and finally part, the one going north, the other south, never again to be united in this life. Immediately after the separation takes place, the woman receives a token, which is made of cast-iron, about an inch and a half square, with a mark upon it resembling the Roman character T. After the marriage has been dissolved, and the woman dismissed from the sacrifice, the heart of the horse is taken out and roasted with fire, then sprinkled with vinegar, or brandy, and eaten by the husband and his friends then present ; the female not being allowed to join in this part of the ceremony. The body of the horse, skin and everything about it, except the heart, is buried on the spot ; and years after the ceremony has taken place, the husband and his friends visit the grave of the animal, to see whether it has been disturbed. At these visits, they walk round the grave, with much grief and mourning."[1]

Simson also mentions that the notorious Captain McDonald who was tried and sentenced to death in 1770, divorced his first wife " over a horse sacrificed for the occasion,"[2] and refers to an " aged man of credibility ", who informed him " that it was

[1] Walter Simson, *A History of the Gipsies*, 1865, pp. 273-274.
[2] Ibid., p. 137.

within his own knowledge, that a Gipsy, of the name of John Lundie, divorced four wives over dead horses."[1]

In England, for centuries, Church and State put every conceivable obstacle in the way of the dissolution of marriage. In certain circumstances divorce was procurable, but a private Act of Parliament was required, involving considerable difficulty and great cost : in consequence such cases were extremely rare, and practically restricted to the wealthy and influential classes. Not until some one hundred years ago, in the year 1857, was this state of affairs altered. In that year the Court for Divorce and Matrimonial Causes came into existence, doing away with the monopoly hitherto possessed by the Ecclesiastical Courts, and at the same time reducing very considerably the cost. This constituted a landmark in the history of marriage, as it paved the way for the provision of additional facilities for the termination of undesirable unions, and foreshadowed the coming of the Matrimonial Causes Act of 1937, which provided for dissolution by divorce or judicial separation, on the grounds of adultery, desertion (three years or more), cruelty, and incurable unsoundness of mind (of at least five years' duration). On all or any of these grounds either husband or wife can apply for a divorce; in addition, the wife can terminate the contract if her husband has, since the celebration of the marriage, been guilty of rape, sodomy, or bestiality.

II

The Suttee

The horrible Hindu rite of Suttee, or widow-burning, is said to have originated as a method of deterring wives from poisoning their husbands, a crime which, at one time, was extremely common in India and other countries. The knowledge that on the death of her husband, a woman had to burn with him, was certainly likely to make the wife do everything in her power to keep the man alive. Other methods, it was said, had been tried without avail. Later, however, the rite was given the sanctity of religion, and the widow instead of being dragged by force to the burning pile, was induced to go to her death

[1] Ibid., p. 270.

voluntarily, and in this way earn her reward in heaven. Her failure to do this subjected her to perpetual infamy, degrading herself and her family to such a degree that she became a social pariah. In this manner, therefore, despite the absence of force, and despite, too, any mention of the rite constituting a penalty for husband-poisoning, it effectually prevented the crime.

The manner in which these heavenly benefits accruing to the widow who so sacrificed herself were expressed in one of the sacred books of the Hindus constitutes a masterpiece of propagandistic incitement, thus : " The woman who mounts the funeral pile of her deceased husband equals herself to Arundhoti, the wife of Vashista, and enjoys bliss in heaven with her husband. She dwells with him in heaven for thirty-five millions of years, which is equal to the number of hairs upon the human body, and by her own power taking her husband up, in the same manner as a snake-catcher would take a snake out of its hole, remains with him in diversion. She who thus goes with her husband to the other world purifies three generations, that is the generations of her mother's side, father's side, and husband's side ; and so she being reckoned the purest and the best in fame among women, becomes too dear to her husband, and continues to delight him during fourteen *Indras*, and although her husband be guilty of slaying a Brahmin or friend, or be ungrateful of past deeds, yet is his wife capable of purifying him from all these sins."[1]

Some indication of the incidence of Suttee is given by the fact that during the decade between 1815 and 1825, the number of widow-burnings reached the astounding total of 5,997, and although the practice was abolished by the British Government in 1829, it continued surreptitiously for many years.

Alexander gives a descriptive account of the rite as practised in the eighteenth century. On February 4, 1742, when Rham Chund, a pundit of the Maharattor tribe died, his widow, aged between 17 and 18, declared her intention to burn with him. Accordingly, says the narrator, " early on the following morning the body of the deceased was carried down to the waterside ; the widow following about ten o'clock, accompanied by three principal Brahmins, her children, relations, and a numerous crowd of spectators. As the order for her burning did not arrive till after one o'clock, the interval was employed in praying

[1] Quoted by James Gardner in *Faiths of the World*. Vol. II, p. 875.

with the Brahmins, and washing in the Ganges : as soon as it arrived, she retired, and stayed about half an hour in the midst of her female relations ; she then divested herself of her bracelets, and other ornaments ; and having tied them in a kind of apron, which hung before her, was conducted by the females to a corner of the pile. On the pile was an arched arbour, formed of dry sticks, boughs, and leaves ; and open only at one end to admit her entrance. In this was deposited the body of the deceased ; his head at the end, opposite to the opening. At that corner of the pile, to which she had been conducted, a Brahmin had made a small fire, round which she and three Brahmins sat for a few minutes ; one of them put into her hand a leaf of the bale tree ; the wood of which a part of the funeral pile is always constructed : she threw the leaf into the fire, and one of the others gave her a second leaf, which she held over the flame, while he, three times, dropped some ghee on it, which melted and fell into the fire ; while these things were doing, a third Brahmin read to her some portions of the *Aughtorrah Beid*, and asked her some questions, which she answered with a steady and serene countenance ; these being over, she was led with great solemnity three times round the pile, the Brahmins reading before her ; when she came the third time to the small fire, she stopped, took her rings off her toes and fingers, and put them to her other ornaments, then taking a solemn and majestic leave of her children, parents, and relations, one of the Brahmins dipped a large wick of cotton in some ghee, and giving it lighted in her hand, led her to the open side of the arbour, where all the Brahmins fell at her feet ; she blessed them, and they retired weeping. She then ascended the pile, and entered the arbour, making a profound reverence at the feet of the deceased, and then advancing, seated herself by his head. In silent meditation, she looked on his face for the space of a minute ; then set fire to the arbour in three places ; but soon observing that she had kindled it to leeward, and that the wind blew the flames from her, she arose, set fire to the windward, and placidly resumed her station ; sitting there with a dignity and composure, which no words can convey an idea of. The pile being of combustible matter, the supports of the roof were soon consumed, and the whole tumbled in upon her, putting an end at once to her courage and her life."[1]

[1] William Alexander, *History of Women*, Vol. II, pp. 399–400.

From the foregoing account it will be noted that the widow acted as her own executioner. This, however, was not always the case. Usually some relative of the deceased actually set the pile alight, as in the following account of a widow-burning. This description of the rite is given, says Gardner, by a native Hindu who not only witnessed but actually took part in it. "Fearing intervention from the British authorities, it was decided that this solemn rite, contrary to the usual practice, should be performed at a distance from the river side; the margin of the consecrated tank was selected for the purpose. After ceremonies of purification had been performed upon the spot, strong stakes of bamboo were driven into the ground, enclosing an oblong space about seven feet in length, and six in breadth, the stakes being about eight feet in height: within this enclosure the pile was built of straw, and boughs, and logs of wood: upon the top a small arbour was constructed of wreathed bamboos, and this was hung with flowers within and without. About an hour after the sun had risen, prayers and ablutions having been carefully and devoutly performed by all, more especially by the Brahmins and Lall Radha, who was also otherwise purified and fitted for the sacrifice, the corpse of the deceased husband was brought from the house, attended by the administering Brahmins, and surrounded by the silent and weeping friends and relations of the family. Immediately following the corpse came Lall Radha, enveloped in a scarlet veil which completely hid her beautiful person from view. When the body was placed upon the pile, the feet being towards the west, the Brahmins took the veil from Lall Radha, and, for the first time, the glaring multitude were suffered to gaze upon that lovely face and form; but the holy woman was too deeply engaged in solemn prayer and converse with Brahma to be sensible of their presence, or of the murmur of admiration which ran through the crowd. Then turning with a steady look and solemn demeanour to her relations, she took from her person, one by one, all her ornaments, and distributed them as tokens of her love. One jewel only she retained, the *tali*, or amulet placed round her neck by her deceased husband on the nuptial day; this she silently pressed to her lips, then separately embracing each of her female relations, and bestowing a farewell look upon the rest, she unbound her hair, which flowed in thick and shining ringlets almost to her feet, gave her right

hand to the principal Brahmin, who led her with ceremony
three times round the pile, and then stopped with her face towards
it, upon the side where she was to ascend. Having mounted
two or three steps, the beautiful woman stood still, and pressing
her hands upon the cold feet of her lifeless husband, she raised
them to her forehead, in token of cheerful submission : she
then ascended, and crept within the little arbour, seating herself
at the head of her lord, her right hand resting upon his head.
The torch was placed in my hand, and overwhelmed with
commingled emotions I fired the pile. Smoke and flame in an
instant enveloped the scene, and amid the deafening shouts of
the multitude I sank senseless upon the earth. I was quickly
restored to sense, but already the devouring element had reduced
the funeral pile to a heap of charred and smouldering timber.
The assembled Brahmins strewed the ashes around, and with
a trembling hand I assisted my father to gather the blackened
bones of my beloved uncle and aunt, when having placed them
in an earthen vessel we carried them to the Ganges, and with
prayer and reverence committed them to the sacred stream.''[1]

Wives are put to death immediately following their husbands'
deaths in other parts of the world besides India, though the
procedure is often devoid of the ceremony characteristic of suttee.
In some parts of the Gold Coast the favourite wife must follow
her husband's corpse to the grave and be buried, either dead
or alive, along with it. Marchais, who actually witnessed such
a burial, says that the marabut took the wife by the arms, and
delivered her to two stout negroes, who tied her hands and feet,
placed her on her back, and then having laid a piece of timber
on her breast, they stamped upon the wood until her breast
was crushed inwards. In a half-dead condition they then threw
the woman, along with her husband's corpse and the body of
a sacrificed goat, into the already prepared grave.[2]

In the Fiji Islands the wives of a chief have to be buried
with their husband. The ceremonial procedure is described by
the missionary, John Williams : " The chiefs have from twenty
to a hundred wives, according to their rank ; and at the
interment of a principal chief, the body is laid in state upon
a spacious lawn, in the presence of an immense concourse of

---

[1] Quoted by James Gardner in *Faiths of the World*, Vol. II, p. 875.
[2] Thomas Little, *The Beauty, Marriage Ceremonies, etc., in all Nations*, 1824.
Vol. III, pp. 153-4.

spectators. The principal wife, after the utmost ingenuity of the natives has been exercised in adorning her person, then walks out, and takes her seat near the body of her husband, when a rope is passed round her neck, which eight or ten powerful men pull with all their strength, until she is strangled and dies. Her body is then laid by that of the chief. This done, a second wife comes and seats herself in the same place. The process is repeated, and she also dies. A third and a fourth become voluntary sacrifices in the same manner : and all of them are then interred in a common grave, one above, one below, and one on either side of the husband. The reasons assigned for this are, that the spirit of the chief may not be lonely in its passage to the invisible world ; and that, by such an offering, its happiness may be at once secured."[1]

Among some savage tribes, the widow was called upon to go through a ceremony which, although it did not inevitably entail her death, nevertheless constituted a terrible ordeal for any living being to be called upon to endure. For instance, the Indians of the Hudson's Bay Territory formerly burned the bodies of the dead upon funeral piles. In the case of a man whose wife survived him, it fell to the widow's lot to set fire to the pile. Having done this she must anoint her breast with the fat that oozed from the body, which meant standing close to the blazing pile, and in the process enduring indescribable agony. There was no such thing as drawing back, for the points of the spears in the hands of the dead man's relations defeated any such attempt. She was compelled to suffer the dreadful torture until the cadaver on the pile was reduced to ashes, or she herself was nearly scorched to death. It would appear indeed that the widow's survival depended largely on the efforts of her own relatives, who attended the ceremony in force with the object of preserving her life. " When no longer able to stand they dragged her away ; and this intervention often led to bloody quarrels."[2]

[1] John Williams, *A Narrative of Missionary Enterprises in the South Sea Islands,* 1837, p. 577.

[2] John McLean, *Notes of a Twenty-Five Years' Service in the Hudson's Bay Territory* 1849. Vol. I, p. 256.

BIBLIOGRAPHY

William Alexander, *The History of Women, from the Earliest Antiquity to the Present time* ; 2 vols., Dublin, 1779.

Capt. Thos. Anburey, *Travels Through the Interior Parts of America in a Series of Letters* ; new edition, 2 vols., London, 1791.

William Andrews (edited by), *Curious Church Customs and Cognate Subjects* ; Hull, 1895.

William Andrews (edited by), *Bygone Church Life in Scotland* ; London, 1899.

Anonymous, *Marriage Ceremonies as now used in all Parts of the World* ; London, 1744.

Anonymous, *Marriage Rites and Ceremonies adopted by All Nations of the World* ; Glasgow, 1856.

Anonymous, *Marriage Rites, Customs and Ceremonies of All Nations of the Universe* ; London, 1824.

Anonymous, *Matrimonial Ceremonies Display'd* ; London, 1748.

Anonymous, *Mormonism Unveiled ; including the Remarkable Life and Confession of the late Mormon Bishop John D. Lee (written by himself), and complete life of Brigham Young* ; Royal Publishing Co., St. Louis, Mo., 1891.

John Ashton, *Social Life Under the Regency* ; new edition, Chatto and Windus, London, 1899.

John Ashton, *The Fleet, Its River, Prison, and Marriages* ; Fisher Unwin, London, 1888.

John Aubrey, *Miscellanies Upon Various Subjects ;* London, 1696.

Lord Avebury, *The Origin of Civilisation and the Primitive Condition of Man* ; sixth edition, Longmans, Green & Co., London, 1902.

S. Baring-Gould, *Curious Myths of the Middle Ages* ; second series, Rivingtons, London, 1868.

Rev. W. Bingley, *North Wales : Delineated from Two Excursions through all the Interior Parts of that Highly Beautiful and Romantic Country, and intended as a Guide to Future Tourists ;* second edition, Longman, Hurst, Rees, Orme and Brown, London, 1814.

Isabella L. Bird, *Unbeaten Tracks in Japan* ; G. P. Putnam's Sons, *c.* 1880.

William George Black, *Folk-Medicine ; a Chapter in the History of Culture* ; Published for the Folk-Lore Society by Elliot Stock, London, 1883.

Capt. John G. Bourke, *Scatologic Rites of all Nations* ; Washington, D.C., W. H. Lowdermilk & Co., 1891.

George Borrow, *The Zincali, or an Account of the Gypsies of Spain* ; second edition, two vols., John Murray, London, 1843.

W. H. Brett, *The Indian Tribes of Guiana : Their Condition and Habits* ; Bell and Daldy, London, 1868.

James Bruce, *Scenes and Sights in the East* ; Smith, Elder & Co., London, n.d.

John Lewis Burckhardt, *Arabic Proverbs ; or the Manners and Customs of the Modern Egyptians.* Illustrated from their proverbial sayings current in Cairo, translated and explained by the late John Lewis Burckhardt ; second edition, Bernard Quaritch, London, 1875.

John Lewis Burckhardt, *Notes on the Bedouins and Wahabys* ; 2 vols., Henry Colburn and Richard Bentley, London, 1831.

Samuel Burder, *Oriental Customs, or an Illustration of the Sacred Scriptures by an Explanatory Application of the Customs and manners of the Eastern Nations, and especially of the Jews therein alluded to, collected from the most celebrated Travellers, and the most Eminent Critics* ; new edition, enlarged and arranged by the Rev. W. Grosser, London, 1840.

John Southerden Burn, *The Fleet Registers : Comprising the History of Fleet Marriages, and some Accounts of the Parsons and Marriage-House Keepers, with Extracts from the Registers : to which are added Notices of the May Fair, Mint, and Savoy Chapels, and an Appendix Relating to Parochial Registration ;* Rivingtons, London, 1833.

John Carr, *The Stranger in Ireland ; or a Tour in the Southern and Western Parts of that Country in the Year 1805 ;* London, 1806.

J. Carver, *Travels Through the Interior Parts of North America, in the Years,* 1766, 1767, *and* 1768 ; third edition, London, 1781.

George Catlin, *Illustrations of the Manners, Customs, and Condition of the North American Indians, with Letters and Notes written during eight years of Travel and Adventure among the Wildest and most Remarkable Tribes now existing ;* 2 vols., Chatto and Windus, London, 1876.

R. Chambers (edited by), *The Book of Days : A Miscellany of Popular Antiquities ;* 2 vols., W. & R. Chambers, Edinburgh.

Ernest W. Clement (edited by), *Hildreth's " Japan As It Was and Is : "* *A Handbook of Old Japan* ; Introduction by Wm. Elliot Griffis ; 2 vols., Kegan Paul, Trench, Trübner & Co., London, 1907.

A. Ernest Crawley, *"Exogamy and the Mating of Cousins,"* in *Anthoroplogical Essays Presented to Edward Burnett Tylor ;* Clarendon Press, Oxford, 1907.

A. Ernest Crawley, *The Mystic Rose* ; new edition, revised and greatly enlarged by Theodore Besterman, 2 vols., Methuen & Co., London, 1927.

William Crooke, *Religion & Folklore of Northern India* ; Prepared for the Press by R. E. Enthoven, Oxford University Press, 1926.

Constance F. Gordon Cumming, *From the Hebrides to the Himalayas : A Sketch of Eighteen Months' Wanderings in Western Isles and Eastern Highlands* ; 2 vols., Sampson Low, 1876.

Colonel Arthur Cunynghame, *An Aide-de-Camp's Recollections of Service in China, a Residence in Hong-Kong, and visits to other Islands in the Chinese Seas* ; Richard Bentley, London, 1853.

James Graham Dalyell, *The Darker Superstitions of Scotland* ; Glasgow 1835.

John Francis Davis, *The Chinese : A General Description of China and Its Inhabitants* ; 3 vols., London, 1845.

F. Depons, *Travels in South America* ; 2 vols., London, 1807.

Eric John Dingwall (edited by), *Woman : An Historical Gynæcological and Anthropological Compendium*, by Hermann Heinrich Ploss, Max Bartels and Paul Bartels ; 3 vols., William Heinemann (Medical Books), London, 1935.

William Hepworth Dixon, *Spiritual Wives* ; 2 vols., Hurst and Blackett, London, 1868.

Rev. Justus Doolittle, *Social Life of the Chinese ; with some Account of their Religious, Governmental, Educational, and Business Customs and Opinions* ; 2 vols., Sampson Low, Son, and Marston, London, 1866.

Nathan Drake, *Shakespeare and His Times* ; 2 vols., London, 1817.

Paul B. Du Chaillu, *A Journey to Ashango-Land : and Further Penetration into Equatorial Africa*, John Murray, London, 1867.

Alice Morse Earle, *Customs and Fashions in Old New England* ; David Nutt, London, 1893.

Robert Elliott, *The Gretna Green Register* ; with an Introduction and Appendix by the Rev. Caleb Brown, London, 1842.

J. S. Forsyth, *The Antiquary's Portfolio, or Cabinet Selection of Historical and Literary Curiosities, on subjects principally connected with the Manners, Customs, and Morals ; Civil, Military, and Ecclesiastical Government, &c. &c. of Great Britain, during the Middle and Latter Ages* ; 2 vols., London, 1825.

R. Forsyth, *The Beauties of Scotland : Containing a clear and full account of the Agriculture, Commerce, Mines, and Manufactures ; of the Population, Cities, Towns, Villages, &c. of each County* ; 5 vols., Edinburgh, 1806.

S. W. Fullom, *The History of Woman, and Her Connexion with Religion, Civilization, & Domestic Manners from the Earliest Period* ; third edition, revised, G. Routledge & Co., London, 1855.

Frederick J. Furnivall (edited by), *Child-Marriages, Divorces, and Ratifications, &c. in the Diocese of Chester, A.D.* 1561-6 ; Published for the Early English Text Society by Kegan Paul, Trench Trübner & Co., London, 1897.

G. F. Gibbs (reported by), *"Mormon" Women on Plural Marriage* ; 1878.

John Henry Gray, *China, A History of the Laws, Manners and Customs of the People* (edited by William Gow Gregor) ; 2 vols., Macmillan, London, 1878.

William Gow Gregor (see under John Henry Gray).

E. J. Guthrie, *Old Scottish Customs, Local and General* ; London and Glasgow, 1885.

James Orchard Halliwell, *Popular Rhymes and Nursery Tales* ; London, 1849.

Alexander Hamilton, *A New Account of the East Indies* ; 2 vols., London, 1744.

Lady Augusta Hamilton, *Marriage Rites, Customs and Ceremonies of all Nations in the Universe*, London, 1824.

E. Sidney Hartland, *"Concerning the Rite at the Temple of Mylitta"* in *Anthropological Essays Presented to Edward Burnett Tylor*, Clarendon Press, Oxford, 1907.

John Harland and T. T. Wilkinson, *Lancashire Folk-Lore*, John Heywood, Manchester, 1882.

Sir George Head, *A Home Tour Through the Manufacturing Districts, and other Parts of England, Scotland, and Ireland, including the Channel Islands and the Isle of Man;* new edition, 2 vols., John Murray, London, 1840.

Samuel Hearne, *A Journey from Prince of Wales's Fort, in Hudson's Bay, to the Northern Ocean,* Dublin, 1796.

Isaac Taylor Headland, *Home Life in China;* Methuen, London, 1914.

Georgiana Hill, *Women in English Life;* 2 vols., Richard Bentley, London, 1866.

A. W. Howitt, *The Native Tribes of South-East Australia;* Macmillan, London, 1904.

M. Huc, *The Chinese Empire;* forming a sequel to the work entitled " Recollections of a Journey Through Tartary and Thibet "; 2 vols., Longman, Brown, Green and Longmans, London, 1855.

Peter Orlando Hutchinson, *Chronicles of Gretna Green;* 2 vols., Richard Bentley, London, 1844.

Sir Edward F. Im Thurn, *Among the Indians of Guiana,* London, 1883.

Washington Irving (Diedrich Knickerbocker), *A History of New York;* Tegg & Son, London, 1836.

John Cordy Jeaffreson, *Brides and Bridals;* 2 vols., Hurst and Blackett, London, 1872.

J. Heneage Jesse, *Literary and Historical Memorials of London;* 2 vols., Richard Bentley, London, 1847.

Peter Kalm, *Travels into North America;* translated in English by John Reinhold Forster, second edition, 2 vols., London, 1772.

Lord Kames, *Sketches of the History of Man;* 4 vols., Edinburgh, 1788.

John Kenrick, *Ancient Egypt Under the Pharoahs;* 2 vols., London, 1850.

A. Henry Savage Landor, *In the Forbidden Land: An Account of a Journey in Tibet, capture by the Tibetan Authorities, Imprisonment, Torture, and Ultimate Release;* William Heinemann, London, 1898.

Edward William Lane, *An Account of the Manners and Customs of the Modern Egyptians, written in Egypt during the Years 1833–34, and –35, partly from notes made during a former visit to that country in the years 1825, –26, –27 and –28;* 2 vols., Charles Knight & Co., London, 1836.

Sir A. H. Layard, *Discoveries in the Ruins of Nineveh and Babylon,* London, 1853.

Thomas Little, *The Beauty, Marriage-Ceremonies, and Intercourse of the Sexes, in all Nations;* 4 vols., second edition, J. J. Stockdale, London, 1824.

John F. McLennan, *Primitive Marriage, An Inquiry Into the Origin of the form of Capture in Marriage Ceremonies;* Adam and Charles Black, Edinburgh, 1865.

John McLean, *Notes of a Twenty-five Years' Service in the Hudson's Bay Territory;* 2 vols., Richard Bentley, London, 1849.

J. P. Malcolm, *Anecdotes of the Manners and Customs of London, from the Roman Invasion to the Year* 1700; 3 vols., London, 1811.

J. P. Malcolm, *Anecdotes of the Manners and Customs of London during the Eighteenth Century*; 2 vols., London, 1810.

W. T. Marchant, *Betrothals & Bridals : with a Chat about Wedding Cakes and Wedding Customs ;* London, 1879.

Henry Mayhew, *German Life and Manners as seen in Saxony at the Present Day*; W. H. Allen, London, 1865.

F. Somner Merryweather, *Glimmerings in the Dark ; or Lights and Shadows of the Olden Time*; Simpkin Marshall, London, 1850.

Louise Jordan Miln, *Wooings and Weddings in Many Lands*; C. Arthur Pearson, London, 1900.

M. Misson, *Memoirs and Observations in His Travels over England*; London, 1719.

C. O. Müller, *The History and Antiquities of the Doric Race*; translated from the German by Henry Tufnel and George Cornewall Lewis, second edition, 2 vols., John Murray, London, 1839.

Eugene O'Curry, *On the Manner and Customs of the Ancient Irish*; Williams and Norgate, London, 1873.

Adam Olearins, *Voyages and Travels of Ambassadors sent by Frederick Duke of Holstein, to the Grand Duke of Muscovy and the King of Persia*; London, 1669.

Mungo Park, *Travels in the Interior Districts of Africa*; 2 vols., John Murray, London, 1816.

Thomas Pennant, *A Tour of Scotland*; London, 1769.

Thomas Pennant, *Of London*; Robt. Faulder, London, 1790.

Ida Pfeiffer, *A Woman's Journey Round the World*; National Illustrated Library, London, *c.* 1852.

Bernard Picart, *Religious Ceremonies of the World*; 6 vols., London, 1731-7.

Marco Polo, *Travels*; with copious notes by High Murray, third edition, Oliver & Boyd, Edinburgh, 1845.

John Potter, *Archæologia Græca, or the Antiquities of Greece*; 2 vols., Edinburgh, 1827.

Eleanor F. Rathbone, *Child Marriage : The Indian Minotaur, An Object-Lesson from the Past to the Future*; George Allen & Unwin, London, 1934.

Sir John Richardson, *Arctic Searching Expedition : A Journal of a Boat-Voyage through Rupert's Land and the Arctic Sea, in search of the Discovery Ships under Command of Sir John Franklin*; 2 vols., Longmans, Brown, Green, and Longmans, London, 1851.

Rev. Charles Rogers, *Scotland, Social and Domestic*; printed for Grampian Club, London, 1869.

Sir Spenser B. St. John, *Life in the Forests of the Far East*; 2 vols., London, 1862.

Father Sangermano, *The Burmese Empire a Hundred Years Ago*; with an Introduction and Notes by John Jardine, Archibald Constable & Co., London, 1893.

George Ryley Scott, *Encyclopædia of Sex : A Practical Encyclopædia arranged in alphabetical order, explanatory of everything pertaining to Sexual Physiology, Psychology and Pathology* ; T. Werner Laurie, London, 1939.

George Ryley Scott, *Marriage in the Melting Pot* ; T. Werner Laurie, London, 1930.

Sir J. G. Scott (Shway Yoe), *The Burman, His Life and Notions* ; Macmillan, London, 1910.

Rev. Joseph Shooter, *The Kafirs of Natal and the Zulu Country* ; E. Stanford, London, 1857.

George R. Sims (edited by), *Living London*, Cassell, London, 1901.

Walter Simson, *A History of the Gipsies* ; edited with Preface, Introduction, and Notes, and a Disquisition on the Past, Present and Future of Gipsydom, by James Simson ; Sampson, Low, Son, and Marston, London, 1865.

Henry Reed Stiles, *Bundling, Its Origin, Progress and Decline in America* ; Book Collectors Association, Inc., New York, 1934.

William Graham Sumner, *Folkways, A Study of the Sociological Importance of Usages, Manners, Customs, Mores, and Morals* ; Ginn & Co., Boston, 1907.

William Connor Sydney, *England and the English in the Eighteenth Century* ; 2 vols., second edition, John Grant, Edinburgh, *c.* 1891.

John Sykes, *Local Records, or Historical Register of the Remarkable Events which have occurred, in Northumberland and Durham, Newcastle-upon-Tyne, and Berwick-upon-Tweed from the Earliest Period of Authentic Record to the Present Time* ; 2 vols., Newcastle, 1833.

William Tegg, *The Knot Tied : Marriage Ceremonies of All Nations* ; Wm. Tegg & Co., London, 1877.

Northcote W. Thomas, "The Origin of Exogamy", in *Anthropological Essays Presented to Edward Burnett Tylor* ; Clarendon Press, Oxford, 1907.

C. J. S. Thompson, *Love, Marriage and Romance in Old London* ; Heath Cranton, London, 1936.

George Thompson, *Travels and Adventures in Southern Africa* ; 2 vols., second edition, Henry Colburn, London, 1827.

Edward Thompson, *Suttee, A Historical and Philosophical Enquiry into the Hindu Rite of Widow-burning* ; Allen & Unwin, London, 1928.

W. M. Thomson, *The Land and the Book, or, Biblical Illustrations drawn from the Manners and Customs, the Scenes and Scenery of the Holy Land* ; Nelson, London, 1862.

Richard Twiss, *A Tour of Ireland in* 1775 ; London, 1776.

Eshwar Chandra Vidyasagar, *Marriage of Hindu Widows* ; Sanscrit Press, Calcutta, 1856.

Edward Walford, *Londoniana* ; 2 vols., Hurst and Blackett, London, 1879.

William Ward, *A View of the History, Literature, and Mythology of the Hindoos : including a minute description of their Manners, and Customs, and Translations from their Principal Works* ; 4 vols., third edition, London, 1820.

Edward Westermarck, *Marriage Ceremonies in Morocco*; Macmillan, London, 1914.

Edward Westermarck, *The History of Human Marriage*; Macmillan, London, 1891.

Lady Wilde, *Ancient Cures, Charms and Usages of Ireland*; Ward and Downey, London, 1890.

John Williams, *A Narrative of Missionary Enterprises in the South Sea Islands; with Remarks upon the natural history of the Islands, Origin, Languages, Traditions, and Usages of the Inhabitants*; London, 1837.

Edward J. Wood, *The Wedding Day in All Ages and Countries*; 2 vols., Bentley, London, 1869

Thomas Wright, *The Homes of Other Days, A History of Domestic Manners and Sentiments in England from the Earliest Known Period to Modern Times*; Trübner & Co., London, 1871.

INDEX

ABDUCTION, formerly prevalent in Great Britain, 61

Abduction in England, legal measures against, 61

Abduction, marriage by, 58

Abduction, sensational cases of, 62, 63

Abyssinia, punishment of adultery in, 277

Account of the Manners and Customs of the Modern Egyptians, An, 119, 176

Adultery, blinding as a punishment for, 275

Adultery, condemnation of, 273

Adultery, punishment of, 274 *et seq.*

Ainsworth, Harrison, 237

Alcibiades, 289

Alexander, William, 40, 48, 69, 123, 129, 148, 293

Alexander, William, quoted, 7, 49, 68, 96, 130, 133, 153, 285

All-Hallows Eve, superstitions connected with, 20

All the Year Round, 134, 136

Along New England Roads, 231

America, bundling at one time practised in, 44, 45, 46, 47

America, corporal punishment of wives in, 152

America, regulations regarding marriage of early settlers in, 235

America, sale of wives at one time in, 138, 139

Anaitis, custom of dedicating virgin girls to, 99

Anburey, Capt. Thomas, quoted, 47, 48, 153

Annals of Scotland, 286

Armenian Marriages, description of, 174

Ashton, John, 230 *n.*

Aubrey, John, quoted, 20

Avebury, Lord, 140, 142, 155, 238, 289

BACHELORS, persecution of, viii

Banns of Marriage as a preventive of clandestine unions, 244

Banns of marriage, original aim of, 212

Barbor, J. T., 43

Barrow, John, 146

Beaumont and Fletcher, 215

Beckherius, 31

"Bedding the bride," curious custom of, 228, 229

Betrothal among the Kaffirs, 6

Betrothal among the Medes, curious method of, 8

Betrothal at birth, 5

Betrothal before birth, 6

Betrothal by cohabitation, 8

Betrothal by means of a ring, 13

Betrothal by word of mouth, 8

Betrothal by written agreement, 7

Betrothal, curious methods of, practised in Persia, 50

Betrothal in Biblical times, 7

Betrothal in China, 12

Betrothal in infancy and childhood, 5 *et seq.*

Betrothal in Lapland, 8

Betrothal in public, evil consequences of, 14

Betrothal in Scotland, 8, 9

Betrothal, manner of, 7, 8

Betrothal that is indistinguishable from marriage, 6

Betrothal, symbols of, 13 *et seq.*

Bible, quotation from, 33, 65, 69, 100, 290

Bingley, Rev. W., quoted, 43

Black, W. G., quoted, 142

Bloch, I., 31

Bœce, Henry, quoted, 144, 145

Boethius, Hector, 119

Borneo, curious wedding ceremonies practised in, 205

Borrow, George, 192, 193

Bourke, Captain John G., 31

Brand, John, 31, 156

Brantôme, 132

Bride-ale, 216

Bride, crowning of the, 161, 162

Bride, custom of carrying across threshold, 124, 166

Bride, stealing of the, 61

Bridegroom, crowning of the, 162

Bridegroom, whip presented to, as token of bride's submission, 195

Brides and Bridals, quotation from, 60

Bride's marriage in a shift, formerly thought to clear husband's responsibility for debts, 230

Britain, reason for child marriages in, 73

Brooke, 214

305

Browne, James, quoted, 93
Bundling, causes of, 40
Bundling, genesis and development of, 39 *et seq.*
Bundling, risk of degeneration into promiscuity, 47
Bundling in Finland, 39
Bundling in Holland, 45
Bundling in Ireland, 44, 45
Bundling in North America, 44
Bundling in Wales, 35, 36
Bundling, modified form of, formerly practised in Massachusetts, 47
Bundling, practised by North American Indians, 40
Burckhardt, John Lewis, quoted, 58, 59, 66, 126, 179
Burder, Samuel, 81, 286
Burma, strange marriage customs observed in ancient, 172
Burn, J. S., 111, 244
Burnaby, Rev. Andrew, 46, 47 *n.*
Burns, Robert, 8, 20, 21
Burton, Sir Richard, 37
Butler, Samuel, 13, 227, 242

CALIZA, ceremony of the, 101, 102
Calmett's Dictionary of the Bible, quotation from, 8
Campbell, Major-General John, quoted, 58
Canute, marriage regulations introduced by, 69
Carr, John, quoted, 44
Carrying bride over threshold, origin due to superstition, 124, 166
Carver, J., quoted, 206
Catlin, George, 82
Cato, 134
" Chaining," curious custom of, 234
Chambers's *Book of Days*, quotation from, 229, 232
Chambers's Journal, quotation from, 55
Charms, use of for predicting or visualizing future husband, 16 *et seq.*
Charms, use of to create love, 25, 26
Chastity, bizarre methods of proving, 273, 274
Chastity, curious method adopted in Africa to ensure, 131
Chastity, different standards of, for men and women, 129
Chastity in marriage, 129
Chastity, methods of ensuring, 130
Chastity, multiple births considered proof of, 274
Chastity, value of, 128, 129
Chastity, varying concepts of, 128
Chaucer, 211, 218

Childbirth, curious practice observed at, in Scotland, 284
Childbirth, magical rites connected with, 126
Child marriages, law relating to Indian, 78
China, attitude towards divorce in, 290
China, concubinage in, 105
China, juvenile marriages in, 74
China, manner of arranging marriage in, 12
China, manner of betrothal in, 12
China, marriage by purchase in, 67, 68
China, marriage rites of, 183 *et seq.*
China, method of warding off evil spirits adopted in, 121
China, polygyny in, 81, 82
China, punishment of adultery in, 277
China, rites for preventing sterility practised in, 117, 118
Church porch marriages, 218, 219
Collier's Wedding, The, 214
Concubinage, 104 *et seq.*
Concubinage, Biblical references to, 104
Connecticut, curious custom of stealing the bride practised in, 61
Consanguinity, prohibition of, 269
Corpses, strange custom of marrying, 172
Council of Trent, 212
Country Wake, 13
Courting in Bed, see Bundling
Courtship among the Gipsies, 9
Courtship, curious methods of, 48 *et seq.*
Courtship, method adopted in Lapland, 8
Courtship, significance of, 3 *et seq.*
Courtship, strange New England method of, 4
Couvade, explanations for practice of, 142, 143
Couvade, widespread practice of, 141, 142
Cranz, D., 59
Crawley, Ernest, 25, 37, 54, 142, 155.
" Creeling the Bridegroom," curious custom known as, 232, 233
Crown, wearing of, at marriage, 161, 162
Cunynghame, Colonel Arthur, quoted, 67, 68

Daily Mail, viii
Daily Post, 255
Dalyell, John Graham, quoted, 28, 99, 124, 232, 281
Davis, John Francis, 12, 183, 184
Davison, 213

Dawson, W. R., 143
Defloration, artificial, 36, 37
Defloration as a sacrificial rite, 37, 38
Defloration, risk thought to be connected with, 36
Dekker, Thomas, 213, 216
Divorce, Biblical attitude towards, 290
Divorce, curious ceremony observed by North American Indians in connexion with, 206
Divorce, curious customs relating to, 288 et seq.
Divorce in England, 292
Divorce, reasons for, in China, 290
Divorce, strange ceremony of the Gipsies in connexion with, 290, 291
Doolittle, Rev. Justus, quoted, 12, 116, 146, 186
Dowry as a form of purchasing a husband, 70 et seq.
Drake, Nathan, 20, 283
Dream, revelation of future husband in a, 16, 17, 18, 23, 24
Dryden, quoted, 15
Du Chaillu, Paul B., 279
Dunmow flitch, 236 et seq.

Earle, Alice Morse, viii, 4, 61, 232
"Eating the Herring," old Scots custom of, 22
Eddy, Mrs., v
Egypt, curious practice to prevent sterility formerly used in, 119
Egypt, juvenile marriage in, 74
Egypt, marriage rites of, 176 et seq.
Egypt, trial marriage in, 92
Elliott, Robert, 263
Ellis, Havelock, 271
England, attitude towards divorce in, 292
England, church porch marriages in, 218
England, curious old wedding custom in, 211 et seq.
England, dowry in, 71
England, juvenile marriages in, 75, 76
England, marriage by purchase in, 68, 69
England, punishment of adultery in, 277
England, sale of wives in, 135 et seq.
England's Helicon, 214
Essay on Fairies, 281
Euripides, 165
Evil spirits, adoption of disguise as protection against, 155
Evil spirits, keeping away at childbirth, 280
Evil spirits, methods of warding off, 120 et seq.
Exogamy, 53

Fairies, evil influence of, 282
Féré, Ch., 143
Fertility, hops as a symbol of, 195
Fertility rites, use of urine in, 31
Fines levied by schoolboys at marriages, 233
Fleet marriages, 243 et seq.
"Flinging the Stocking," curious custom of, 228
Flitch of Bacon, A, 237
Forsyth, R., quoted, 94, 259
France, Church porch marriages in, 218
France, marriage rites in, 192
France, symbolic marriage by capture formerly practised in, 60
Free love, doctrine of, 103
Frommann, 31
Fullom, S. W., 7, 173
Furnivall, F. J., 75, 76

Gardner, Dr. James, quoted, 81, 101, 146, 161, 295
Gay, John, 13, 19, 31, 125
Gentleman's Magazine, 112, 137, 229
German Life and Manners, quotation from, 197
Germany, marriage customs formerly observed in, 196, 197
Gimmal ring, 14
Gipsy marriages, 192, 193, 219, 220
Gipsy divorce, curious ceremony formerly observed, 290, 291
Girdle of chastity, 132, 133
Girdles, magical, used to promote childbirth, 119
Gopalsami, worship of, 116
Gray, John Henry, 12, 82
Grey, Lady Elizabeth, 31
Gretna Green, marriages of, 258 et seq.
Gretna Green Memoirs, The, 263
Grub Street Journal, 252
Guthrie, E. J., 22, 94, 124, 233, 282
Guy Mannering, quotation from, 284

Hailes, Lord, 102, 286
Halliwell, J. O., 16, 23
Hamilton, Alexander, 144
Handfasting, 93 et seq.
Handfasting, origin of, 94
Happy Village, 214
Hardwicke, Lord, 257
Head, Sir George, 224, 225, 260
Health's Improvement, 238
Hearne, Samuel, 6
Herodotus, 65, 71, 99
Herrick, 227, 232, 238
Hesperides, quotation from, 227, 238
History of Eastern Vermont, 231
History of New York, 45
History of Two Maids of Moreclacke, 216

History of Women, The, 48, 274
Holland, bundling in, 45
Homer, 164
Horace, quoted, 26
Hottentots, strange marriage cere-
monies of the, 199
Howett, A. W., 145, 148
Huc, M., quoted, 67, 188
Hudibras, quotation from, 227
Humours of the Fleet, The, 246
Humphrey Clinker, quotation from, 238
Husband, virtual purchase of by
means of dowry, 70
Hutchinson, Peter Orlando, 260, 263

ICELAND, means to overcome de-
population adopted in, 129
Inbreeding, dangers connected with
careless, 272
Incest, definition of, 269
Incest, laws relating to, 269, 270, 271
India, ancient practice of marrying
girls to deities in, 99, 100
India, corporal punishment of wives
in, 152
India, ceremonial marriage in, 167, 168
India, infanticide in, 147, 148
India, infantile marriage in, 77 *et seq.*
India, law relating to child marriage
in, 78
India, marriage by capture in, 58
India, method of driving away evil
spirits adopted in, 123
India, punishment of adultery in, 274
India, remarriage of widows prohibi-
ted in, 286
Infanticide, 145 *et seq.*
Infibulation, 132
Ireland, marriage gifts in ancient, 70, 71
Irving, Washington, 45
Ireland, bundling in, 44, 45
Ireland, symbolic marriage by capture
formerly practised in, 60, 61

JAPAN, marriage ceremony in, 189 *et
seq.*
Java, marriage ceremonies in, 175, 176
Java, punishment of adultery in, 275,
276
Jeaffreson, John Cordy, 60, 111, 112,
213, 218, 238
Jonson, Ben, quoted, 19, 214, 216
Josephus, 289
Joshi Report, 78
Jus Primæ Noctis, 143, 144
Jus Primæ Noctis in ancient Scotland,
144
Juvenal, 289

KALE, use of, for divinatory purposes,
24
Kalm, Peter, quoted, 231, 234
Kames, Lord, quoted, 60
Kendrick, John, 81
King's Bench prison, clandestine
marriages celebrated at, 257
Kirk, Robert, 281

LAING, David, 62, 262
Landor, A. Henry Savage, 82, 83
Lane, Edward William, quoted, 10,
11, 176, 177
Laneham, Robert, 216
Lapland, method of courtship in, 8
Lay of the Last Minstrel, 213
Lee, John, 31
*Letter on the Queen's Entertainment at
Kenilworth Castle*, 216
Letters of a Frenchman, 250
Levirate, antiquity of, 100
Lindsay, Judge Ben, 95
Little, Thomas, quoted, 36, 37, 167,
234, 275, 296
Liver, used as a love charm, 25
Lives of the Berkeleys, 76
Love charms, 25, *et seq.*
Love induced by occult practices,
admitted in witchcraft trials, 29
Love, use of charms and philtres for
arousing, 24 *et seq.*
Love philtre, cow's dung used by
American Indians as a, 32
Love philtres, alluded to by Shakes-
peare, 30, 31
Love philtres, death following use of,
27
Love philtres used in ancient Ireland,
29
Love philtres, use of pansy in connec-
tion with, 30
Love philtres, use of, punishable, 27,
28
Love philtres, use of urine in com-
pounding, 31
Lucina, worship of, by pregnant
women in ancient Rome, 118
Lycurgus, 97

MACARTNEY, 286
Magic, its connexion with marriage,
115 *et seq.*
Magic, sympathetic, 25
Magnetick Lady, 216
Magnus, Olaus, 54, 60, 64
Malcolm, J. P., 71
Malinowsky, B., 6
Mandrake used as love charm, 29

Manu, Laws of, 73
Marchant, W. T., 219
Marriage Act of 1754, 257, 258
Marriage and magic, 115 *et seq.*
Marriage as a means of averting execution of condemned criminal, belief in, 155, 156
Marriage at sea, fallacies concerning, 156
Marriage banns, publication of, 212
Marriage by capture, 53 *et seq.*
Marriage by capture among the Eskimos, 57
Marriage by capture as a ceremonial procedure, 57 *et seq.*
Marriage by capture, distinction between abduction and, 58
Marriage by capture in South America, 57
Marriage by capture, practised by Australian Blacks, 55, 56
Marriage by proxy, 192, 235
Marriage by purchase, 64 *et seq.*
Marriage by purchase, antiquity of, 64, 65
Marriage by purchase, Biblical references to, 65, 69
Marriage by purchase in China, 67, 68
Marriage ceremonies in Africa, 202, 203
Marriage ceremonies, in Germany, 196, 197, 198
Marriage ceremonies in Great Britain, curious old, 211 *et seq.*
Marriage ceremonies in Mexico, 208
Marriage ceremonies in South Sea Islands, 204, 205, 210
Marriage ceremonies of the Gipsies, 219, 220
Marriage ceremonies of the Hindus, 167 *et seq.*
Marriage ceremonies of the Kaffirs, 201
Marriage ceremonies of the North American Indians, 205, 206
Marriage ceremonies of the Jews, 159, 160, 161
Marriage ceremonies, wearing of crown by bride at, 161, 162
Marriage ceremonies, wearing of crown by bridegroom at, 162
Marriage ceremony, reason for untying knots before, 120
Marriage, companionate, 95
Marriage customs founded on superstition, 9, 10
Marriage customs in Great Britain, curious old, 211 *et seq.*
Marriage days, unlucky, 10
Marriage, disadvantages of, 1
Marriage, fallacies concerning, 155, 156

Marriage, favoured days for, 124, 163, 165, 167, 194
Marriage, group and communal, 96 *et seq.*
Marriage, infantile, evils of, 77 *et seq.*
Marriage in the Melting Pot, quotation from, 272
Marriage of a woman in her shift, curious belief respecting, 230, 231
Marriage, morganatic, 105
Marriage, part-time, 155
Marriage, primitive forms of, 199 *et seq.*
Marriage rites in China, 183 *et seq.*
Marriage rites in Egypt, 176 *et seq.*
Marriage rites in Japan, 189 *et seq.*
Marriage rites in Morocco, 182
Marriage rites of Gipsies, 192, 193
Marriage rites of primitive and savage tribes, 199 *et seq.*
Marriage rites of the ancient Babylonians, 162, 163
Marriage rites of the ancient Greeks, 163
Marriage rites of the ancient Romans, 165
Marriage, secret celebration of as a means of eluding evil spirits, 123
Marriage, spiritual, 103, 104
Marriage, state idealization of, vii
Marriage, superstitions connected with, 123 *et seq.*
Marriage, taboos relating to, 269 *et seq.*
Marriage, temporary, with a stranger, 36
Marriage to a corpse, 172
Marriage to gods and devils, 98
Marriage, trial, 91, 95
Marriage, unfavourable months for, 124, 163, 165
Marriage, women sold for at public auction in ancient Assyria, 64
Marriage, women sold for in North American Indian tribes, 68
Marriage, women sold for under Anglo-Saxon law, 68
Marriages, blackmailing tactics adopted at, 234
Marriages, church porch, 218, 219
Marriages, clandestine, 243
Marriages, clandestine, efforts to suppress, 245, 254
Marriages, clandestine, of Gretna Green, 258 *et seq.*
Marriages, fines levied by schoolboys at, 233
Marriages, juvenile, 72 *et seq.*
Marriages, juvenile, in Britain, 75, 76
Marriages, juvenile, in China, 74
Marriages, juvenile, origin and incidence of, 72 *et seq.*

Marry, disinclination to, vi
Masochism displayed to inspire love, 49
Masson, Charles, 40, 192, 228
Matchmaker, role of the, 10 *et seq.*
Match Me in London, 213
Matrimonial Causes Act of 1937, 292
Maximus, Valerius, 71
May, considered unlucky month in which to marry, 10
May Fair, clandestine marriages celebrated at, 257
Mayhew, Henry, quoted, 196, 197
McLean, John, quoted, 297
M'Lennan, John F., quoted, 53, 54, 60
Menstrual blood, belief in pernicious effects of, 35
Menstruation, taboos concerning, 279
Mexico, strange marriage ceremony observed in, 208
Middleton, 216
Midsummer Night's Dream, quotation from, 30
Midwifery, practice of by women in ancient Greece, 153
Miles, Arthur, 123, 171
Miln, Louise Jordan, 57, 183
Moffet, Thomas, 238
Monogamy, advantages of, to women, 91
Monogamy and equality of sexes, 91
Monogamy as an ideal system of marriage, 91
Monogamy, genesis of, 90, 91
Montagu, Lady, quoted, 49
Montfaucon, 166
Moore, Theophilus, quoted, 8, 174, 193, 200, 279, 288
Mormonism, 83 *et seq.*
Mormonism, methods formerly used to compel adherence to polygamous principles of, 86, 88, 89
Mormonism Unveiled, quotation from, 86, 88
Morocco, concubinage in, 106, 107
Morocco, marriage rites in, 182
Müller, C. O., vii, 58
Multiple weddings, 224, 225, 226
Mutunus, 38

News of the World, 133
Notes and Queries, 284
No Wit, No Help like a Woman's, 216
Noyes, John Humphrey, 97
Nudity, marriage in a state of, 230
Nuts, burning of, for divinatory purposes, 125

O'curry, Eugene, 70
Ode on the Popular Superstitions of the Highlands of Scotland, 282
Olearius, Adam, quoted, 102
Oneida Community, 97, 98
Orkney Islands, curious wedding ceremony formerly practised in the, 234
Orkney Islands, times considered favourable for weddings in, 123
Outbreeding, effects of, 272

Pall Mall Gazette, The, 136
Paracelsus, 31
Park, Mungo, quoted, 34, 151, 202, 203
Parturition, superstitions relating to, 281
Pay weddings, 198
Pennant, Thomas, quoted, 247, 259
Penny Bridals, see Penny Weddings
Penny Weddings, regulations concerning, 222
Pepys' *Diary*, 75, 228
Pericles, 134
Persia, curious method of betrothal practised in, 50
Persia, description of royal wedding in, 173
Persia, description of strange rites of the desert dwellers in, 173
Persia, marriage ceremonies in ancient, 172, 173
Pfeiffer, Ida, quoted, 37, 172
Phallicism in relation to sterility, 115
Philtres for arousing love, 25
Plato, 145
Pliny, 31, 281, 284
Ploss and Bartels, 133
Plural marriage, 80 *et seq.*
Plutarch, 58, 124, 155, 288
Polyandry, definition of, 80, 84 *n.*
Polyandry, in Tibet, 82
Polygamy, definition of, 80, 84 *n.*
Polygamy, evidence of unhappiness caused by, 86
Polygamy, origin and incidence of, 80 *et seq.*
Polygamy, testimony in favour of, 83, 85
Polygyny among the North American Indians, 82
Polygyny and polygamy, importance of distinction between, 80
Polygyny, definition of, 80, 84 *n.*
Polygyny, development into monogamy, 90
Polygyny, evils of, 83
Polygyny, in Biblical times, 81

Polygyny in China, 81
Polygyny in Tibet, 82
Polygyny, prohibited by the Justinian Code, 81
Polygyny, reasons for restriction of, 90
Popular Rhymes and Nursery Tales, quotation from, 16 *et seq.*
Pregnancy, taboos concerning, 280
"Pricking the Egg," old Scots custom of, 22
Prostitution, temporary, as a means of obtaining a dowry, 71
Pseudo-marriages, 111, 112
Public Advertiser, 137
Punishment of Incest Act of 1908, 271

QUEESTING, see Bundling

RABELAIS, 132
Ramsay, Allan, 228
Rice, reasons for throwing at weddings, 120
"Riding the Stang," 151
Rogers, Rev. Charles, quoted, 8, 9, 94, 221, 222
Rowe, 214

SABINE virgins, rape of, 53, 57
St. Paul, v
Sangermano, Father, 126, 172
Satirio-Mastix, 216
Savoy Chapel, clandestine marriages celebrated at, 257
Scornful Lady, 215
Scotland, corporal punishment of wives in, 151
Scotland, curious practice observed at childbirth in, 284
Scotland, former practice of *jus primæ noctis* in, 144, 145
Scotland, handfasting in, 93, 94
Scotland, law relating to marriage in, 258
Scotland, strange method of betrothal formerly practised in, 8
Scotland, punishment of adultery in, 278
Scot, Reginald, 31
Scott's Encyclopædia of Sex, quotation from, 271
Scott, Sir Walter, quoted, 93, 262, 284
Shakespeare, 20, 30, 215
Shakespeare and His Times, quotation from, 20, 21
Shepherd's Week, quotation from, 19, 31

Shooter, Rev. Joseph, 201, 202
Simson, Walter, quoted, 219, 220, 291
Smith, George, 214
Smith, Joseph, 85
Smollett, 239
Social Life Under the Regency, 230 *n.*
Society of Perfectionists, see Oneida Community
Socrates, 140
Sororate, custom of, 82
South America, marriage by capture in, 57
Sparta, symbolic marriage by capture in ancient, 58
Spiritual wives, 103
Stamford Mercury, 228
Sterility in women and witchcraft, 119, 120
Sterility in women, curious Egyptian custom to prevent, 119
Sterility in women, measures for preventing, 115 *et seq.*
Sterility, its connexion with phallicism, 115
Straffado of the Divell, 213
Stranger in Ireland, The, 44
Stiles, Henry Reed, 44
Sumner, W. G., 35
Sunday Chronicle, 237
Sunday Pictorial, 79
Superstitions connected with marriage, 9, 10, 123 *et seq.*
Superstition connected with number seven, 171
Suttee, 292 *et seq.*
Sweden, equality of sexes in, 91
Swedenborg, Emanuel, v
Sydney, William Connor, 230
Sykes, John, quoted, 240

Taming of the Shrew, 215
Tarrying, 45, 47
Tavernier, 126
Tegg, William, 111, 236
Tennyson, 127
Tertullian, 13, 212, 270
Thompson, C. J. S., 96
Thompson, George, quoted, 6, 120, 269
Thomson, Dr. W. M., 270
Thurn, Sir E. F. Im, 141
Tibet, system of polygamy practised in, 82
Times, The, 137
Tour of Ireland in 1775, *A*, 45
Tour Through Greece, 70
Transvestism, practice of, at weddings, 200
Travels in North America, 46
Travels in Siberia, 59

Travels of Marco Polo, 105
Travels of Van Egmont and Heyman, 45
Tree marriage, advantages of, 155
Trial marriage, 92 *et seq.*
Tryall of a Man's Own Selfe, 31
Twelfth Night, quotation from, 13
Twins, strange African belief concerning, 280
Twiss, Richard, 45
Tylor, 142

Urine used in connexion with marriage rites, 32, 200, 202, 219
Urine, use of as a fertility rite, 31

Vaspasian, 162
Virginity as a despised possession, 35 *et seq.*
Virginity, curious old test for, 35
Virginity, high value placed upon, 33
Virginity, punishment for loss of, 33
Virginity, simulation of, 35
Virgins, anciently considered unfit to marry, 37
Voltaire, 132

Wakefield, Edward Gibbon, 61, 262
Wales, corporal punishment of wives in ancient, 152
Wales, symbolic marriage by capture formerly practised in, 60
Wales, trial marriage in, 95
Walpole, Horace, 255
Ward, William, quoted, 168
Webster, John, 213
Wedding cake, kinds of, 239
Wedding cake, origin of, 238
Wedding cake, superstitions connected with, 238, 239
Wedding favours, custom of handing out, 214
Wedding feasts, 239, 240

Wedding feasts as a proof of marriage, 164
Wedding ring, 240 *et seq.*
Weddings, throwing money at English, 214
Weddings, wine-drinking in church at English, 215
Welsh biddings, 223
Westermarck, 37, 54, 118, 142, 155, 271
White Devil, The, 213
Widow burning, see Suttee
Widowers, remarriage of, disapproved in early days of Christianity, 286
Widows, Christianity's attitude towards remarriage of, 286, 287
Widows, remarriage of, prohibited in India, 286
Widows, strangling of, 297
Widows, superstitions relating to, 126
Widows, taboo in connexion with remarriage of, 285 *et seq.*
Widows, torture of, 297
Wife-barter, 137
Wife-beating, 150 *et seq.*
Wife, gift to, on morning after wedding, 196
Wife, purchase of, by service instead of money, 69
Wilde, Lady, 29
Williams, Rev. John, quoted, 149, 150, 204, 296
Witchcraft, curious Scots method of thwarting power of, 124
Witches, power of, to cause sterility, 119, 120
Witch of Edmonton, 213
Wives, exchange of, 140
Wives, exchange of, antiquity of practice, 140
Wives, loan of, 139, 140
Wives, sale of, 134 *et seq.*
Wood, Edward J., quoted, 166, 173, 192, 223
Wrestling as a means of securing a wife, 154

Young, Brigham, 85, 86, 128